OECD Environmental Performance Reviews: The Netherlands 2015

OECD
BETTER POLICIES FOR BETTER LIVES

Please cite this publication as:
OECD (2015), *OECD Environmental Performance Reviews: The Netherlands 2015*, OECD Publishing.
http://dx.doi.org/10.1787/9789264240056-en

ISBN 978-92-64-23999-9 (print)
ISBN 978-92-64-24005-6 (PDF)

Series: OECD Environmental Performance Reviews
ISSN 1990-0104 (print)
ISSN 1990-0090 (online)

Photo credits: © gigra – Fotolia.com; © ValES1989 – Fotolia.com.

Corrigenda to OECD publications may be found on line at: *www.oecd.org/publishing/corrigenda*.

Preface

Long recognised as a forerunner in environmental policy, the Netherlands has continued to make important strides in dealing with environmental pressures in what is a very densely populated country with the sixth largest economy in the euro area. In the context of modest growth over 2000-14, it managed to decouple greenhouse gas emissions, all major pollutants and waste generation from economic activity. Yet, the Netherlands still has the fifth-highest share of fossil fuels in its energy mix among OECD countries, and around 95% of habitat types and 75% of species are considered threatened. The country needs, therefore, to push the frontier of environmental policy even further and in innovative ways to maintain growth while ensuring conservation and sustainable use of environmental assets.

This third *OECD Environmental Performance Review* of the Netherlands assesses the country's progress in achieving its environmental policy objectives since the last review carried out in 2003. It identifies what is working well and what can be improved, providing 29 recommendations to help green the economy and improve environmental governance and management. The current drive to modernise environmental policy provides an opportunity for the Netherlands to build on the impressive progress already made in streamlining environmental legislation, regulations and permits. The modernisation effort explores new ways of working with the private sector and civil society, such as in the promising "Green Deals" programme.

The *Environmental Performance Review* pays special attention to the issues of sustainable mobility and waste and materials management. The report underlines that the Netherlands is an important global transport hub. The trends are largely positive, with air pollution emissions, noise and congestion declining, while traffic safety has improved. Yet, as the easy wins in terms of better road management have largely been exhausted, other policies, such as road pricing should be re-considered to address the expected increase in road traffic in the very densely populated Randstad. The *Review* recommends the introduction of distance-based road charging for trucks, in line with the trend in neighbouring countries.

The Netherlands is also one of the OECD's best performers in the area of waste management. Since 2000, landfilling has been virtually eliminated and there has been a marked shift towards incineration with energy recovery. The transition from traditional waste management towards a circular economy is underway, bringing new challenges. The *Review* provides recommendations for supporting this transition.

This study is the result of a constructive policy dialogue between the Netherlands and the countries participating in the OECD Working Party on Environmental Performance. The Dutch experience provides a number of valuable lessons for countries promoting greener and more sustainable growth. I am confident that this collaborative effort will be useful to tackle the many shared environmental challenges faced by other OECD members and partner countries.

Angel Gurría
OECD Secretary-General

Foreword

The principal aim of the OECD Environmental Performance Review programme is to help member and selected partner countries improve their individual and collective performance in environmental management by:

- *helping individual governments assess progress in achieving their environmental goals*
- *promoting continuous policy dialogue and peer learning*
- *stimulating greater accountability from governments towards each other and public opinion.*

This report reviews the environmental performance of the Netherlands since the previous OECD review in 2003. Progress in achieving domestic objectives and international commitments provides the basis for assessing the country's environmental performance. Such objectives and commitments may be broad aims, qualitative goals or quantitative targets. A distinction is made between intentions, actions and results. Assessment of environmental performance is also placed within the context of the Netherlands' historical environmental record, present state of the environment, physical endowment in natural resources, economic conditions and demographic trends.

The OECD is indebted to the government of the Netherlands for its co-operation in providing information, organising the review mission to The Hague and Rotterdam (13-17 October 2014) and the policy mission to The Hague (12 May 2015), as well as facilitating contacts both inside and outside government institutions.

Thanks are also due to the representatives of the two examining countries: Mr István Pomázi (Hungary) and Professor Takashi Matsumura (Japan).

The authors of this report were Nils Axel Braathen, Kathleen Dominique, Alexa Piccolo and Frédérique Zegel from the OECD Environment Directorate, and Niall Lawlor, Milieu Limited, Law and Policy Consulting and Professor Stef Proost, Catholic University of Leuven. Rob Visser, independent consultant, provided expert advice and inputs. Brendan Gillespie and Nathalie Girouard provided oversight and guidance. Carla Bertuzzi provided statistical support. Mark Foss copy-edited the report. Jennifer Humbert and Clara Tomasini assisted with production and publication.

The OECD Working Party on Environmental Performance discussed the draft Environmental Performance Review of the Netherlands at its meeting on 18 June 2015 in Paris, and approved the Assessment and recommendations.

Table of contents

Boxes

Tables

Figures

Reader's guide

General notes

Signs

The following signs are used in Figures and Tables:

. . : not available

– : nil or negligible

. : decimal point

Country Aggregates

OECD Europe: This zone includes all European member countries of the OECD, i.e. Austria, Belgium, the Czech Republic, Denmark, Estonia, Finland, France, Germany, Greece, Hungary, Iceland, Ireland, Italy, Luxembourg, the Netherlands, Norway, Poland, Portugal, the Slovak Republic, Slovenia, Spain, Sweden, Switzerland, Turkey and the United Kingdom.

OECD: This zone includes all member countries of the OECD, i.e. the countries of OECD Europe plus Australia, Canada, Chile, Israel, Japan, Korea, Mexico, New Zealand and the United States.

Country aggregates may include Secretariat estimates.

Currency

Monetary unit: Euro (EUR).

In 2014, USD 1.00 = EUR 0.75

Disclaimer

The statistical data for Israel are supplied by and under the responsibility of the relevant Israeli authorities. The use of such data by the OECD is without prejudice to the status of the Golan Heights, East Jerusalem and Israeli settlements in the West Bank under the terms of international law.

This document and any map included herein are without prejudice to the status of or sovereignty over any territory, to the delimitation of international frontiers and boundaries and to the name of any territory, city or area.

Abbreviations and acronyms

CAP	European Union's Common Agricultural Policy
CBS	Statistics Netherlands
CCS	CO_2 capture and storage
CDKN	Climate Development and Knowledge Network
CPB	Bureau for Economic Policy Analysis
CSO	Civil society organisation
DAC	OECD Development Assistance Committee
DANK	Digital Atlas of Natural Capital
DMC	Domestic material consumption
DSU	Dutch Sustainability Unit
ECA	European Court of Auditors
ECN	Energy Research Centre of the Netherlands
EEA	European Environment Agency
EGS	Environmental goods and services
ELD	Environmental Liability Directive
ELV	End-of-life vehicles
EMA	Environmental Management Act
EMAS	Environmental management systems
EPR	Extended producer responsibility
ETS	Emissions trading system
EZ	Ministry of Economic Affairs
GBR	General binding rules
GDP	Gross domestic product
GHG	Greenhouse gas
GNI	Gross national income
HDO	Waste from business, government and services
ICCT	International Council on Clean Transportation
IEA	International Energy Agency
ILT	Human Environment and Transport Inspectorate
IMPEL	EU's Network for the Implementation and Enforcement of Environmental Law
IPO	Association of Provincial Authorities
IPPC	Integrated Pollution Prevention and Control
KiM	Netherlands Institute for Transport Policy Analysis
KNMI	Royal Netherlands Meteorological Institute
LNS	Liquefied natural gas
MFA	Ministry of Foreign Affairs
MSW	Municipal solid waste
NAS	National Adaptation Strategy
NCA	Natural Capital Accounting
NCEA	Netherlands Commission for Environmental Assessment
NCP	National contact point for OECD guidelines
NEA	Netherlands Environmental Assessment Agency
NGO	Nongovernmental organisation
NEN	National Ecological Network
NH_3	Ammonia
NMP4	Fourth national environmental policy plan

NMVOC	Non-methane volatile organic compounds
NO_x	Nitrogen oxides
NVWA	Netherlands Food and Consumer Product Safety Authority
NWMP	National Waste Management Plan
OD	Environmental Services
PAS	Integrated Approach to Nitrogen
PBL	Netherlands Environmental Assessment Agency
PFC	Perfluorocarbon
PM	Particulate matter
PROs	Producer responsibility organisations
RBMP	River Basin Management Plan
RD&D	Research, development and demonstration
RES	Renewable energy supply
RIVM	National Institute for Public Health and the Environment
RSL	Regional Air Quality Co-operation Programmes
RWA	Regional Water Authority
SCI	Sites of Community Importance
SCP	Netherlands Institute for Social Research
SDE+	Renewable energy producers subsidy
SEA	Strategic environmental assessment
SER	Social and Economic Council of the Netherlands
SO_x	Sulphur oxides
SPA	Special Protection Areas
SVIR	National Policy Strategy for Infrastructure and Spatial Planning
TEEB	The Economics of Ecosystems and Biodiversity
TKI	Top Consortia for Knowledge and Innovation
TNO	Organisation for Applied Scientific Research
TPES	Total primary energy supply
UNEP	United Nations Environment Programme
UNFCCC	United Nations Framework Convention on Climate Change
USD	United States dollars
UvW	Union of the Regional Water Authorities
VAT	Value-added tax
VNG	Association of Netherlands Municipalities
VSL	Value of a statistical life
WABO	Act on General Provisions for Environmental Law
WEEE	Waste electrical and electronic equipment
WFD	Water Framework Directive
WHO	World Health Organization
WRI	World Resources Institute
WSR	European Waste Shipment Regulation

BASIC STATISTICS OF THE NETHERLANDS (2013 or latest available year)

(Number in parentheses refer to the OECD averages*)

PEOPLE AND SOCIETY

Population (million)	16.9		Population density per km^2	405.7	(34.8)
Share of population by type of region:			Population growth (%, latest 5-year yearly average growth)	0.5	(0.6)
Predominantly urban (%)	85.1	(48.0)	Income inequality (Gini coefficient, 2012)	27.8	(31.4)
Intermediate (%)	14.9	(26.2)	Poverty rate (% population with less than 50% med. income)	7.8	(11.5)
Predominantly rural (%)	0.0	(25.1)	Life expectancy	81.4	(80.4)

ECONOMY AND EXTERNAL ACCOUNTS

Total GDP (GDP, EUR billion)	603		Imports of goods and services (% of GDP)	71.6	(28.9)
Total GDP (GDP, USD billion)	801		Main exports (% of total merchandise exports)		
GDP, latest 5-year average real growth (%)	-0.7	(0.8)	Machinery, transport equipment	20.3	
GDP per capita (1 000 USD current PPP)	46.2	(37.9)	Mineral fuels, lubrificants	19.8	
Value added shares (%)			Chemicals	13.6	
Primary sector	2.0	(1.4)	Main imports (% of total merchandise imports)		
Industry including construction	22.2	(23.8)	Mineral fuels, lubrificants	24.8	
Services	75.9	(74.7)	Machinery, transport equipment	22.1	
Exports of goods and services (% of GDP)	82.6	(28.6)	Chemicals	11.2	

GENERAL GOVERNMENT

Percentage of GDP

Expenditure	46.8	(41.9)	Education expenditure	5.4	
Revenue	44.5	(37.7)	Health expenditure	8.1	
Gross financial debt	77.0	(109.3)	Environmental protection expenditure	1.5	
Fiscal balance	-2.3	(-4.2)	Environmental taxes: (% of GDP)	3.4	(1.6)
			(% of total tax revenue)	9.2	(5.1)

LABOUR MARKET, SKILLS AND INNOVATION

Unemployment rate (% of civilian labour force)	7.2	(7.9)	Patent applications in environment-related technologies (% of all technologies, average 2009-11)[a]	10.4	(11.3)
Tertiary educational attainment of 25-64 years-olds (%, 2012)	34.4	(32.2)	Environmental management technologies	4.6	(4.9)
Gross domestic expenditure on R&D, (% of GDP)	2.2	(2.4)	Water-related adaptation technologies	0.6	(0.5)
			Climate change mitigation technologies	7.1	(8.5)

ENVIRONMENT

Energy intensity: TPES per capita (toe/cap.)	4.6	(4.2)	Road vehicle stock (veh./100 inhab.)	53	(57)
TPES per GDP (toe/1 000 USD, 2005 PPP)	0.13	(0.13)	Water stress (Netherlands 2012) (abstraction as % of available resources)	11.7	(9.5)
Renewables (% of TPES)	4.2	(8.8)	Water abstraction per capita (Netherlands 2012) (m^3/cap./year)	640	(830)
Carbon intensity (energy-related CO_2, 2012):			Municipal waste per capita (kg/cap.)	520	(520)
per capita (t/cap.)	10.4	(9.7)	Material productivity (2011) (USD, 2005 PPP/kg)	3.2	(1.8)
per GDP (t/1 000 USD, 2005 PPP)	0.3	(0.3)	Land area (1 000 km^2, 2012)	34	
GHG intensity (2012):[b]			% of arable land and permanent crops	31	(12.2)
per capita (t/1 000 USD, 2005 PPP)	11.4	(12.5)	% of permanent meadows and pastures	24	(23)
per GDP (t/1 000 USD, 2005 PPP)	0.31	(0.40)	% of forest area	11	(30)
Exposure to air pollution ($PM_{2.5}$) (2012, µg/m^3)	15.8		% of other land (built-up and other land)	35	(34)

* Where the OECD aggregate is not provided in the source database, a simple OECD average of latest available data is calculated where data exist for at least 29 member countries.

a) Higher-value inventions that have sought patent protection in at least two jurisdictions.

b) Excluding emissions/removals from land use, land-use change and forestry.

Source: Calculations based on data extracted from databases of the following organisations: OECD, IEA, IMF, UN, World Bank.

Executive summary

A forerunner in environmental policy that has recently reined in ambitions

As a small, densely populated country with a very open economy, the Netherlands became a forerunner in environmental policy decades ago when it was confronted with acute environmental pressures. More recently, the government has reined in ambitions for environmental policy objectives to levels set by the European Union (EU), with a view to promoting a level playing field. Given its strong track record, it may be tempting for the Dutch government to wait and let other countries catch up in areas where it is already doing well. But, the country still faces some persistent environmental challenges, including addressing diffuse pollution (such as nitrogen deposition in nature areas) and securing significant improvements in the quality of ecosystems and biodiversity, and new issues continue to emerge.

Since 2000, the Netherlands achieved absolute decoupling of greenhouse gas (GHG) emissions and all major air pollutants from economic growth. The economy's carbon intensity has decreased although, the country still has one of the largest shares of fossil fuels in its energy mix in the OECD, ranking fifth-highest. Air quality in zones with intensive road traffic has strongly improved, although some hot spots remain. As of 2013, about 95% of habitat types and 75% of species were considered threatened, a higher share than in many other OECD member countries. Nutrient surpluses have declined, but from a high baseline. The quantity of nitrogen fertiliser and pesticides used per square kilometre of agricultural land remain significantly higher than the OECD average. As a delta country, flood management has long been a strength, but stresses on freshwater supply are emerging in some areas and non point sources of pollution continue to strain water quality.

Environmental governance saw significant streamlining and modernising efforts

Impressive progress in streamlining included a major legislative overhaul to consolidate all of the national environmental legislation into the Environment and Planning Act. Many environmental competencies were decentralised over the review period, but this was not necessarily accompanied by additional resources. In 2014, to address some major deficiencies that had emerged in policy implementation, the Netherlands established 29 Environmental Services to consolidate and reinforce expertise in environmental licensing and enforcement. It will be important that these newly established services secure sustainable funding and have access to strong mechanisms for exchanging good practice. The quality of their performance should be closely monitored.

The current drive to modernise environmental policy has a strong focus on public health, particularly on new potential risks (such as nanotechnology and micro-contaminants in water). The government is also looking for opportunities to tap into the energy of civil society by building new coalitions among various partners. The recent "Green Deals" programme is a promising way to make the most of the distinctive Dutch polder approach by removing obstacles to implementing environmental efforts by industry and agriculture.

Greening growth at a moderate pace, with opportunities for more cost-effective policies

The 2013 Energy Agreement for Sustainable Growth provides the cornerstone for Dutch climate and energy policy. It succeeded in creating a common understanding around shared goals across a broad range of stakeholders. Objectives include improving energy efficiency, scaling up renewable energy, reducing CO_2 emissions from transport and promoting employment, innovation and investment. However, early assessments indicate that the agreed policy measures may not be sufficient to reach stated objectives. For example, the Netherlands is not on track to meet renewable energy and energy efficiency objectives under the agreement. The assessment planned for 2016 will provide an important opportunity to review the set of instruments and step up efforts as necessary.

Measured as a percentage of gross domestic product (GDP), the Netherlands raised more revenue from environmental taxes in 2013 than most other OECD member countries. However, there is scope to improve the design of these taxes. For example, Dutch energy taxes do not adequately reflect the relevant environmental damages and there are a number of exemptions and refund mechanisms that mainly benefit large-scale users. The planned tax exemption for coal used in electricity generation is also regrettable from an environmental perspective.

The country has a comparative advantage in several environmentally related technologies, yet it is lagging behind the most eco-innovative OECD member countries. Various initiatives, such as the Top Sector policy, support green innovation. However, there is concern that larger firms and incumbents benefit more from them than do small and medium-sized enterprises. The Netherlands could benefit from an ambitious framework for promoting eco-innovation.

Dutch policies effective at promoting sustainability mobility, but at a very high cost in some cases

The Netherlands has managed to maintain a high share of environmentally friendly modes of transport. Over the past ten years, air pollution emissions declined, noise from transport went down, congestion decreased and traffic safety improved. In the coming years, congestion is expected to increase in the very densely populated Randstad. As the easy wins have largely been exhausted, a further increase of road traffic is unlikely to be solved by additional road capacity alone. Thus, road pricing, the principal policy option to address congestion cost-effectively, should be re-considered. The Netherlands enjoys the highest penetration of electric cars in the EU and declining CO_2 emissions from new cars. The policies in place to stimulate low-polluting vehicles are a very costly approach to reduce CO_2 emissions, however, they also aim to foster innovation and green growth and at the moment they are the only way to achieve the EU objective to decarbonise urban transport.

A strong track record in waste management, with new challenges to transition to a circular economy

The Netherlands is one of the OECD's best performers in the area of waste management, having successfully achieved progressively ambitious targets while keeping charges at relatively low levels. The Dutch economy is one of the most resource-efficient in the OECD. Since 2000, absolute decoupling of waste generation from GDP has been achieved, landfilling has been virtually eliminated and there has been a marked shift towards incineration with energy recovery. Yet ongoing efforts to increase material recycling and composting have only resulted in marginal improvements. The transition from traditional waste management towards a circular economy is underway. This will require developing new business models, finding new ways of working across the whole product chain and dealing with commodity price volatility. A detailed roadmap to promote the circular economy, tailored indicators and stronger product policies can help spur this transition towards a circular economy.

Assessment and recommendations

The Assessment and recommendations presents the main findings of the OECD Environmental Performance Review of the Netherlands *and identifies 29 recommendations to support the country's further progress towards its environmental policy objectives and international commitments. The OECD Working Party on Environmental Performance reviewed and approved the Assessment and recommendations at its meeting on 18 June 2015. Actions taken to implement selected recommendations from the 2003* OECD Environmental Performance Review *are summarised in the Annex.*

The statistical data for Israel are supplied by and under the responsibility of the relevant Israeli authorities. The use of such data by the OECD is without prejudice to the status of the Golan Heights, East Jerusalem and Israeli settlements in the West Bank under the terms of international law.

1. Introduction

As a small, densely populated country with a very open economy, the Netherlands felt acute environmental pressures early on. To tackle these pressures, it became a forerunner in environmental policy decades ago and has long been considered a leader in a number of areas. However, more recently, the government recalibrated ambitions for environmental policy objectives to levels set by the European Union, with a view to promoting a level playing field. While the temptation may be to wait and let other countries catch up in areas where it is already doing well, the Netherlands still faces some persistent environmental challenges, and new ones are emerging. Hajer (2011) stressed the scale of the task ahead when he highlighted that resource use and the resulting pressures on the environment need to be scaled back by a factor of five. This equates to operating 80% to 90% more efficiently. The challenge for the Netherlands in the coming years will be to push the frontier of environmental policy even further and in new ways.

Over the period 2000-14, the country experienced modest growth in real gross domestic product (GDP) of 15%, with an annual rate of 1%. From 2000 to 2008, the economy grew steadily before facing a severe drop in 2009 due to the global economic and financial crisis. Economic activity gradually recovered in 2014 and real GDP is expected to increase further in 2015 and 2016. Important structural reforms are underway, namely in the labour market, health care and pension systems. Significant fiscal consolidation has also been achieved and the budget deficit lowered to 2.3% of GDP in 2014 (OECD, 2015, 2014a, 2014b). Living standards in the Netherlands are significantly higher than the OECD average, as measured by real GDP per capita. Both income inequality and relative poverty are low compared to other OECD member countries.

International trade plays a significant role in the economy. With the Port of Rotterdam, the largest in Europe, the country is a major global trading hub. Transport is a key sector and large-scale investments in infrastructure, including road, rail, aviation and maritime transportation, have been made over the years (IEA, 2014). Yet, like in any densely populated country, there is a constant tension between the available transport capacities, the demand for mobility and the associated pressure on the environment.

The Netherlands has one of the largest shares of fossil fuels in its energy mix among OECD member countries, ranking fifth-highest. Natural gas, oil and coal together accounted for more than 90% of total primary energy supplied (TPES). The pursuit of a regional and international approach to energy markets and technology innovation, notably for the deployment of renewable and other clean energy technologies is among the key elements that will shape the future success of Dutch energy and climate policies (IEA, 2014). Renewable energy growth in Europe depends on additional electrical grid infrastructure, with a special focus on interconnection of national networks (OECD, 2014c). Thus, deepening the European Union (EU) internal energy market is important for the achievement of energy and climate goals in the Netherlands.

2. The Netherlands' environmental performance

2.1. Transition to an energy-efficient and low-carbon economy

Since 2000, the Netherlands has achieved absolute decoupling of greenhouse gas (GHG) emissions from economic growth. The carbon intensity of the economy decreased, driven by energy savings, higher imports of electricity and the impact of the economic crisis, as the fall in emissions was larger than the decline in GDP spurred by the crisis (Figure 1). The energy sector, the largest producer of GHG emissions, is the sector with the lowest decrease in emissions over the period 2000-12, reflecting the large share of fossil fuels in the energy mix. GHG emissions from other sectors, including agriculture, industrial processes, solvents and waste decreased significantly. The country's commitments under the Kyoto Protocol have been fulfilled through the acquisition of carbon credits under the Protocol's flexible mechanisms (the Clean Development Mechanism and Joint Implementation) to complement domestic reductions.

Figure 1. **Absolute decoupling of GHG emissions from economic growth**

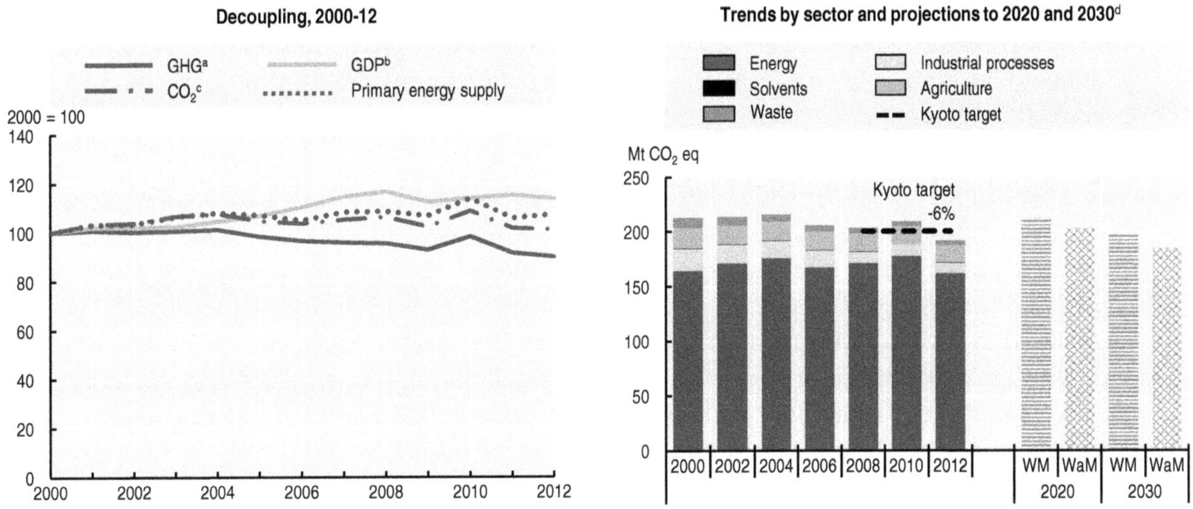

a) Excluding emissions/removals from land use, land-use change and forestry.
b) GDP at 2005 prices and purchasing power parities.
c) CO_2 emissions from energy use only; sectoral approach; excludes international marine and aviation bunkers.
d) National projections based on scenarios with existing measures (WM) and with additional measures (WaM).
Source: IEA (2014), *IEA CO_2 Emissions from Fuel Combustion Statistics* (database); IEA (2014), *IEA World Energy Statistics and Balances* (database); OECD (2014), *OECD Economic Outlook No. 95", OECD Economic Outlook: Statistics and Projections (database);* UNFCCC (2015), *GHG Data Interface* (database).

StatLink http://dx.doi.org/10.1787/888933279980

Over the past decade, emissions of all major air pollutants have been decoupled from economic growth. Despite the overall positive trend, average concentrations of fine particles (PM_{10}) in 2010 and 2011 were higher than in previous years, but continued their downward trend thereafter. The number of deaths from outdoor air pollution has declined since 2005, and in 2010 was significantly lower than the OECD average.

2.2. Managing the natural asset base

The Netherlands is the second most densely populated country in the OECD area after Korea. Despite efforts to prevent the expansion of residential areas, increased pressure from urbanisation has resulted in the loss of natural habitats and landscapes. Around 42% of the overall increase in urban and other artificial areas between 2000 and 2006 was taken by the housing, services and recreation sectors. Around one-third of the country's territory is used for agricultural purposes; meadows and pastures account for about one-fourth, and forests cover only about one-tenth.

The rate of decline of biodiversity has slowed or shown some improvement for certain species. Overall, however, gains have been weak and some species populations are still in decline. The 2013 monitoring results of the EU Habitat Directive reveal that about 95% of habitat types and 75% of species are threatened, a share higher than in many other OECD member countries. The main pressures on biodiversity are increasing urbanisation and transport, as well as industrial, agricultural and fishery activities. The land area under some form of nature protection is slightly lower than the OECD average, covering about one-fifth of the territory.

Situated in the delta of four international rivers, with a quarter of its territory below sea level, the Netherlands faces a number of water-related challenges, especially flood control. The country is classified as medium water-stressed. Non-point sources of pollution from agriculture, atmospheric deposition, traffic and infrastructure and run-off have the largest impact on water quality. Both surface and groundwater quality are improving. Nevertheless, recent analysis shows that the implementation of River Basin Management Plan between 2009 and 2021 will result in only 15% of all water bodies meeting the Water Framework Directive (WFD) ecological targets in 2027 (PBL, 2015a).

2.3. Transition to a resource-efficient economy

The Dutch economy is one of the most resource-efficient among OECD member countries. The country's material productivity (defined as the amount of economic wealth generated per unit of material used) grew by almost 50% between 2000 and 2013. This positive trend was driven by an overall decrease in material consumption and well-functioning waste management strategies. Municipal solid waste (MSW) generation showed significant decoupling, decreasing by 7% between 2000 and 2013 against a slight increase in private final consumption. The country has very high levels of recovery (including reuse, recycling and incineration for energy recovery) across all waste streams.

Despite positive developments in reducing nutrient surpluses, the amount of nitrogen fertiliser and the quantity of pesticides used per square kilometre of agricultural land remain significantly higher than the OECD average. Due to stringent application standards for fertilisation, agricultural nutrient surpluses (nitrogen and phosphorous) showed a continuous downward trend, although from a relatively high level. Nutrient surpluses declined both in absolute tonnes of nutrients and in terms of nutrient surpluses per hectare of agricultural land, resulting in decoupling from agricultural production. In addition, organic farming increased by around 60% between 2000 and 2012 (from 1.6% to 2.6% as a share of total agricultural land).

3. Environmental governance and management

3.1. Environmental policy framework and legislation

Currently, there is a drive to modernise environmental policy, with a strong focus on public health, particularly on new, emerging risks. The government outlined the approach in a Memorandum to the House of Representatives from the State Secretary for the Environment (Government of the Netherlands, 2014). The document recognises the important advances in environmental policy made over the past decades, but signals a new era for environmental policy given that the major environmental issues being encountered today and that lie ahead are of a different order and require a new approach. The modernisation approach emphasises more active international co-operation and continued efforts to streamline environmental legislation and regulations. It also advocates a new role for the government as a facilitator of "new coalitions" to tap into the energy of civil society and the private sector.

Although the Netherlands was a pioneer in the elaboration of long-term comprehensive visions for environmental policy and planning as early as the 1980s, an effective long-term vision has been lacking over the review period. As a result, short-term actions may not have been the most effective in light of longer-term aims. This may have also contributed to some instability in environmental policy over the period. For example, there have been numerous shifts in climate and energy policy, environmentally related taxation and policy visions for sustainable mobility. At the same time, significant strides were made in some areas, such as water management and external safety policy, following major accidents. In the area of water management, the Delta Programme sets out a comprehensive vision and a long-term policy agenda. Such an approach could provide a good model for developing a long-term strategy for environmental policy.

The Netherlands made impressive progress in streamlining environment legislation, regulations and permitting requirements. A major legislative overhaul is currently taking place to consolidate all of the national environmental legislation under one framework in the Environment and Planning Act. The new act will contain integrated rules on the wide array of activities affecting the environment, including land-use planning, urban and rural development, water management, environmental protection, nature conservation, construction, cultural heritage, mining and the development of major public and private works. This marks an important shift from environmental law dispersed across sectorial legislation (13 acts and parts of 14 other acts) into a consolidated piece of legislation. The act is expected to take effect in 2018. In the process of introducing secondary legislation to support its implementation, it will be important to establish a strong footing for the environment in the context of the recent decentralisation trend providing greater discretion to sub-national authorities in balancing economic, social and environmental considerations.

This consolidation of environmental legislation builds on other important efforts over the review period to streamline environmental regulations, while maintaining the level of environmental protection. For example, the Activities Decree, which came into effect in 2008, drastically reduced the number of installations that require an environmental permit, providing for greater reliance on general binding rules. In addition, "all-in-one" permitting established in 2010 provides a single procedure to apply for environmental permits, replacing requirements for multiple permits. These efforts have significantly reduced the administrative burden, resulting in cost and time savings. In addition, the Netherlands has launched the "Make it Work" initiative to identify opportunities for making the EU environmental *acquis* more coherent and consistent. This initiative should also contribute to better implementation of EU environmental legislation, while maintaining the level of ambition in terms of environmental protection.

Recent OECD analysis (Botta and Koźluk, 2014) of the stringency of select environmental policies (mainly related to the electricity sector) ranks the Netherlands among the most stringent. Yet considering the significant consolidation and streamlining efforts over the period, it would be valuable for the government to assess the impact of these changes, as has been done with the Activities Decree. This would ensure that, collectively, they meet the aim of maintaining (or increasing) the overall level of environmental protection in practice.

3.2. Multi-level environmental governance

In the context of a broader decentralisation trend, the Netherlands decentralised many environmental competencies, including environmental permitting and supervision, spatial planning and nature policy. The reforms sought to provide more discretion and authority to provinces and municipalities to allow for more tailored policies and experimentation with various approaches. However, the decentralisation of tasks has not necessarily been accompanied by additional resources. As a result, sub-national governments might not have the necessary financial, managerial, human and technical capacity to manage their new functions, leading to inconsistent policy implementation. Alarming reports from the Dutch Safety Board (2013, 2012) about high-profile incidents at chemical facilities highlighted major deficiencies in policy implementation and spurred action to address them.

The establishment of the 29 Environmental Services (ODs) in 2014 were an important part of the response to address existing weaknesses. The ODs bring together experience and expertise on environmental licensing, compliance assurance and enforcement. They work at the request of and are funded by the competent authority (municipalities or provinces). The Netherlands faces a challenge to ensure the ODs operate effectively and achieve strong and consistent environmental performance. A large and experienced OD, like the DCMR in Rijnmond, is generally performing well. However, there is uncertainty about the capacity, knowledge and expertise of some of the recently established ODs. Their effectiveness could be improved by putting in place national mandatory quality criteria, strengthening financing arrangements to ensure stable and sufficient funding, and strengthening oversight at national level. Building on the co-operation and mechanisms to share experience already in place for the six ODs responsible for Seveso sites could facilitate the exchange of expertise among all the ODs. The evaluation of the ODs planned in the coming years will be important to assess the quality of their performance and to identify further opportunities for improvement.

3.3. Voluntary agreements

The Netherlands has a long and distinctive tradition of consensus-based decision making, known as the "polder approach". This approach, carried out through dialogue and negotiation, is used to reach decisions in which more than one level of government is involved. Given this strong tradition, the use of voluntary agreements (e.g. negotiated "covenants" or "gentlemen's agreements") is commonplace. This has produced mixed results in achieving environmental aims. Reliance on voluntary agreements may undermine environmental performance in some cases, such as situations where low-hanging fruit have already been harvested and the scope for "win-wins" is limited. Voluntary agreements cannot guarantee that agreed-upon goals will be met, and they also lack effective sanctions. More difficult commitments have to be monitored more closely.

As part of the current drive to modernise environmental policy in the Netherlands, the government is exploring new ways of working with society and business. A prominent example is the "Green Deals" programme launched in 2011. This is an innovative way of getting the best out of the "polder approach" by removing obstacles to implementing environmental efforts by industry (including small and medium-sized enterprises [SMEs]) and agriculture. The deals consist of agreements between the government and various private parties that focus mainly on removing non-financial barriers related to regulations, legislations or licensing. Nearly 200 Green Deals have been concluded so far. The

Netherlands Environmental Assessment Agency (PBL) has been positive about the Green Deals approach, noting there are opportunities to improve and extend the programme (PBL, 2014, 2011a), by, for example, improving project selection.

3.4. *Environmental compliance and enforcement*

The Netherlands has made effective use of a risk-based approach in the area of enforcement and compliance, putting limited, and shrinking, resources to best use. For example, the Human Environment and Transport Inspectorate (ILT) and the Netherlands' Food and Consumer Product Safety Authority (NVWA) use a risk-based approach to profile potentially non-compliant installations with significant risks. This approach is also applied by the ODs specialised in the enforcement of the Seveso Directive. There is also a robust approach to avoid and deter chemical accidents. There is an increasing use of covenants with companies based on trust, combined with regular oversight and periodic auditing. This new approach should be carefully monitored to ensure that it contributes to increased compliance and avoids undue accommodation of poorly performing companies. Further, spending cuts for supervision and enforcement of environmental regulations have raised concerns and their impact should also be monitored.

The government is also exploring changes to the existing liability regime as part of efforts to better deal with the potential impacts of new, emerging risks (from new substances and technologies). The aim is to make companies liable for negligence in the case of negative impacts arising from these risks to act as an incentive for them to identify and control such emerging risks. This could also help save resources dedicated to enforcement.

3.5. *Environmental information and policy evaluation*

The Netherlands has a very comprehensive system of environmental information and strong policy evaluation mechanisms, which could be further exploited. The country is privileged to have world-class, independent research institutions (e.g. the Netherlands Environmental Assessment Agency, Central Bureau of Statistics, universities, etc.), which provide a strong scientific evidence basis for the formulation and evaluation of environmental policy. However, the outcome of the work of these institutions is not always used in policy making to the extent that it could be. The country uses a high quality strategic environmental assessment (SEA) and environmental impact assessment (EIA) for plans and projects with possible environmentally-sensitive consequences. The Netherlands Commission for Environmental Assessment (NCEA), which reviews and reports on the scope and quality of environmental assessments, exerts significant influence.

Recommendations on environmental governance and management

Environmental governance framework

- Develop a clear, comprehensive, long-term vision for environmental policy that provides a coherent framework for specific medium- and short-term action plans. The vision should reinforce and support the cross-sectorial approach embodied in the Environment and Planning Act.
- Seize the window of opportunity provided by the introduction of the Environment and Planning Act and the introduction of secondary legislation to establish a strong footing for securing environmental performance in the context of the recent decentralisation

Recommendations on environmental governance and management *(cont.)*

trend, providing greater discretion to sub-national authorities in balancing economic, social and environmental considerations.

- Continue to strengthen efforts related to external safety (including preventing chemical accidents). This may include improving guidance for companies on how to deal with specific external safety issues; extending the enforcement of rules and considering the performance of SMEs; improving the transparency of the permitting process to promote accountability and public participation; and working with (large) companies to enhance their safety culture.
- Better exploit potential synergies between the Water Framework Directive and Natura 2000 by, for example, giving greater weight to ecological considerations in water management.
- Ensure the newly established Environmental Services (ODs) carry out their tasks in an effective manner that will support strong and consistent environmental performance. This could be supported by: consolidating the number of ODs (considering economies of scale, possible specialisation and the relevant ecological scale); ensuring sustainable funding; strengthening mechanisms for the exchange of good practice and expertise among ODs; establishing national mandatory quality criteria; and monitoring the quality of performance.

Voluntary agreements

- Consider using voluntary agreements such as covenants and "Green Deal" projects in a more selective manner by limiting their use to circumstances where "win-win" solutions can lead to expected policy outcomes without reliance on regulatory sanctions.

Environmental compliance and enforcement

- Continue to explore the possibility to improve the existing liability regime as part of efforts to better deal with the potential impacts of new, emerging risks.

Environmental information and policy evaluation

- Strengthen the link between science, policy analysis and policy evaluation, while reinforcing the capacity and knowledge base for environmental policy within relevant ministries by making better use of the available research outcomes. In particular, reinforce the independence of public research institutes, strengthen the use of independent policy assessment and cost-benefit analysis, and broaden the use of explicit carbon values in policy evaluation.

4. Towards green growth

The Netherlands has made progress towards green growth over the review period, but at a moderate pace. Building on the Sustainability Agenda launched in 2011, the government further elaborated its green growth aspirations in a Memorandum to the House of Representatives in March 2013. The document set out the four pillars of the government's policy for green growth: smart use of market incentives; an incentivising framework with legislation that promotes dynamism; innovation; and the government as a network partner (Government of the Netherlands, 2013).

The 2013 Energy Agreement for Sustainable Growth of the Social and Economic Council of the Netherlands (the Energy Agreement) provides the cornerstone for Dutch climate and energy policy. The agreement succeeded in creating a common understanding around shared goals for energy and climate policy among a broad spectrum of stakeholders. It spells out objectives and policy instruments for the energy sector, aiming to secure a high degree of stability in climate and energy policy for the longer-term. Objectives include improving energy efficiency, scaling up renewable energy, phasing out the least efficient coal-fired power plants and reducing CO_2 emissions from transport, as well as promoting employment, innovation and investment. However, early assessments indicate the policy measures agreed may not be sufficient to reach the stated objectives.

4.1. *Environmentally related taxes*

As part of the green growth toolbox, the Netherlands continues to use a number of potentially cost-effective economic instruments, such as emissions trading systems and indexed environmentally related taxes, which are raising a significant amount of revenue. Measured as a percentage of GDP, only three other OECD member countries (Denmark, Turkey and Slovenia) raised more revenue from environmental taxes in 2013 (Figure 2). Further, the share of this revenue coming from tax bases other than energy and motor vehicles was among the highest across the OECD.

Figure 2. **The Dutch raise more revenue from environmentally related taxes as a share of GDP than most OECD member countries, 2013**

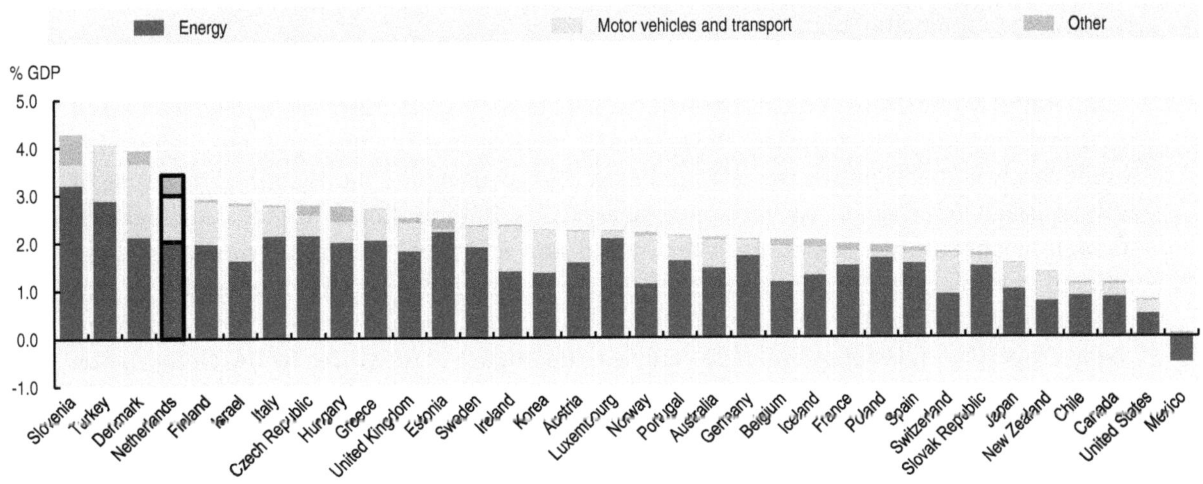

a) Until 2014, the system used to stabilise end-use prices of motor fuels caused tax revenue to turn negative (i.e. become a subsidy) in years when the international oil price was high. Mexico's 2013 Tax Reform corrected this mechanism and introduced a tax on fossil fuels based on their carbon content, which will yield positive revenue.

Source: OECD (2015), *OECD Database on Instruments Used for Environmental Policy and Natural Resources Management.*

StatLink http://dx.doi.org/10.1787/888933279993

There is scope to improve the design of several environmentally related taxes, including energy taxes, to enhance both their environmental effectiveness and cost efficiency. Currently, energy taxation has been designed primarily taking into account the climate impacts of energy consumption of small users, particularly households. Large energy users – and greenhouse gas emitters – face much lower tax rates at the margin than small-scale users. This is largely due to the fear of negative competitiveness impacts of higher taxes on the energy use or carbon emissions of large companies. However, recent OECD studies (Arlinghaus, 2015; Flues and Lutz, 2015) have indicated that such fears are not well founded, at least for taxes not much higher than current levels.

Further, energy taxation is applied unevenly across energy sources and there are large differences in the effective carbon tax rates on energy use. Thus, energy tax rates do not reflect well the relevant environmental damages, including local air pollution. For example, the current tax rate on coal is very low, when considering the environmental damages of coal use on air quality, even before a planned exemption for the use of coal in electricity generation is taken into account. The OECD has recently estimated that the social cost of mortalities due to outdoor air pollution in the Netherlands was about USD 25 billion in 2010.

While it is important to address negative impacts on low-income households of the relatively high tax rate on electricity, the lump-sum compensation of EUR 312 per electricity network connection results in a negative electricity tax for about 10% of households. This can be explained in part by the fact that lump-sum compensation is supposed to cover taxes on both electricity and natural gas, but for administrative reasons, it is deducted only from the electricity bill. On the other hand, the surcharge on the electricity tax introduced to finance the increasing subsidies for renewable electricity (for which no additional lump-sum compensation will be provided) is expected to cause a 50% increase in electricity bills for households up to 2020. This increase will come on top of already high electricity costs, compared to other OECD member countries.

Further, the distributional impacts of the subsidies to renewable electricity generation could be problematic, as low-income households generally have limited scope to take advantage of the subsidies (by installing solar panels, for example), but will have to contribute to financing them.

The country has a large share of low-polluting modes of transport, including a comparatively low share of diesel cars due in part to the higher purchase and annual taxes on diesel than on petrol vehicles. However, it is notable that the total tax rate on petrol is significantly higher than the tax rate on diesel. The government has encouraged the use of low-emission vehicles via the very progressive CO_2 differentiation of motor vehicle taxes, as well as specific tax preferences for hybrid and electrical vehicles. These measures caused the average CO_2 emissions of newly registered passenger vehicles in the Netherlands to be the lowest across EU countries in 2014. Yet, given the EU-wide "cap" on the average CO_2 emissions of all new vehicles, the impact of measures by the Netherlands on EU-wide emissions will be small or non-existent if the EU-wide fuel economy constraint is binding, but these measures impose fiscal losses on the Netherlands.

The fiscal sustainability of environmentally related taxes is an important consideration, given that they raise a significant share of tax revenue. Energy and motor vehicle taxes alone represent about 8% of total tax revenue. Environmentally related tax rates in the Netherlands are indexed to inflation, securing their environmental effectiveness and contributing to their fiscal sustainability over time. However, measures leading to low-polluting modes of transport, along with rapidly improving vehicle fuel efficiencies, have caused significant tax-base erosion for vehicle taxes. The Netherlands, therefore, needs to consider an alternative design of its vehicle taxes, including considering road pricing, taking foreseen technological changes into account.

Environmentally harmful subsidies in the Netherlands in 2010 amounted to between EUR 5-10 billion according to estimates by PBL (2011b). Although environmentally harmful subsidies to the agriculture sector have been greatly reduced over the past years, around one-third of the subsidies estimated by PBL relate to agriculture. This contributes to a very intensive livestock sector in the Netherlands, leading to important nutrient run-off.

There are also a number of exemptions and refund mechanisms in Dutch energy taxes mainly benefiting large-scale users. These include a refund of the energy tax for large industrial electricity consumers under certain conditions; reduced natural gas tax rates for the horticulture sector when participating in energy efficiency agreements; and rebates and subsidies for energy distribution firms to deploy combined heat and power, energy-saving technologies and renewable electricity.

4.2. *Environment-related investment and financing*

The Netherlands has implemented a complex system of instruments, including feed-in-tariffs, regulatory standards, tax incentives, accelerated depreciation and energy tax rebates for companies entering into long-term agreements with the government. While these instruments have stimulated large investments in clean energy, mainly biomass co-firing until 2013 and onshore wind energy, the Netherlands is not on track to meet its objectives on renewable energy and energy efficiency under the 2013 Energy Agreement. Further, support measures have not been effective enough to achieve interim targets under the EU's Renewable Energy Directive. With the implementation of support scheme SDE+ in 2011, the share of renewable energy is expected to grow significantly from 2017 onwards (ECN, 2014). However, this positive forecast is subject to favourable development of uncertainties surrounding co-firing of biomass in coal-fired plants and operation of delayed large offshore wind projects.

Since the early 2000s, several changes in targets and support measures have made the investment framework for renewable energy and energy efficiency unstable. There are questions about whether clean energy investments would have been made without public support and the resulting windfall gains. There are also questions about cost effectiveness of tax relief to promote better environmental outcomes. The evaluation of the Energy Agreement, planned in 2016, should provide the basis for reviewing the set of instruments.

Between 2000 and 2011, environmental expenditure remained at around 2% of GDP, a relatively high level compared with other European countries. As in other OECD member countries, waste and wastewater management are the main expenditure items, accounting for more than half of the total. Investment in wastewater treatment has grown faster than all other areas, helping the country to comply with the EU Urban Wastewater Treatment Directive and to meet the highest treatment standards. The Netherlands has a solid system for financing water resources management. Nearly all financial costs of service provision are recovered through charges, levies and taxes. However, the contribution from the various sectors (households, agriculture and industry) to cost recovery is unclear as is the extent to which price incentives stimulate efficient water use.

4.3. *Promoting eco-innovation and environmental goods and services*

The environmental goods and services sector grew faster than the whole economy in the past decade, in particular since 2005. In 2012, it accounted for 2.1% of GDP and 1.8% of employment, broadly in line with the EU average. As in other OECD member countries, waste and wastewater management, renewable energy and energy saving are the most important activities. The production of renewable energy has been the fastest growing activity both in terms of value added and employment. The number of jobs in government administration related to environmental protection has been noticeably reduced since the global economic crisis.

Since the 1970s, strong environmental and innovation policies have helped the Netherlands develop innovation capacity in environment-related technologies, which boosted the economy's productivity and competitiveness. Over 2000-11, the Netherlands has developed a comparative advantage in technologies related to energy efficiency in lighting, energy generation from biofuels and waste, and CO_2 capture and storage. It is still one of the world leaders in water technologies. However, it is lagging behind the most eco-innovative OECD member countries, which could affect its competitiveness in the future. Public investment in energy research development and demonstration (RD&D) rose between 2005-10, dropped sharply in 2011 and only partially recovered in 2012 (IEA, 2014) (Figure 3). While the government R&D budget is set to fall in the period to 2018, the share of environment- and energy-related R&D spending (already below the OECD average at the start of the 2010s) is planned to be further reduced. This will weaken some of the country's world-class environment and energy research institutes.

Figure 3. **Strong fluctuations in public RD&D spending on energy**

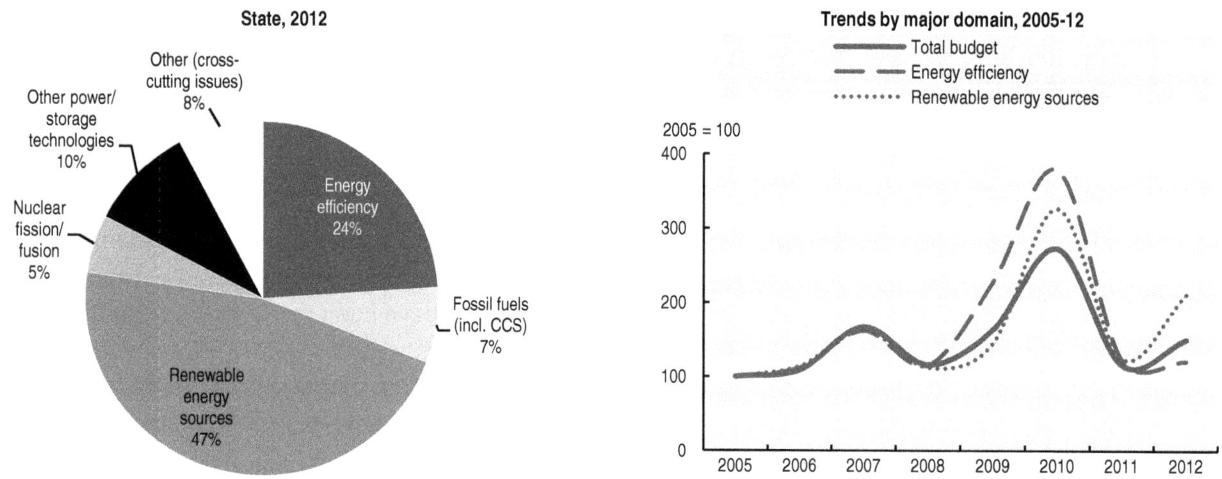

Note: Government budgets for research, development and demonstration (RD&D).
Source: IEA (2015), *IEA Energy Technology and RD&D Statistics* (database).

StatLink http://dx.doi.org/10.1787/888933280001

Although there is no specific eco-innovation plan, green innovation activities have been supported under various initiatives such as the 2011 Top Sector policy, the 2013 Energy Agreement and the Green Deals programme. However, there are concerns that their leverage effect on private investment may not be sufficient to achieve the Dutch 2020 R&D objectives or its targets under the Energy Agreement. Another concern is that larger firms and existing industries are better organised than SMEs and emerging industries, and can thus gain from a "first-mover" advantage in dealing with public support schemes. In 2013, a specific scheme (MIT) was introduced to strengthen innovative SMEs in top sectors; a positive development. There is a need for providing longer-term direction to research and a potential for better focusing support on green innovation. Adopting ambitious commitments such as those on the circular economy, ensuring the stability of the regulatory framework and public acceptance of renewable energy and energy efficiency policies are opportunities for boosting green innovation.

The system of investment support and tax incentives for R&D and environment-related technologies could be reviewed to ensure its consistency and efficiency in fostering the most innovative technologies, while achieving environmental objectives. For example, the subsidy for renewable energy has favoured low-cost and proven technologies. More attention could also be given to non-technological innovation, for example, in the water sector. The Netherlands is among the most advanced EU countries in green public procurement. However, there is potential to shift rewards to reap greater environmental gains and to apply life-cycle costing.

4.4. *Trade, development and environment*

In 2013, the Netherlands was the sixth-largest donor of the OECD Development Assistance Committee (DAC) with 0.67% of its gross national income given as official development assistance (ODA). This is below the United Nations target of 0.7% for the first time since 1975 and the development budget is planned to be further cut by EUR 3.3 billion over 2014-17. Since 2000, environment-focused aid decreased to 10% of total sector allocable aid in 2012-13, a very low share compared with the DAC average of more than 30%. In contrast, Dutch aid related to climate change has risen with a strong focus on adaptation, notably for water management, climate-smart agriculture and emergency preparedness in least developed countries. All Dutch-supported interventions are screened for environment and climate issues. However, the recent focus on climate should not crowd out other important environmental issues, particularly biodiversity, forests and broader natural resource management.

Recommendations on green growth

- Ensure the assessment of the 2013 Energy Agreement planned for 2016 is carried out in a thorough, independent and transparent manner. If this assessment indicates that it is unlikely that the agreed objectives will be met, or if the cost effectiveness of certain instruments is low, changes should be made to increase the environmental effectiveness and economic efficiency of Dutch climate and energy policy.
- Consider a partial switch from taxation of electricity towards taxation of natural gas use in households. As natural gas use is not covered by the EU ETS, this would lead to lower EU-wide GHG emissions. Consider contributing to effectively making the "cap" of the ETS stricter by buying and retiring some emission allowances. Reconsider the planned tax exemption for coal used in electricity generation, taking into account the impact of such a tax on local air pollution. Carefully consider the long-term fiscal sustainability of the current vehicle taxes.
- When assessing the introduction – or reintroduction – of environmentally related taxes, the environmental benefits that these taxes can stimulate should be considered on par with their administrative cost and their revenue generation potential. Even if the revenue generation potential of some taxes may be small, the environmental advantages they might contribute to could justify their implementation.
- Develop an ambitious framework for promoting eco-innovation that includes a balanced and consistent mix of increased public support for R&D, demand-side measures and partnerships with the private sector, with a focus on frontrunner SMEs; maintain a stable and clear policy and investment framework for innovation to support policy objectives, such as those for the circular economy and renewable energy; continue to refine criteria for public procurement to reap greater environmental gains and encourage green procurement approaches in the private sector.
- Ensure a strong and balanced commitment to the environment and climate within an increased volume of official development assistance, in line with international commitments.

5. Sustainable mobility

The Netherlands has managed to achieve and maintain a high share of environmentally friendly modes of transport. There is a relatively low share of diesel cars, biking is an important mode of urban transportation and goods transport on inland waterways is almost as important as road freight. The country is an important global transport hub, with the Port of Rotterdam the largest port in Europe. Since 2000, overall, freight and passenger transport volumes have been stable (except for rail freight, but this is a small share of the total transport per rail), as is the case in many high-income countries. Incoming freight transit traffic has increased, however, due to the growing internationalisation of economic activity; national freight traffic has decreased due to the shift in economic activity towards services.

In the coming years, the very densely populated Randstad (the metropolitan area with the four largest cities of Amsterdam, Rotterdam, The Hague and Utrecht) will continue to attract more inhabitants and commuters. This will raise congestion issues for road, rail and local public transport. With one of the most dense and congested road networks in Europe, the Netherlands has benefited from road capacity-enhancing measures. However, as the easy wins in terms of better road management have largely been exhausted, a further increase of road traffic is unlikely to be solved by additional road capacity alone, leaving road pricing as a principal policy option to address congestion. A proposal for road pricing had been considered as early as 2005, but was set aside when the government resigned for unrelated reasons, resulting in a missed opportunity. Evaluations of the proposal at the time indicated the cost of implementation, as well as a lack of public acceptance and support in Parliament posed significant barriers. The 2013 Energy Agreement includes plans to begin studying road pricing again as of June 2016.

All air pollution emissions from transport have declined significantly since 2004, except for CO_2 emissions, which have decreased only slightly since 2008 (Figure 4). Stricter emission standards for cars, as well as the economic recession and subsidies for more fuel-efficient cars, have driven emission reductions. Air quality in zones with intensive road traffic has strongly improved, although some hot spots remain, in particular around major cities and transportation corridors. The EU annual limit concentrations of particulate matter (PM_{10}) and nitrogen dioxide (NO_2) are only exceeded along a limited number of roads. There has been a clear improvement compared to 2004.

Fewer hours have been lost to congestion in nearly all congestion-prone regions over the last three years. This is explained, in part, by a 42% decrease in travel time losses due to more road capacity in heavily congested areas despite a 30% increase in travel time losses due to an increase in traffic volumes since 2004. The latter was caused by growth in population, employment and car ownership. The 2013 Energy Agreement includes a number of mostly voluntary measures to reduce congestion. An example of a voluntary measure agreed under a previous programme included a system of 16 regional covenants to reduce the number of car trips. This agreement has fallen short; the number of trips has dropped by 1.5% instead of 5% over several years.

Noise hindrance from transport has declined, with the number of houses exposed to "high noise levels" (more than 65 decibels) along national roads reduced by over one-third between 2006 and 2011. The country has an ambitious plan to continue reducing noise levels of road, rail and air transport, in line with the rising sensitivity and attention of the population to noise issues. This is important, given the country's high population density

Figure 4. **Air pollution emissions from transport declined, 2004-13**

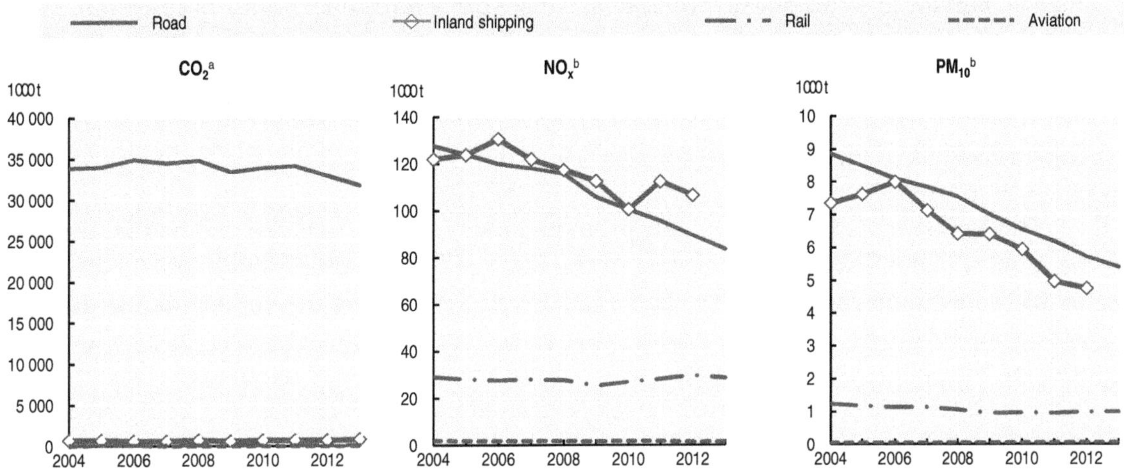

a) Emissions from road, water, rail and air transport reported according to the IPCC guidelines and calculated on the basis of motor fuel sales in the Netherlands.
b) Emissions from mobile sources, excluding emissions from mobile machinery, fishery and seagoing shipping.
Source: CBS (2015), *StatLine* (database).

StatLink http://dx.doi.org/10.1787/888933280010

and the fact that health damage of noise could well be underestimated. A noise innovation programme resulted in cheaper solutions to reduce noise at the source. As the main airport is in a densely populated area, the Netherlands faces a challenge in managing noise levels around airports at acceptable levels for residents.

The Dutch road system performs well in international comparisons of traffic safety. Over the last 12 to 15 years, improvements include better car technologies, road design (for instance, the building of roundabouts) and traffic regulation, which have helped reduce car fatalities by more than half.

Successive governments have put forward many different policy visions for sustainable mobility over the last ten years. Policy changes are needed when external conditions change dramatically, such as the revision of tax and subsidy programmes due to the recession. It is less clear why policy has changed significantly to deal with other issues, such as climate change and road and congestion management. The Netherlands can build on a strong tradition of scientific excellence and independent policy assessment by its public agencies. This is an important input for mobility policies and plans, and the independence of these institutes should be reinforced and maintained. There is traditionally strong co-operation and co-ordination between local, provincial and national authorities.

Policies to contribute to climate mitigation goals in the transport sector were not always cost effective. For example, the Netherlands restructured vehicle purchase taxes into a progressive carbon tax. The reform has been very effective at inducing the purchase of vehicles with lower CO_2 emissions, but has come at a very high cost per tonne of CO_2 abated. It also resulted in substantial tax base erosion. In addition, the net saving of CO_2 emissions has been smaller than expected, due to a rebound effect. Furthermore, monitoring studies have revealed a significant and growing discrepancy between actual CO_2 emission reductions and those calculated on the basis of emission data from the European driving cycle test results; actual emission reductions turned out to be only half of what was estimated by test values (PBL, 2015b). On the positive side, contrary to most other EU countries, the Netherlands did not inadvertently encourage the purchase of diesel cars by maintaining a specific annual vehicle tax for diesel cars. These vehicles may offer a small advantage in terms of GHG emissions, but are more harmful in terms of conventional emissions (NMVOC, NO_x and PM_{10}) than gasoline cars. A car scrapping scheme was implemented for a short period from 2009 to 2010. Analysis has shown, not surprisingly, that the net effect of such schemes on CO_2 emissions is low or even negative, as well as being very costly. The country will continue to face a challenge in preparing the transport sector for ambitious EU 2030-50 carbon emission targets.

The Netherlands has very actively promoted low-emission vehicles and has achieved the highest penetration of electric cars in the EU. The Netherlands aims to put 15-20 000 electric vehicles on the road by the end of 2015 and 1 million by the end of 2025. In 2014, more than 31 000 low-polluting vehicles were already on the road. However, most of these vehicles were plug-in hybrid vehicles, which drive only a portion of kilometres electrically. Because the electricity for electric charges is covered by the EU emissions trading system cap, when driven electrically, they do not contribute to additional carbon emissions (outside of the cap) nor do they emit almost any conventional air pollution (NMVOC, NO_x and PM_{10}). While low-emission vehicles may be a technology of the future, any cost-benefit analysis will show they are a very costly approach to reduce CO_2 emissions. However, stimulating low-polluting modes also aims to create an ecosystem that fosters innovation and green growth. The Netherlands has made electric vehicles a strategic priority and aims to be a frontrunner. In addition, at present, they are the only way to achieve the EU objective to decarbonise urban transport.

A recent study by Mandell and Proost (2015) suggests that countries that do not implement distance-based road charging for trucks, like the Netherlands, could risk losing a lot of their excise tax revenues if they decline to do so, as neighbouring countries have already done or are doing. As international trucks can decide where to take fuel, countries with a distance charge can always increase slightly their distance charge and lower their diesel excise, thereby undercutting the diesel excise of neighbours without distance charges. The gradual adoption of distance-based charges in the EU has arguably improved the effectiveness of taxation in addressing the externalities of road transport (Van Dender and Parry, forthcoming).

The number of passengers using Dutch airports has grown by 33% since 2004 and growth is likely to continue if real incomes grow. An air passenger tax was introduced in July 2008, but abolished a year later largely due to concerns that it would cause potential passengers to fly from neighbouring countries. However, soon after the Dutch tax was abolished, Germany introduced a similar tax. A tax on extra-European flights could help internalise some of the externalities caused by aviation, at least until a global system to address such externalities is agreed. Such a tax would need to be considered in the broader international context of the airline industry.

Recommendations on sustainable mobility

- Allocate efforts to reduce carbon emissions across sectors based on a cost-efficiency analysis. For example, consider reducing the progressive CO_2 emission differentiation in the motor vehicle purchase tax; this would bring the abatement incentives per tonne of CO_2 emitted from high-emission vehicles more in line with the marginal abatement cost found in other parts of the economy.

Recommendations on sustainable mobility *(cont.)*

- Reconsider the introduction of road pricing for cars, differentiated across place and time, possibly limited to the most congested zone of the country (Randstad). This can be done in a revenue-neutral way by substituting the vehicle purchase and ownership taxes and reducing motor fuel taxes.
- As long as road pricing is not introduced, the second-best option is to continue discouraging car use in urban areas through very high parking charges.
- Reconsider the pricing of public transport (local and rail) so it can cope with growing demand in the peak periods in the Randstad.
- Consider the introduction of distance-based road charging for trucks, as all neighbouring countries have already done or are doing. Trucks have become more fuel efficient and their options to fuel abroad limits the regulating and financing function of diesel charges.
- Consider the introduction of a passenger tax on extra-European aviation, together with neighbouring countries that have not already done so, taking into account potential competitiveness impacts in the broader international context of the airline industry.
- Continue efforts to reduce negative environmental impacts of transport, including through the ambitious plan for noise reduction. Evaluate the potential net benefits of further emission reductions in remaining air pollution hot spots.

6. Waste and materials management

The Netherlands is one of the OECD's best performers in the area of waste prevention and management. Since 2000, the country has considerably reduced the amount of waste it has generated, achieving absolute decoupling of waste generation from GDP. The amount of municipal solid waste (MSW) produced on a per capita basis fell by around 10% between 2000 and 2013, but remains just slightly above the OECD average. Over the review period, there has been a continuous move from waste disposal operations towards very high levels of recovery (including reuse, recycling and incineration for energy recovery) across all waste streams.

The Netherlands is one of the pioneers of sustainable waste management planning in the OECD. It has successfully achieved progressively ambitious targets set out in its National Waste Management Plans, but maintaining this trend may become increasingly difficult. For example, the impact of the global economic crisis dampened overall consumption, leading to reduced waste generation. As the economy recovers, one of the main challenges will be to ensure that waste generation does not rebound. Ongoing efforts to increase material recycling and composting of MSW and waste from business, government and services have resulted in marginal improvements; the proportion of waste recycled and composted has barely changed since 2000. As recycling rates are already relatively high compared to other OECD member countries, making further gains is difficult, but results from several local communities are promising.

Since 2000, emissions of most air pollutants from the waste sector declined, although nitrous oxide (NO_X) emissions increased from 2005. Greenhouse gas emissions from the waste sector dropped sharply (around 60%), largely due to minimising landfilling and the shift towards incineration of waste for energy recovery, since the emissions from these facilities are attributed to the energy sector. The Netherlands' status as a major importer and exporter of waste expanded considerably during the review period. In 2013, between 1.6-1.7 million tonnes (Mt) of waste was imported for incineration, most of it coming from the United Kingdom.

There has been a marked shift from landfilling to incineration, and within incineration, a shift from disposal to energy recovery. Incineration for energy recovery helps the Netherlands meet its EU renewable energy targets. One of the main drivers of investment in incineration capacity has been the application of high and increasing landfill taxes up to 2011, along with a landfill ban on many types of waste. High levels of investment in incineration resulted in overcapacity in the sector and also may have discouraged greater recycling rates. Recently, the government re-introduced the landfill tax and extended the coverage for the first time to include the incineration of Dutch residual waste; imported waste is exempt. The tax rate for incineration has been set primarily with an objective to generate a stable stream of revenue. But it may be too low to deliver sufficient incentives for more recycling and further reductions in waste generation.

The review period saw the successful liberalisation of the waste treatment market, improving market competition. The cost of waste management increased less than inflation, while the environmental performance of the sector increased across most, but not all, measures. Declining incineration gate charges led to lower waste management costs for municipalities and customers. The country is one of the best performers in the OECD in MSW management, while keeping MSW charges at some of the lowest levels in OECD Europe and attaining nearly full cost recovery; this is a considerable achievement.

The use of "pay as you throw", or "Diftar", charging schemes has generally improved the efficiency of waste management. These schemes allow for lower waste levies compared to non-differentiated rate schemes, as well as promote higher levels of waste separation. This reduces the amount of separation involved for municipalities and increases the value of the waste collected. There is further scope for use of Diftar schemes, especially in large and medium-sized cities. Another promising development is the use of reverse collection schemes in which the service offered for separated waste is better than that offered for unseparated waste.

The Netherlands excels in areas that have presented problems for other countries, such as the provision of high quality waste data, monitoring and enforcement, and awareness raising for the public. It was one of the first OECD member countries to introduce extended producer responsibility (EPR) schemes in the 1990s and has benefited from experimentation with various approaches and extensive dialogue with stakeholders. Currently, it has a system based on charging schemes set up by producer responsibility organisations (PROs). Overall, the current approach enjoys both greater economies of scope (compared with having a large number of PROs) and reduced administrative costs (compared with a taxation-based system), although some systems, like the one for plastic packaging, remain very expensive.

The Netherlands has taken significant and quite innovative steps to discourage illegal waste shipments, such as implementing risk-based information technology tools. At the same time, the high and increasing levels of trade coming through Dutch ports make it challenging to monitor and discourage illegal shipments. This may call for further increased investment to strengthen efforts to enforce EU and international laws on waste shipments.

Over the past several years, the Netherlands has been laying the groundwork for a transition beyond traditional waste management towards a circular economy. It is already one of the most resource-efficient members of the OECD in terms of GDP per unit of domestic material consumption (DMC) (Figure 5). The government has set out ambitious strategic objectives and broad lines of action to stimulate this transition, although policy

Figure 5. **The Netherlands is one of the most resource-efficient economies in the OECD**

DMC per capita versus GDP per capita, 2011[a]

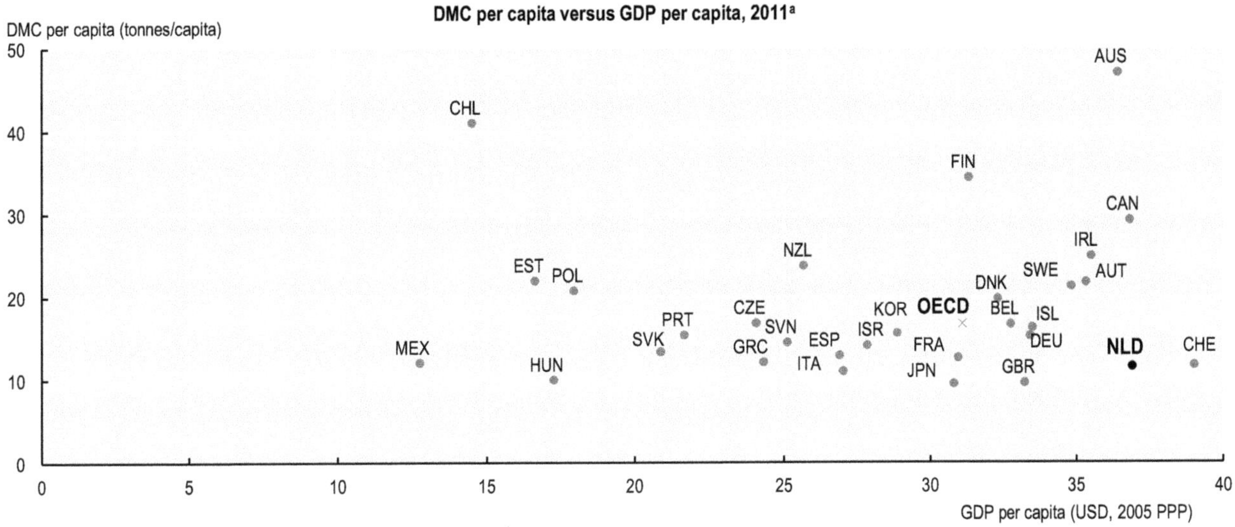

a) Domestic material consumption (DMC) designates the sum of domestic extraction of raw materials used by an economy and the physical trade balance (imports minus exports of raw materials and manufactured products).

Source: OECD (2015), "Material resources", *OECD Environment Statistics* (database).

StatLink http://dx.doi.org/10.1787/888933280023

development remains in early stages, as in other OECD member countries. The government is working with a range of Dutch stakeholders to draw lessons from pilot projects and to consider targets that could be set, monitored and measured. Putting the vision for the circular economy into action in a cost-effective way will require realistic targets informed by cost-benefit analysis. It will also require overcoming challenges presented in this new area, such as the need to develop new business models and dealing with commodity price volatility. The transition also requires new ways of working across the whole product chain and new product design and ownership models.

Recommendations on waste and materials management

- Maintain absolute decoupling of waste generation from GDP to avoid a potential rebound as the economy recovers by reinforcing efforts to reduce waste generation in the next iteration of the National Waste Management Plan. Consider an objective for the reduction of hazardous waste in the next iteration of the National Waste Management Plan, which was not done in previous plans.
- Consider the design of an emission-based tax as an alternative to the input-based tax now in place for the waste tax. This would provide a much more direct incentive to operators of incinerators to limit the environmental damages related to the combustion process as much as possible. Since environmental damages occur regardless of the origin of the waste treated, removing the exemption on imported waste could also be considered.
- Encourage broader uptake of schemes, such as "Diftar" charging schemes and reverse collection, which have been shown to promote greater separation of waste and lower the cost of treatment. There is significant scope for uptake in large and medium-sized cities. Encourage measures to promote further separate collection of plastic waste, without increasing waste treatment costs.

Recommendations on waste and materials management *(cont.)*

- Explore ways for EPR schemes to support the circular economy by going beyond just waste management and promoting systems that have an influence on sourcing, design and consumption phases; improve the quality of recycling within EPR schemes.
- Continue to support and reinforce efforts to minimise illegal waste trade, such as through the use of the risk-based approach to identify possible waste shipments, as well as to ensure that such waste is properly handled once identified. This may call for further increased investment over the coming years to strengthen efforts to enforce EU and international laws on waste shipments.
- Develop a roadmap for specific actions to promote the circular economy and a timeline for implementation; strengthen product policies to deliver stronger incentives for designs that are conducive to the circular economy, such as through product labelling and information, as well as specific design criteria where appropriate; promote reuse and remanufacturing, including through fiscal incentives (such as lower VAT for repair services), minimum quality standards and warranties, legal requirements on the availability of information and spare parts for repair and facilitating (as appropriate) recycling, refurbishment, reuse and repair in the relevant legislation.
- Encourage innovation through the Green Deals approach; develop policies that can support the emergence of new business models conducive to the circular economy, such as those based on services rather than the sale of goods; explore dynamic standard setting that can spur innovation; use green public procurement to support the circular economy.
- Put in place policies and measures that help to overcome information barriers and issues with access to finance, in particular for SMEs where the capacity to identify and implement resource efficiency opportunities is more constrained.
- Prioritise the development of indicators to monitor resource productivity and progress towards a circular economy; consolidate and further develop material flow accounts by industry and improve the coherence between waste and material flow statistics (especially for secondary raw materials and recycling rates); encourage the inclusion of circular economy and resource productivity indicators (physical and financial data) in reporting by businesses and financial institutions.

References

Arlinghaus, J. (2015), "Impacts of carbon prices on indicators of competitiveness: A review of empirical findings", *OECD Environment Working Papers*, No. 87, OECD Publishing, Paris, *http://dx.doi.org/10.1787/5js37p21grzq-en*.

Botta, E. and T. Koźluk (2014), "Measuring environmental policy stringency in OECD countries: A composite index approach", *OECD Economics Department Working Papers*, No. 1177, OECD Publishing, Paris, *http://dx.doi.org/10.1787/5jxrjnc45gvg-en*.

Dutch Safety Board (2013), "Odfjell Terminals Rotterdam Safety during the 2000-2012 period", Dutch Safety Board, The Hague, June 2013, *www.onderzoeksraad.nl/en/onderzoek/1883/odfjell-terminals-rotterdam-safety-during-the-2000-2012-period* (accessed 14 May 2015).

Dutch Safety Board (2012), "Fire at Chemie-Pack Moerdijk", Dutch Safety Board, The Hague, February 2012, *www.onderzoeksraad.nl/uploads/items-docs/1805/Rapport_Chemie-Pack_EN_def.pdf* (accessed 14 May 2015).

ECN (2014), *Nationale Energieverkenning 2014* [National Energy Outlook 2014], Energy Research Centre of the Netherlands, Petten, *www.ecn.nl/publicaties/ECN-O--14-036*.

Flues, F. and B.J. Lutz (2015), "Competitiveness impacts of the German electricity tax", *OECD Environment Working Papers*, No. 88, OECD Publishing, Paris.

Government of the Netherlands (2014), "Modernisation of environmental policy", Parliamentary document: Letter to the House of Representatives, 10 March 2014, *www.government.nl/documents-and-publications/parliamentary-documents/2014/03/10/modernisation-environmental-policy.html* (accessed 5 October 2014).

Government of the Netherlands (2013), "Green Growth: for a strong, sustainable economy", Parliamentary document: Memorandum to the House of Representatives, 28 March 2013, Minister of Economic Affairs and the State Secretary for Infrastructure and the Environment.

Hajer, M. (2011), "The energetic society: In search of a governance philosophy for a clean economy", Netherlands Environmental Assessment Agency, The Hague, ISBN: 978-90-78645-78-8.

IEA (2014), *Energy Policies of IEA Countries, The Netherlands, 2014 Review*, IEA/OECD Publishing, Paris, *http://dx.doi.org/10.1787/9789264210462-en*.

Mandell S. and S. Proost, (2015), "Why truck distance charges are contagious and drive fuel taxes to the bottom", *Discussion Paper Series*, March DPS 15.04, KU Leuven, Center for Economic Studies, Leuven, Belgium.

OECD (2015), "Development in individual OECD countries and selected non member economies", [ECO/CPE(2015)5].

OECD (2014a), *OECD Economic Outlook*, Vol. 2014/1, OECD Publishing, Paris, *http://dx.doi.org/10.1787/eco_outlook-v2014-1-en*.

OECD (2014b), *OECD Economic Surveys: Netherlands 2014*, OECD Publishing, Paris, *http://dx.doi.org/10.1787/eco_surveys-nld-2014-en*.

OECD (2014c), *OECD Economic Surveys: European Union 2014*, OECD Publishing, Paris, *http://dx.doi.org/10.1787/eco_surveys-eur-2014-en*.

PBL (2015a), *Waterkwaliteit nu en in de toekomst* [Water Quality Now and in the Future], Netherlands Environmental Assessment Agency, The Hague, *www.pbl.nl/publicaties/waterkwaliteit-nu-en-in-de-toekomst* (accessed 11 June 2015).

PBL (2015b), *Assessment of the Dutch Human Environment 2014 – The Future is Now*, Netherlands Environmental Assessment Agency, The Hague.

PBL (2014), *Green Gains: In Search of Opportunities for the Dutch Economy*, Netherlands Environmental Assessment Agency, The Hague.

PBL (2011a), Het effect van 59 Green Deals op het aandeel hernieuwbare energie en de uitstoot van niet-ETS-broeikasgassen: een quick scan, [The Effect of 59 Green Deals on the Share of Renewable Energy and Greenhouse Gas Emissions from Non-ETS: A Quick Scan], Netherlands Environmental Assessment Agency, The Hague.

PBL (2011b), *Environmentally Harmful Subsidies*, Netherlands Environmental Assessment Agency, The Hague, *www.pbl.nl/sites/default/files/cms/publicaties/PBL_2011_Environmentally%20Harmful%20Subsidies_500209002.pdf*.

Van Dender, K. and I. Parry (forthcoming), "How should countries tax road fuels, vehicles, and usage?", OECD and IMF.

ANNEX

Actions taken to implement selected recommendations from the 2003 OECD Environmental Performance Review of the Netherlands

RECOMMENDATION	ACTIONS TAKEN
Chapter 2: Environmental governance and management	
Retain and refine quantitative policy targets for reducing environmental pressures, and strengthen efforts to see that they are attained without slippage.	The Rutte I government (2010-12) explicitly announced it would redress environmental policy objectives to levels prescribed by the EU in order to establish a level playing field. The Rutte II cabinet has made one exception for the share of renewable energy in final energy consumption (16% in 2023, while the EU prescribes 14% in 2020).
Continue efforts to reduce emissions of NO_x, particulate matter and NMVOCs (e.g. from transport, energy and industry) in light of persistent problems with concentrations of NO_2, PM_{10} and ozone in some areas; implement the proposed NO_x emission trading scheme.	The emissions of all substances showed a downward trend in 1990-2012. The major overall drivers for this trend are emission reductions in the industrial sectors, cleaner fuels and cleaner cars. The main contributors to the decrease of NO_x emissions are the road-transport and energy sectors, despite a growth in road transport. The decrease is mainly attributable to European emission regulations for new road vehicles. Also for NO_x, standards have been set for installations by tightening the extent of emission stocks of heating installations. In meeting these requirements, Dutch industrial plants have reduced NO_x emissions by 62% since 1990. NMVOC emissions decreased for all major source categories. For transport, this is mainly due to introduction of catalysts and cleaner engines. For product use, the Netherlands implemented an intensive programme to reduce NMVOC content in consumer products and paints. In the industry sector, a specific abatement for NMVOC emissions was introduced. For particulate matter, standards have been set for installations by tightening limits on emissions from heating installations. In meeting these requirements, Dutch industrial plants have reduced PM emissions by 93% since 1990. Cleaner fuels in refineries, along with the side effect of emission abatement of SO_2 and NO_x in traffic and transport, also helped reduce emissions. The National Air Quality Cooperation Programme (NSL) is designed to ensure the Netherlands meets the targets for concentrations of fine particulates (PM_{10}) and NO_x. The NSL programme will run until 1 January 2017.
Strongly pursue implementation of policies to allocate "more space for water", establish ecological networks and better protect areas at risk (e.g. from floods); in particular, integrate water management, nature management and spatial planning.	The "Room for Rivers" programme was adopted in 2006. It sets out how more space for rivers can be provided to enhance safety and spatial quality in the area around the main rivers. The programme contains 35 measures that will contribute to 1 500 acres of nature area. There are also measures in the River Basin Management Plans (2009) to improve water quality, which aim to have a positive effect on ecological values. The measures seek synergies by combining different water tasks with Natura 2000 goals. For example, the construction of parallel channels in flood plains and the construction of natural banks (environmentally friendly banks). There has been a small cutback in the available budget. New water retention areas in the regional water system help to prevent flooding or retain water for dry periods. In these areas, the functions of water and nature are often combined. Also, measures have been taken to improve water quality in regional systems. As in rivers and lakes, these measures often also enhance nature.

RECOMMENDATION	ACTIONS TAKEN
Further reduce nitrogen loads from intensive agriculture (livestock and crop production) in line with related international commitments (EU Nitrates Directive, North Sea Action Programme).	Various Nitrate Action Programmes contain measures taken to further reduce nitrate leaching. The fifth Nitrate Action Programme (2014-17) further tightens nitrogen application levels for certain regions by a maximum of 20% for crops prone to leaching. N-levels are relaxed for grassland in clay regions from 350 to 385 kg N/ha.
Strengthen efforts to integrate biodiversity, nature and landscape conservation among themselves and with spatial planning.	Natura 2000 management plans focus on maintaining and restoring favourable conservation status of listed species and habitats. Urbanisation and the urban-rural interface has traditionally been the main theme of national spatial planning. Against the background of less housing demand and lower demand for offices, the "new" urban question is one of transformation of existing cities, more than expansion. This will be addressed by the Minister for Housing (without the prospect of new funding). The "ladder for sustainable urbanisation" is available as a guideline: Rung 1: Is there regional demand for housing, offices, amenities, etc.? Rung 2: Can demand be met by restructuring or transforming existing locations? Rung 3: New locations should be accessible to multiple transport modes.
Extend the use of spatial planning and regulation to serve pollution abatement, nature, biodiversity and landscape conservation, as well as risk prevention.	Legislation concerning external safety has been implemented. The National Air Quality programme (NSL) contains elements of spatial planning: minimal distances between roads and buildings with vulnerable people (schools, hospitals). The Programme-based Approach to Nitrogen (PAS) seeks to reduce nitrogen deposition (NO_x from traffic and industry and NH_3 from farming) on nature areas, using technical abatement measures, as well as spatial planning, to meet deposition targets. The programme seeks co-operation between stakeholders on national, regional and local levels. The National Policy Strategy for Infrastructure and Spatial Planning (SVIR) focuses on 13 national interests. Three of these interests are most relevant in this field: i) improvement of environmental quality (air, soil, water) and provide protection from noise pollution and external safety risks; ii) room to preserve and strengthen nationally and internationally unique cultural heritage and natural values; and iii) room for a national network of wildlife habitats to aid the survival and development of flora and fauna.
Enhance the role of provinces as a key level of policy integration, including environmental policy planning, land-use planning and water management planning.	The SVIR has been in force since June 2012. Central government intends to bring decision making on spatial planning closer to the stakeholders, delegating more to local and provincial authorities (through deregulation and decentralisation as the first option). Local and regional authorities will be able to make their own policy decisions, although they will be expected to contribute to simplifying and integrating spatial planning regulations. National-level planning policy focuses on 13 interests of national importance.
Further maintain a high-quality environmental information base and ensure continuity in environmental reporting activities.	The Minister of Infrastructure and Environment has commissioned a group of institutes to develop the "Atlas Leefomgeving", a web-based tool to integrate spatial information and make it accessible to the general public. See www.atlasleefomgeving.nl/home.
	Chapter 3: Towards green growth
Extend the use of economic instruments (e.g. waste, water and transport management) and their incentive effects, in line with the user and polluter pays principles.	Progress has been made on the use of economic instruments, but in some cases taxes were introduced only to be later abolished. In most cases, this was linked to a reduced tax base or competitiveness concerns.
Refine market-based instruments and extend the environmental tax system, having regard to simplicity, effectiveness, transaction costs and carrying out cost-benefit analysis.	The Netherlands is one of the frontrunners in the OECD in terms of the revenue raised from environmentally related taxes as a share of GDP. Many changes have taken place over the last ten years. Simplicity and effectiveness have been of concern. There appears to be tension between solid revenues and effectiveness from an environmental perspective.
Couple the regulatory energy tax with pollutant emissions (carbon tax) and consider its extension to large companies in the case of non-compliance with environmental targets.	The regulatory energy tax has expanded since 2003. Tariffs differ between target groups. There is no direct link to the CO_2 content. The Netherlands complies to a large extent with European emission targets.
Continue to work towards increased energy efficiency.	Energy efficiency has been a priority over the last decade and has been increased accordingly. An overview of the measures taken can be found in IEA country reviews of 2008 and 2014. The 2013 Energy Agreement aims to achieve a saving in final energy consumption averaging 1.5% annually.
Expand the use of renewable energy sources (e.g. in municipalities and large firms).	The use of renewable energy has been expanded mainly by subsidy schemes. The SDE+ is the latest such scheme. A full review of the policy measures can be found in the 2014 IEA country review. The 2013 Energy Agreement contains initiatives to raise production of renewable energy to 14% in 2020 (EU objective) and 16% in 2023 (national objective).

RECOMMENDATION	ACTIONS TAKEN
Strengthen and generalise requirements concerning environmental impact assessment to apply to all major projects financed through international assistance (ODA and non-ODA).	There are several examples of actions taken to support this recommendation. The Ministry of Foreign Affairs (MFA) has renewed its agreement with the Netherlands Commission for Environmental Assessment (NCEA) until 2017. The NCEA is an independent expert body that provides advisory services and capacity development on environmental assessment. In international co-operation, the NCEA has operated under an agreement with the MFA since 1993, with a special focus on 18 countries eligible for Dutch international co-operation. In addition, the NCEA works in several other countries, under agreement with donors such as the Dutch Ministry of Infrastructure and the Environment, Dutch embassies, the World Bank, European Union, etc. The core of the NCEA's international work is to assist environment and sector ministries, environmental assessment professionals and nongovernmental organisations to achieve better environmental assessment practice. It provides advice, capacity development and improved knowledge and learning resources on environmental assessment (EIA/SEA). In this way, EIA requirements will be strengthened for both national and internationally (donor) financed projects and plans in those countries. The Dutch Sustainability Unit (DSU), established at the NCEA, supports the Ministry of Foreign Affairs in making its international interventions in the domain of water and food security more sustainable. The DSU pays particular attention to environment (including EIA and SEA), climate and gender equality issues.
	Chapter 4: Sustainable mobility
Strengthen or revive efforts to integrate environmental and sustainable development concerns into transport policy.	The Netherlands has a multiple-year programme to facilitate the planning and building of spatial, infrastructural and transportation projects ("MIRT"). The spatial aspect was included in the process to ensure that infrastructural and transportation projects are well-embedded in their environment. The government is working on incorporating sustainability into the MIRT-system explicitly, by trying to take this into account in every phase of the project (from planning to building, maintenance and renovation). One measure to integrate environmental and sustainable development is the environment-index (*omgevingswijzer*) in infrastructural projects. This tool helps stakeholders gain insights in 12 aspects of sustainability, based on the "people-planet-profit" triangle. This enables them to consider the various options for a project more effectively. In the Getting Ahead Programme (*Meer Bereiken*), eight MIRT-research projects will be started, in which the aspect of sustainability will be strongly embedded. The government, local governments and public parties will work together even more closely than before. Basisnet, the national basic network for the transport of hazardous substances, sets legal risk limits for routes transporting dangerous goods on railways, roads or water. The same applies to the building code in the security zones along these routes. Municipalities must include these statutory building regulations in their spatial zoning plan, so developers and residents know exactly where they stand.
Further internalise externalities into transport operation and pricing: strengthen the use of existing economic instruments and introduce new ones, such as the suggested per-kilometre tax on lorries and cars (with differentiated rates according to time, place and the environmental impact of each vehicle) or other relevant instruments.	In 2007, the ruling administration decided to implement a pay-per-kilometre tax (*Anders betalen voor mobiliteit*). To prepare this legislation, the potential and possibilities (both technical options and public attitudes) were extensively investigated and a concept-plan was developed. Due to both lack of public acceptance and political coalitions, it was not desirable to implement a pay-per-kilometre tax. According to the current political coalition, there is no need to implement a pay-per-kilometre tax until 2020. One of the activities in the 2013 Energy Agreement is to further research a pay-for-use system. The first step will be taken by private parties. Nevertheless, a pay-for-use-system is still one of the possible measures for the future. A series of fiscal measures has been taken to stimulate the sale and use of (very) efficient and low-emission cars. In the Optimising Use Programme (*Beter Benutten*), measures have been taken to encourage people to avoid certain roads at certain times. The goal is to reduce congestion at the busiest points by 20% in 2014 with a great number of (sometimes small) measures. One of them is giving people a temporary financial reward to avoid the rush hours. This is an incentive to travel at different times and with different transport modes.
Pursue efforts to reduce noise emissions from road, rail and air traffic (e.g. emission reduction at source).	In 2012, new legislation came into force (SWUNG), ensuring there will be no increase in noise emissions on national infrastructure road and rail. Even when the amount of traffic increases, the emissions must remain the same. The latest SWUNG legislation is an addition and an improvement on earlier noise legislation. In the legislation, source measures are preferred above noise barriers. Only when necessary, additional measures can be taken. There are situations where noise levels are not increasing, but are already very high. For such situations, the SWUNG legislation included a single, large-scale measure to ensure noise abatement operations continue and to reduce existing high noise levels.

RECOMMENDATION	ACTIONS TAKEN
Urgently define and implement a package of measures to reduce CO_2 emissions from freight and passenger transport.	With the 2013 Energy Agreement, the government, a large number of companies, environmental organisations and financial institutions committed to a series of goals to reduce CO_2 emissions. For transport, they agreed on maximum CO_2 emissions of 25 Mt, which means a reduction of 6 Mt (17%) on top of earlier goals. Parties to the agreement are working on a large number of measures to achieve the goals. A selection of activities follows: • developing a sustainable fuel vision to aim for efficient use and alternatives • ensuring all new sold cars are zero emission in 2035 • introducing fiscal incentives for the use of electric cars and creating infrastructure to enable the use of electric cars • stimulating use of bikes and public transportation or making mobility more efficient through different measures. Since the "Green Deals" programme was launched in 2011, over 160 deals have been agreed, many of them related to transport. The aim of Green Deals is to enable companies, local governments and other organisations to develop sustainable initiatives by removing barriers such as legislation, a shortage of (investments) funds or lack of co-operating partners. The Green Deals "Zero Emission City Distribution" and "Personal Mobility" aim to significantly reduce CO_2 emissions. The Optimising Use Programme has reduced congestion on roads. A follow-up on this programme (*Beter Benutten 2*) is in preparation for the period 2014-17.
Chapter 5: Waste and materials management	
Take steps to ensure full implementation and enforcement of new international commitments concerning port reception and ship-generated wastes and cargo residues.	Directive 2000/59/EC on port reception facilities came into force in Dutch law on 1 January 2005. Adequate port reception facilities are available in all Dutch ports. Furthermore, indirect user charges and waste handling and management plans are implemented in all ports.

Source: Country submission.

PART I

Progress towards sustainable development

PART I

Chapter 1

Key environmental trends

This chapter provides a snapshot of key environmental trends in the Netherlands since 2000. It highlights the main achievements and remaining challenges on the path towards a greener economy. The chapter examines the Netherlands' progress in reducing the energy, carbon and material intensities of its economy; in managing the natural asset base; and in improving the environmental quality of life.

The statistical data for Israel are supplied by and under the responsibility of the relevant Israeli authorities. The use of such data by the OECD is without prejudice to the status of the Golan Heights, East Jerusalem and Israeli settlements in the West Bank under the terms of international law.

1. Introduction

This chapter provides a snapshot of key environmental trends in the Netherlands since 2000. Drawing on indicators from national and international sources, the chapter assesses progress towards the country's national and international targets. To the extent possible, it compares the state of the environment in the Netherlands with that of other OECD member countries. It highlights some of the main environmental achievements and remaining challenges on the path towards green growth and sustainable development.

The chapter first examines the Netherlands' main economic and social developments, including economic and fiscal performance, the structure of the economy, urbanisation patterns and the quality of life of the population. It then discusses the country's transition towards a low-carbon economy, especially focusing on energy use, as well as trends for greenhouse gas (GHG) and air emissions. It analyses progress towards a resource-efficient economy, paying particular attention to material consumption, waste management and agricultural inputs. It then examines the natural resource base of the country, looking at fossil fuel resources, as well as biodiversity and water issues.

2. The economic and social context

2.1. Economic performance

The Netherlands is the sixth-largest economy in the euro area and experienced an increase in real gross domestic product (GDP) of about 15% over 2000-14, with an annual growth rate of 1%. The economy grew steadily between 2000-08 at a rate in line with the OECD average (Figure 1.1) before facing a severe drop in 2009, when GDP decreased by 3.6% in just one year. Since then, GDP slightly recovered between 2010 and 2011, but has been falling almost continuously since mid-2011, driven by fluctuating domestic demand. Private consumption has been weakened by falling purchasing power, large declines in real house prices and insufficient liquid assets held by banks to support spending. Recently, however, nominal house prices appear to have stabilised at 20% below their peak, and the private sector is gaining some confidence.

Economic activity gradually recovered in 2014, with GDP growing by about 1% and expected to increase further in 2015 and 2016 (OECD, 2014a). With real GDP per capita at USD 46 200 (in current prices and purchasing power parity [PPP]) in 2013, living standards in the Netherlands are significantly higher than the OECD average (USD 37 900) (OECD, 2014b).

Macroeconomic indicators are traditionally strong for the Dutch economy. However, the fiscal balance of the Netherlands worsened during the economic crisis to a deficit of 5.6% of GDP in 2009, lower than the 8.4% average deficit among OECD member countries (OECD, 2013a). Public debt has increased since 2008, reaching 77% of GDP in 2013. Significant structural reforms are underway, namely in the labour market, health care and

Figure 1.1. **The Dutch economy is gradually recovering**

GDP trends,[a] 2000-13

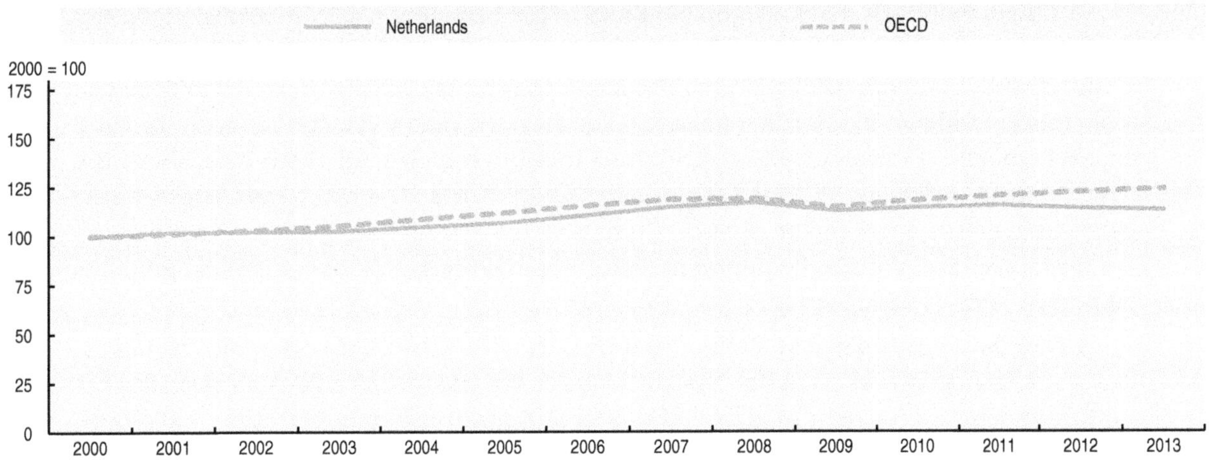

a) GDP expressed at 2005 prices and purchasing power parities.
Source: OECD (2014), "OECD Economic Outlook No. 95", *OECD Economic Outlook: Statistics and Projections* (database).

StatLink http://dx.doi.org/10.1787/888933280039

pension systems. In addition, distortions in the housing market are expected to be reduced through better targeting of social housing, lowering the property transfer tax and limiting tax benefits on mortgages, among other measures. Fiscal consolidation has also been achieved and the budget deficit lowered to 2.3% of GDP in 2014 (OECD, 2015a, 2014a, 2014b).

Government spending has generally been high over the last decade, accounting for about 47% of GDP in 2013. Dutch taxation levels are slightly lower than those in other OECD member countries. In 2012, the tax-to-GDP ratio stood at 39%, compared to the average of 39.4% among European Union (EU) member countries. The Netherlands has a rather centralised tax structure as local government taxes account for merely 3.8% of total tax revenues. In 2013, environmental protection accounted for 1.5% of GDP (see Table of Basic Statistics).

Environmentally related taxes generate around 3.5% of GDP, a level significantly higher than in most other OECD member countries (Chapter 3). They consist mainly of energy taxes, although the Netherlands raises significant revenue from transport taxes (excluding fuel taxes). It is also one of the few countries in the EU with a non-negligible contribution from pollution taxes (a tax on pollution of surface waters and sewerage charges). These pollution taxes account for around 0.5% of GDP, compared to an EU average of 0.1% (European Commission, 2014a).

2.2. Structure of the economy, employment and trade

In the Dutch economy, the services sector accounts for the largest share of GDP in value added (76%), followed by the industry and construction sector (22%), and by the agriculture sector (2%). All shares are close to the OECD average (see Table of Basic Statistics). The services sector employs the vast majority of the workforce. Economic activities are relatively dispersed geographically in the Netherlands compared to the OECD average (OECD, 2014c). In 2012, 75% of the population aged 15-64 years-old was employed, although the rate was 9% higher for men (OECD, 2014b). Job vacancies have been steadily declining and have reached their lowest level in nearly ten years. The unemployment rate, which stands at about 7%, is expected to stabilise by mid-2015 (OECD, 2014a). It is, however, lower than the OECD average of nearly 8% (see Table of Basic Statistics).

International trade plays a significant role in the economy. The Netherlands is a very open economy with a level of exports over GDP above the OECD average, and above that of countries of similar size (OECD, 2014c). The share of exports over GDP declined in 2009 due to a global slowdown in international trade, but has returned to positive growth. In 2013, exports amounted to some 83% of GDP, while imports represented about 72%, above the OECD averages of about 29% for both imports and exports. The country's major trading partners are Germany, Belgium, France, China and the United Kingdom. The core exports are machinery and transport equipment (20%), mineral fuels (20%) and chemical products (14%) (see Table of Basic Statistics).

Given the country's role as a major trading hub, with the Port of Rotterdam the largest in Europe, transport is an important sector in the Dutch economy. Large-scale investments in infrastructure, including road, rail, aviation and maritime transportation, have been made over the years to meet the country's needs (IEA, 2014). Overall freight and transport volumes have remained relatively stable since 2000. A significant share of freight transport in the Netherlands occurs via inland waterways, while passenger transport is largely dominated by road, a trend similar to many other OECD member countries. However, the use of rail increased by 25% over 2004-13. Bicycle use has traditionally represented a significant share in passenger transport, and currently some 10% of total distance is travelled by bicycle (Chapter 4).

2.3. Urbanisation

The Netherlands is highly urbanised and densely populated, with 85% of the population living in urban areas covering almost 66% of the country's territory. Like most other OECD member countries, urbanisation has increased, reducing the number of rural inhabitants. This was driven in part by modernisation of the agriculture sector, but also by growth of the services sector. As a result, no Dutch region is considered predominantly rural, according to the OECD typology[1], which classifies regions as being predominantly urban, intermediate or rural (OECD, 2014c). Spatial planning has traditionally been an important policy area for the country, with the aim of configuring its dense urban structure (Chapter 2).

With 16.9 million inhabitants in 2013 and a relatively small surface area of 33 720 square kilometres (km^2), the Netherlands has a markedly higher population density than the OECD Europe average (405.7 inhabitants per km^2 compared to 109.5 inhabitants per km^2). It is the second most densely populated country in the OECD after Korea. The population density is particularly high in the Randstand (the metropolitan area with the four largest cities – The Hague, Rotterdam, Amsterdam and Utrecht). The population grew by some 6% over 2000-12, a faster rate than the OECD Europe average, but slower than the OECD average. The number of households is also increasing, which results in higher infrastructure and housing needs (IEA, 2014).

The Netherlands' location in the delta of four international rivers (the Scheldt, Meuse, Rhine and Ems) has consequences for flood protection, water supply and water quality (OECD, 2014d). A large proportion of the country's territory has been reclaimed from the sea, with a quarter of the territory below sea level. The country is vulnerable to flooding from both the sea and major rivers, requiring careful flood management to ensure water security.

2.4. Quality of life

The Netherlands scores well on many measures of well-being (OECD, 2012), in particular work and life balance, life satisfaction and social network quality. It performs slightly below the OECD average with respect to the perception of the quality of the local living environment, but in general, it is above or in line with the OECD average for most indicators. Overall, the Dutch liveability index (*Leefbarometer*) shows that the Dutch are satisfied with the quality of their surroundings (PBL, 2015a). The latest assessment by the World Health Organization (WHO) indicates that environmental factors represent 13% of the total burden of disease in the Netherlands, down by 1% from the previous assessment. This is among the lowest levels in the European region (WHO, 2009, 2007). A more recent study by the Dutch National Institute for Public Health and the Environment (RIVM) investigated environmental factors conducive to disease development and estimated that such factors account for 6% of the overall burden of disease (RIVM, 2014).

The population is generally well educated: 73% of the working age population (25 to 64 years-old) has at least upper secondary education, close to the OECD average of almost 76%. The share of tertiary graduates within the same age group is slightly higher than the OECD average (see Table of Basic Statistics). The percentage of youth neither in employment nor in education or training, aged 15 to 24 years, is about 10%, relatively low compared to other OECD member countries.

Life expectancy at birth in the Netherlands was 81.4 years in 2013, slightly higher than the OECD average of 80.4 years (see Table of Basic Statistics). Gains in life expectancy are connected to higher health care spending, which in the Netherlands accounts for 11.9% of GDP, the second highest rate in the OECD (OECD, 2012).

Both income inequality (as measured by the Gini coefficient) and relative poverty are low compared to the OECD average (see Table of Basic Statistics). Relative income poverty has remained stable, despite an increase in the poverty rate of youth. Still, there is a considerable gap between the richest and the poorest in terms of wealth; the top 10% of Dutch households own more than 60% of domestic net wealth, a high ratio among advanced economies (OECD, 2014b).

3. Transition to an energy-efficient and low-carbon economy

3.1. Energy use and intensity

Energy mix

The Netherlands has significant natural gas reserves and smaller oil deposits. Natural gas accounts for almost 90% of energy produced, twice as much as the country's consumption needs; therefore, large quantities of gas are exported. The Netherlands also produces energy from biofuels and waste (around 6%). Significant quantities of oil are imported, since domestic production accounts for less than 3% of energy produced. Nuclear energy, together with renewable sources such as wind, solar and geothermal energies, account for about 2% of energy produced (IEA, 2014).

The Netherlands has one of the largest shares of fossil fuels in the energy mix among OECD member countries, ranking fifth-highest. More than 80% of energy supplied in the Netherlands is produced locally. Fossil fuels represent more than 90% of total primary energy supplied (TPES), with natural gas accounting for the largest source at almost 42% of total energy supply in 2013. Oil represents almost 39%, while the remainder is made up of coal, renewables and nuclear (Figure 1.2). Total energy supply has increased since 2000,

Figure 1.2. **Fossil fuels account for the largest share of energy supply**

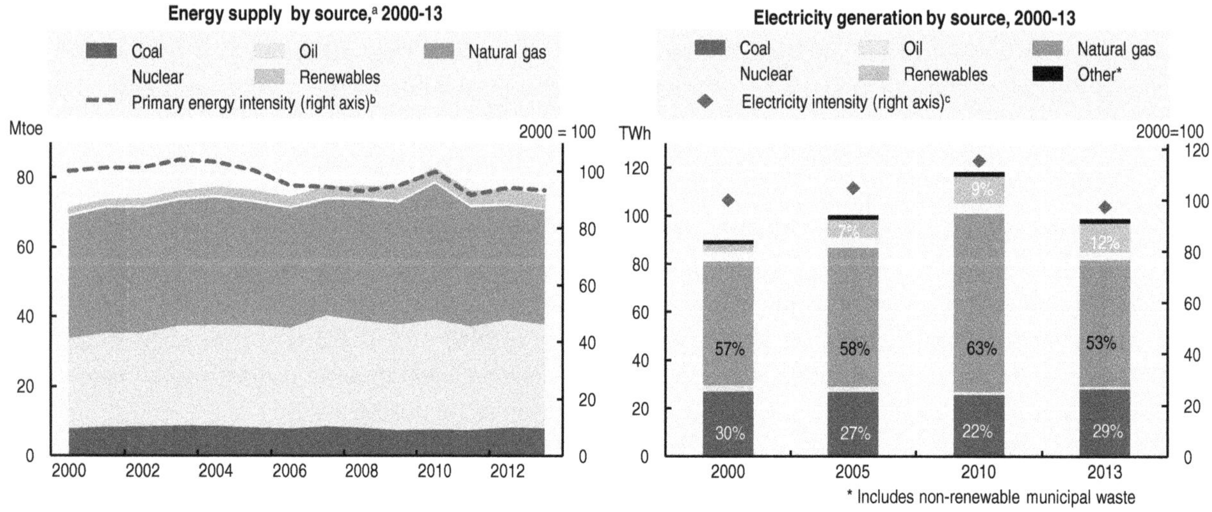

a) Total primary energy supply. Breakdown excludes electricity trade and non-renewable municipal waste.
b) Index of relative change since 2000 of total primary energy supply per unit of GDP (at 2005 prices and purchasing power parities).
c) Index of relative change since 2000 of electricity consumption per unit of GDP (at 2005 prices and purchasing power parities).
Source: IEA (2014), *IEA World Energy Statistics and Balances* (database); OECD (2014), "OECD Economic Outlook No. 95", *OECD Economic Outlook: Statistics and Projections* (database).

StatLink http://dx.doi.org/10.1787/888933280040

with drops in 2005 and 2010. Over 2000-12, the share of gas and renewables increased at the expense of coal and oil.

Renewable energy supply (RES) has increased significantly since 2000, especially since 2003. However, RES still accounted for only 4.2% of energy supply in 2013. Supply from all renewable sources has increased, largely benefiting from imports, except for hydropower, which accounts for a negligible share. The two main renewable energy sources are solid biomass and renewable municipal waste (Figure 1.3). Under the EU's Renewable Energy Directive (2009/28/EC), the Netherlands has a target for renewable sources in gross final consumption[2] of 14% by 2020. The 2013 SER Energy Agreement for Sustainable Growth also includes a target of 16% by 2023. Significant additional contributions of RES will be needed to achieve both the 14% and the 16% targets (EZ, 2013; ECN, 2014). The country failed to meet the EU directive's interim target for 2011-12, as well as the 2012 National Renewable Energy Action Plan target.

The country has nearly reached its target for the share of renewables in transport. According to the EU Renewables Directive, a minimum of 10% of all energy consumption in transport must come from renewable sources by 2020. The Netherlands reached over 5% in 2012, mainly due to the contribution of alternative biofuels, such as biodiesel from residues and waste, which count twice as much compared to other biofuels when determining compliance with the target. The aim for the Netherlands is to maximise the share of biofuels that are not produced from food crops (I&M, 2013).

The energy mix used for electricity generation has changed since 2000 with the share of oil products declining in favour of renewables. The latter went from 3% of electricity generation to 12% in 2000-12. Among renewable sources, wind power represents the largest share (nearly half), followed by biomass and renewable waste (Figure 1.3).

Figure 1.3. **Renewables have significantly increased**

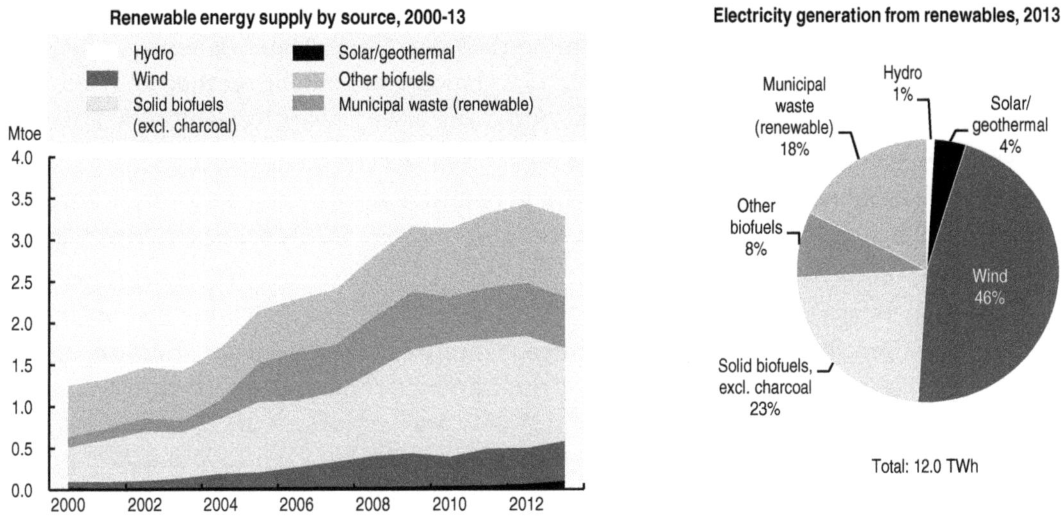

Source: IEA (2014), *IEA World Energy Statistics and Balances* (database).

StatLink http://dx.doi.org/10.1787/888933280054

Energy intensity

Over the last decade, both total primary energy supply and total final energy consumption increased. Nevertheless, their intensities (measured as the amounts of primary energy supply and final consumption per unit of GDP) decreased, showing a relative decoupling to GDP growth. Overall, primary energy intensity decreased by 7.3% over 2000-13, less than the OECD average decrease of almost 16% (Figure 1.2).

Energy consumption remained steady until 2005, then showed an irregular trend over the following five years, with a low in 2009 due to the recession. Energy consumption reached 2005 levels again in 2011 and has since remained stable (Figure 1.4). The Dutch government considers energy efficiency as an important means to reduce energy

Figure 1.4. **Energy consumption grew, but its intensity decreased**

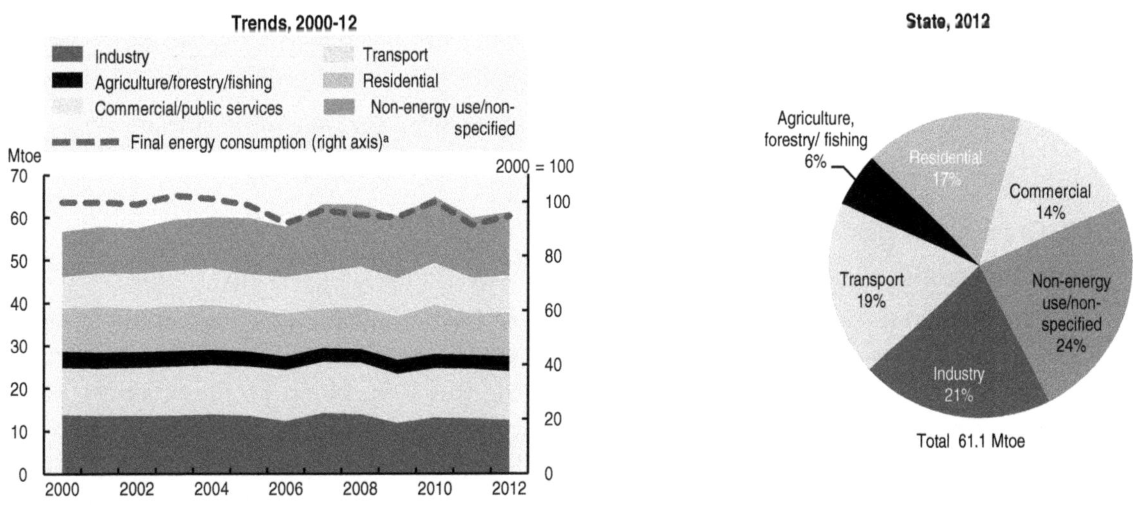

a) Index of relative change since 2000 of total final consumption of energy per unit of GDP (at 2005 prices and purchasing power parities).
Source: IEA (2014), *IEA World Energy Statistics and Balances* (database).

StatLink http://dx.doi.org/10.1787/888933280068

consumption. Energy savings achieved by 2010 pursuant to the EU Directive on Energy End-Use Efficiency and Energy Services (2006/32/EC) surpassed the intermediate target of 2% (European Commission, 2014b). According to the 2014 Dutch National Energy Outlook, however, the indicative EU target of 9% by 2016 will most likely not be reached with existing measures. In addition, the national target under the 2013 Energy Agreement will not be achieved with currently known policy measures (ECN, 2014).

Similar to the energy trends, electricity generation grew by some 10% over 2000-13. Electricity intensity (the ratio of electricity consumption over GDP) decreased slightly in the same period (Figure 1.2).

The transport sector accounts for 19% of total final energy consumption in the Netherlands. Similar to other OECD member countries, road transport dominates the sector's energy use, representing 96% of final energy consumption (Figure 1.5). GHG emissions from the sector represented 18% of total emissions in 2012 (Figure 1.6). Emissions, primarily of CO_2, are projected to decrease by 8% between 2010 and 2020 due to the effects of the economic recession and stricter emission standards for cars, as well as subsidies for more fuel-efficient cars (Chapter 4).

Figure 1.5. **Road transport accounts for almost all of the energy consumption of the sector, but CO_2 emissions from new cars are decreasing**

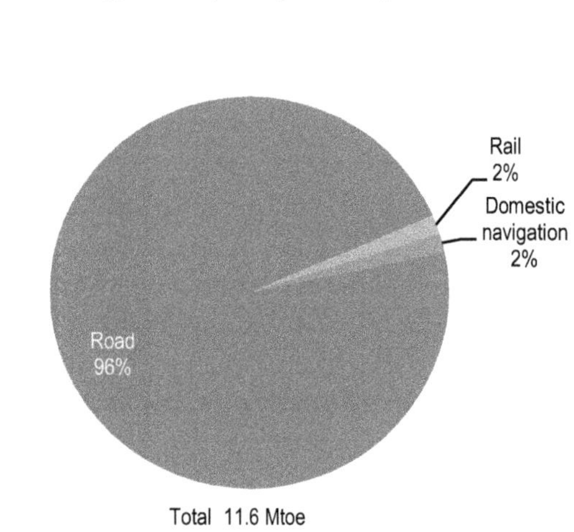

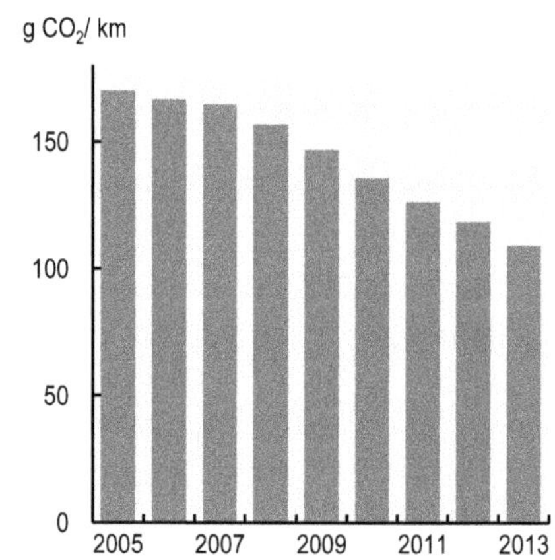

Source: Eurostat (2014), *Environment and Energy Statistics* (database); IEA (2014), *IEA World Energy Statistics and Balances* (database).

StatLink http://dx.doi.org/10.1787/888933280077

3.2. Greenhouse gas emissions

Emissions profile

The Netherlands decoupled economic growth from domestic GHG emissions. Over 2000-12, total GHG emissions[3] decreased by 10%, while overall GDP growth was about 14% (Figure 1.6). The energy sector strongly defines the Dutch emission profile, making the economy emissions-intensive. Energy, the largest contributor to national GHG emissions (84%), is the sector that showed the smallest decrease in emissions since 2000 (-2%). Emissions from other sectors decreased more significantly compared to 2000 levels, especially in the waste (-60%), industrial processes (-50%) and solvents (-35%) sectors. The agriculture sector decreased its emissions by 16% (Figure 1.6).

Figure 1.6. **GHG emissions decoupled from economic growth**

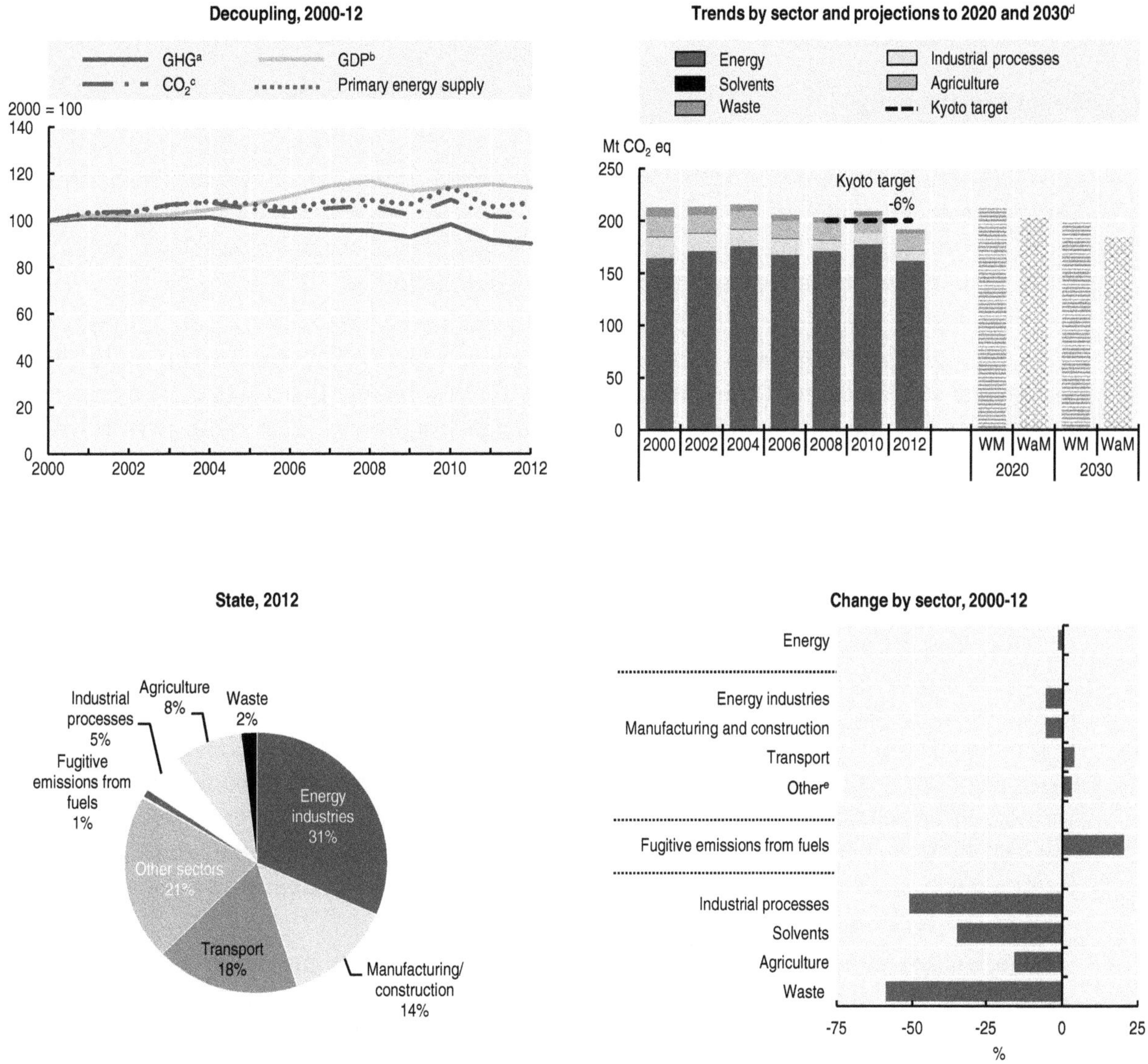

a) Excluding emissions/removals from land use, land-use change and forestry.
b) GDP at 2005 prices and purchasing power parities.
c) CO_2 emissions from energy use only; sectoral approach; excludes international marine and aviation bunkers.
d) National projections based on scenarios with existing measures (WM) and with additional measures (WaM).
e) Emissions from fuel combustion of residential, commercial/institutional and agriculture/forestry/fisheries sectors, and emissions from military use of fuels.
Source: IEA (2014), *IEA CO_2 Emissions from Fuel Combustion Statistics* (database); IEA (2014), *IEA World Energy Statistics and Balances* (database); OECD (2014), "OECD Economic Outlook No. 95", *OECD Economic Outlook: Statistics and Projections* (database); UNFCCC (2015), *GHG Data Interface* (database).

StatLink http://dx.doi.org/10.1787/888933280087

As in other OECD member countries, CO_2 represents the bulk of GHG emissions (85%). The energy sector emits the largest share of CO_2, with natural gas being the largest source followed by oil and coal. In terms of sectors, power generation and heat is the largest contributor to CO_2 emissions, followed by manufacturing and construction, and the transport sector (IEA, 2014).

The Netherlands has complied with the Kyoto Protocol target for 2008-12 of reducing GHG emissions by 6% below 1990s levels (RIVM, 2013). To that end, it relied on the flexible mechanisms provided under the protocol (i.e. purchasing emission reduction credits from other countries) (EEA, 2014a). By 2020, the Netherlands aims to reduce emissions inside and outside the EU ETS by 21% and 16% respectively compared to 2005 levels (Government of the Netherlands, 2014).

Emissions intensity

The GHG emissions intensity of the Dutch economy (the ratio between GHG emissions and GDP) declined by more than 20% between 2000 and 2012, albeit at a lower rate than the OECD average. The country's GHG intensity is low, at 0.3 tonnes of CO_2 equivalent (CO_2-eq) per USD 1 000 of GDP (at 2005 PPP) in 2012, compared to an OECD average of over 0.4 tonnes. GHG emissions per capita are lower than the OECD average (Annex 1.B).

The carbon intensity of the Netherlands, measured as the ratio of CO_2 emissions from fuel combustion over GDP[4], also decreased. It was down 12% in 2000-12 against an average decrease of 21% among OECD member countries. This is mainly the result of a carbon-intensive energy mix, the increase in supply and consumption rates, and the growth in population. In per capita terms, the carbon intensity of the Dutch economy is higher than the OECD average (IEA, 2014).

3.3. Air emissions and air quality

Air emissions

Over the past decade, emissions of all major air pollutants have been decoupled from economic growth. In 2000-13, while GDP grew, emissions of SO_X decreased by almost 60% and emissions of NO_X and non-methane volatile organic compounds (NMVOC) decreased by around 40%. In 2012, both SO_X and NO_X emissions per unit of GDP were significantly lower than the OECD averages of 0.4 kg/USD 1 000 and 0.8 kg/USD 1 000, respectively (Annex 1.B). Emissions of ammonia (NH_3) declined by 26%, much less than other pollutants (Figure 1.7). However, between 1990 and 2010, the Netherlands registered the largest ammonia emissions reduction among EU member countries (-68%), which was primarily due to a change in agricultural practices (Eurostat, 2012).

Stationary sources account for almost all SO_X emissions, with industrial combustion contributing the largest share (more than 60%). Mobile sources represent 60% of NO_X emissions, with road transport the largest source and stationary sources (mainly combustion) accounting for the rest.

The Netherlands met the 2010 target under the National Emission Ceiling Directive (NEC) for all pollutants except for NO_X. Emissions of NO_X subsequently improved and the NEC target was fully met in 2013 (Figure 1.7). According to national projections, the 2020 emission reduction targets under the amended Gothenburg Protocol to the Convention on Long-range Transboundary Air Pollution will be met for all pollutants except for NO_X and $PM_{2.5}$ (UNECE, 2012).

Emissions of heavy metals, following the trend of other pollutants, have decreased since 2000. Although emissions from heavy metals are generally at a lower atmospheric concentration than those of other gases, they are deposited in soils and organisms; as such, they cannot be degraded or destroyed and thus progressively accumulate in food chains with harmful effects on human health. Emissions of lead registered the most significant drop (-50%), followed by mercury (-49%), the latter mostly due to fewer transport emissions. Cadmium emissions decreased as well over 2000-13 (-34%), but peaked in 2010, when the level was four times higher than in 2013 (Figure 1.7).

Figure 1.7. **Air emissions decreased**

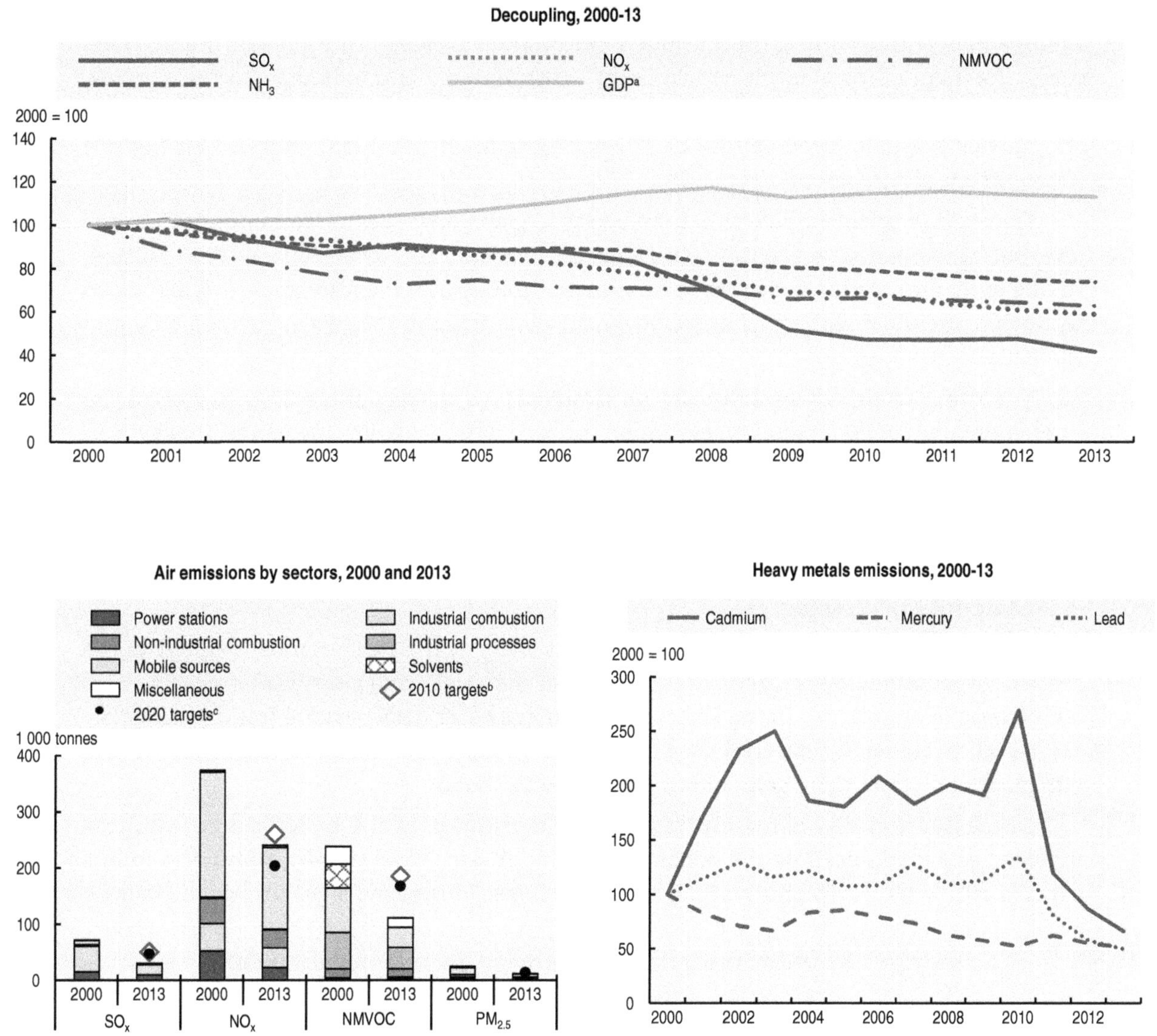

a) At 2005 prices and purchasing power parities.
b) Targets set by EU Directive 2001/81/EC (NEC Directive) on National Emission Ceilings for Certain Atmospheric Pollutants.
c) Targets set by the Gothenburg Protocol to Abate Acidification, Eutrophication and Ground-level Ozone.
Source: UNECE-EMEP (2015), National Submission to the LRTAP Convention; OECD (2014), OECD Economic Outlook No. 95", *OECD Economic Outlook: Statistics and Projections* (database).

StatLink http://dx.doi.org/10.1787/888933280099

Air quality

In 2010, some 6 700 people were estimated to have died from ambient air pollution, down 16% from 2005 levels. During the same period, the economic cost of deaths from ambient air pollution decreased by 7% to USD 25 billion, compared with a 7% increase in the OECD on average (OECD, 2014e).

Particulate matter ($PM_{2.5}$ and PM_{10}), also collectively known as aerosols, consists of particulates suspended in the air that pose severe health risks even when found at concentrations below current air quality guidelines set by the EU (EEA, 2013a). Emissions of particulate matter decreased by 48% for $PM_{2.5}$ and by 32% for PM_{10} over 2000-12.

Despite the overall positive trend, average PM_{10} concentrations showed a significant increase in 2010 and 2011, but continued their downward trend thereafter. The annual average concentration in 2012 remained below target levels at all measuring stations except for 4 km of roads in the provinces of South Holland and Limburg. On these roads, average concentrations of particulate matter were above the hourly targets (measured as an equivalent annual average rate of 31.2 microgrammes per cubic metre of air ($\mu g/m^3$) (Government of the Netherlands, 2014).

Exposure to urban air pollution from ozone (O_3) was lower in the Netherlands than the level set by EU legislation in 2011, in keeping with the trend over 2002-11 (EEA, 2013a). Unlike other air pollutants, ozone is not emitted directly into the atmosphere; it is formed through a chemical reaction that follows emissions from other gases, such as NO_x and NMVOCs.

The main factor influencing overall trends in air quality since 2000 has been the implementation of EU air quality legislation through national policy measures. However, in the case of transport, while newer vehicles are becoming less polluting, traffic levels have increased and more heavy vehicles are in use (Government of the Netherlands, 2014).

4. Transition to a resource-efficient economy

4.1. Material consumption

Between 2000 and 2013, the material productivity of the Netherlands (defined as the amount of economic wealth generated per unit of material used) grew by almost 50%, with an increase of almost 30% in the last two years (Figure 1.8). This positive trend is driven by an overall decrease in material consumption and generally well-functioning resource efficiency and waste management strategies (OECD, 2015b).

Domestic material consumption (DMC), measured as the sum of domestic raw material extraction used by the economy and its physical trade balance (imports minus exports of raw materials and manufactured products), decreased significantly in 2000-13.

Figure 1.8. **Dutch material productivity grew faster than GDP**

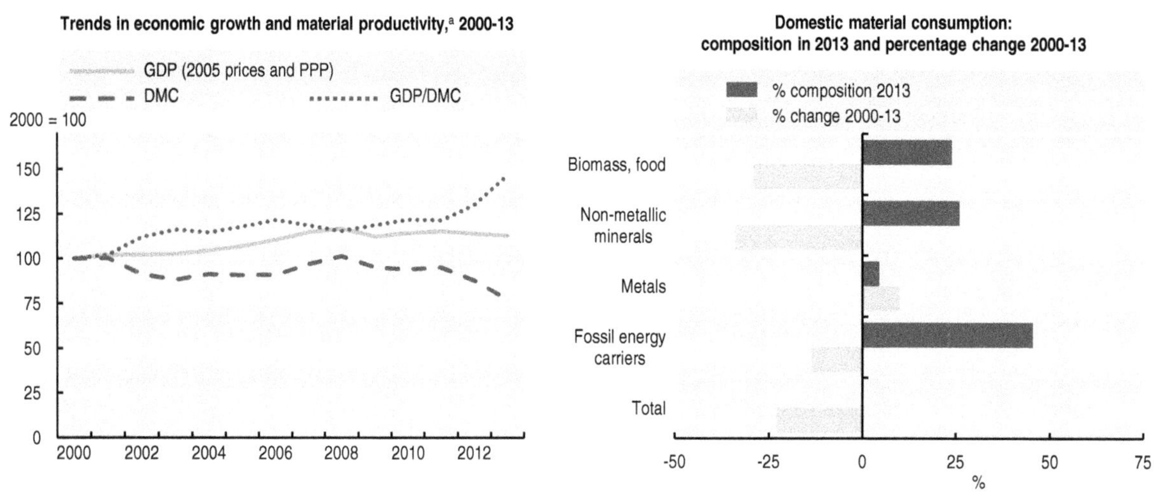

a) Material productivity designates the amount of GDP generated per unit of materials used. It refers to the ratio of GDP to domestic material consumption (DMC), where DMC is the sum of domestic extraction of raw materials used by an economy and the physical trade balance (imports minus exports of raw materials and manufactured products). A rise in material productivity is equivalent to a decline in material intensity (i.e. DMC/GDP).

Source: OECD (2015), "Material resources", *OECD Environment Statistics* (database).

StatLink http://dx.doi.org/10.1787/888933280106

Total Dutch DMC broken down by different categories shows that the consumption of fossil fuels and their derivatives (referred to as "fossil energy carriers") as a share of DMC is higher than in most OECD member countries. It accounts for the largest share (45%) of DMC, followed by non-metallic minerals (26%) and biomass (24%). Consumption of metals accounted for 5% of total DMC in 2013, the lowest share in the DMC composition. The largest decline was registered in the consumption of non-metallic minerals; this decreased by 34% in 2000-13, and by almost 30% since 2011 (Figure 1.8).

Much of the natural gas, sand and gravel used by the Netherlands is extracted domestically. The same is true for crops, biomass and non-metallic minerals, although to a lesser extent. For materials not extracted domestically, such as metals, the Netherlands depends on other countries; these imports are mainly re-exported or used as inputs for exports (CBS, 2014).

4.2. *Waste management*

The Netherlands generated almost 122 million tonnes of primary waste in 2012, corresponding to more than 7 000 kilogrammes (kg) per capita. The construction sector is responsible for the largest share, accounting for 66% of total waste, followed by manufacturing industries (12%). Water supply accounts for 5%; agriculture, forestry and fishing account for 4%; and energy production accounts for only 1% (Figure 1.9).

The Dutch waste management strategy is based on the waste hierarchy principle: avoid as much waste as possible through recovery and recycling. Municipal-generated waste, which decreased by 7% in 2000-13, showed significant decoupling with private final consumption, which increased by 1% (Figure 1.9); municipal waste per capita reached 525 kg in 2013, in line with the OECD average of about 520 kg (Annex 1.C).

Incineration with energy recovery is the main treatment for municipal waste (48%), followed by composting (26%) and recycling (24%) (Figure 1.9). The 50% recycling target set out in the EU Waste Framework Directive was reached in 2009, 11 years ahead of the deadline. Landfilling has been banned since 1995 for 35 waste categories. In addition, a landfill tax has been increasing progressively since 1995, becoming the highest in Europe in 2010. The tax was abolished in 2012, but re-introduced in 2014. The second National Waste Management Plan introduced a target to further increase the recovery and recycling of waste (Chapter 5).

4.3. *Agricultural inputs*

Following a general trend in the OECD, overall agricultural nutrient surpluses (nitrogen and phosphorous) in the Netherlands declined in 1990-2011, both in absolute tonnes of nutrients and in terms of nutrient surpluses per hectare of agricultural land. This is particularly significant, considering that the Netherlands had relatively high levels of nutrient surpluses in the past (OECD, 2014d). While agricultural production has increased by 7% since 2000, phosphorous surpluses declined by around 9% a year over the course of the 2000s, more than the OECD average decline of around 5%. Nitrogen surpluses declined more slowly, by an average of around 5% a year over the same period, compared to an average decrease of 1.4% in the OECD (OECD, 2013b) (Figure 1.10).

The decline in agricultural inputs is due to more stringent standards for fertilisers and, to a lesser extent, to the growth of organic farming. Agricultural land area under certified organic management increased by some 60% between 2000 and 2012, although

Figure 1.9. **Waste generation declined and incineration with energy recovery increased**

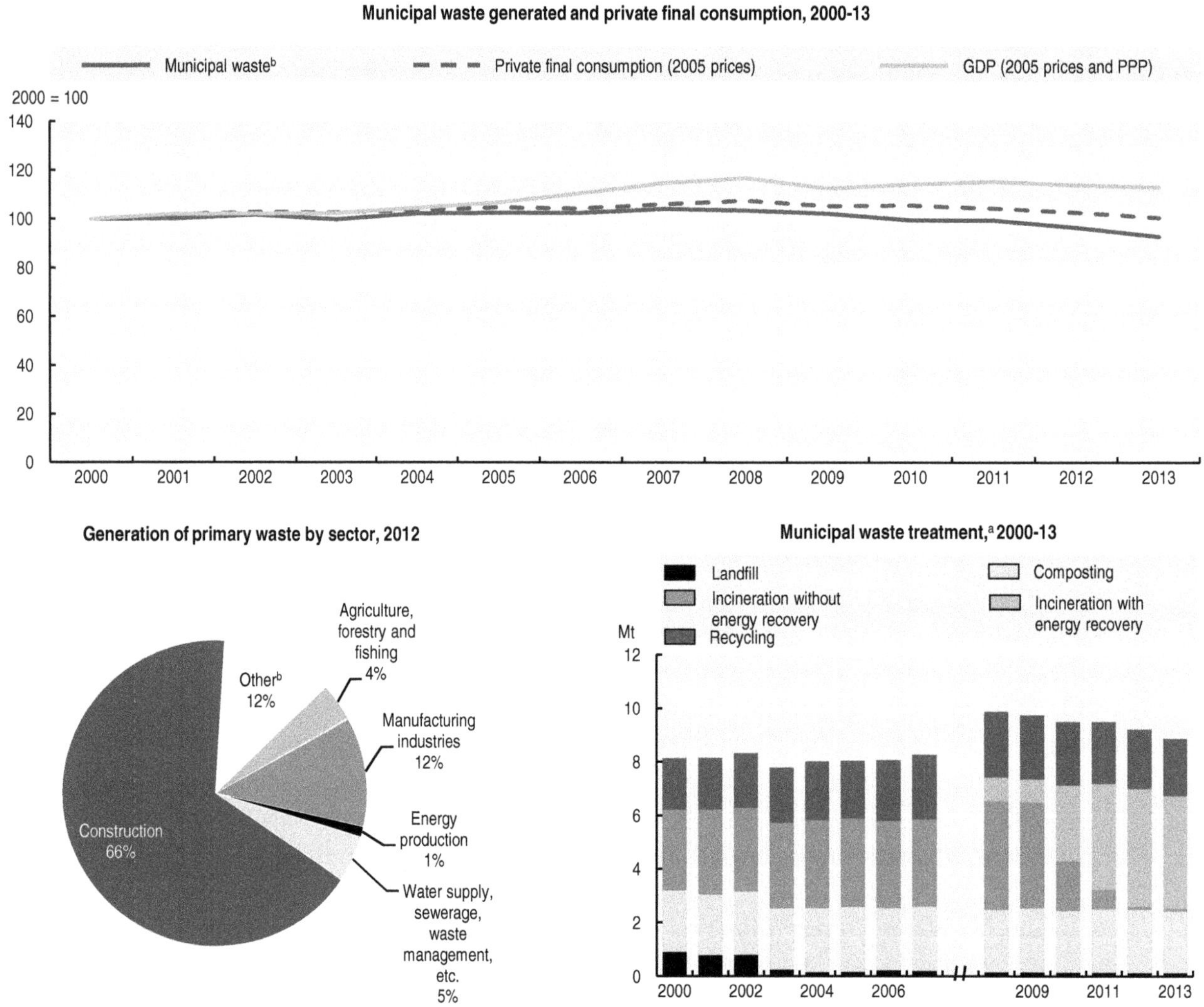

a) Waste collected by or for municipalities including household, bulky and commercial waste, and similar waste handled at the same facilities. Includes separate collection for recycling purposes. Up to 2008, data for total treatment exclude amounts undergoing mechanical sorting before further treatment/disposal.

b) Including municipal waste.

Source: Eurostat (2015), *Eurostat Environmental Data Centre on Waste* (database); OECD (2015), *OECD Environment Statistics* (database); OECD (2014), "OECD Economic Outlook No. 95", *OECD Economic Outlook: Statistics and Projections* (database).

StatLink http://dx.doi.org/10.1787/888933280111

starting from a low base (1.6% of total agricultural land). In 2012, the 2.6% share of organic land area was lower than the European average of 5.7% (Eurostat, 2014a).

Despite the positive trends, however, the amount of nitrogen fertiliser used per square kilometre of agricultural land accounted for almost 13 tonnes, significantly higher than the OECD average of about 2.4 tonnes (Annex 1.C). Over the past decade, growth in crop production has been decoupled from the sale of pesticides. This was due to a decline in the amount of pesticides sold per tonne of crop output, a trend also observed in other OECD member countries (OECD, 2013b). However, the quantity of pesticides sold increased over 2009-11 and their use per square kilometre of agricultural land is above the OECD average (Annex 1.C).

Figure 1.10. **Nutrient surpluses decoupled from agricultural production**

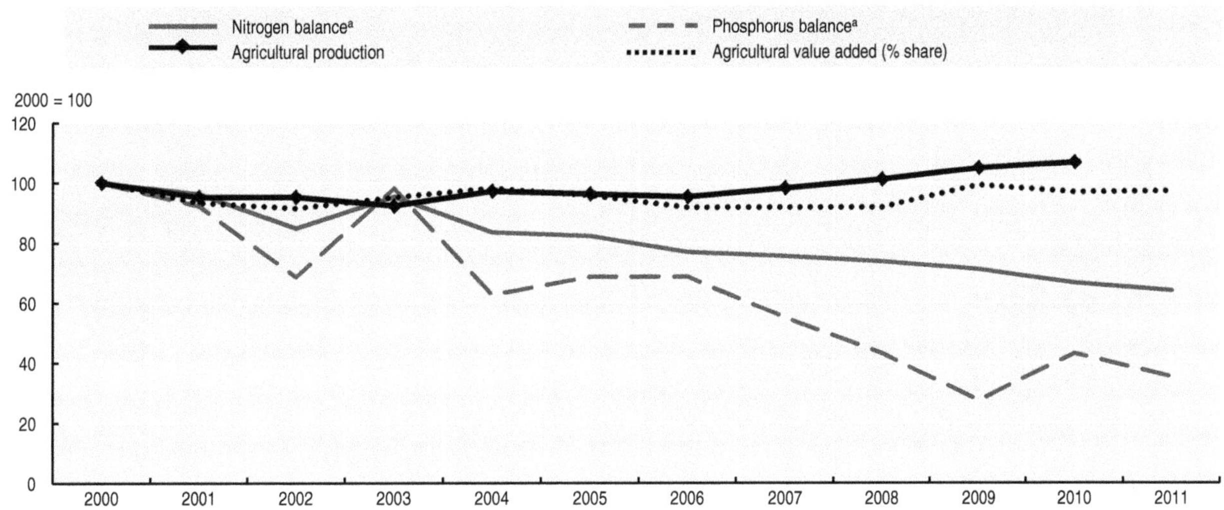

a) Gross nutrient balances.
Source: CBS (2014), *Environmental Data Compendium* (website); OECD (2015), *OECD Agriculture Statistics* (database).

StatLink http://dx.doi.org/10.1787/888933280122

5. Managing the natural asset base

5.1. *Fossil fuels*

The Netherlands has significant deposits of natural gas, as well as some smaller oil reserves. Therefore, it is a major producer of natural gas, as well as a trade and transit hub for oil, gas, electricity and coal.

The country is the second-largest gas producer in Europe, even though production levels from the largest gas field (Groningen) and from other smaller ones are falling. At the end of 2013, natural gas reserves, in continuous decline since the 1970s, were estimated at 1 044 billion cubic metres (CBS, 2014). The development of unconventional gas reserves was put on hold due to public opposition and the need for environmental impact assessments (IEA, 2014).

Proven oil reserves were 47 million cubic metres at the end of 2013, 2% less than in 2012 (CBS, 2014). Oil production in the Netherlands decreased by more than half compared to the beginning of the century (IEA, 2014).

5.2. *Biodiversity and ecosystems*

Land use and forests

In the Netherlands, the annual urban land take is slightly higher than the average level in the OECD. The largest area was taken by the housing, services and recreation sector, which made up 42% of the overall increase in urban and other artificial area over 2000-06. Construction was a dominant driver as well, covering 40% of the newly developed land. Commercial and industrial sites represented 14% of the taken area, while new mines, quarries and dumpsites, as well as transport infrastructure, accounted for the rest (Figure 1.11).

The highest share of urban areas is in South Holland, the most densely populated province in the country, which includes both The Hague and Rotterdam. The province with the highest share of green spaces is Drenthe, which is in the northeast and mostly agricultural (Figure 1.11).

Figure 1.11. **Dutch urban land take is higher than the OECD average**

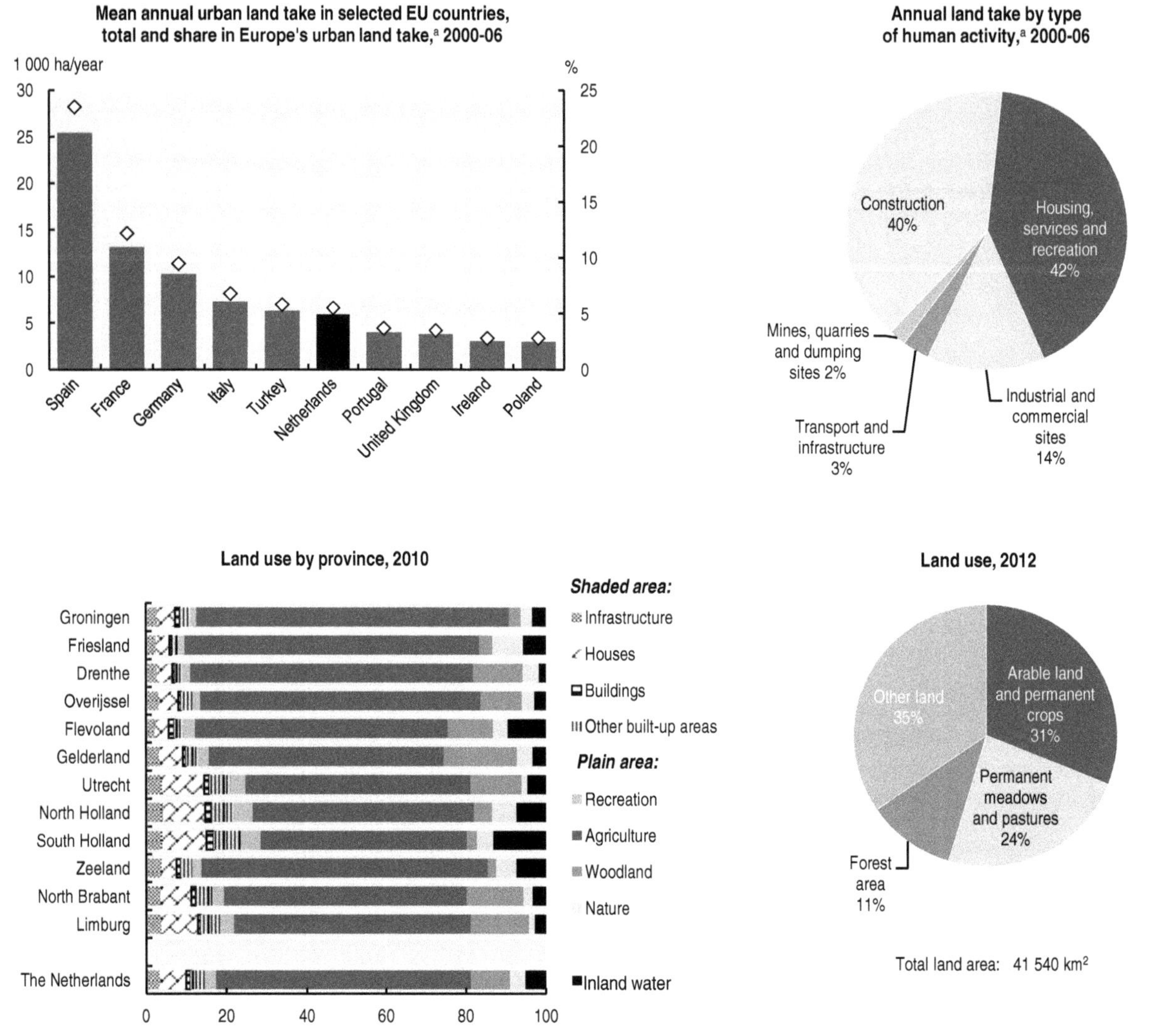

a) Annual land take by the expansion of residential and construction sites.

Source: CBS (2014), *Environmental Data Compendium* (website); EEA (2013), *Land Take Assessment*; FAO (2015), *FAOSTAT* (database).

StatLink http://dx.doi.org/10.1787/888933280131

In terms of land use, 31% of the Netherlands' territory consists of arable land and croplands; meadows and pastures account for some 24% and forests cover only 11% of the country. Arable areas increased significantly in 2004 at the expense of meadows and pastures, a trend that has remained stable. Agricultural products represent 17.5% of total Dutch exports, making the Netherlands one of the largest exporters of agricultural products in the world (in terms of value). The government supports multifunctional agriculture, which consists of farms that provide nature management services (such as leaving fields fallow to provide breeding grounds for birds), as well as agricultural products.

The growing stock in forests and other wooded land is slightly higher than the OECD average. Tree fellings remained almost unchanged over 2000-05, while natural losses decreased by some 20% in the same period.

Protected areas

The land area under some form of nature protection in the Netherlands covers almost 20% of the territory, slightly below the OECD average of 22.5%. The area under the highest level of nature protection (IUCN category I-II: strict nature reserves, wilderness areas and national parks) accounts for 2.2% of total area, compared to an OECD average of 4.4%. It consists exclusively of national parks (Figure 1.12).

Figure 1.12. **A small share of land is under the highest level of nature protection**

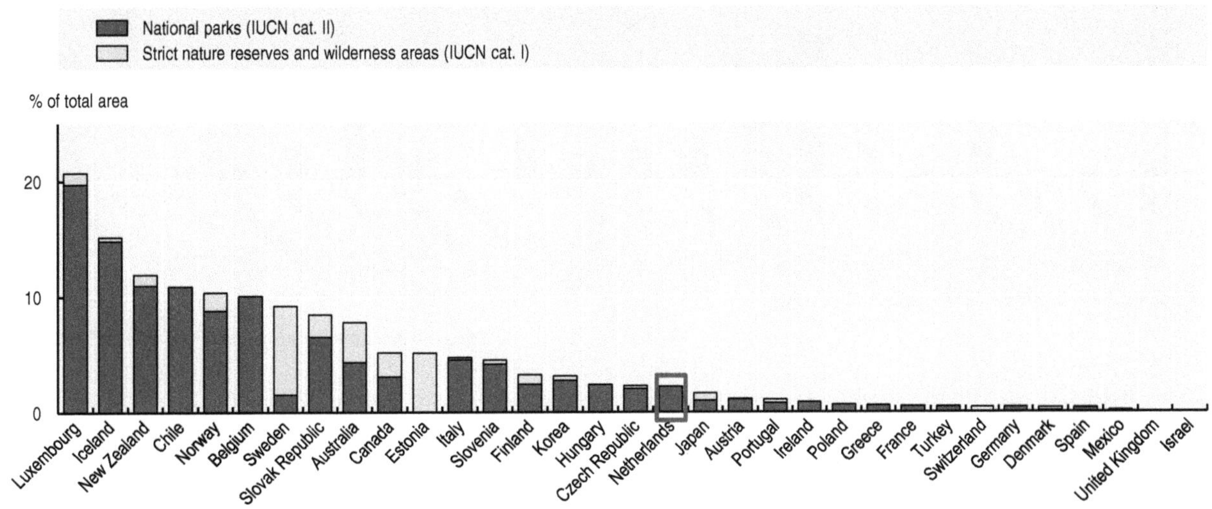

Source: OECD (2013), *Environment at a Glance 2013: OECD Indicators.*

StatLink http://dx.doi.org/10.1787/888933280144

Until the designation of the National Ecological Network (NEN) in the framework of the Nature Policy Plan (*Natuurbeleidsplan*) approved in 1990, Dutch policy on protected areas focused mainly on specific species, habitats and designated areas. Today, the focus has shifted towards whole landscapes to provide more consistent environmental management of protected areas and their surroundings (EZ, 2014a) (Chapter 2). Half of NEN areas are Natura 2000 sites, a network that includes Sites of Community Importance (SCI) and Special Protection Areas (SPAs). The network covers only about 13% of the country's territory, below the EU average of 19%, although it is still being extended. In the Netherlands, the Natura 2000 network is made up of approximately one-third of terrestrial areas and two-thirds of marine sites (Figure 1.13).

With the NEN and 164 Natura 2000 sites, the Netherlands has already reached the 2020 Aichi targets of the United Nations Convention on Biological Diversity. The targets aim to protect at least 17% of the terrestrial area and inland waters, and 10% of the coastal and marine areas of the convention's parties. The number of protected areas is expected to increase once the NEN is completed in the coming years (Government of the Netherlands, 2014).

Threatened species

The 2013 monitoring results of the European Union Habitat Directive (Directive 92/43/EEC) reveal that about 95% of habitat types and 75% of species are threatened in the Netherlands. The main causes of environmental pressures on biodiversity are increasing urbanisation and transport, as well as industrial, agricultural and fishery activities.

Figure 1.13. **The Natura 2000 network covers a smaller share of land compared to other countries**

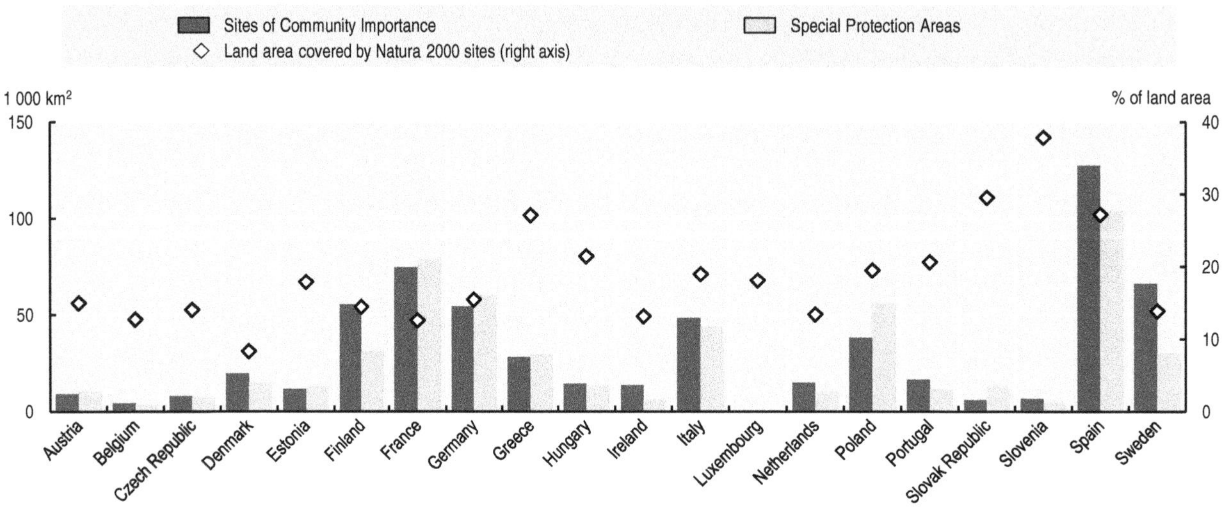

Source: European Commission (2014), *Natura 2000 Barometer.*

StatLink http://dx.doi.org/10.1787/888933280154

Another major threat to terrestrial biodiversity is desiccation, which occurs in over 90% of the natural areas that rely on groundwater for their sustenance (EZ, 2014b).

The share of threatened species in the Netherlands is higher than in many other OECD member countries, accounting for around 28% of fish, 25% of mammals, 22% of vascular plants, 21% of birds and 71% of reptiles (Annex 1.D) (Figure 1.14). One of the main challenges, especially in the agricultural sector, concerns the bird population on farmland, which has dramatically declined by almost 50% in 10 years. This decrease, due primarily to increasingly intensive agricultural practices, is the largest in the OECD (OECD, 2014d) (Figure 1.15).

Figure 1.14. **The share of threatened species is high**

Threatened species,[a] late 2000s

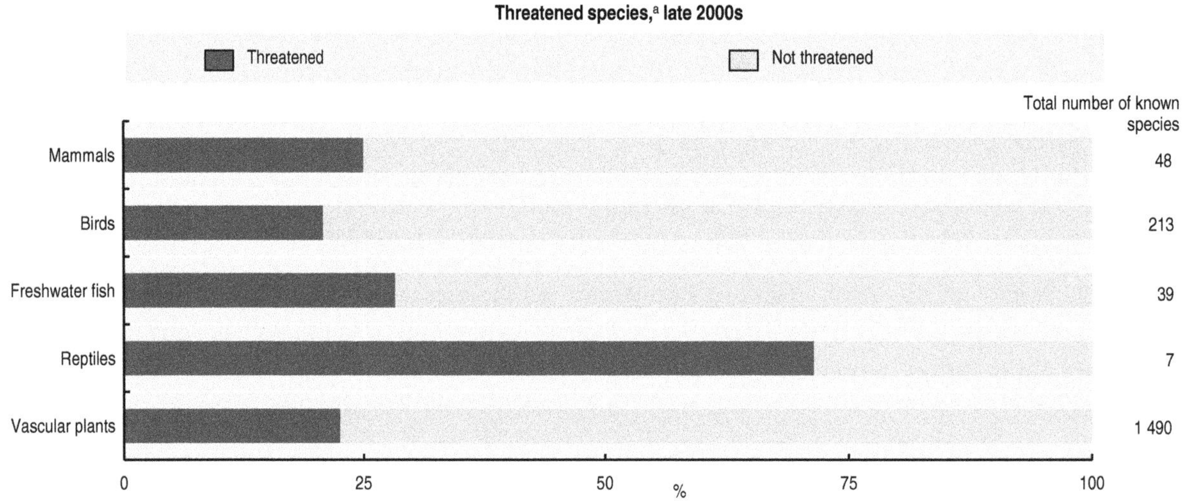

a) IUCN categories "critically endangered", "endangered" and "vulnerable" in % of known species.
Source: OECD (2015), "Threatened species", *OECD Environment Statistics* (database).

StatLink http://dx.doi.org/10.1787/888933280160

Figure 1.15. **Farmland bird population decreased significantly**

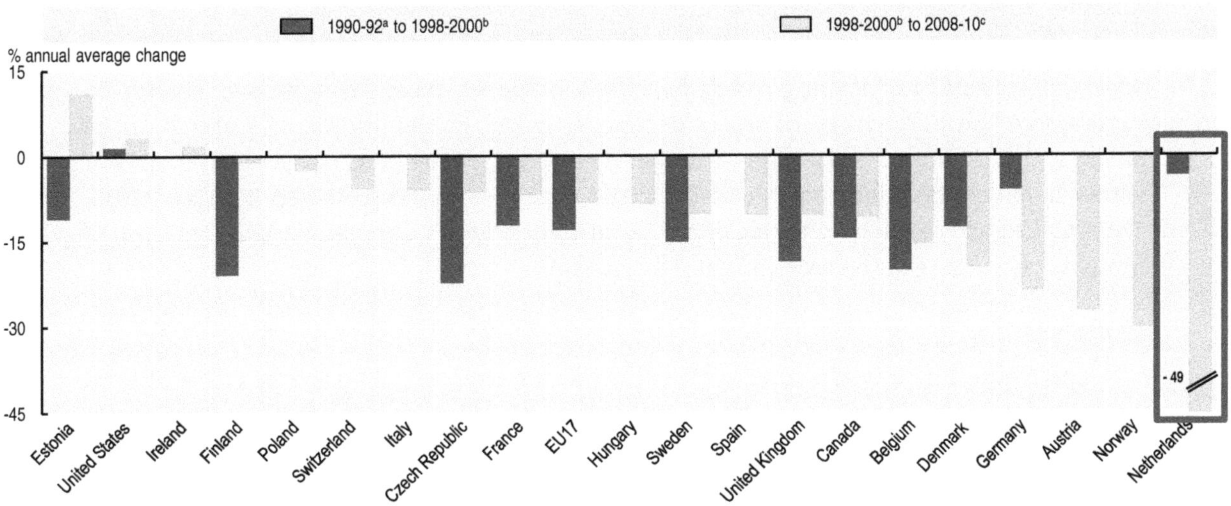

Note: Aggregated index of population trend estimates of a selected group of breeding bird species that are dependent on agricultural land for nesting or feeding. The index only represents grassland breeding birds in the United States and Canada.

a) 1991-93 average for Germany.

b) 1999-2001 average for Hungary and Switzerland and 2000-02 average for Italy and Poland.

c) 2004-06 average data for Estonia, 2005-07 average for the United States, 2007-09 average for Hungary and 2006-08 average for Belgium, Denmark, Finland, France, Germany, Ireland, Spain, Sweden, Switzerland and the United Kingdom.

Source: OECD (2013), *OECD Compendium of Agri-environmental Indicators.*

StatLink http://dx.doi.org/10.1787/888933280173

The Netherlands is trying hard to find new systems to improve biodiversity on farmland, while developing the agricultural sector business (EZ, 2014b).

While biodiversity loss in some ecosystems still continues, there are a number of success stories that show positive results in stabilising this trend. For example, the number of Red List animals and plants has stabilised in recent years, most commercial fish stocks are recovering and important animal species, such as otter (*Lutra lutra*) and beaver (*Castor fiber*), are being reintroduced in the country (EZ, 2014b).

The Netherlands territory also comprises three islands and marine areas within the Caribbean, which are home to hundreds of species and large ecosystems. The Saba Bank, for example, is the Caribbean's largest sub-marine coral atoll. Here, the status of biodiversity and ecosystems is particularly vulnerable, due to the same kind of issues faced by all Caribbean Small Island Developing States (SIDS). Challenges include high vulnerability to climate change, presence of invasive alien species, overgrazing, nutrient loads and overfishing. The Netherlands has been very active in supporting local governments to ensure progress towards the achievement of the Aichi targets, but to date large improvements are still needed (EZ, 2014b).

5.3. *Water resources*

Located in the delta of four major international rivers with half of its territory prone to flooding, the Netherlands faces persistent water challenges, such as the risk of flood, water shortages and water quality. The four Dutch river basin districts comprise surface and groundwater bodies that are shared with other countries, so transboundary aspects of water management are important. Even prior to the adoption of the River Basin Management Plans (RBMPs) under the Water Framework Directive (WFD) in 2009, the country was trying hard to improve water management (European Commission, 2012) (Chapter 2).

Over time, the country has developed a strong water management system, which proved successful in "keeping Dutch feet dry". However, recent trends have shown an increase in the percentage of water defences (dykes, dunes, dams and storm-surge barriers) that do not meet the high Dutch safety standards. The percentage of kilometres of water defences classified as sub-standard rose from 15% to 35% between 2001 and 2013. This can be partly explained by use of new information on water defences and inclusion of more infrastructure in the assessment (PBL, 2015a).

Water use

The Netherlands is classified as medium water-stressed, abstracting 11.7% of total available renewable freshwater in 2012. Gross freshwater abstraction was 640 m^3 per capita in 2012, lower than the OECD average of 830 m^3 (Annex 1.D). Overall, abstraction of freshwater has not shown a decoupling from economic growth over 2001-12 (Figure 1.16). Cooling in electricity production still represents the largest share of freshwater abstraction (56%), followed by manufacturing (28%) and public water supply (11%). According to CBS (2014), abstraction of groundwater (which may include freshwater, but also brackish or salt water) has declined by nearly 20% over 2003-12, thus showing a decoupling from economic growth.

Figure 1.16. **A medium water-stressed country, with electricity cooling abstracting the largest share of freshwater**

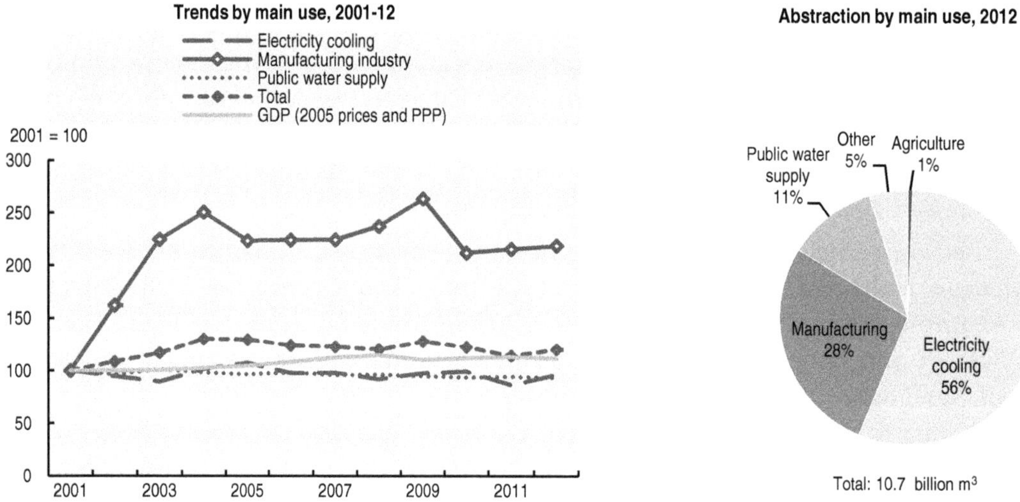

Note: Data exclude underground flows, estimated at 2 billion m^3.
Source: OECD (2015), "Freshwater abstractions", *OECD Environment Statistics* (database).

StatLink http://dx.doi.org/10.1787/888933280180

Water quality

The largest share of surface water bodies (44%) had poor ecological status (based on a combination of biological, physical and chemical indicators) in 2013, and 19% registered bad ecological status. In the remaining 37% of surface water bodies, the ecological status was moderate. In general, the standards agreed under the WFD for water quality of regional surface waters were not achieved, nor will they likely be met in 2015 (as in many other EU member countries). Analysis shows that even though the quality of surface water is improving, the implementation of water management plans over 2009-21 will result in only 15% of all water bodies meeting the WFD ecological targets in 2027 (Government of the Netherlands, 2014; PBL, 2015b).

For all river basin districts, non-point sources of pollution have the largest impact on water quality. These include pollution from agriculture, atmospheric deposition, traffic and infrastructure, and run-off. The Netherlands has performed well in reducing point sources of water pollution, but effluents from urban wastewater plants and sewage outlets are still considered to have a significant impact on surface water bodies. The load from transboundary origins is considered an important source for nearly all threshold-exceeding substances. The Meuse River, in particular, does not meet sufficient water quality levels, in contrast to the overall quality of national-scale surface waters (European Commission, 2012). Recent studies have shown, however, that nutrient concentrations in the Rhine and Meuse Rivers have decreased considerably over the last decade (PBL, 2015b).

Another pressure on water quality comes from human activities in general, which have significantly altered river morphology and hydrological conditions. Consequently, the Netherlands has the highest percentage of heavily modified (40%) or artificial (50%) water bodies as a share of total surface water bodies in the EU (European Commission, 2012).

Groundwater quality is generally good. Some 61% of groundwater bodies have good quantitative status, while only nine groundwater bodies risk failing to reach a good chemical status in 2015. For groundwater quality, the main pressures are due to nutrients, pesticides and heavy metals (European Commission, 2012). In 2001-12, emissions of heavy metals to water decreased significantly, to a higher extent than the decrease of nutrients from agriculture. The largest contributor of heavy metal emissions to water was zinc, followed by copper. In 2012, heavy metal emissions increased for the first time since 2001, due mainly to the manufacturing of metal products and chemical products (CBS, 2014).

In 2013, the quality of about 87% of total bathing waters was good or excellent. The remaining bathing waters did not meet minimum standards established by the relevant EU directives because of poor microbiological conditions (OECD, 2014d). Bathing waters (of which 13% are coastal and 87% inland) account for about 3.2% of total EU bathing waters (EEA, 2014b).

Water supply and sanitation

Water abstraction for public supply decreased by 7% in 2000-10, and accounted for only 11% of total freshwater abstraction in 2010. The majority of drinking water comes from groundwater, while less than 40% comes from surface water. Households account for more than 70% of drinking water use, but this share has declined by 2% since 1990 due to water saving. This represented a significant decoupling with population growth, which rose by 13% in the same period (CBS, 2014).

Over 99% of household wastewater is treated before it is discharged into surface waters (OECD, 2014d). Targets for wastewater management have been shaped by the European Directive on Urban Wastewater (Directive 91/271/EEC and Directive 98/15/EC). In implementing the directive, the Netherlands has increasingly addressed point sources of water and chemical pollution. The share of the population connected to public wastewater treatment plants increased by only 1% in 2000-10, as the country was starting from an already high baseline. Nearly all of the population is connected to a wastewater treatment facility that implements tertiary treatment.

Notes

1. The OECD typology, which classifies territorial level 3 regions (TL3), is based on the percentage of regional population living in rural or urban communities and therefore allows for meaningful comparisons among regions of the same type and level (OECD, 2014c).
2. The gross final consumption of energy from renewable sources is calculated as the sum of: a) gross final consumption of electricity from renewable energy sources; b) gross final consumption of energy from renewable sources for heating and cooling; and c) final consumption of energy from renewable sources in transport (Directive 2009/28/EC).
3. Excluding land use, land-use change and forestry.
4. In 2012, the overall CO_2 intensity in the Netherlands was 0.28 kg CO_2/USD GDP PPP, which represents a median level in the OECD.

References

CBS (2014), *Environmental Accounts of the Netherlands 2013*, Statistics Netherlands, The Hague.

ECN (2014), *Netherlands National Energy Outlook 2014*, Energy Research Centre of the Netherlands, Petten.

EEA (2014a), *Progress Towards 2008-2012 Kyoto Targets in Europe*, European Environment Agency, Copenhagen.

EEA (2014b), *European Bathing Water Quality in 2013*, European Environment Agency, Copenhagen.

EEA (2013a), *Air Quality in Europe – 2013 Report*, European Environment Agency, Copenhagen.

European Commission (2014a), "Taxation trends in the European Union – Country Chapters", *The Netherlands, 2014 edition*, Taxation and Customs Union, European Commission, Brussels, *http://ec.europa.eu/taxation_customs/resources/documents/taxation/gen_info/economic_analysis/tax_structures/country_tables/nl.pdf* (accessed 30 September 2014).

European Commission (2014b), *Commission Staff Working Document, Accompanying the documents: Report from the Commission to the European Parliament and the Council, Progress Report on the Application of Directive 2006/32/EC on Energy End-use Efficiency and Energy Services and on the Application of Directive 2004/8/EC on the Promotion of Cogeneration based on a Useful Heat Demand in the Internal Energy Market*, COM (2013) 938 Final, SWD (2013) 541 Final, European Commission, Brussels.

European Commission (2012), *Commission Staff Working Document, Member State: Netherlands, Accompanying the document: Report from the Commission to the European Parliament and the Council on the Implementation of the Water Framework Directive (2000/60/EC): River Basin Management Plans*, COM (2012) 670 Final, SWD (2012) 379 Final, European Commission, Brussels.

Eurostat (2014a), database, *http://ec.europa.eu/eurostat/data/database* (accessed 7 May 2015).

Eurostat (2012), "Agri-environmental indicator – ammonia emissions", *Factsheet*, Eurostat, Luxembourg.

EZ (2014a), *The Natural Way Forward – Government Vision 2014*, Ministry of Economic Affairs, The Hague.

EZ (2014b), *Convention on Biological Diversity – Fifth National Report of the Kingdom of the Netherlands*, Ministry of Economic Affairs, The Hague.

EZ (2013), *Energy from Renewable Sources in the Netherlands 2011-2012 – Progress Report*, Ministry of Economic Affairs, The Hague.

Government of the Netherlands (2014), "Answers to OECD Environmental Performance Review Questionnaire" (internal document).

IEA (2014), *Energy Policies of IEA Countries – The Netherlands: 2014 Review*, IEA/OECD Publishing, Paris, *http://dx.doi.org/10.1787/9789264210462-en*.

I&M (2013), *Sixth Netherlands National Communication under the United Nations Framework Convention on Climate Change*, Ministry of Infrastructure and the Environment, The Hague, The Netherlands.

OECD (2015a), "Netherlands", in OECD Economic Outlook, Vol. 2015 Issue 1, OECD Publishing, Paris, *http://dx.doi.org/10.1787/eco_outlook-v2015-1-31-en*.

OECD (2015b), *Material Resources, Productivity and the Environment*, OECD Publishing, Paris, *http://dx.doi.org/10.1787/9789264190504-en*.

OECD (2014a), *OECD Economic Outlook*, Vol. 2014/1, OECD Publishing, Paris, *http://dx.doi.org/10.1787/eco_outlook-v2014-1-en*.

OECD (2014b), *OECD Economic Surveys: Netherlands 2014*, OECD Publishing, Paris, *http://dx.doi.org/10.1787/eco_surveys-nld-2014-en*.

OECD (2014c), *OECD Territorial Reviews: Netherlands 2014*, OECD Publishing, Paris, *http://dx.doi.org/10.1787/9789264209527-en*.

OECD (2014d), *Water Governance in the Netherlands: Fit for the Future?*, OECD Studies on Water, OECD Publishing, Paris, *http://dx.doi.org/10.1787/9789264102637-en*.

OECD (2014e), *The Cost of Air Pollution: Health Impacts of Road Transport*, OECD Publishing, Paris, *http://dx.doi.org/10.1787/9789264210448-en*.

OECD (2013a), *OECD Economic Outlook*, Vol. 2013/2, OECD Publishing, Paris, *http://dx.doi.org/10.1787/eco_outlook-v2013-2-en*.

OECD (2013b), *OECD Compendium of Agri-environmental Indicators*, OECD Publishing, Paris, *http://dx.doi.org/10.1787/9789264186217-en*.

OECD (2012), *OECD Better Life Index*, *www.oecdbetterlifeindex.org*.

PBL (2015a), *Assessment of the Dutch Human Environment 2014 – The Future is Now*, PBL Netherlands Environmental Assessment Agency, The Hague.

PBL (2015b), *Waterkwaliteit nu en in de toekomst* [Water Quality Now and in the Future], Netherlands Environmental Assessment Agency, The Hague, *www.pbl.nl/publicaties/waterkwaliteit-nu-en-in-de-toekomst* (accessed 11 June 2015).

RIVM (2014), *Een gezonder Nederland: Kernboodschappen van de Volksgezondheid Toekomst Verkenning 2014* [A Healthier Netherlands: Key Findings from the Dutch 2014 Public Health Status and Foresight Report], National Institute for Public Health and the Environment, Bilthoven, the Netherlands, *www.eengezondernederland.nl/en/English_version/Key_Findings* (accessed 29 June 2015).

RIVM (2013), *National Inventory Report 2013 – Greenhouse Gas Emissions in the Netherlands 1990-2011*, National Institute for Public Health and the Environment, Bilthoven, the Netherlands.

UNECE (2012), *1999 Protocol to Abate Acidification, Eutrophication and Ground-level Ozone to the Convention on Long range Transboundary Air Pollution, as amended on 4 May 2012*, United Nations Economic Commission for Europe, Geneva, *www.unece.org/fileadmin/DAM/env/documents/2013/air/eb/ECE.EB.AIR.114_ENG.pdf*.

WHO (2009), *Country Profiles of Environmental Burden of Disease: The Netherlands*, World Health Organization, Geneva.

WHO (2007), *Country Profiles of Environmental Burden of Disease: The Netherlands*, World Health Organization, Geneva.

ANNEX 1.A

Energy and transport data

Figure 1.A1. **Energy structure and intensity**

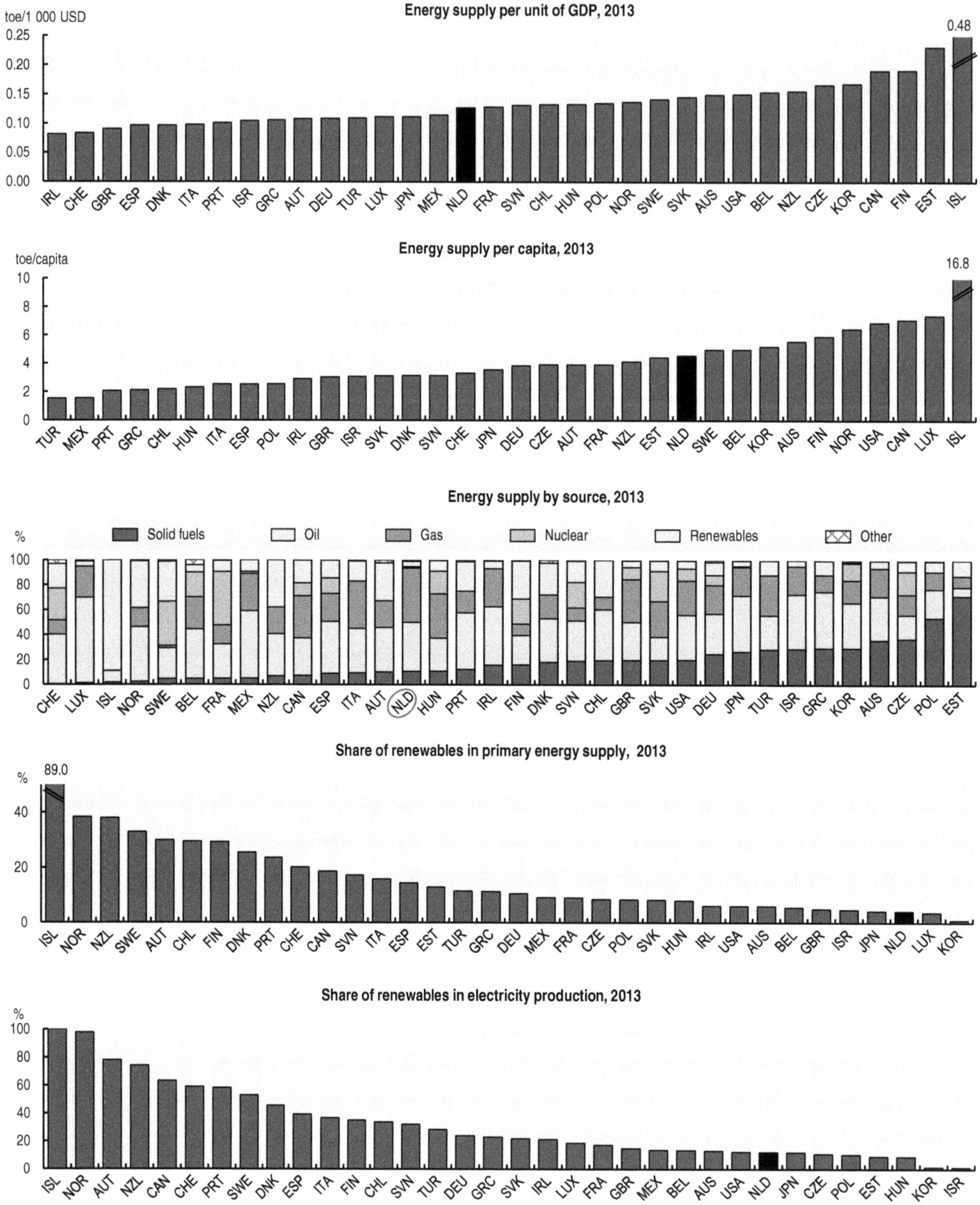

Notes: Data may include provisional figures and estimates. Total primary energy supply; the breakdown excludes electricity trade. GDP at 2005 prices and purchasing power parities.

Source: IEA (2014), *IEA World Energy Statistics and Balances* (database); OECD (2014), "OECD Economic Outlook No. 95", *OECD Economic Outlook: Statistics and Projections* (database).

StatLink http://dx.doi.org/10.1787/888933280476

Figure 1.A2. **Road transport**

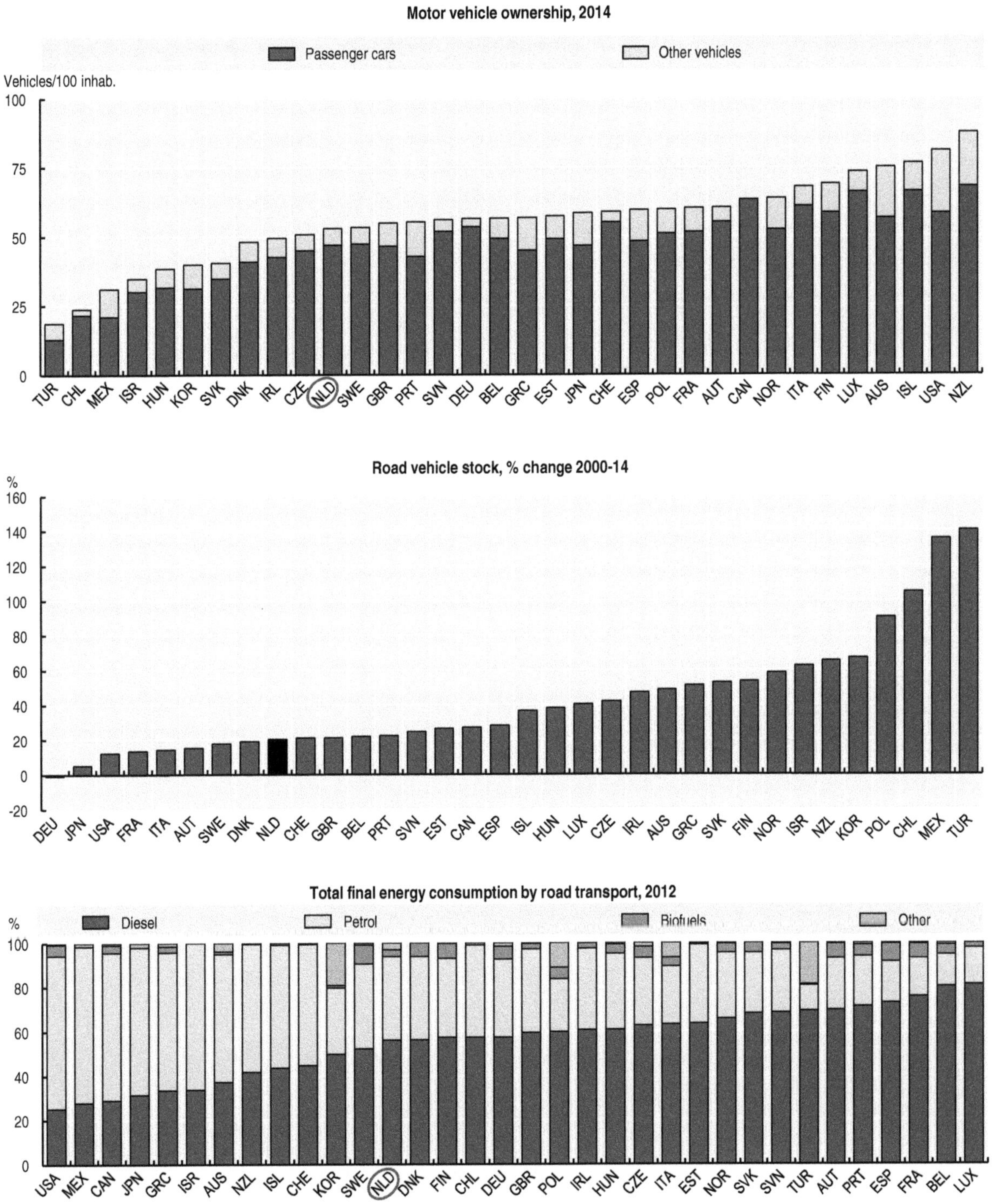

Notes: Data refer to the indicated year or to the latest available year. They may include provisional figures and estimates.
Motor vehicles with four or more wheels. Canada: data refer to total vehicles.
Source: IEA (2014), *IEA World Energy Statistics and Balances* (database); OECD (2015), *OECD Environment Statistics* (database).

StatLink http://dx.doi.org/10.1787/888933280486

ANNEX 1.B

Climate change and air pollution data

Figure 1.B1. **GHG emissions and intensity**

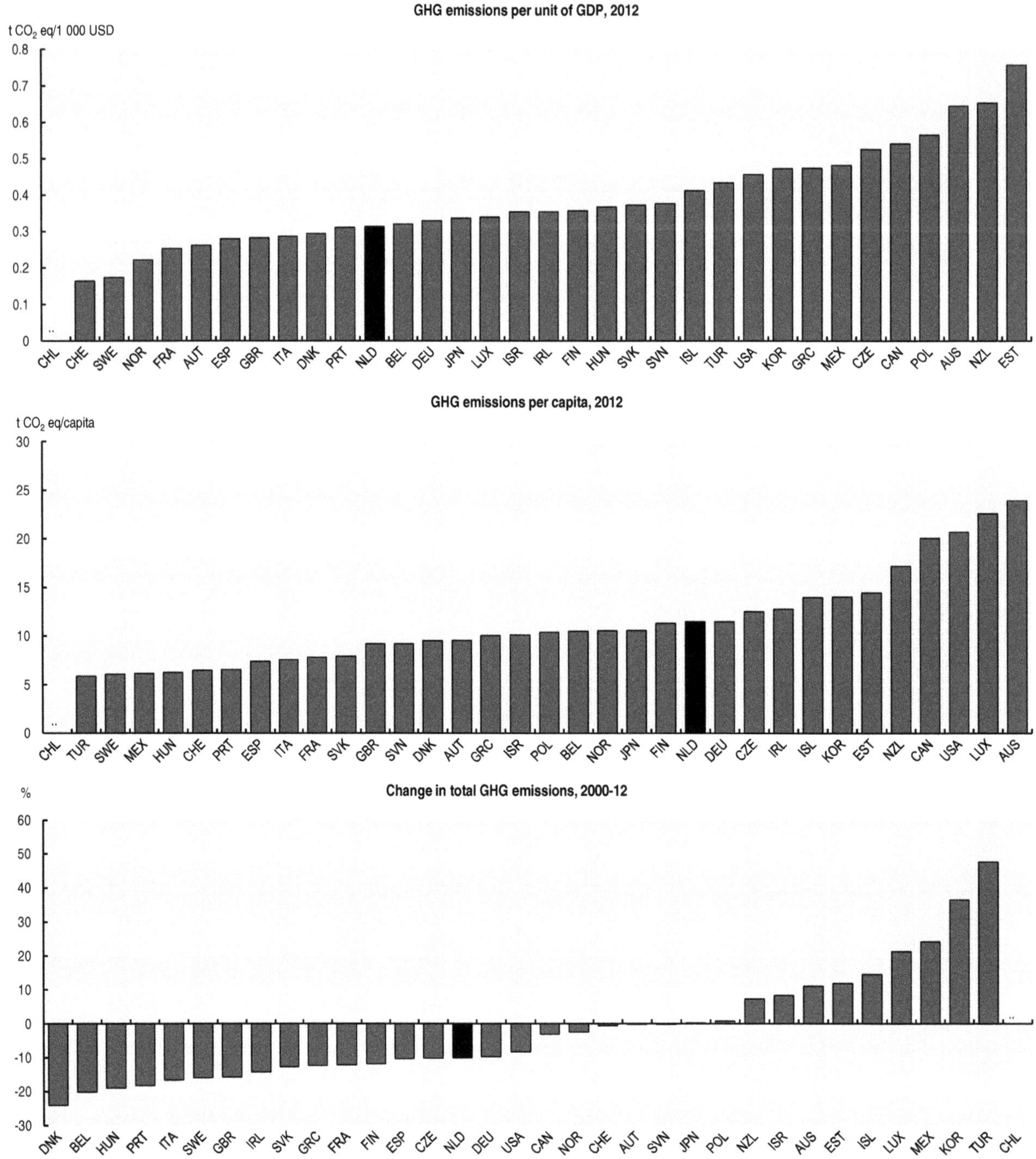

Notes: Data refer to the indicated year or to the latest available year. They may include provisional figures and estimates.
GHG emissions excluding emissions/removals from land use, land-use change and forestry. Israel: 2000 data exclude F-gases.
GDP at 2005 prices and purchasing power parities.
Source: OECD (2015), "Greenhouse gas emissions by source", *OECD Environment Statistics* (database); OECD (2014), "OECD Economic Outlook No. 95", *OECD Economic Outlook: Statistics and Projections* (database).

StatLink http://dx.doi.org/10.1787/888933280498

Figure 1.B2. CO_2 emissions and intensity

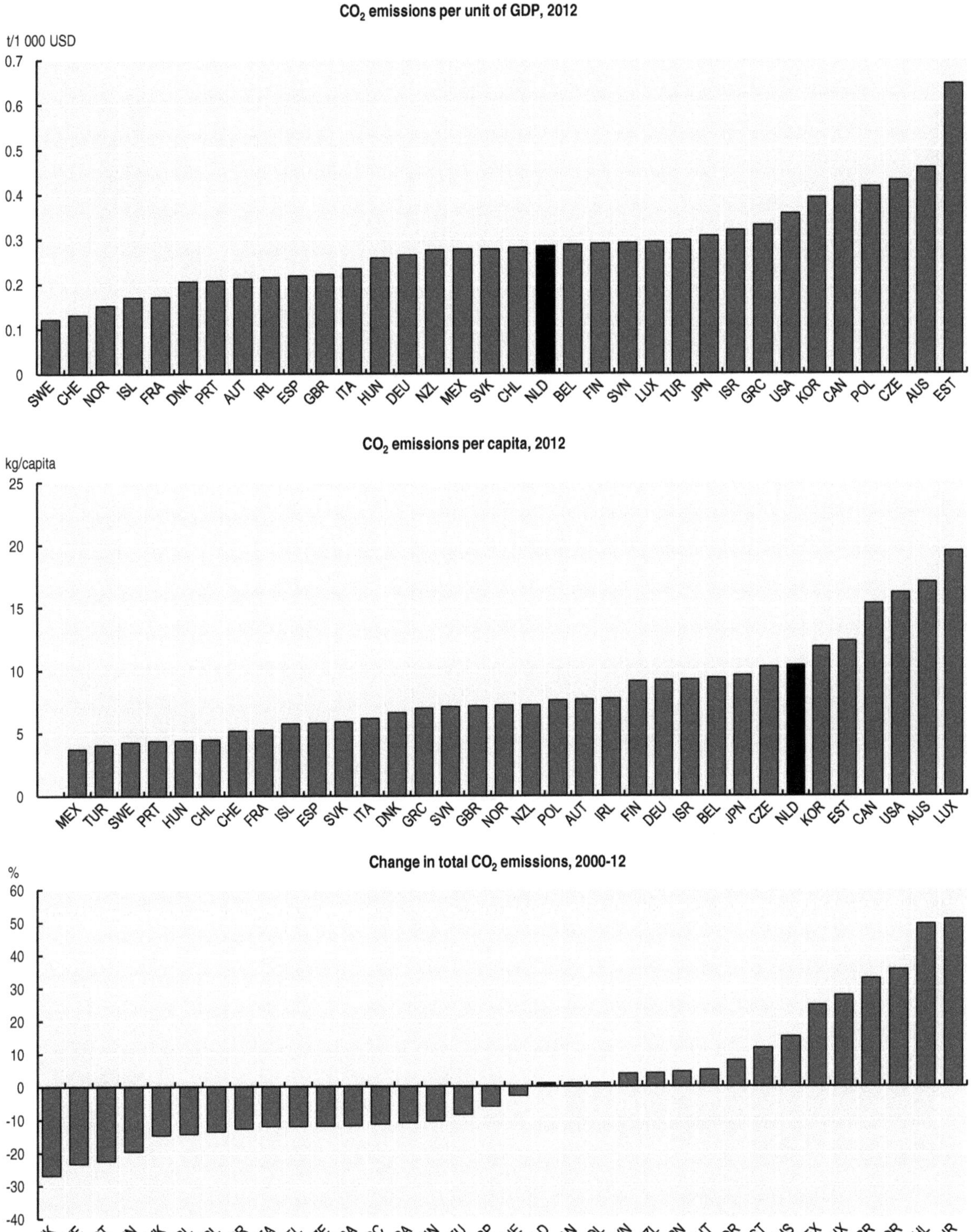

Notes: Data refer to the indicated year or to the latest available year. They may include provisional figures and estimates.
CO_2 emissions from energy use only; excluding international marine and aviation bunkers; sectoral approach. GDP at 2005 prices and purchasing power parities.
Source: IEA (2014), *IEA CO_2 Emissions from Fuel Combustion Statistics* (database); OECD (2014), "OECD Economic Outlook No. 95", *OECD Economic Outlook: Statistics and Projections* (database).

StatLink http://dx.doi.org/10.1787/888933280502

Figure 1.B3. **SO_x emissions and intensity**

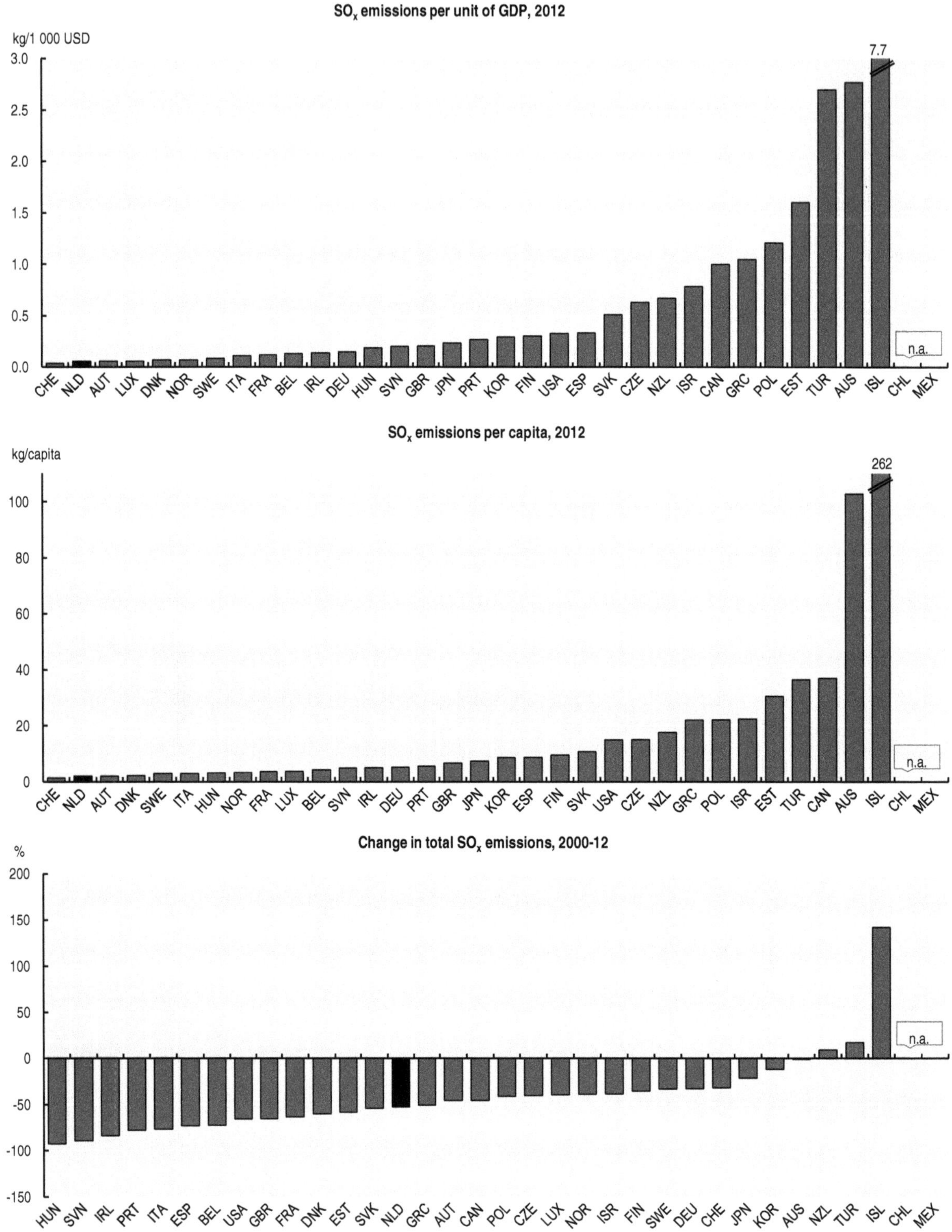

Notes: Data refer to the indicated year or to the latest available year. They may include provisional figures and estimates.
GDP at 2005 prices and purchasing power parities.
Source: OECD (2015), "Air emissions by source", *OECD Environment Statistics* (database); OECD (2014), "OECD Economic Outlook No. 95", *OECD Economic Outlook: Statistics and Projections* (database).

StatLink http://dx.doi.org/10.1787/888933280512

Figure 1.B4. NO_x emissions and intensity

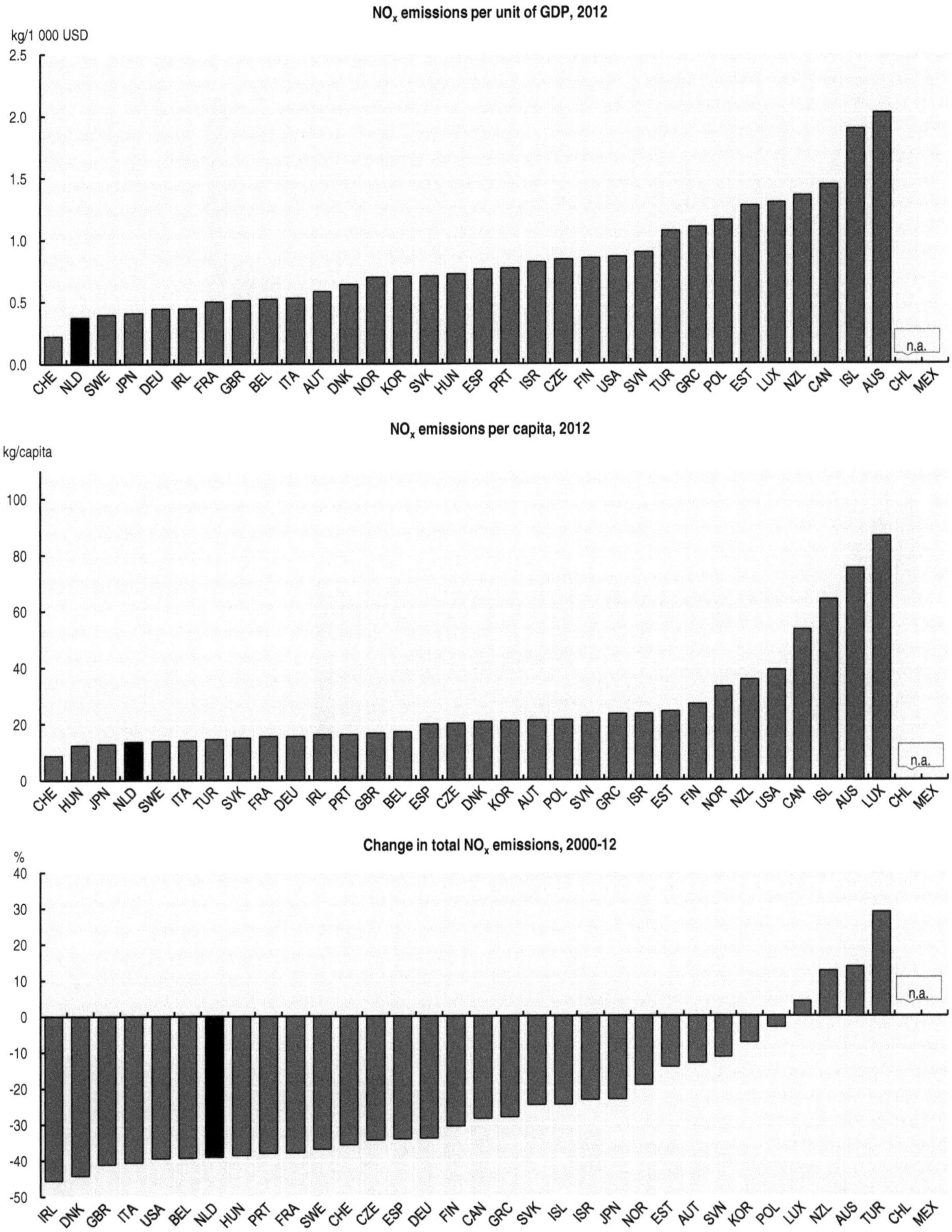

Notes: Data refer to the indicated year or to the latest available year. They may include provisional figures and estimates.
GDP at 2005 prices and purchasing power parities.
Source: OECD (2015), "Air emissions by source", *OECD Environment Statistics* (database); OECD (2014), "OECD Economic Outlook No. 95", *OECD Economic Outlook: Statistics and Projections* (database).

StatLink http://dx.doi.org/10.1787/888933280529

Figure 1.B5. **$PM_{2.5}$ emissions and pollution**

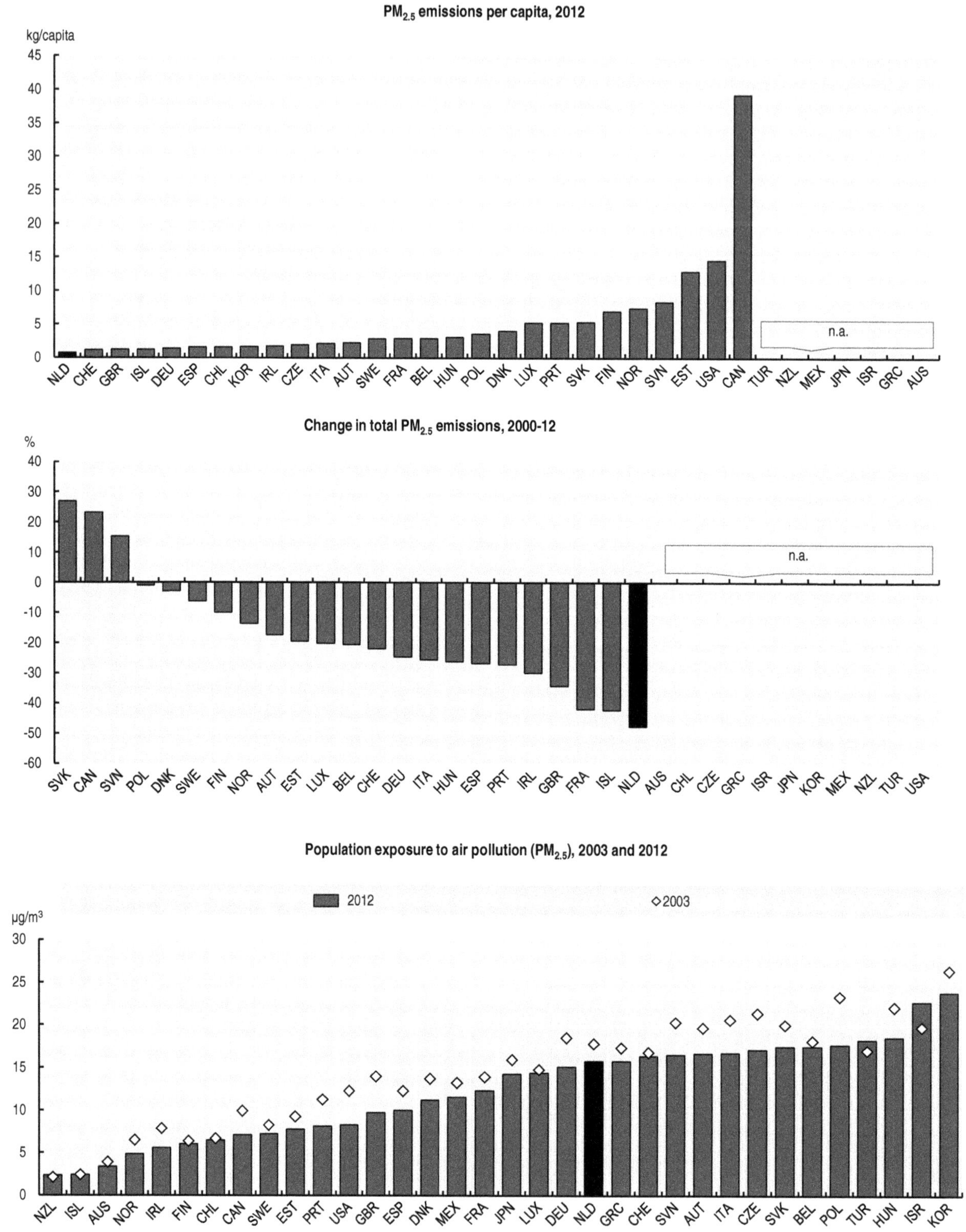

Notes: Data refer to the indicated year or to the latest available year. They may include provisional figures and estimates.
Population exposure to air pollution: estimates based on satellite imagery data; three-year average data.
Source: OECD (2015), "Air emissions by source", *OECD Environment Statistics* (database); OECD (2015), *OECD Regional Statistics* (database).

StatLink http://dx.doi.org/10.1787/888933280531

ANNEX 1.C

Waste and resource management data

Figure 1.C1. **Waste generation and management**

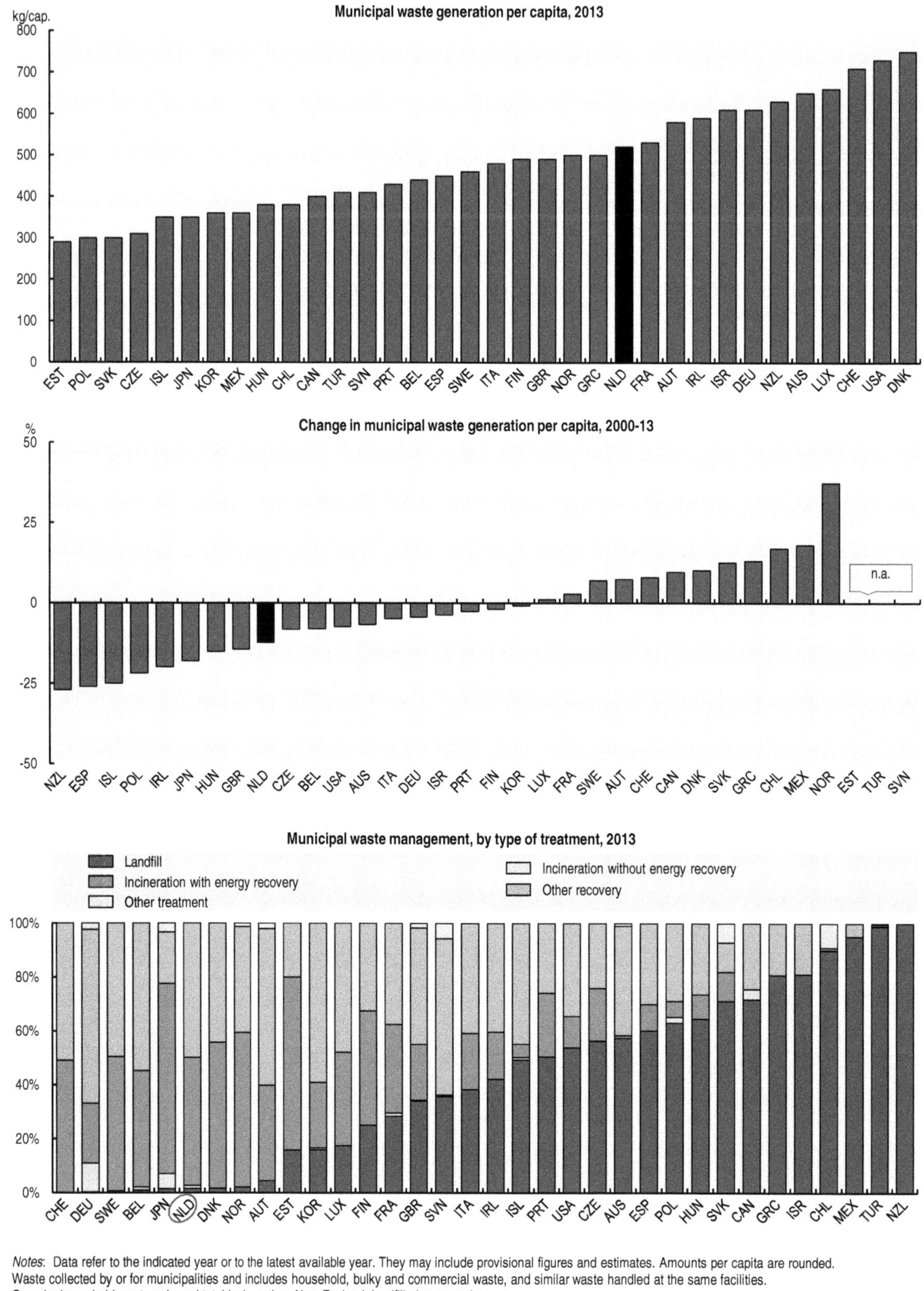

Notes: Data refer to the indicated year or to the latest available year. They may include provisional figures and estimates. Amounts per capita are rounded.
Waste collected by or for municipalities and includes household, bulky and commercial waste, and similar waste handled at the same facilities.
Canada: household waste only and total incineration; New Zealand: landfilled waste only.
Source: OECD (2015), "Municipal waste", *OECD Environment Statistics* (database).

StatLink http://dx.doi.org/10.1787/888933280541

Figure 1.C2. **Material consumption and productivity**

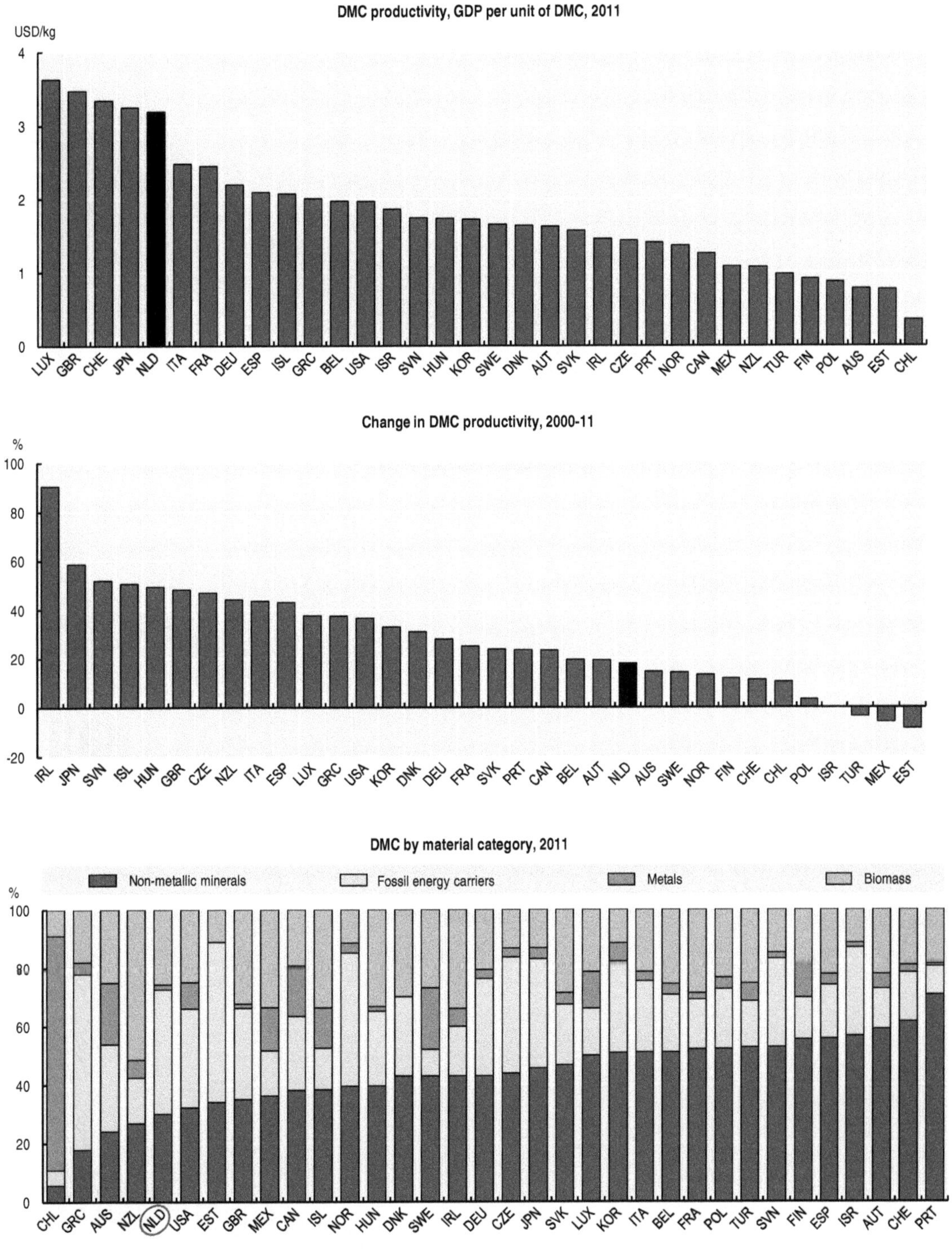

Notes: Data refer to the indicated year or to the latest available year. They may include provisional figures and estimates.
Domestic material consumption (DMC) equals the sum of domestic extraction of raw materials used by an economy and their physical trade balance (imports minus exports of raw materials and manufactured products). DMC productivity designates the amount of GDP generated per unit of materials used and is calculated as the ratio of GDP to DMC. GDP at 2005 prices and purchasing power parities.
Non-metallic minerals: domestic extraction and trade of minerals used in industry and construction, plus trade of derived processed products; fossil energy carriers: coal, crude oil, natural gas, peat and traded-derived products; metals: domestic extraction of metal ores, plus trade of metal ores, metal concentrates, refined metals, products mainly made of metals, and scrap; biomass: domestic production from agriculture, forestry and fisheries, plus trade of raw and processed products from these sectors.
Source: OECD (2015), "Material resources", *OECD Environment Statistics* (database); OECD (2014), "OECD Economic Outlook No. 95", *OECD Economic Outlook: Statistics and Projections* (database).

StatLink http://dx.doi.org/10.1787/888933280553

Figure 1.C3. **Agricultural inputs and livestock density**

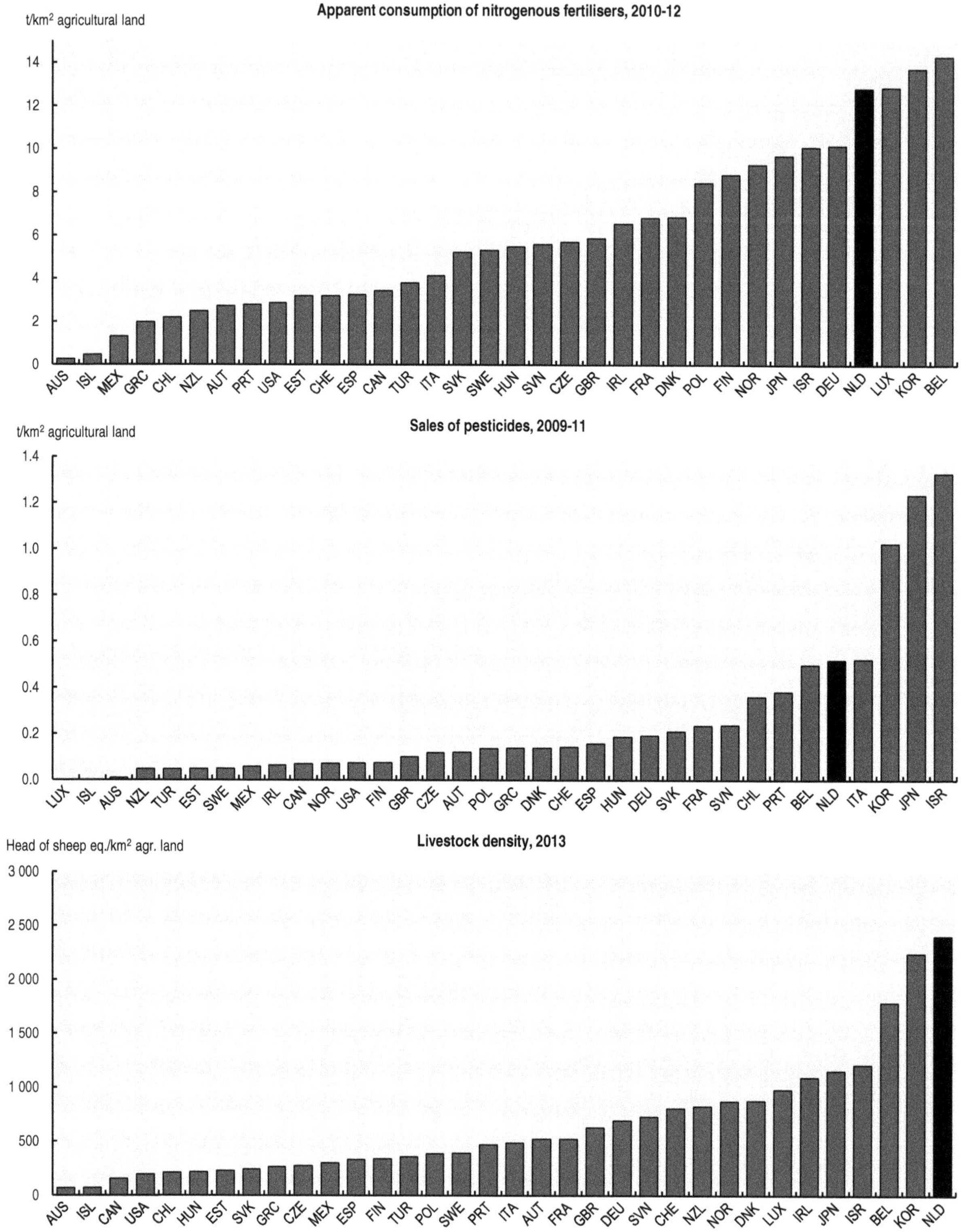

Notes: Data refer to the indicated year or to the latest available year. They may include provisional figures and estimates.
Source: FAO (2015), *FAOSTAT* (database); OECD (2015), *OECD Environment Statistics* (database).

StatLink http://dx.doi.org/10.1787/888933280562

ANNEX 1.D

Biodiversity and water data

Figure 1.D1. **Fish catches and threatened species**

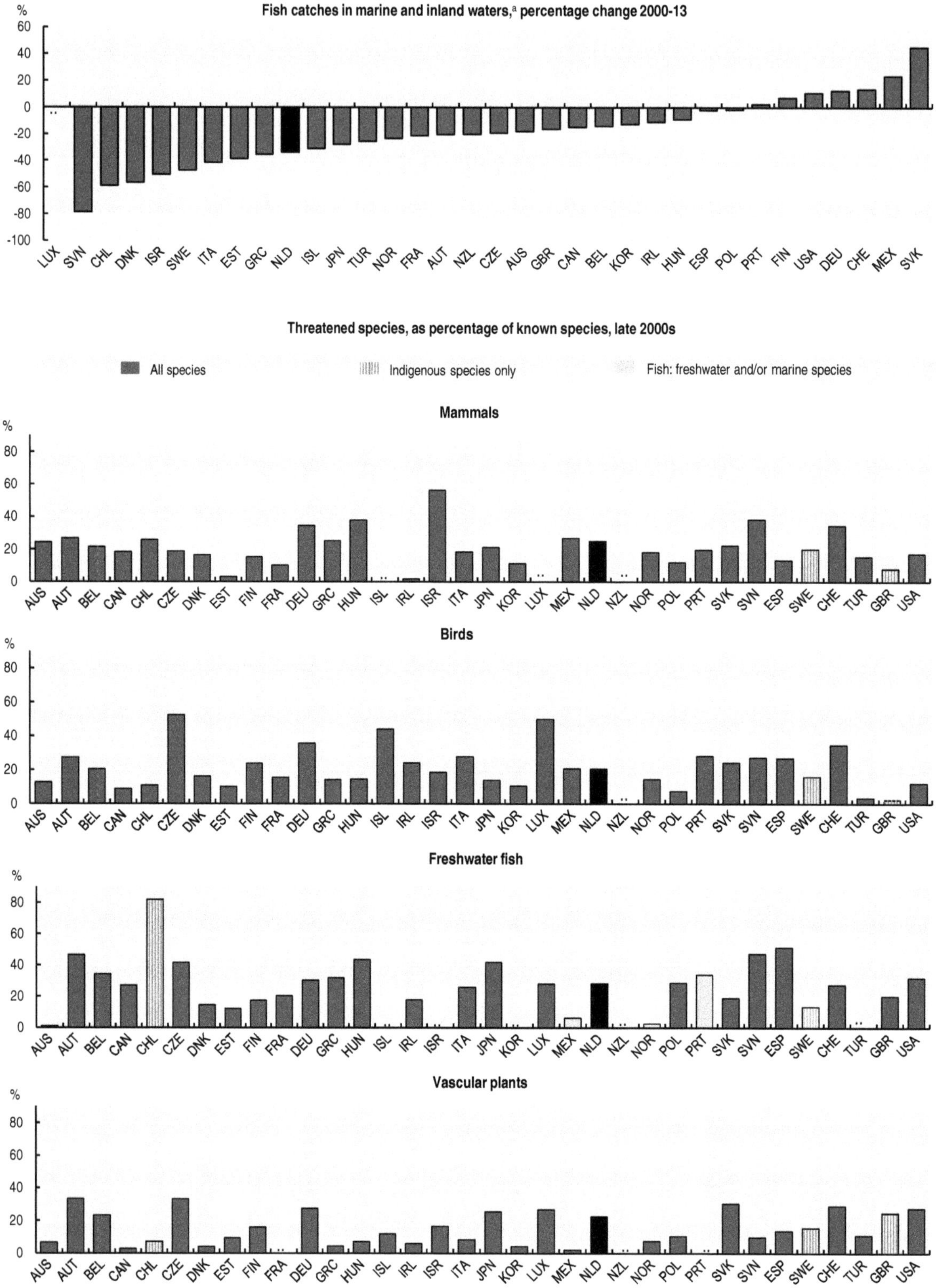

Notes: Data refer to the indicated year or to the latest available year. They may include provisional figures and estimates.

a) Includes fish, crustaceans, molluscs and other aquatic animals. Excludes marine mammals, crocodiles and alligators, and miscellaneous aquatic products.

Source: FAO (2015), *Global Capture Production* (database); OECD (2015), "Threatened species", *OECD Environment Statistics* (database).

StatLink http://dx.doi.org/10.1787/888933280575

Figure 1.D2. **Water abstraction and wastewater treatment**

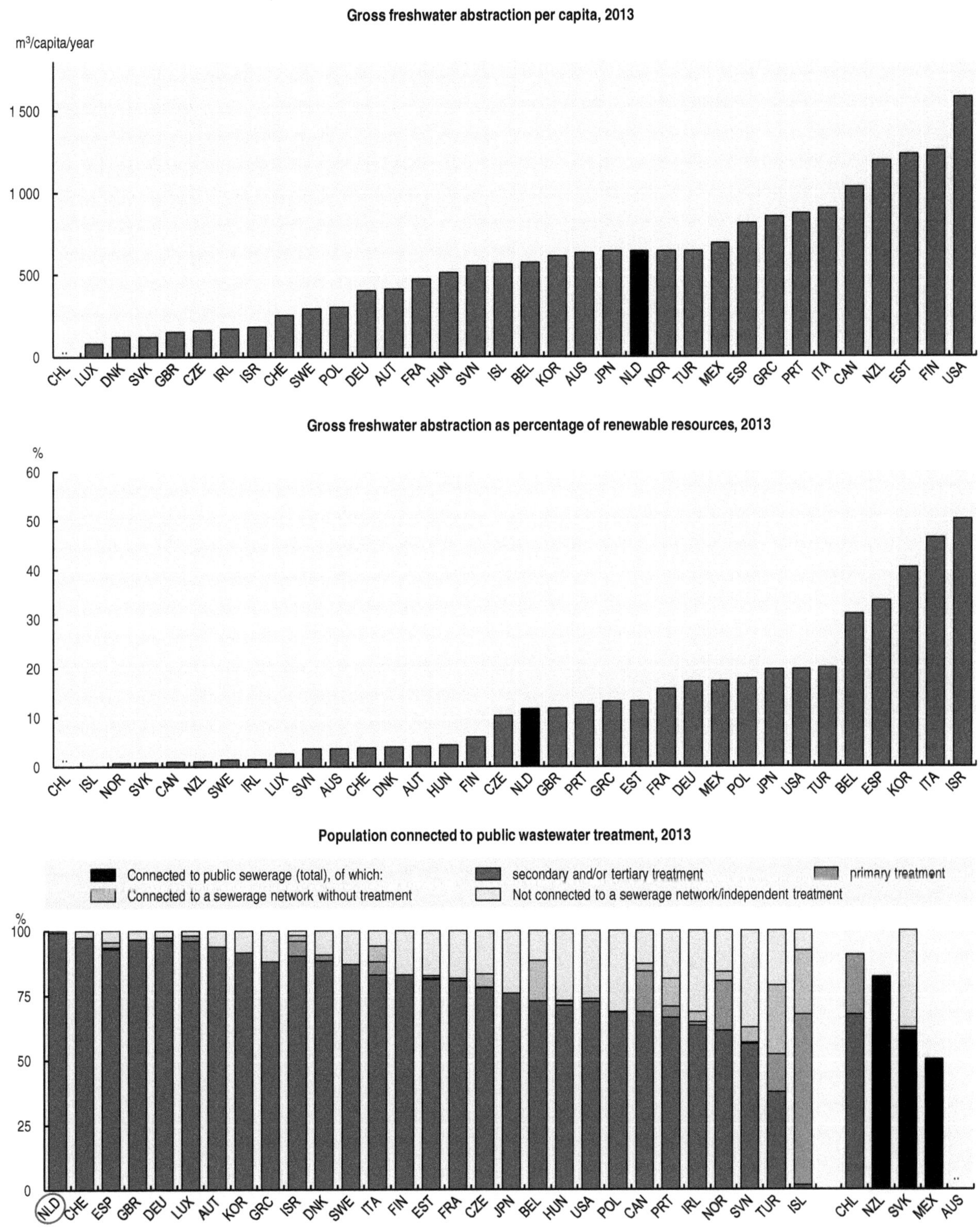

Notes: Data refer to the indicated year or to the latest available year. They may include provisional figures and estimates. United Kingdom: England and Wales only. Freshwater abstraction: for some countries, data refer to water permits and not to actual abstractions. Amounts per capita are rounded.

Source: OECD (2015), "Water: Freshwater Abstractions", "Water: Freshwater Abstractions", "Wastewater Treatment (% Population Connected)", OECD (2015), "Water: Freshwater Resources", *OECD Environment Statistics* (database).

StatLink http://dx.doi.org/10.1787/888933280583

PART I

Chapter 2

Environmental governance and management

This chapter examines the Netherlands' environmental governance and policy framework for environmental management. It documents important advances in environmental policy, particularly in streamlining environmental legislation, regulations and permitting requirements. It also summarises key developments in specific areas, including climate change, air, water, biodiversity and nature, spatial planning and external safety. Finally, the chapter discusses environmental permitting, enforcement and compliance, as well as the tools in place to ensure a comprehensive system of environmental information and strong policy evaluation mechanisms. The recommendations on environmental governance and management are summarised in a box at the end of the chapter.

1. Introduction

As a small, densely populated country with a very open economy, the Netherlands felt acute environmental pressures early on. To tackle these pressures, it became a forerunner in environmental policy decades ago and has long been considered a leader in a number of areas. However, more recently, the government recalibrated ambitions for environmental policy objectives to levels set by the European Union (EU), with a view to promoting a level playing field. While the temptation may be to wait and let other countries catch up in areas where it is already doing well, the Netherlands still faces some persistent environmental challenges, and new ones are emerging. Hajer (2011) stressed the scale of the challenge ahead when he highlighted that resource use and the resulting pressures on the environment need to be scaled back by a factor of five. This equates to operating 80% to 90% more efficiently.

This chapter assesses the environmental governance and management of the Netherlands over the review period. It provides an overview of the policy framework and strategic vision for environmental management and briefly summarises key developments in specific areas, including climate change, air, water, biodiversity and nature, spatial planning, external safety and environmental liability. The chapter examines the multi-level governance arrangements and approaches to vertical and horizontal co-operation. It also assesses the approach to environmental permitting, enforcement and compliance, as well as environmental information systems and policy evaluation.

2. Policy framework and strategic vision for environmental management

The Netherlands was a pioneer in the development of comprehensive environmental plans, which set out a long-term, strategic vision. The first plan was developed in the 1980s, while the fourth and most recent (NMP4) was released in 2001. The NMP4 committed the government to a "transition" agenda with a horizon to 2030 to restructure production and consumption systems and sharply reduce resource use and emissions. However, according to PBL (2013), the plan's effectiveness was limited as it lacked a clear vision of the policy instruments to be used (and at which level) and did not spell out a clear role for government and its relationship to society. For example, it did not consider which issues would best be dealt with at the EU level rather than at the national level or how best to harness the power of innovation in society.

Over the review period, in addition to this "transition" agenda, the government set out a number of different initiatives to promote environmental objectives focused on various themes and environmental media. These included the Sustainability Agenda launched in 2011 along with the overarching strategy for green growth set out in a letter to the House of Representatives in March 2013 (Chapter 3). Major initiatives include the Netherlands Social and Economic Council (SER) 2013 Energy Agreement for Sustainable Growth (the Energy Agreement) and the Delta Programme launched in 2010 to focus on water management. These and other key developments are briefly summarised later in this chapter.

Currently, there is a drive to modernise environmental policy, with a focus on public health, particularly on new risks. The government outlined the approach in a Memorandum to the House of Representatives from the State Secretary for the Environment (Government of the Netherlands, 2014a). The document recognises the important advances in environmental policy over the past decades, while signalling a new era for environmental policy given that major environmental issues today and in the future are of a different order and require a new approach. The modernisation approach emphasises more active international co-operation, in recognition of both the global nature of environmental issues, such as climate change, and the influence of international forums (in particular the EU) on environmental policy. Continued efforts to streamline and consolidate environmental legislation and regulations will aim to support the cross-sectorial focus in the integrated Environment and Planning Act. This move towards an integrated legislative framework seeks to make implementation easier and reduce discrepancies between sectors. Finally, the approach stresses the role of government as a facilitator of "new coalitions" to tap into the energy of civil society organisations (CSOs), the private sector and the general public in promoting sustainability. The Sustainable Action programme (*Duurzaam Doen*) was launched to encourage such initiatives.

2.1. *Legal and regulatory framework for environmental management*

The Environmental Management Act (*Wet milieubeheer*, EMA) provides the foundation for environmental legislation in the Netherlands. The act covers all environmental aspects, including transposing the requirements of EU environmental directives. Around 80% of environmental legislation in the Netherlands is linked to European law. Compliance with the EU environmental *acquis* has been consistent, as reflected in the relatively low number of infringement procedures compared to the average across EU countries (Figure 2.1).

Figure 2.1. **Few Dutch infringements on EU environmental legislation, 2007-14**

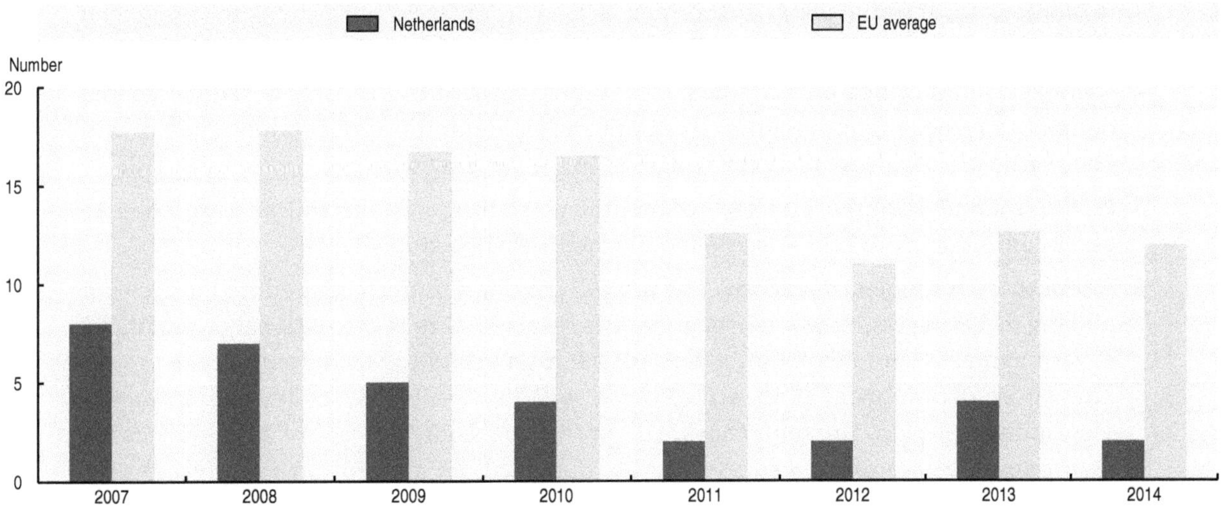

Source: European Commission (2015), Statistics on environmental infringements.

StatLink http://dx.doi.org/10.1787/888933280192

The Netherlands made impressive progress in streamlining environment legislation, regulations, and permitting requirements over the review period. The government is undertaking a major legislative overhaul to consolidate its environmental legislation.

The legislative streamlining will integrate all national legislation for the protection of the natural environment under one framework: the Environment and Planning Act (*Omgevingswet*), which is expected to enter into force in 2018. This marks an important shift from environmental law dispersed across sectorial legislation (13 acts and parts of 14 other acts) into a consolidated piece of legislation. The consolidated act will transpose more than 30 EU directives related to the environment previously transposed in other legislation. A similar streamlining process is taking place for the underlying regulations.

The Environment and Planning Act aims to improve the quality, coherence and application of environmental law, streamline policy and legal instruments, and create conditions for improved and expedited decision making. The new act will contain integrated rules on land-use planning, urban and rural development, water management, environmental protection, nature conservation, construction of buildings, cultural heritage, mining and earth removal, as well as the development of major public and private works. Whether the integration of these diverse areas will be effective will depend on how the secondary legislation is elaborated and how it is implemented in practice.

The Environment and Planning Act is based on six pillars (Ministry of Infrastructure and Environment, 2014):

1. **Development of an environmental vision:** The act will require the central government and provincial authorities to each produce an environmental vision, which will replace the existing array of plans and visions relating to the living environment.
2. **Programmes:** Programmes will be used to set out concrete measures for protection, management, use and development of the environment that can reach environmental aims.
3. **Decentralised regulation:** A core tenet of the act is decentralised regulation. Each local government authority will need to consolidate all of its environmental rules into a single regulatory document: an environmental plan for municipalities, water management regulations for regional water authorities and environmental regulations for provincial authorities.
4. **General national rules on activities:** General national rules for some activities will be defined to remove requirements to submit multiple permit applications. The act will have some provisions to allow for flexibility in the general rules.
5. **Environmental permits:** The environmental permitting system will be simplified to avoid contradictory or burdensome requirements ("a one stop shop").
6. **A procedure for project decisions.** The act will provide a uniform procedure for decision making regarding complex projects under the responsibility of the national or provincial governments. Where incompatibilities between an economic or infrastructure project and an environmental plan arise, there will be flexibility to deviate from the environmental plan. In some cases, the project decision procedure may replace an environmental permit procedure. Finally, there will be a statutory requirement for participation in the course of project decisions.

As a part of the preparation of the new Environment and Planning Act, a comprehensive review of environmental legislation, including the environmental *acquis* of the EU, took place (Box 2.1).

In addition to the legislative overhaul underway, the Netherlands has taken other important steps to consolidate and streamline environmental regulations over the review

Box 2.1. "Make it Work": Reviewing the EU environmental *acquis*

The preparation of the Environment and Planning Act included an analysis of EU environmental directives (*aquis communautaire*), as around 80% of environmental legislation in the Netherlands links to European law (Wöltgens and Stoop, 2012). The analysis revealed the *acquis* appears to be consistent at a high level; however, upon closer examination, some inconsistencies emerge. These inconsistencies may have developed in the course of negotiations on individual instruments. Other issues potentially affecting effective implementation of the *acquis* include contradictory, overlapping or accumulating obligations, different timelines for reporting and the complexity of the *acquis* itself, as it has grown over time.

To further investigate these issues, the Netherlands launched the "Make it Work" project, along with nine other EU member countries, including the United Kingdom and Germany. The project seeks to identify opportunities for improving the coherence and consistency of environmental legislation and to propose concrete recommendations. The overall aim is to improve the effectiveness of the *acquis*, while maintaining the level of ambition in terms of environmental protection.

Source: Government of the Netherlands (2014b), "Make it Work", *https://omgevingswet.pleio.nl/file/download/26694012* (accessed 22 October 2014).

period. This includes the adoption of the Activities Decree, which came into effect in 2008. The decree reduced the number of required environmental licences, providing for a greater reliance on general binding rules (GBRs). It trimmed the volume of legislation and drastically reduced the number of installations that required an environmental permit. Of the 412 000 establishments in the Netherlands that have an environmental impact, the large majority (more than 390 000) are now covered by GBRs, while a smaller share (22 000) require an environmental permit. The government estimated that as of 2013, this change resulted in a reduction of administrative burden in the order of EUR 354 million (Ministry of Infrastructure and Environment, 2013).

Streamlining efforts continued with the 2010 Act on General Provisions for Environmental Law (*Wet algemene bepalingen omgevingsrecht*, WABO), which established "all-in-one" permitting for environmental permits. The act allows applicants to use a single procedure to apply to one competent authority for permits for activities that affect the physical environment. This replaced requirements for around 25 separate permits for activities such as construction, demolition, spatial planning and buildings. In so doing, it reduced administrative burden and costs for the public and private companies.

Given the significant consolidation and streamlining efforts over the period, it would be valuable for the government to assess the impact of these changes to ensure that, collectively, they meet the aim of maintaining (or increasing) the level of environmental protection in practice. Such an evaluation has been undertaken in the case of the Activities Decree. The evaluation concluded that the decree's system of GBRs has only a minimal impact (positive or negative) on the level of environmental protection that can be seen in certain practical cases (Ministry of Infrastructure and Environment, 2015).

Ensuring the level of environmental protection is maintained or improved in the context of ongoing streamlining efforts is important for continued environmental performance. A related, but distinct, concept is that of the stringency of environmental policy. Recent OECD analysis has examined the stringency of selected environmental policies, which ranks the Netherlands among the most stringent (Botta and Koźluk, 2014) (Figure 2.2). In this study, stringency was defined as a higher, explicit or implicit, cost of polluting or environmentally harmful behaviour (which is distinct from attempting to measure the level of environmental protection). The analysis does not provide a comprehensive picture of the stringency of environmental policies in OECD member countries; it only covers certain instruments related mainly to the electricity sector, along with two transport policy instruments and one waste policy instrument. The analysis shows that stringency in the Netherlands, as measured by this analysis, has increased significantly over time, in line with the broader trend in OECD member countries.

Figure 2.2. **Relatively high stringency of select environmental policies in the Netherlands**

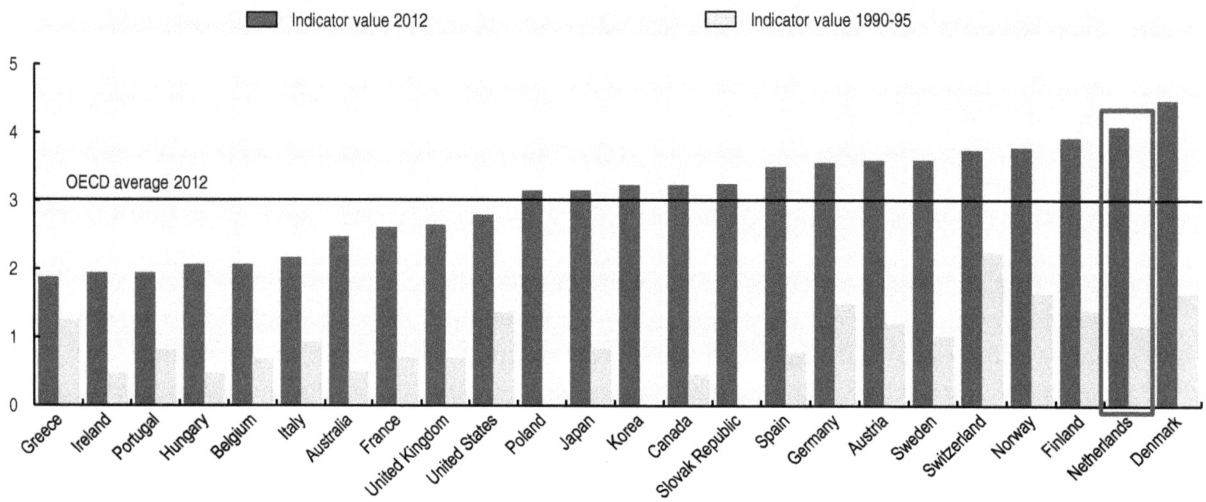

Source: Botta, E. and T. Koźluk (2014), "Measuring Environmental Policy Stringency in OECD Countries: A Composite Index Approach", *OECD Economics Department Working Papers, No. 1177.*

StatLink http://dx.doi.org/10.1787/888933280208

2.2. *Key environmental strategies, policies and programmes*

Over the review period, the government developed a number of different environmental strategies, policies and programmes focused on specific environmental media. Overall, the Netherlands made successful advances over the last decade in traditional environmental policy domains, where it has long been considered a forerunner. Yet the country has faced persistent difficulties in addressing diffuse pollution and securing significant improvements in the quality of ecosystems and biodiversity. Several key initiatives are briefly discussed in this section.

Climate change mitigation and adaptation

The policy and investment framework for renewable energy and energy efficiency to support climate mitigation goals in recent years has been characterised by relative instability (IEA, 2014). The 2007 Clean and Efficient Programme and the 2008 Energy Strategy called for a 30% reduction in greenhouse gas (GHG) emissions from 1990 levels, 20% renewables in the energy mix and annual energy efficiency improvements of 2% by 2020 (IEA, 2009). Since 2010, the government has revised downward these ambitious climate policy targets and programmes. The aim has been to use EU policy as the ceiling on ambition (with the exception of the 2023 target on renewable energy) to establish a level playing field within the EU. The 2020 EU Climate and Energy package translates into the national targets of a 14% share of renewables in gross final energy consumption and a 16% reduction in GHG emissions (for the non-ETS sector) by 2020, below 2005 levels. The 2013 Energy Agreement set targets to save 1.5% in final energy consumption annually until 2020[1] and increase the share of renewable energy in final energy consumption to 14% by 2020 and 16% by 2023. For the transport sector, the target is to reduce CO_2 emissions by 17% by 2030 and by 60% by 2050 (below 1990 levels) (see Chapter 3).

In addition to instruments deriving from EU climate policy (EU emissions trading system, CO_2 standards for passenger cars and light commercial vehicles, as well as buildings), the Netherlands has a feed-in-tariff system that subsidises renewable energy producers (SDE+) (see Chapter 3). Sectorial agreements continue to play an important role in Dutch climate policy, as reflected in the 2013 Energy Agreement spearheaded by the SER (discussed below).

Building on the Energy Agreement, the government put forth a "Climate Agenda" in October 2014 covering mitigation and adaptation policy with a horizon to 2030. The agenda covers a broader range of sectors than the Energy Agreement, such as agriculture. Within the EU, the Dutch Cabinet is advocating for at least a 40% reduction of GHG emissions compared with 1990.

Climate change adaptation has been considered in some specific policy areas, such as water management, but a comprehensive approach to adaptation has been lacking to date. In 2012, the Court of Audit (*Algemene Rekenkamer*) reviewed adaptation policy, including the Spatial Planning and Climate Adaptation Programme that ran from 2006-10 and the 2007 National Adaptation Strategy (NAS). The court's findings highlighted a number of shortcomings. For example, in 2008, Parliament was told the NAS would be developed into a national adaptation agenda, with specific actions, a timetable and allocation of responsibilities; this never happened. Neither a comprehensive assessment of risks and vulnerabilities nor concrete measures have been developed. Further, adaptation policy lacks co-ordination and is not monitored and evaluated in a systemic way. This increases the risk that the Netherlands will not be well prepared for the impacts of climate change. It can also make adaptation more costly if measures are delayed too far into the future and require costly retrofitting and adjustments (Algemene Rekenkamer, 2012).

Since the establishment of the Delta Programme in 2012 (discussed below), climate change adaptation has been mainstreamed into key areas of water management, in particular flood safety and freshwater supply. Taking an integrated and adaptive approach, the Delta Programme has re-evaluated water management in light of long-term challenges, including climate change, with a horizon to 2100. In September 2014, key decisions ("Delta Decisions") were presented to Parliament. These decisions included a new flood risk management policy, a new nationwide approach to freshwater supply and a decision on spatial adaptation that sets out a new, targeted approach to water-robust and climate-proof development in the built environment.

A new National Adaptation Strategy to update the 2007 NAS is expected to be presented to Parliament in 2016. It will go beyond the water-related focus of the Delta Programme, to address a range of sectors, in particular health, energy, infrastructure, information and communications technologies, transport, nature, agriculture and fisheries. It will also examine cross-sectorial interactions and the potential effects of climate change outside of the Netherlands, which could nonetheless have impacts on Dutch society and the economy.

Air pollution

EU limit values for concentrations of air pollutants were incorporated into Dutch law via the Environmental Management Act. Air quality has improved significantly in recent decades. However, the country requested a derogation to extend the date to comply with the limit values for PM_{10} and NO_2 set out in the EU Directive on Ambient Air Quality and Cleaner Air (2008/50/EC). According to a report from the National Institute for Public Health and the Environment (RIVM), the limit values for particulate matter were exceeded at a limited number of locations (in 20 of the 403 municipalities in the Netherlands) in industrial areas and regions with intensive livestock farming, resulting in a failure to comply with EU limit values in 2013. Projected NO_2 exceedances for 2015 are expected to occur mostly in the Randstad, close to locations with high road traffic intensity (RIVM, 2014).

The National Air Quality Co-operation Programme (*Nationaal Samenwekingsprogramma Luchtkwaliteit*, NSL) addresses areas that are expected to exceed limit values for air quality. The programme was intended to run through August 2014, but was extended until 1 January 2017. The NSL is a co-operation programme between the national government and local authorities. Regional Air Quality Co-operation Programmes (RSLs), under the responsibility of the provinces and municipalities, are also part of the NSL. The government provided more than EUR 1.55 billion to reduce background and peak concentrations of air pollution emissions. For example, some EUR 554 million was used to subsidise particulate filters on diesel-powered vehicles. In addition, EUR 45 million was provided in grants to livestock farmers (mainly poultry farms) to help reduce PM_{10} emissions through measures such as the installation of air scrubbers. While the programme has been effective in helping to meet PM_{10} standards in most areas, it has resulted in little additional health benefit, as it does not focus on exposure to finer particulate matter, the most harmful type (PBL, 2013).

Water management

Flood protection standards in the Netherlands are among the highest in the world. While not all flood defence structures currently meet safety standards, efforts are underway to address this (OECD, 2014a). Despite being a water-abundant country, the risk of drought and shortage of freshwater is expected to grow in the future, especially in a changing climate. Increasing salinity in some regions and longer and more frequent dry spells have contributed to the increasing risk of shortage. There are currently few formal arrangements for water allocation in the Netherlands and no explicit limit on abstraction (OECD, 2015). Shortage incidents are handled through priority regime banning, where access to lower priority use is temporarily restricted. Inadequate water quality as a result of diffuse pollution and stresses on freshwater ecosystems are persistent issues, making the targets under the EU Water Framework Directive (WFD) difficult to reach (OECD, 2014a). The revised draft EU WFD River Basin Management Plans covering the period 2015-21 were presented at the end of 2014. Based on these plans, only about 15% of water bodies will reach EU WFD objectives by 2027 (PBL, 2015a).

For decades, Dutch water management has relied on large structural solutions and an engineering approach to provide flood protection and ensure freshwater supply. Recently, a new approach known as "Room for the River" has emerged, combining innovative architecture, urbanisation and landscape solutions to build with nature and live with water. Re-naturalising waterways and using multi-functional water management infrastructures can improve the environmental benefits associated with water management (OECD, 2014a). Further, these approaches can be more cost effective than traditional, engineered approaches. Building on these positive developments, water management could further consider impacts on ecosystem functioning and nature objectives. This will require close co-operation between the Ministry of Economic Affairs, the Ministry of Infrastructure and Environment, and sub-national authorities, in particular the regional water authorities. Strong collaboration between the Nature Vision Strategy of the Ministry of Economic Affairs and the development of the next iteration of the River Basin Management Plans could help promote coherence between water and nature objectives (PBL, 2015b).

An important advance in water policy occurred in 2012 with the adoption of the Delta Act on Flood Risk Management and Freshwater Supplies. This was driven by growing concerns about the potential impacts of climate change and the long-term water security of the country. The act established the Delta Programme as the national planning instrument to respond to the country's current and future challenges on water safety and freshwater supply. The Delta Commissioner, appointed by the government, leads the programme and submits a yearly proposal for action to the cabinet; this provides an overview of all measures, studies and ambitions related to flood risk management and freshwater supplies. The Delta Fund provides financial resources for measures of national importance related to flood risk management and freshwater supplies (as well as the water quality measures directly related to these tasks). Up until 2020, the money earmarked for water safety and freshwater supply has been transferred from the Infrastructure Fund to the Delta Fund, with an average annual budget of EUR 1 billion until the end of 2028 (Ministry of Infrastructure and Environment and Ministry of Economic Affairs, 2014).

Nature and biodiversity policy

With few remaining "natural" areas, biodiversity in the Netherlands co-exists with high population density and economic activity, including intensive agricultural production. At the same time, the long Dutch coastline and low-lying delta create unique conditions for biodiversity. Although the rate of decline has slowed or improved for a number of species, some populations are still in decline. The 2013 monitoring results of the European Union Habitat Directive reveal that about 95% of habitat types and 75% of species are threatened, a share higher than in many other OECD member countries.

The Netherlands put in place the National Ecological Network (NEN) to promote biodiversity and fulfil international commitments under the UN Biodiversity Convention and EU directives for birds and habitats (Natura 2000). The NEN, a programme running until 2027, consists of 162 designated Natura 2000 land areas, as well as national parks and other forest and nature areas. It seeks to extend and better connect ecosystem areas, including via a national programme to address fragmentation related to infrastructure. The 2014 budget for the NEN (including terrestrial Natura 2000 sites) was EUR 415 million, funded mainly by the national government. Efforts also continue to reduce pressures on biodiversity and improve nature management on farmland. The protection of the nature areas in the NEN exist under a "qualified no" regime. This means that actions with significant negative impact on the NEN are not permitted unless they are clearly in the public interest and there are no realistic alternatives (Ministry of Infrastructure and Environment, 2011).

Of the more than 160 Natura 2000 areas, 117 are affected by nitrogen levels (Ministry of Economic Affairs, 2015). Nitrogen deposition arises from multiple sources, NO_x from traffic and industry, and NH_3 from farming. The Integrated Approach to Nitrogen (PAS) was developed to help address this and reduce the amount of nitrogen in nature areas. From 1 July 2015, the permitting of new economic activities (e.g. agriculture, industry, traffic) will be conditional upon assessing the impact of nitrogen deposition on surrounding Natura 2000 areas (as estimated by the new AERIUS calculation tool from RIVM).

Since 2010, nature policy has been largely decentralised and deregulated (PBL, 2015b). The Natural Capital Agenda, launched in 2013, shifted the focus of nature policy from conservation of nature areas to the sustainable use of ecosystem services provided by nature. The 2014 Nature Conservation Act replaced existing acts concerning nature (the Nature Conservation Act of 1998 and the Flora and Fauna Act of 2002, which transposed the relevant EU directives into national legislation). The act, considered more flexible and less detailed than previous legislation, will be incorporated into the new Environment and Planning Act.

The Ministry of Economic Affairs outlined a new government vision for nature policy in 2014 (Ministry of Economic Affairs, 2014). It marks a shift in nature policy, emphasising a change in role for the national government from "managing" to "facilitating". Green Deals (discussed below) play a prominent role. In line with the decentralisation trend underway, the Pact for Nature transfers large parts of nature policy to provincial authorities. Under the pact, provincial authorities have entered into agreements with key stakeholders to define their role in implementing nature policy.

Spatial planning

The Netherlands' high population density and dense transportation networks contribute to intense competition for physical space. Spatial planning thus has an important impact on the living environment and quality of ecosystems. Since 2012, the National Policy Strategy for Infrastructure and Spatial Planning (SVIR) has provided a reference framework for all government policy with implications for spatial planning, replacing a number of diverse plans and strategies. It represents a strategic agenda for spatial planning policies, which guides a programme of investments. A related instrument, the Multi-Year Plan for Infrastructure, Spatial Planning and Transport (MIRT), aims to promote coherence between investments in spatial planning, economic development, mobility and quality of life at the national level. The total national budget of the MIRT in 2013 was EUR 6.4 billion (Government of the Netherlands, 2014c).

A core feature of the SIVR is decentralisation, delegating more responsibilities to local and provincial authorities, to provide them with greater flexibility. To this end, the central government has eliminated the national landscape policy and reduced the number of nature management regimes (OECD, 2014b). Provincial authorities have been given responsibility for balancing urban and green areas at regional level, while land-use planning has largely been decentralised to the municipalities. Municipalities prepare local regulations and land-use plans, designating land use for residential areas, industrial estates, business parks, agricultural production, nature and other purposes. They may also authorise and finance compulsory land purchase. In cases where zoning plans extend beyond a given municipality, consultation with neighbouring municipalities is required. Examples include the siting of windmill parks, transportation infrastructure and the designation of nature areas. Municipal and inter-local co-ordination are left to local authorities.

In cases where regional or national interests are at stake in land-use decisions, responsibility lies with the provinces or national government, respectively. The central government focuses on 13 areas of national interest, including space for the main sustainable energy supply network and room for a national network of wildlife habitats. For example, the central government and provincial authorities will plan space for more onshore wind farms, aiming to generate at least 6 000 megawatts (MW) by 2020 (Ministry of Infrastructure and Environment, 2011) and 6 000 MW from offshore wind in the longer term.

External safety

External safety policy is concerned with limiting risks to people and the environment from the possible effects of hazardous activities (e.g. industrial installations and hazardous substance transport routes). This is particularly important in the Netherlands, given its high population density and dense transport networks. Hazardous substances are present at over 5 000 establishments; nearly half of these are liquefied petroleum gas (LPG) tank filling stations, 1 000 are chemical storage sites and 300 are "Seveso" sites (Government of the Netherlands, 2011). According to the EU directives on the control of major accident hazards involving dangerous substances (generally known as the Seveso directives) these Seveso sites require special attention.

Two major accidents, the Bijlmer airplane crash in 1992 and the Enschede fireworks explosion in 2000 spurred a major revision in external safety policy. The Enschede explosion caused 22 deaths, injured nearly 1 000 people and inflicted substantial physical damage. An independent commission found that both the security arrangements of the fireworks facility (including compliance with government regulations) and the external security provisions set by the government, including regulations, licensing requirements and monitoring, were inadequate (Fireworks Investigation Commission, 2001). Among its recommendations, the commission suggested the government explicitly task the Environment Minister, or another, with the primary responsibility for external safety, including interdepartmental co-ordination.

The overhaul of external safety policy included new legislation and more than doubled programme financing from 2004 to 2006. Financing reached EUR 20 million per year over 2006-10 (Government of the Netherlands, 2011). The legal framework consists of several decrees covering external safety for establishments, pipelines, transport routes and situations involving hazardous substances.[2] An annual report on the safety performance of the top 400 risk-generating companies is produced for Parliament in collaboration with local authorities and industry. Legislation ensuring a basic transport network for dangerous substances (Basisnet) took effect on 1 April 2015. In addition to existing instruments, a new instrument called the "Safety Deal" is being used to build coalitions of public- and private-sector actors around a common safety agenda. For example, the LNG Safety Deal, which was signed in 2015 by the government, private companies and research institutes, promotes the safe use and transport of liquefied natural gas (LNG) in the Netherlands (Nationaal LNG Platform, 2015).

External safety policy focuses on the most significant risks in terms of potential impact and likelihood. This risk-based approach aims to ensure a minimum level of safety for the public and uniformity across the territory. It is also used to promote safety awareness in spatial planning. Drawbacks of the approach include limited incentives to go beyond minimum safety levels and significant requirements in terms of expertise (Government of the Netherlands, 2011).

Environmental liability

The Netherlands has transposed the EU Environmental Liability Directive (ELD) (2004/35/EC) via the Environmental Management Act. The ELD establishes a framework based on the polluter pays principle to prevent and remedy environmental damage. The ELD, which is based on administrative law, is distinct from a civil liability regime (e.g. the ELD does not include provisions for private parties to seek compensation as a result of environmental damage). The transposition of the ELD across EU member states has been greatly affected by the existing liability law and environmental legislation in individual countries, and has resulted in widely varying liability systems (European Commission, 2013). There has been no application of the implementing legislation reported in the Netherlands since 2008, including the major fire in 2011 at the firm ChemiePack in Moerdijk. The rules of the ELD have not been applied in any cases either, due to the application of pre-existing legislation.

The government is exploring changes to the existing liability regime as part of efforts to better deal with the potential impacts of new, emerging risks (from new substances and technologies). The aim is to make companies liable for negligence in the case of risks, as an incentive to take responsibility for identifying and controlling such emerging risks.

2.3. Voluntary agreements

The Netherlands has a long tradition of consensus-based decision making, known as the "polder approach". The use of voluntary agreements (e.g. negotiated "covenants" or "gentlemen's agreements") is commonplace. In principle, voluntary agreements lack sanctions and are not enforceable. Yet, in some cases, covenants include a sanction that applies if parties fail to meet the targets established in the agreement. For example, firms participating in energy efficiency agreements may under strict conditions receive an energy tax exemption if they meet agreed targets for improving energy efficiency. If they fail to reach the targets, they lose the tax exemption. Other ways to encourage parties to fulfil commitments in voluntary agreements include "naming and shaming" or "naming and faming", whereby the party receives either negative or positive public attention related to their actions vis-à-vis the agreements.

A recent prominent example of the use of voluntary agreements is the "Green Deals" programme launched in 2011. The programme is an innovative way to get the best of the "polder approach" by removing obstacles for industry (including SMEs) and agriculture to implement environmental efforts. The deals consist of agreements between the government and various private parties that focus mainly on removing non-financial barriers related to regulations, legislations or licensing.

Close to 200 Green Deals have been concluded so far. The energy sector accounted for around 75% of all deals in 2011 and 50% in 2012. Green Deals have also been concluded for a range of other themes, including water, mobility, biodiversity, the bio-based economy, construction and food. The government is using the experience gained so far to refine criteria used to select opportunities for Green Deals.

The Netherlands Environmental Assessment Agency (PBL) has been positive about the Green Deals approach. An *ex ante* assessment in 2011 highlighted that the approach could inspire others to follow the examples set out in the Deals (PBL, 2011). A more recent report referred to the deals as a "clear step towards defining the obstacles encountered by companies, with a view to removing them wherever possible" (PBL, 2014). The report also noted opportunities to improve and extend the programme. In particular, it suggested that Green Deals can play a key role in supporting green innovation by providing opportunities for experimentation through temporary licences or providing exceptions to standard operating practice.

Another prominent example of voluntary agreements is the 2013 Energy Agreement spearheaded by the SER. An influential advisory and consultative body of private sector associations and independent experts, the SER advises the Dutch government and Parliament on social and economic policy. In the Energy Agreement, more than 40 organisations jointly set out targets and actions to achieve energy and climate policy goals. The diverse range of organisations includes central, regional and local government, employers' associations and unions, financial institutions, environmental groups and other CSOs. The objectives of the agreement are summarised in Chapter 3.

The SER has set up a committee to support implementation of the agreement. An evaluation is planned for 2016, but early assessment indicates goals are unlikely to be met. This was most recently confirmed by a report from the National Audit Agency, which concluded it was unrealistic to expect that with current efforts the Netherlands would reach the Energy Agreement objectives of 14% sustainable energy by 2020 and 16% by 2023 (Algemene Rekenkamer, 2015). As part of the evaluation in 2016, a decision will be taken on the need for supplementary measures to achieve the targets for 2020 and 2030.

Covenants have also been extensively used to promote sustainable agriculture. The Gentlemen's Agreement for Clean and More Efficient Agriculture is one such example. This covenant was agreed between several ministries and associations representing the agricultural, horticultural and livestock industries. The agreement sets out a number of commitments to meet sustainability targets and emission levels for the sector (Government of the Netherlands, 2008). The Multi-annual Agreement on Glass Horticulture of 2014 commits parties to ensuring that new greenhouses from 2020 are carbon neutral and that existing ones reduce fossil fuels by half, as compared to 2011 (Government of the Netherlands, 2014d). The Implementation Agenda on Sustainable Livestock sets objectives to improve the sustainability of livestock farming by 2023.

Overall, the use of voluntary approaches has produced mixed results in achieving environmental aims. PBL (2013) indicates covenants agreed with various industrial sectors failed to achieve significant emission reductions, given their lack of enforceability. Reliance on voluntary agreements may undermine environmental performance, especially in situations where low-hanging fruit has already been harvested and the scope for "win-wins" is limited. While voluntary agreements can provide a platform to set out a common agenda among diverse stakeholders, they cannot guarantee that the goals agreed will be met and they lack effective sanctions. Thus, more difficult commitments have to be monitored more closely.

2.4. *Environmental certificates*

The use of environmental management systems (EMAS) has increased in the Netherlands over the past years, with the number of certified organisations growing by 15% per year since 2008. More than 2 200 organisations with more than 4 500 sites in the Netherlands have an ISO 14001 certified environmental management system (Government of the Netherlands, 2014c). A range of different sectors has become certified, with some reaching 50% of firms certified. The use of ISO 14001 certificates in procurement has been cited as a key driver for the uptake of EMAS. Companies are increasingly integrating environmental reporting into their sustainability reporting. The top 200 Dutch companies typically publish an integrated sustainability report with environmental data. While such systems can help strengthen environmental management procedures, it is less clear that they result in improved environmental outcomes, particularly the ISO 14000 system.

3. Environmental governance: Institutional arrangements and co-ordination

3.1. *Multi-level governance*

The Dutch government consists of three levels: state, provincial and municipal, with a mix of autonomy and dependence in the relations between sub-national authorities and the central government. In addition to these three levels, regional water authorities (RWAs) have the same position as municipalities, but their authority is limited to water safety and quality. Each level is autonomous in terms of regulation and administration of its own internal affairs in addition to taxation power (OECD, 2014b). National legislation limits the autonomy of provinces and municipalities, while provincial legislation limits municipal autonomy (Box 2.2).

Box 2.2. **Multi-level governance in the Netherlands**

In the Netherlands, the structure, tasks and supervision of the government are regulated in several parliamentary acts, including the Municipalities Act, the Provinces Act and the Act on the Regional Water Authorities. The Act on Financial Relations regulates the financial relations between national government and sub-national government authorities. The national government is responsible for the unity of the government.

There are 12 provinces, which are the authority at the regional level. They act as "area manager" (*gebiedsregisseur*), monitoring and supervising the finance and governance of municipalities. Provinces play a role in inter-regional and inter-sectorial co-operation.

There are 393 municipalities, which operate most closely to citizens. To perform their own tasks effectively and reap the benefits of economies of scale, municipalities co-operate voluntarily in public bodies for implementation of one or more public services. In urban areas, municipalities co-operate, for example, in planning for infrastructure and the development of industrial areas.

There are 24 regional water authorities. They also operate at the local level, with responsibility for specific functions related to water safety and water quality. They are governed by elected councils and can raise funds for their activities through taxes.

At the national level, the Ministry of Infrastructure and Environment is responsible for most areas of environmental policy. The ministry was formed in 2011 through the merger of the former Ministry of Housing, Spatial Planning and the Environment with the former

Ministry of Transport and Water Management. One minister is responsible for water and transport policy, while the State Secretary of the Environment is responsible for the environment. Responsibility for nature and biodiversity policy lies with the Ministry of Economic Affairs, which was created by a merger of the former Ministry of Agriculture, Nature and Fisheries and the former Ministry of Economic Affairs.

One of the peculiarities of Dutch multi-level governance is its resemblance to an "hourglass" structure with the comparatively weak provincial level "squeezed" between the stronger national and municipal levels (OECD, 2014b). This structure is reflected in budgetary arrangements. Provincial budgets represent 1% of GDP and 11% of total sub-national government expenditure, while municipal budgets account of 10% of GDP and nearly 75% of the total. However, following transfer of new responsibilities in recent years, provincial expenditure grew by 50% (in nominal terms) between 2007 and 2010 (OECD, 2014b).

Overall, the financial situation of sub-national governments deteriorated in 2008 due to the direct effects of the economic crisis and the impact of the central government's fiscal consolidation measures. Since 2010, sub-national governments have adjusted by cutting expenditure on goods and services, staff and investment. The reduction in transfers from the central government was offset somewhat by increasing sub-national tax rates and user charges (OECD, 2014b).

3.2. Decentralisation trend

Over the review period, there has been a marked trend to decentralise responsibility for environmental policy and implementation. This has taken place in the context of a broad reform of the sub-national governance system. The reforms seek to provide more discretion and authority to provinces and municipalities, and allow for more tailored policies and experimentation with various approaches. However, decentralisation may also lead to inconsistent policy implementation and an uneven playing field across jurisdictions. Further, the decentralisation of tasks is not necessarily accompanied by the provision of additional resources. As a result, sub-national governments might not have the necessary financial, managerial, human and technical capacity to manage their new functions (OECD, 2014b).

Alarming reports from the Dutch Safety Board following high-profile incidents (see Dutch Safety Board, 2013, 2012) highlighted major deficiencies in policy implementation and spurred action to address them. The need to consolidate expertise and experience to support the implementation of environmental requirements at an appropriate scale spurred the establishment of the 29 Environmental Services (*Omgevingsdiensten*, ODs) on 1 January 2014. This was an important part of the response to addressing existing weaknesses in policy implementation at the local level. The ODs bring together experience and expertise on environmental licensing, compliance assurance and enforcement. They implement environmental legal requirements, including enforcement of environmental permits, at the request of the competent authority (provincial and municipal authorities). Six of the ODs are responsible for Seveso sites.

The Netherlands faces a challenge to ensure the ODs operate effectively and promote strong and consistent environmental performance. A large and experienced OD, like the DCMR in Rijnmond, is generally performing well. However, there is uncertainty about the capacity, knowledge and expertise of recently established ODs. Moreover, budget cuts for supervision and enforcement are a cause for concern. Funding for the ODs will be provided by municipalities and regional authorities, which already face fiscal constraints. The ODs were designed based on administrative considerations (via a bottom-up process of negotiating specific co-operation arrangements between provincial and municipal authorities) rather than on ecological considerations or economies of scale or scope. Furthermore, shared oversight for ODs that cross provincial boundaries could be problematic. The current *ad hoc* co-operation among the various ODs may miss opportunities to share experience and good practice. Building on the co-operation mechanisms to share experience already in place for the six ODs responsible for Seveso sites could facilitate the exchange of expertise among all of the ODs. Although quality criteria for the performance of the ODs are being developed, it has not yet been decided whether they will be mandatory or optional. The effectiveness of the ODs could also be improved through national mandatory quality criteria, strengthening financing arrangements to ensure stable and sufficient funding and monitoring the quality of their performance.

Overall, the decentralisation trend can create opportunities for better integration of environmental policies and spatial policies, providing a tailored balance of local interests and needs. Conversely, it can compromise environmental objectives in cases where short-term economic considerations prevail. Sufficient financial and human resources are essential to ensure that competent authorities can execute their functions, or properly finance the ODs that execute them on their behalf. The establishment of the ODs to bring together specialised expertise is a step in the right direction. However, further improvements are needed to ensure quality of the performance of the ODs.

3.3. Horizontal and vertical co-ordination

Over the review period, the trend has been towards more *ad hoc* co-operation on specific issues and less formal co-ordination and co-operation. This takes place through periodic meetings, *ad hoc* teams and negotiated agreements on specific issues. For example, arrangements for co-ordinating environmental policy between the national and regional levels of government include the Multi-level Governance Meeting on Spatial Issues (*Bestuurlijk overleg Ruimte*) and the Accessibility and Multi-level Governance Meeting on Water Affairs (*Bereikbaarheid, bestuurlijk overleg Milieu en de stuurgroep Water*). Convened since 2013, these meetings take place between the Minister of Infrastructure and Environment and representatives of the Association of Provincial Authorities (IPO), the Association of Netherlands Municipalities (VNG), the Union of the Regional Water Authorities (UvW) and the Urban Regions under Traffic and Transport (SkVV).

To develop a common position for EU proposals, co-ordination takes place in *ad hoc* intergovernmental or inter-ministerial teams. The teams develop a brief to inform Parliament on the Dutch common position. These briefs are discussed in an interdepartmental working group chaired by the Ministry of Foreign Affairs.

Co-ordination also occurs through negotiated agreements. An example of this type of arrangement is the Administrative Agreement on Water Affairs (*Bestuursakkoord Water*), concluded by the national government, provincial authorities, municipalities, regional water authorities and water companies in 2011. The agreement set out a financing arrangement for the High Water Protection Programme and set targets to achieve EUR 750 million in efficiency gains, shared among the various parties (Government of the Netherlands, 2014e).

4. Environmental permitting, enforcement and compliance

The Netherlands has long been at the forefront of enforcement and compliance practice. In the 1990s, the Dutch Ministry of Justice developed the "Table of Eleven" factors that influence regulatory compliance, which have widely influenced the compliance practices of other countries. More recently, the Netherlands led the EU's Network for the Implementation and Enforcement of Environmental Law (IMPEL) 2006 programme "Doing the Right Things" and subsequent follow-up work. The programme explored how inspection authorities set priorities (one of the key steps in setting up inspection plans) and resulted in the development of a step-by-step guidance book for planning environmental inspections.

The WABO Act provides the main basis for environmental permitting in the Netherlands. All installations with an impact on the environment either fall under general binding rules (GBRs) or require a specific permit (Box 2.3). All environmental aspects are covered in these permits or GBRs, with the exception of direct discharges to surface water, which are addressed in the Water Act. The Activities Decree transposes requirements of the EU Industrial Emissions Directive, covering rules for emissions of large combustion plants, waste incineration plants, plants categorised in the Integrated Pollution Prevention and Control (IPPC) installations and volatile organic compounds (VOCs). The Emissions Guidelines for Air provide limits for most air emissions from industrial sources.

Box 2.3. **General binding rules in the Netherlands**

In the Netherlands, the regulatory changes introduced as of 2008 establish different requirements for three categories of installations (defined in the Activities Decree):

- Type A facilities, characterised by minimal environmental impact, are regulated by general, not activity-specific provisions; they do not need to notify the competent authority of their operations.
- Type B installations have a moderate environmental impact, are covered by activity-specific GBRs and are required to notify the competent (local or provincial) authority of the nature and size of its activities four weeks before starting operations.
- Type C installations have a potentially important impact and require an environmental licence that must be complied with along with applicable activity-specific GBRs (this category includes large installations subject to the EU Industrial Emissions Directive and that need an integrated permit/licence).

GBRs establish "quantitative target-based provisions" (i.e. emission limit values) that can be achieved by any "recognised" measure without prior consent from the competent authority. They also establish "qualitative" provisions that require certain specific techniques or management practices that can be modified only with the competent authority's consent.

GBRs have been developed for activities related to hazardous substances, plastics, metals, paper and textiles, food products, vehicles and other motorised equipment, etc. The range of activities subject to GBRs covered by the Activities Decree is expanding every year until 2016. GBRs currently cover about 400 000 companies.

Source: Mazur, E. (2012).

Environmental permitting and supervision have been mainly decentralised. Prior to the 2010 WABO Act, several different authorities granted applications for environmental permits. As discussed above, the act provided for an "all-in-one-permit", which has significantly streamlined the process. Now, only one authority – most often the municipal executive body – is competent to issue permits. In some cases, the provincial executive body has the authority; in a small number of instances (such as military installations), the minister holds the authority. The authority that issues the all-in-one-permit is also responsible for enforcing it. Since their establishment in 2014, the ODs now execute the enforcement of environmental permits on behalf of the provinces and municipalities. In case of non-compliance, the competent authority may impose sanctions, which include measures based on administrative law (such as warnings, recommendations, fines, revocation of a licence, publication of inspection results) or measures based on criminal law (fine or prosecution).

The Human Environment and Transport Inspectorate (the "Inspectorate") was formed in 2012 following a merger of the former Inspectorate for Housing, Spatial Planning and the former Environment and the Transport and Water Management Inspectorate. The Inspectorate monitors and encourages compliance with national and European legislation and regulations; its environmental departments are charged with maintaining a safe and healthy living environment. The Inspectorate may advise on the compliance of WABO permits with national and European environmental law. In 2013, for example, it advised on 214 WABO permits, mainly concerning external safety and air emissions.

The Inspectorate operates on a basis of mutual trust with the supervised organisation and focuses on reducing the burden of supervision. A risk-based approach is used to profile potentially non-compliant installations with significant risks. The aim is to exploit available inspection capacity in the most effective and efficient way. Quality criteria for supervisory authorities with regard to knowledge, experience and availability have been revised recently (Ministry of Infrastructure and Environment, 2012). The legal status of the criteria is under discussion.

The Netherlands is also exploring the use of private compliance assurance in which "private parties (the regulatee and other third private parties) systematically assure compliance with formal regulations" (de Bree et al., 2013). The Inspectorate has begun to use covenants with companies that enjoy good compliance records. The approach, based on trust, regular oversight and periodic auditing, aims to increase compliance and reduce the regulatory burden for companies. The Ministry of Infrastructure and Environment commissioned a comprehensive study of private compliance assurance (see de Bree et al., 2013). The study identified indicators for promising conditions for such an approach relating to the suitability and willingness of the target population. It also set out conditions for success of the meta supervision required by the public regulator.

Spending cuts for supervision and enforcement of environmental regulations have raised concerns as have recent reports from the Dutch Safety Board. For instance, the review of the Odfjell Terminals' safety record over 2000-12 points to significant shortcomings in the company's internal operations and the actions of supervisory authorities (Dutch Safety Board, 2013). The Safety Board's report expressed surprise that a company handling large quantities of hazardous substances could "muddle on" for such a long time. As noted by PBL (2013), given the government only monitors at the system level, it requires a high degree of trust in compliance and in the compliance assurance procedures. Care should be taken to ensure that constructive working relationship between supervisory authorities and the companies they supervise contribute to improved compliance and avoid unacceptable levels of tolerance for poorly performing companies.

5. Environmental information and policy evaluation mechanisms

The Netherlands has a very comprehensive system of environmental information and strong policy evaluation mechanisms. It has been a party to the UN Aarhus Convention on Access to Information, Public Participation in Decision-Making and Access to Justice in Environmental Matters since 25 June 1998 and accepted the convention on 29 December 2004 (UN, 2015). Public access to environmental information is ensured by the 1991 Government Information Act and also by the EMA.

Overall, the public has a positive view of the living environment in the Netherlands. The Dutch liveability index (*Leefbarometer*) provides information about quality of life based on 49 indicators. Results show the population is satisfied with the quality of its environment.

In a recent survey, Statistics Netherlands (CBS) documented a sharp drop in level of concern for the environment and willingness to pay for environmental protection over the review period (2012). The number of people who think that air, water and soil are strongly polluted decreased from around 60% to 40% between 2002 and 2012.[3] Over the same period, concern for the economic situation and security/crime increased, while the share of the population willing to pay more taxes to protect the environment dropped from 44% to 24%. Only 30% of people who thought that air, water and soil are strongly polluted were willing to pay more taxes for environmental protection (CBS, 2012).

5.1. *Environmental information and stakeholder engagement*

The Netherlands benefits from the expertise of world-class, independent research institutions and universities that produce high quality, policy-relevant outputs, which could be further exploited. Examples include PBL, the Netherlands Organisation for Applied Scientific Research (TNO), the Energy Research Centre of the Netherlands (ECN), the Netherlands Institute for Transport Policy Analysis (KiM), the Royal Netherlands Meteorological Institute (KNMI) and RIVM, along with a number of institutes specialising in water management, such as Deltares, as well as universities. The data and analysis produced by these research institutes provide a strong scientific evidence basis for the formulation and evaluation of environmental policy, as well as providing information to the public. However, the outcome of these institutions is not always used in policy making to its full potential. Several key sources of environmental information are briefly summarised below.

One of the most prominent and comprehensive reviews of environmental policy is PBL's report series "The Balance of the Living Environment" (*Balans van de Leefomgeving*).[4] These reports are an authoritative overview of environmental policy in the Netherlands. They have a high political profile, as they are presented to the minister and to Parliament. The reports assess the present state of the environment and nature, as well as the impacts of existing policies on environmental pressures and quality, now and in the near future. The report is supported by a dedicated website with forward-looking indicators comparing expected developments to quantifiable policy objectives. After producing this report annually in 1995-2009, PBL switched to bi-annual publication.

Since 1999, the Environmental Data Compendium (www.environmentaldata.nl) has provided indicators on the state of the living environment in the Netherlands. It is a joint publication of CBS, PBL and the Wageningen University Research Centre.

The Knowledge Centre InfoMil is a key source of information on environmental legislation and policy. It was established in 1995 to provide practical information to policy makers who are responsible for implementation of environmental policy and legislation. InfoMil, hosted by the Ministry of Infrastructure and Environment, also serves as a forum of exchange between the ministry and environmental authorities at provincial, regional and local levels.

The Dutch Sustainability Monitor, published every two years since 2009, quantifies progress in sustainable development. The report presents historic trends (and comparisons with EU-averages) for a range of composite indicators capturing the dimensions of quality of life and resource use. The report is produced by CBS, the Bureau for Economic Policy Analysis (CPB), PBL and the Netherlands Institute for Social Research (SCP).

More recently, the Minister of Infrastructure and Environment commissioned a group of institutes to develop the "Atlas of our Living Environment" (*Atlas Leefomgeving*). This is an innovative online platform to integrate spatial information about the quality of the living environment and make it publicly accessible. The Atlas makes it possible to view various environmental aspects at a certain location or to compare various locations. It uses maps and background information about noise, air pollution, green spaces, external safety, soil, asbestos, cultural heritage, perception of the living environment and regional planning programmes (Atlas Leefomgeving, 2015).

In addition to the various sources of environmental information available for decision makers and the public, there are established institutions to engage stakeholders in environmental policy making. For example, the Participation Directorate of the Ministry of Infrastructure and Environment advises on stakeholder participation. In the context of modernising environmental policy, the government is also exploring new ways of engaging stakeholders and civil society. For example, the "Sustainable Action" programme seeks to expand opportunities for the private sector and civil society to help reach environmental goals.

5.2. *Policy and project evaluation mechanisms*

Large government investments in infrastructure require a social cost-benefit analysis (SCBA) from CPB. PBL often provides second opinions to these SCBAs. In 2013, CPB and PBL released an updated SCBA protocol, endorsed by the government, with special provisions for quantifying (and possibly monetising) environmental and nature benefits (see Romijn and Renes, 2013).

Since public policies and investment projects can have large impacts on GHG emissions (especially in the transport and energy sectors), project and policy assessments should take them into account. According to a recent OECD survey, the Netherlands uses a monetary carbon value to assess investment projects in the transport sector. However, this is not the case in the energy sector; given that these emissions are covered by the EU ETS, the net impact of GHG emissions is close to zero. Monetary carbon values are not taken into account in *ex ante* or *ex post* policy assessments more broadly (OECD, 2014c).

In the Netherlands, it is common practice to invite research institutes to conduct *ex-post* and *ex-ante* evaluation studies of policy proposals. Mechanisms for engaging the scientific community in policy analyses and the policy development process include the Council for the Environment and Infrastructure (RLI), an independent advisory board for the government and Parliament. In certain cases, the government requests monitoring studies to support specific policies or initiatives. For example, CBS produced a document series on Green Growth, while PBL and ECN launched a new Energy Policy Monitor in 2014 to support the 2013 Energy Agreement.

A national programme, the Economics of Ecosystems and Biodiversity (TEEB), was launched in 2012. It focuses on national, regional, city and overseas cases, as well as trade flow impacts on ecosystem services abroad and business dependencies on ecosystem services (Wilson et al., 2014). The first version of the Digital Atlas of Natural Capital (DANK) became available at the end of 2014. The programme aims to increase awareness of, and methods for, economic evaluation of ecosystem services in decision making. There have also been recent efforts to develop Natural Capital Accounting (NCA), with some experiments to integrate natural capital into national and regional accounts, as well as support business initiatives to account for natural capital.

Until recently, CPB and PBL assessed political parties' election manifestos with respect to their impact on the economy and the environment (CPB and PBL, 2012). This assessment provided voters with a uniform comparison of party promise issues. However, CPB announced it will no longer provide the service due to budget restrictions.

Environmental impact assessment and strategic environmental assessment

The Netherlands has a strong tradition of high quality environmental impact assessment (EIA) for projects with possible impacts on the environment. Formal regulations on EIA were introduced as early as 1986 in the Environmental Protection Act (now the Environmental Management Act). Current procedures are based on EU directives for strategic environmental assessment (SEA) (2001/42/EC) and for EIA (2011/92/EC). The Environmental Assessment Modernisation Act of 2010 updated Dutch legislation to limit administrative costs associated with environmental assessments (Arts and Schijf, 2014).

EIAs show how proposals will affect the environment and whether alternatives would achieve goals in a more sustainable way. The EIA is linked to mandatory evaluation procedures for major plans or decisions about "complex" projects. As such, it is a prerequisite for the construction of major infrastructure, such as oil refineries, nuclear power plants, chemical plants, roads, railways, and oil and gas pipelines. Stakeholder participation in the EIA and decision making is required. There are also provisions allowing for appeals of final decisions.

Since 2010, a simplified EIA procedure is available for projects with limited environmental impacts, with the aim of limiting administrative costs. In such cases, the competent authority has discretion to tailor the requirements of the EIA. For example, the authority can decide when to start the EIA, how it will be linked to planning or decision making, how alternatives will be developed, how the quality will be guaranteed and how stakeholders will be engaged.

From the 1980s, when EIA became a formal requirement, it was required at both project and strategic levels. As such, the Netherlands was an early adopter of SEA and has benefited from a long experience in application (Arts and Schijf, 2014). SEA considers environmental consequences in plans and programmes, with specific emphasis on the strategic phase.

The Netherlands Commission for Environmental Assessment (NCEA), an independent advisory body that reviews and reports on the scope and quality of environmental assessments, exerts significant influence (Box 2.4).

Several studies have evaluated the use of EIA and SEA in the Netherlands. Arts (2014) reviewed several and drew a number of conclusions that point to the positive influence of these assessments in the Netherlands. Overall, evaluations have shown clearly that EIA and

Box 2.4. The Netherlands Commission for Environmental Assessment

The Netherlands Commission for Environmental Assessment (NCEA) is an independent advisory body of experts established by decree in 1987. Its responsibilities are set out in the Environmental Management Act. The commission advises governments and competent authorities (both in the Netherlands and abroad) on the quality of environmental assessments (both EIA and SEA reports). It does not produce environmental assessments itself, which are usually completed by government authorities, consultants or other private parties. Instead, it reports on the scope and quality of the assessments. Its advice is a mandatory component of the SEA procedure for plans and of the EIA procedure for "complex" projects (Arts and Schijf, 2014). Over the past 25 years, some 2 600 EIAs and SEAs have been reviewed (NCEA, 2012). The commission exerts significant influence through its independence, expertise and transparency.

As of 2014, the commission's secretariat had about 35 staff, led by a chair and a small management team (NCEA, 2015). It is able to leverage the expertise of several hundred Dutch and international experts in environment and other fields (economics, social issues, etc.). The commission may advise competent authorities at any stage during the process, including after it ends. It operates independently from government and does not become involved in decision making. All of its reports are publicly available on its website.

In addition to its work in the Netherlands, the commission also advises other countries on issues such as strengthening assessment systems for both EIA and SEA, and capacity building. The commission regularly documents lessons learned in the application of EIA and SEA, accumulating a significant body of experience.

Source: NCEA (2015, 2012, 2011); Arts and Schijf (2014).

SEA are highly effective, although there is some disagreement about their efficiency as measured by delays and costs imposed. Studies have demonstrated that EIA and SEA influence decision making and enhance environmental awareness. The status of legal requirements, transparency of decision making and quality of the study were singled out as the most important factors for the performance of EIA and SEA. The NCEA is considered instrumental in improving the quality of EIA and SEA. In general, procedures are seen as an obligation; in practice, stakeholders typically only implement measures that are legally required.

Recommendations on environmental governance and management

Environmental governance framework

- Develop a clear, comprehensive, long-term vision for environmental policy that provides a coherent framework for specific medium- and short-term action plans. The vision should reinforce and support the cross-sectorial approach embodied in the Environment and Planning Act.
- Seize the window of opportunity provided by the introduction of the Environment and Planning Act and the introduction of secondary legislation to establish a strong footing for securing environmental performance in the context of the recent decentralisation trend, providing greater discretion to sub-national authorities in balancing economic, social and environmental considerations.

Recommendations on environmental governance and management *(cont.)*

- Continue to strengthen efforts related to external safety (including preventing chemical accidents). This may include improving guidance for companies on how to deal with specific external safety issues; extending the enforcement of rules and considering the performance of SMEs; improving the transparency of the permitting process to promote accountability and public participation; and working with (large) companies to enhance their safety culture.
- Better exploit potential synergies between the Water Framework Directive and Natura 2000 by, for example, giving greater weight to ecological considerations in water management.
- Ensure the newly established Environmental Services (ODs) carry out their tasks in an effective manner that will support strong and consistent environmental performance. This could be supported by: consolidating the number of ODs (considering economies of scale, possible specialisation and the relevant ecological scale); ensuring sustainable funding; strengthening mechanisms for the exchange of good practice and expertise among ODs; establishing national mandatory quality criteria; and monitoring the quality of performance.

Voluntary agreements

- Consider using voluntary agreements such as covenants and "Green Deal" projects in a more selective manner by limiting their use to circumstances where "win-win" solutions can lead to expected policy outcomes without reliance on regulatory sanctions.

Environmental compliance and enforcement

- Continue to explore the possibility to improve the existing liability regime as part of efforts to better deal with the potential impacts of new, emerging risks.

Environmental information and policy evaluation

- Strengthen the link between science, policy analysis and policy evaluation, while reinforcing the capacity and knowledge base for environmental policy within relevant ministries by making better use of the available research outcomes. In particular, reinforce the independence of public research institutes, strengthen the use of independent policy assessment and cost-benefit analysis, and broaden the use of explicit carbon values in policy evaluation.

Notes

1. Dutch target under the EU Directive on Energy Efficiency (2012/27/EU).
2. External Safety (Establishments) Decree (*Bevi, Besluit externe veiligheid inrichtingen*) May 2004; Decree on the External Safety of Pipelines (*Bevb, Besluit externe veiligheid buisleidingen*) July 2010; External Safety (Transport Routes) Decree (*Bevt, Besluit externe veiligheid transportroutes*) January 2015; Registration Decree on Risk Situations Involving Hazardous Substances (*Registratiebesluit externe veiligheid*) November 2006.
3. Note that there were some differences in the surveys for 2000-02 and 2012. Nevertheless, the general trend has been corroborated by other studies (see PBL [2010], *Prioritering maatschappelijke vraagstukken*, 2006-10, The Hague).
4. Prior to 2010, these reports were called *Milieubalans* (Environmental Balance).

References

Algemene Rekenkamer (2015), "Doelen duurzame energie niet haalbaar zonder miljarden extra voor windmolens op zee of projecten in buitenland" [Renewable Energy Goal is not Feasible without Additional Billions for Wind Turbines at Sea or Projects Abroad], 16 April 2015, Algemene Rekenkamer [Court of Audit], *www.rekenkamer.nl/Nieuws/Persberichten/2015/04/Doelen_duurzame_energie_niet_haalbaar_zonder_miljarden_extra_voor_windmolens_op_zee_of_projecten_in_buitenland* (accessed 30 April 2015).

Algemene Rekenkamer (2012), "Aanpassing aan klimaatverandering:strategie en beleid", [Adapting to Climate Change: Strategy and Policy], Second House of Representatives, 2012-2013, 33 470, No. 2, ISBN 9789012576277, Algemene Rekenkamer [Court of Audit], the Hague.

Arts, J. (2014), "Research into SEA effectiveness in the Netherlands", *Strategic Environmental Assessment Effectiveness: Learning from Experience in China and the Netherlands,* Appraisal Center for Environment and Engineering, Ministry of Environmental Protection of China and the Netherlands Commission for Environmental Assessment, *http://api.commissiemer.nl/docs/mer/diversen/sea-effectiveness-china-nl2014.pdf* (accessed 10 January 2015).

Arts, J. and B. Schijf (2014), "Introduction to SEA in the Netherlands", *Strategic Environmental Assessment Effectiveness: Learning from Experience in China and the Netherlands,* Appraisal Center for Environment and Engineering, Ministry of Environmental Protection of China and the Netherlands Commission for Environmental Assessment, *http://api.commissiemer.nl/docs/mer/diversen/sea-effectiveness-china-nl2014.pdf* (accessed 10 January 2015).

Atlas Leefomgeving (2015), "Atlasleefomgeving" [Environment Atlas], *www.atlasleefomgeving.nl/en/home* (accessed 7 May 2015).

Botta, E. and T. Koźluk (2014), "Measuring environmental policy stringency in OECD countries: A composite index approach", *OECD Economics Department Working Papers*, No. 1177, OECD Publishing, Paris, *http://dx.doi.org/10.1787/5jxrjnc45gvg-en.*

CBS (2012), *Green Growth in the Netherlands 2012*, Statistics Netherlands, *www.cbs.nl/NR/rdonlyres/2C613080-F668-439C-B12C-98BF361B5ADF/0/2013p44pub.pdf* (accessed 5 October 2014).

CPB and PBL (2012), *Charted Choices: 2013-17*, English translation of Chapter 2: The Headlines, Statistics Netherlands and Netherlands Environmental Agency, The Hague, August 2012, *www.pbl.nl/sites/default/files/cms/publicaties/CPB_PBL_2012_charted-choices-2013-2017.pdf* (accessed 7 April 2015).

De Bree, M. et al. (2013), "Private Borging van Regelnaleving in het Omgevingsrecht", [Private Assurance of Regulatory Compliance in Environmental Law], Rotterdam School of Management Erasmus University, 21 June 2013, Ministry of Infrastructure and Environment, ISBN 978-1-291-45644-8.

Dutch Safety Board (2013), "Odfjell Terminals Rotterdam Safety during the 2000-2012 period", Dutch Safety Board, The Hague, June 2013, *www.onderzoeksraad.nl/en/onderzoek/1883/odfjell-terminals-rotterdam-safety-during-the-2000-2012-period* (accessed 14 May 2015).

Dutch Safety Board (2012), "Fire at Chemie-Pack Moerdijk", Dutch Safety Board, The Hague, February 2012, *www.onderzoeksraad.nl/uploads/items-docs/1805/Rapport_Chemie-Pack_EN_def.pdf* (accessed 14 May 2015).

European Commission (2013), "Environmental liability directive: A short overview", European Commission, *http://ec.europa.eu/environment/legal/liability/pdf/Summary%20ELD.pdf* (accessed 5 May 2015).

Fireworks Investigation Commission (2001), *Fireworks Commission Report*, Enschede and the Hague, 28 February 2001, *www.vuurwerkramp.enschede.nl/.../Eindrapport.../manage.download.html* (accessed 6 February 2015).

Government of the Netherlands (2014a), "Modernisation of environmental policy", (Letter to Parliament), 10 March 2014, *www.government.nl/documents-and-publications/parliamentary-documents/2014/03/10/modernisation-environmental-policy.html* (accessed 5 October 2014).

Government of the Netherlands (2014b), "Make it work", *https://omgevingswet.pleio.nl/file/download/26694012* (accessed 22 October 2014).

Government of the Netherlands (2014c), "Answers to the OECD Environmental Performance Review Questionnaire" (internal document).

Government of the Netherlands (2014d), "Nieuwe meerjarenafspraak duurzame glastuinbouw" [New agreement on sustainable horticulture], 3 July 2014, *www.rijksoverheid.nl/onderwerpen/landbouw-en-tuinbouw/nieuws/2014/07/03/nieuwe-meerjarenafspraak-duurzame-glastuinbouw.html* (accessed 6 February 2015).

Government of the Netherlands (2014e), "Administrative agreement on water affairs", *www.government.nl/issues/water-management/administrative-agreement-on-water-affairs* (accessed 9 February 2015).

Government of the Netherlands (2011), "Risk-based external safety regulations in the Netherlands", presentation at the Seveso Conference, 25 May 2011, Stockholm.

Government of the Netherlands (2008), "Convenant Schone en zuinige Agrosectoren" [Covenant for Cleaner and More Efficient Agriculture], 31 December 2008, *www.rijksoverheid.nl/onderwerpen/landbouw-en-tuinbouw/documenten-en-publicaties/convenanten/2008/12/03/convenant-schone-en-zuinige-agrosectoren.html* (accessed 6 February 2015).

Hajer, M. (2011), "The energetic society: In search of a governance philosophy for a clean economy", PBL Netherlands Environmental Assessment Agency, The Hague, ISBN: 978-90-78645-78-8.

IEA (2014), *Energy Policies of IEA Countries, The Netherlands, 2014 Review*, IEA/OECD Publishing, Paris, *http://dx.doi.org/10.1787/9789264210462-en.*

IEA (2009), *Energy Policies of IEA Countries: Netherlands 2008*, IEA/OECD Publishing, Paris, *www.oecd.org/bookshop?lang=en&pub=9789264043398.*

Mazur, E. (2012), "Green transformation of small businesses: Achieving and going beyond environmental requirements", *OECD Environment Working Papers*, No. 47, OECD Publishing, Paris, *http://dx.doi.org/10.1787/5k92r8nmfgxp-en.*

Ministry of Economic Affairs (2015), *Programmatische Aanpak Stikstof* [Programmatic Approach to Nitrogen], *http://pas.natura2000.nl/pages/home.aspx* (accessed 5 May 2015).

Ministry of Economic Affairs (2014), *The Natural Way Forward: Government Vision 2014*, Ministry of Economic Affairs, the Hague, April 2014.

Ministry of Infrastructure and Environment (2015), "Aanbieding rapport Evaluatie milieueffecten Activiteitenbesluit" [Environmental Impact Assessment Report of the Activities Decree], (Letter to Parliament), 16 April 2015.

Ministry of Infrastructure and Environment (2014), *The Environmental Planning Act in Brief: Scope for Development, Safeguards for Quality*, Ministry of Infrastructure and Environment, June 2014, the Hague.

Ministry of Infrastructure and Environment (2013), "Evaluatie Activiteitenbesluit milieubeheer" [Environmental Assessment of the Activities Decree], (Letter to Parliament), 17 December 2013.

Ministry of Infrastructure and Environment (2012), "Uitvoeringmet ambitie.nl: Kwaliteitscriteria 2.1" [Ambitious Version: Quality criteria 2.1], 7 September 2012, *www.infomil.nl/onderwerpen/ruimte/wet-algemene/vth/* (accessed 20 January 2015).

Ministry of Infrastructure and Environment (2011), *Summary National Policy Strategy for Infrastructure and Spatial Planning*, Ministry of Infrastructure and Environment, March 2011, the Hague, *www.government.nl/documents-and-publications/publications/2013/07/24/summary-national-policy-strategy-for-infrastructure-and-spatial-planning.html* (accessed 15 November 2014).

Ministry of Infrastructure and Environment and Ministry of Economic Affairs (2014), *Delta Programme 2015: Working on the Delta*, September 2014, *www.deltacommissaris.nl/english/Images/Delta%20Programme%202015%20English_tcm310-358177.pdf* (accessed 10 April 2015).

Nationaal LNG Platform (2015), Nationaal LNG Platform website, *www.nationaallngplatform.nl/lng-safety-deal-in-the-netherlands/* (accessed 21 April 2015).

NCEA (2015), "Views and experiences 2015", *Series*, No. 16, Netherlands Commission for Environmental Assessment, *http://api.commissiemer.nl/docs/mer/diversen/views-experiences2015.pdf* (accessed 23 June 2015).

NCEA (2012), "Views and experiences 2012", *Series*, No. 11, Netherlands Commission for Environmental Assessment, *http://api.commissiemer.nl/docs/mer/diversen/views_experiences_2012.pdf* (accessed 13 April 2015).

NCEA (2011), "Key Sheet: About the NCEA" (brochure), Netherlands Commission for Environmental Assessment, May 2011.

OECD (2015), Water Resources Allocation: Sharing Risks and Opportunities, OECD Studies on Water, OECD Publishing, Paris, *http://dx.doi.org/10.1787/9789264229631-en.*

OECD (2014a), *Water Governance in the Netherlands: Fit for the Future?*, OECD Studies on Water, OECD Publishing, Paris, *http://dx.doi.org/10.1787/9789264102637-en.*

OECD (2014b), *OECD Territorial Reviews: Netherlands 2014*, OECD Publishing, Paris, *http://dx.doi.org/10.1787/9789264209527-en*.

OECD (2014c), "Questionnaire on the use of monetary values of carbon in public policy assessments", (internal document), OECD Working Party on Integrating Environmental and Economic Policies, March 2014 [ENV_EPOC_WPIEEP(2014)12], OECD, Paris.

PBL (2015a), *Waterkwaliteit nu en in de toekomst [*Water quality now and in the future*]*, PBL Netherlands Environmental Assessment Agency, The Hague, *www.pbl.nl/publicaties/waterkwaliteit-nu-en-in-de-toekomst* (accessed 11 June 2015).

PBL (2015b), *Assessment of the Dutch Human Environment 2014 – The Future is Now*, PBL Netherlands Environmental Assessment Agency, The Hague.

PBL (2014), *Green Gains: In Search of Opportunities for the Dutch Economy*, Netherlands Environmental Assessment Agency, the Hague.

PBL (2013), *Changing track, Changing Tack*, Netherlands Environmental Assessment Agency, the Hague.

PBL (2011), Het effect van 59 Green Deals op het aandeel hernieuwbare energie en de uitstoot van niet-ETS-broeikasgassen: een quick scan, [The Effect of 59 Green Deals on the Share of Renewable Energy and Greenhouse Gas Emissions from Non-ETS : A Quick Scan], Netherlands Environmental Assessment Agency, the Hague.

RIVM (2014), "NSL Monitoring Report 2014: State of affairs of National Air Quality Cooperation Programme (NSL)", RIVM Report 2014-0092, 17 December 2014.

Romijn and Renes (2013), "Algemene leidraad voor maatschappelijke kosten-batenanalyse" [General Guidance for Cost-Benefit Analysis], CPB and PBL, The Hague, ISBN: 978-90-5833-619-4.

SER (2013), "Energy Agreement for Sustainable Growth", 6 September 2013, English summary, Social and Economic Council of the Netherlands, *www.ser.nl/en/publications/publications/2013/energy-agreement-sustainable-growth.aspx* (accessed 5 May 2015).

UN (2015), "United Nations Treaty Collection", *Chapter XXVII: Environment* (database), *https://treaties.un.org/Pages/ViewDetails.aspx?src=TREATY&mtdsg_no=XXVII-13&chapter=27&lang=en* (accessed 8 April 2015).

Wilson, L. et al. (2014), "The role of national ecosystem assessments in influencing policy making", *OECD Environment Working Papers*, No. 60, OECD Publishing, Paris, *http://dx.doi.org/10.1787/5jxvl3zsbhkk-en*.

Wöltgens and Stoop (2012), "EU as starting point for the Environmental Planning Act", Operational implementation by chapter, Official working document version 4.0.

PART I

Chapter 3

Towards green growth

This chapter reviews the Netherlands' efforts to mainstream environmental considerations into economic policy and to promote green growth. It analyses the use of taxation and other economic instruments to pursue environmental objectives. The chapter also discusses environmentally harmful subsidies, efforts to promote renewable energy and energy efficiency, and the role of the environmental goods and services sector as a source of employment and green growth. Finally, the chapter examines the country's eco-innovation performance and spending on research and development, as well as efforts to mainstream the environment into development co-operation programmes. The recommendations on green growth are summarised in a box at the end of the chapter.

The statistical data for Israel are supplied by and under the responsibility of the relevant Israeli authorities. The use of such data by the OECD is without prejudice to the status of the Golan Heights, East Jerusalem and Israeli settlements in the West Bank under the terms of international law.

1. Introduction

Between 2000 and 2008, real gross domestic product (GDP) in the Netherlands grew on average 4.6% per year, one of the highest growth rates among all OECD member countries. Following the economic crisis, the Netherlands has been gradually emerging from a protracted double-dip recession. Real GDP in the fourth quarter of 2014 was only about the same as in the fourth quarter of 2007, prior to the crisis. Pre-crisis growth was partly driven by banks' use of international capital markets to fund mortgage expansion. Rising house prices boosted household wealth and consumption, but the subsequent correction exposed imbalances in the economy. Growth is improving but remains weak, which contributes to the persistence of a very high current account surplus of about 10% of GDP (OECD, 2014a).

The authorities have implemented, or are preparing, significant structural reforms. Fiscal sustainability has been strengthened, notably with recent reforms of the pension system, health care and long-term care. Better targeting of social housing and tax provisions on mortgages are expected to reduce distortions in the housing market. Planned enhancements to the labour market aim to diminish segmentation, limit unemployment benefits to two years, simplify child benefits and improve integration of the disabled. Product market regulation is the least restrictive in the OECD, which contributes to firm creation. The country has launched an approach based on two complementary pillars to promote a healthy entrepreneurial system with innovation at its core. The aim is to enhance framework conditions for the entire business sector (the first pillar) and to develop sector-specific policies to unleash research and development (R&D) and address bottlenecks hampering the growth of nine "top sectors" (the second pillar) (OECD, 2014a).

2. Green growth initiatives

The Netherlands has made progress towards green growth over the review period, but at a moderate pace. Government initiatives to spur green growth include the Sustainability Agenda launched in 2011 to examine how key sectors could help the country attain green growth. For example, targets included an aim to recycle nearly 85% of waste and to have 15 000 to 20 000 electric cars on the road by 2015. The government also sought to pursue greener production outputs by switching to a bio-based economy. To do so, it co-operates with sectors such as the chemical, energy and water industries, as well as academia, to develop the use of biomass for materials, chemicals and biofuel products. By reducing dependency on fossil fuels, it aims to protect the natural asset base and reduce carbon emissions.

The government elaborated further on its green growth aspirations in a letter to the House of Representatives in March 2013, which also represented an update of the Sustainability Agenda. The letter indicated that "[t]he Government wants to make the Netherlands more competitive and, at the same time, reduce the burden on the environment and our reliance on fossil fuels. That is why, at international level, we are striving to achieve a fully sustainably energy supply by 2050, and have adopted the target of 16% sustainable energy by 2020" (Government of the Netherlands, 2013).

The letter set out the four pillars of the government's policy for green growth: smart use of market incentives; an incentivising framework with legislation that promotes dynamism; innovation; and the government as a network partner. In June 2015, the government provided a mid-term update of green growth policy in a letter to the House of Representatives (Government of the Netherlands, 2015). It added a fifth pillar related to greening through aid, trade and investment and provided an update on progress across the eight domains considered important for green growth:

1. Energy: towards a sustainable, affordable and reliable energy supply
2. Bio-based economy: substituting green raw materials (biomass) for fossil fuels
3. Climate: towards an ambitious national and international climate policy
4. Waste: from waste to raw material
5. Construction: towards an energy-efficient built environment
6. Food: towards a sustainable agricultural industry and food supply
7. Mobility: towards sustainable transport
8. Water: sustainable use of water.

Whereas the government as a whole is responsible for green growth, a co-ordinating minister or state secretary has been appointed for each domain. The Minister of Economic Affairs has the lead on energy, bio-based economy and food, the Minister for Housing and the Central Government Sector has the lead on construction, and the Minister and State Secretary for Infrastructure and the Environment leads on climate, waste to resource, mobility and water. The Minister for Foreign Trade and Development Co-operation is responsible for co-ordinating international environmental policy and sustainability, including international climate funding.

The 2013 Energy Agreement for Sustainable Growth provides the cornerstone for Dutch climate and energy policy. It spells out the objectives and policy instruments to be used in relation to energy, aiming to secure a high degree of stability in climate and energy policy for the longer-term (Box 3.1 provides further details). However, as pointed out by PBL (2015), the agreement focuses mainly on targets for 2020 and 2030 and lacks a strong, universally supported greenhouse gas emission target for 2050.

3. Greening the tax system

As part of the green growth toolbox, the Netherlands uses a number of potentially cost-effective economic instruments to address environmental challenges, including indexed environmentally related taxes (Table 3.1). In 2013, only Slovenia, Turkey and Denmark among OECD member countries raised more revenue from environmentally related taxes as a share of GDP than the Netherlands (Annex 3.A). Revenue from energy products and motor vehicles dominates total environmentally related tax revenues in the OECD. However, the Netherlands is one of the few countries that also raises a significant amount of revenues (about 0.5% of GDP) from other tax bases of environmental relevance; this includes tap water and municipal sewerage treatment. Further, contrary to a number of OECD member countries, environmentally related tax rates in the Netherlands are indexed to inflation, securing their environmental effectiveness over time.

Revenue from environmentally related taxes as a share of GDP has remained relatively stable since 1994 (Figure 3.1). The share was quite similar in 2013 to that of 2002-03 and slightly higher than in the mid-1990s. In between, however, revenues were even higher compared to GDP in some years (Figure 3.2). As a share of total tax revenue, revenues from environmentally related taxes increased from just under 8% in 1994 to peak at just over 10% in 2004 and again in 2006 before tapering down to just above 9% in 2012 (Figure 3.1).

Figure 3.1. **Revenue from environmentally related taxes relatively stable since 1994**

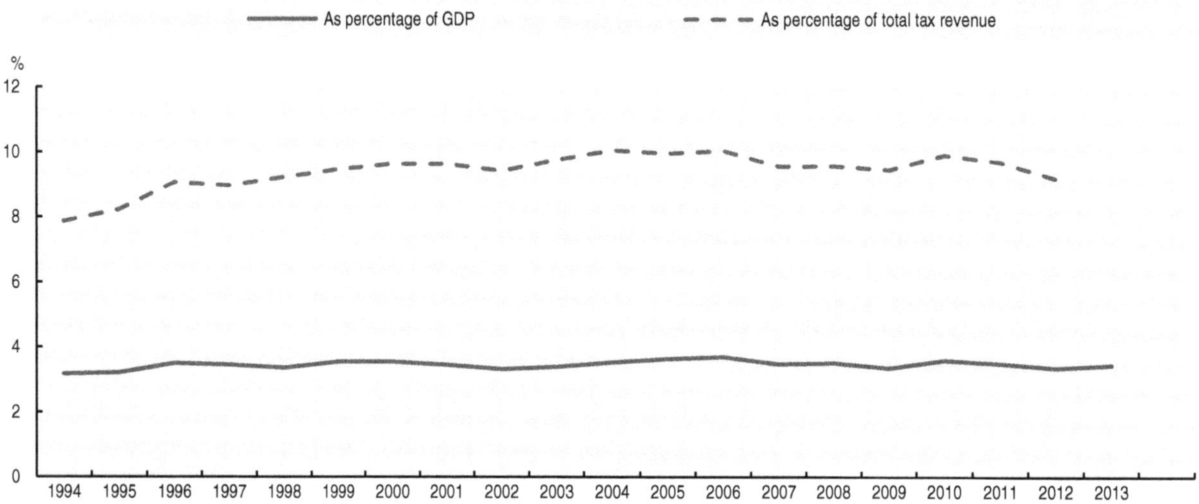

Source: OECD (2015), *OECD Database on Instruments Used for Environmental Policy and Natural Resources Management.*

StatLink http://dx.doi.org/10.1787/888933280210

Figure 3.2. **Increase in Rotterdam petrol price dampened revenues from environmentally related taxes**

As percentage of GDP and indices (2005 = 100)

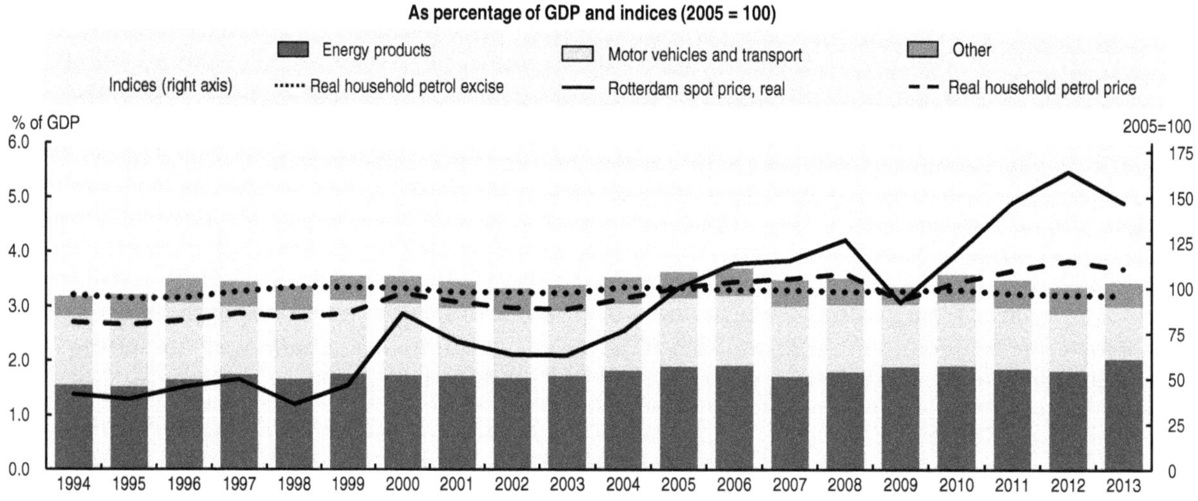

Source: OECD (2015), *OECD Database on Instruments Used for Environmental Policy and Natural Resources Management.*

StatLink http://dx.doi.org/10.1787/888933280229

The amount of tax revenue generated from energy products – including vehicle fuels – decreased as a share of GDP from 2010 to 2012. International fuel prices increased significantly over those years; Figure 3.2 illustrates the pre-tax price increases for petrol in the harbour of Rotterdam. Between 2009 and 2012, that price increased well over 60%, which led to substitution away from fuel use towards other (generally less taxed) goods and services, which, in isolation, reduces the share of revenues from environmentally related taxes in GDP. However, from 2012 to 2013, international crude oil prices started to decrease, and the reduction in real household petrol prices contributed to larger fuel sales and increasing tax revenues. Given the strong further decrease in crude oil prices since 2013, revenues from energy taxes will also likely have increased from 2013 to 2015.

In recent years, revenue raised from motor vehicles and transport activities also decreased. This may be explained in part by the changes to motor vehicle taxes that penalised vehicles with high CO_2 emissions; these changes stimulated the purchase of low-emitting vehicles, which are taxed less than high-emitting ones. In addition, the economic crisis probably made potential car buyers more reluctant to take on major new financial obligations. All in all, while taxes on vehicles and transport activities raised an amount equal to 1.29% of GDP in 2007, that share had declined to 0.97% in 2013. If the share had remained the same as it was in 2007 – and everything else also remained unchanged – revenues in 2013 would have been more than EUR 2 billion higher. Such a reduction in tax revenues certainly represents a major fiscal challenge.

In 2013, households paid more than 62% of the total environmentally related tax revenues and 78% of the environmentally related fees, of which municipal sewage fees were most important. Companies paid the remainder (CBS, 2014a).

3.1. *Taxes on energy products*

The Netherlands applies a number of different taxes on energy products summarised in Table 3.1. Motor fuel taxes are discussed in further detail in Chapter 4, but it is notable that the total tax rate on petrol is significantly higher than the tax rate on diesel.

While all uses of coal are being taxed in 2015, the use of coal for electricity generation will be exempted from 2016 as part of the 2013 Energy Agreement. While such an exemption could be motivated by the fact that electricity generation is covered by the European Union's emissions trading system (ETS) for greenhouse gases (GHGs), the use of coal in electricity generation also causes a number of other negative environmental impacts, which clearly makes the exemption regrettable.

The energy tax is levied on electricity and natural gas, with highly regressive rates. With respect to natural gas, for example, the first 170 000 cubic metres (m^3) of use per year is taxed at EUR 0.1911 per m^3. The marginal tax rates decrease rapidly, reaching EUR 0.0118 per m^3 for uses larger than 10 million m^3 per year. For electricity, while the first 10 000 kilowatt hour (kWh) per year are taxed at EUR 0.1196 per kWh, the tax rate per kWh declines significantly with increasing use; it reaches EUR 0.0005 per kWh for electricity use for the largest business users. The regressive tax rates on electricity and natural gas need to be seen in the context of the EU ETS, which covers larger energy users in particular. As long as the overall "cap" of this trading system remains unchanged, higher taxes on the energy use of firms covered by the system will not change total EU-wide emissions of the GHGs covered (Braathen, 2011).

The effective carbon tax rates on energy use in the Netherlands and the OECD are presented in Figure 3.3. Although some Dutch tax rates have been modified since May 2012, the figure still presents large differences in the energy taxes within the country and reveals several important differences between the Netherlands and the OECD average. The tax

Table 3.1. **Environmentally related taxes in the Netherlands**

Tax rates as of 1 January 2015

Name of tax	Tax base	Tax rate
Duty on petrol	Leaded petrol	EUR 0.8531 per L
	Unleaded petrol	EUR 0.7661 per L
Duty on oil other than petrol	Diesel and kerosene used as a motor fuel	EUR 0.4821 per L
	Diesel and kerosene used for heating purposes	EUR 0.4821 per L
	Liquefied petroleum gas	EUR 0.3347 per kg
	Heavy fuel oil	EUR 0.0362 per kg
Tax in connection with oil stocks	Leaded petrol	EUR 0.0080 per L
	Unleaded petrol	EUR 0.0080 per L
	Diesel and kerosene for all purposes	EUR 0.0080 per L
	Liquefied petroleum gas	EUR 0.0080 per kg
Tax on coal	Coal	EUR 14.40 per 1 000 kg
Energy Tax	Tax per electricity connection	EUR -311.84 per connection
	Consumption of up to 10 000 kWh electricity per year	EUR 0.1196 per kWh
	Consumption of between 10 000 and 50 000 kWh electricity per year	EUR 0.0469 per kWh
	Consumption of between 50 000 and 10 million kWh electricity per year	EUR 0.0125 per kWh
	Consumption of more than 10 million kWh electricity per year for non-business use	EUR 0.0010 per kWh
	Consumption of more than 10 million kWh electricity per year for business use	EUR 0.0005 per kWh
	Consumption of up to 170 000 m^3 natural gas per year	EUR 0.1911 per m^3
	Consumption of between 170 000 m^3 and 1 million m^3 natural gas per year	EUR 0.0677 per m^3
	Consumption of between 1 million and 10 million m^3 natural gas per year	EUR 0.0247 per m^3
	Consumption of more than 10 million m^3 natural gas per year	EUR 0.00118 per m^3
Sustainable energy surcharge	Consumption of up to 10 000 kWh electricity per year	EUR 0.0036 per kWh
	Consumption of between 10 000 and 50 000 kWh electricity per year	EUR 0.0046 per kWh
	Consumption of between 50 000 and 10 million kWh electricity per year	EUR 0.0012 per kWh
	Consumption of more than 10 million kWh electricity per year	EUR 0.000055 per kWh
	Consumption of up to 170 000 m^3 natural gas per year	EUR 0.0074 per m^3
	Consumption of between 170 000 m^3 and 1 million m^3 natural gas per year	EUR 0.0028 per m^3
	Consumption of between 1 million and 10 million m^3 natural gas per year	EUR 0.0008 per m^3
	Consumption of more than 10 million m^3 natural gas per year	EUR 0.0006 per m^3
Motor vehicles tax	The ownership of a motorcycle	EUR 95.40 per year
	The ownership of diesel-driven passenger cars	EUR 669.76 at 1 000 kg net weight per year + EUR 105.00 per extra 100 kg
	The ownership of LPG-driven passenger cars	EUR 260.08 at 900 kg net weight per year + EUR 112.52 per extra 100 kg
	The ownership of petrol-driven passenger cars	EUR 201.84 at 1 000 kg net weight per year + EUR 54.28 per extra 100 kg
	The use of a coach (bus)	EUR 335.52 at 2 700 kg net weight per year + EUR 1.10 per extra 100 kg
Tax on passenger cars	Registration of a passenger car emitting between 0 and 82 gramme (g) CO_2 per km	EUR 6 per g CO_2 emitted per km above 0 g/km, plus EUR 175
	Registration of a passenger car emitting between 82 and 110 g CO_2 per km	EUR 69 per g CO_2 emitted per km above 82 g/km, plus EUR 667
	Registration of a passenger car emitting between 110 and 160 g CO_2 per km	EUR 112 per g CO_2 emitted per km above 110 g/km, plus EUR 2 599
	Registration of a passenger car emitting between 160 and 180 g CO_2 per km	EUR 217 per g CO_2 emitted per km above 160 g/km, plus EUR 8 199
	Registration of a passenger car emitting more than 180 g CO_2 per km	EUR 434 per g CO_2 emitted per km above 180 g/km, plus EUR 12 539
	Surcharge for cars with a diesel engine emitting more than 70 g CO_2 per km	EUR 86 per g CO_2 emitted
Tax on tap water	Tap water delivered to a consumer	EUR 0.333 per m^3
Waste tax	Landfilling	EUR 13 per 1 000 kg
	Incineration	EUR 13 per 1 000 kg

Source: OECD (2015), *OECD Database on Instruments Used for Environmental Policy and Natural Resources Management.*

Figure 3.3. **Large differences in the effective carbon tax rates on energy use**

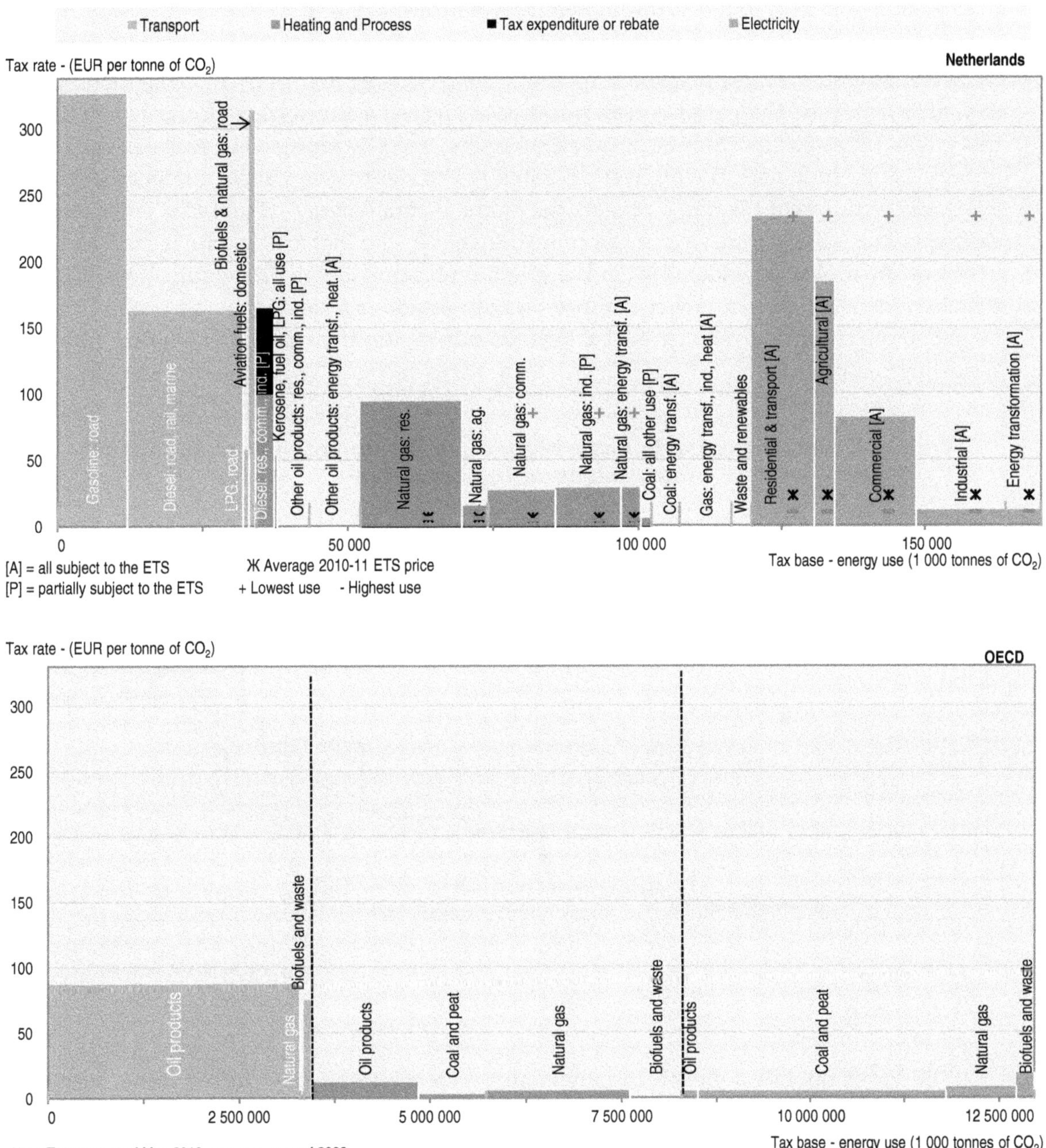

Note: Tax rates as of May 2012; energy use as of 2009.
Abbreviations: Res. = residential; comm. = commercial; ind. = industrial; ag. = agricultural; fish. = fishery; energy transf. = energy transformation; heat = merchant heat.
Source: OECD (2013), *Taxing Energy Use: A Graphical Analysis.*

rates for various fossil fuels have been converted to taxes on CO_2, taking the average carbon content of each fuel into account. For electricity tax rates, the carbon content of the fuels used to generate the electricity is reflected in the graph. The tax rates are generally much higher in the Netherlands than elsewhere in the OECD. The difference in tax rates between transport fuels and other energy products is lower in the Netherlands than elsewhere. This is especially the case for taxes on electricity, and within this category, especially in relation to residential, transport and agricultural use of electricity. For heating and process uses of energy, tax rates for residential natural gas use are significantly higher than what is generally found in OECD member countries.

Figure 3.4 compares the taxation of energy products on a carbon basis in the Netherlands with the three neighbouring countries of Belgium, Germany and Luxembourg, as well as Japan and Hungary, the two countries acting as peer reviewers for this review. In this graph, tax rates (as of May 2012) on all energy-related CO_2 emissions have been sorted in increasing order, with the highest tax rates at the right-hand part of the graph. The width of the different tax bases reflects the share of total energy-related CO_2 emissions caused by this tax base. In each of the countries shown, the highest tax rate is applied to petrol, while the "next (wide) step" in the graph represents diesel. The graph shows that the Netherlands applies a higher tax rate on both petrol and diesel than do each of the neighbouring countries; the rate is also significantly higher than the rates applied in the reviewing countries.

Figure 3.4. **The Netherlands has a higher tax rate on both petrol and diesel than neighbouring countries**

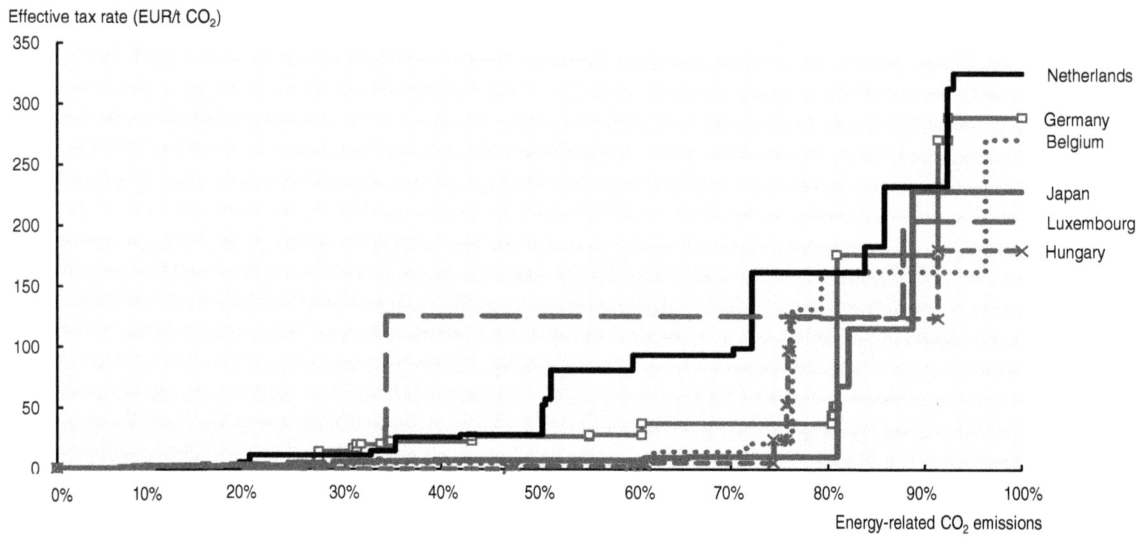

Source: OECD (2013), *Taxing Energy Use: A Graphical Analysis.*

The lower tax rates applied in neighbouring countries already causes some cross-border trade in motor fuels,[1] and makes it difficult for Dutch authorities to raise fuel tax rates further. From an environmental point of view, it would be desirable to gradually phase out the current tax preference given to diesel. However, the very low tax rate applied on diesel in Luxembourg, in particular, makes it challenging to implement such a reform.[2]

The Netherlands Environmental Assessment Agency (PBL) recently prepared an in-depth assessment of Dutch energy taxes (Vollebergh, 2014). According to the report, the design of energy taxes has emphasised the climate impacts of energy consumption of small users, particularly households. The focus on small users is largely due to fears that higher environmental taxes could drive large companies out of the country. As stated in the report, it is more difficult for households to avoid taxes by moving abroad. The report also points out that a disadvantage of taxing energy consumption is that this addresses the negative environmental impacts rather indirectly. Moreover, energy products are not taxed based on emissions released during combustion. It is also important to take into account the effects of fuel combustion on air quality, especially in relation to motor fuels and biomass. The latter causes very significant emissions of particulate matter and nitrogen oxides (NO_x) during combustion.

The air quality impacts of motor fuels, particularly diesel, are considerable. OECD (2014c) estimates the social cost of mortalities due to outdoor air pollution in the Netherlands was about USD 25 billion in 2010 taking into account estimated mortalities due to outdoor air pollution from the 2010 Global Burden of Disease study and country-specific estimates of "values-of-statistical-lives" (VSL). The report estimates that for OECD as a whole, road transport caused about half of mortality costs. As opposed to the trend in most OECD member countries, total estimated social costs of air pollution declined in the Netherlands from 2005 to 2010; this occurred due to a stronger-than-average reduction in the estimated mortalities, even if the VSL was estimated to increase more than 10% over that period.

Vollebergh (2014) compared the Dutch energy tax rates to the direct and indirect environmental damages (emissions of GHGs and local air pollutants) caused by different energy products and uses (Figure 3.5). In monetary terms, the dominant effect is, in most cases, damage to human health. In contrast to greenhouse gases, the impact of air-polluting emissions depends on time and place. Hence, an adjustment factor for emissions in densely populated regions was used to calculate air pollution damage costs. Figure 3.5 includes uncertainty bars to reflect important uncertainties in estimating these damages. It demonstrates clearly that current energy tax rates do not vary according to relevant environmental damages, as would be desirable. For example, they do not reflect well the very different environmental impacts of various ways of generating electricity (e.g. natural gas, coal, biomass, nuclear).

The report argues that the current tax rate on coal is too low, even before the planned exemption for the use of coal in electricity generation from 2016 is taken into account. It noted that even if a tax on coal does not contribute much to reduce EU-wide CO_2 emissions in the short term (due to interactions with the EU ETS), such a tax can help reduce emissions of sulphur dioxide (SO_2), particulate matter and NO_x, among others. Hence, the tax could still have a positive effect on air quality. Further, the report suggests that a tax on biomass used for electricity production could have positive air quality impacts, as biomass combustion causes considerable emissions of particulate matter and NO_x. The report found it remarkable that no tax had been levied to date on the incineration of combustible waste, including products made from fossil fuels such as plastics. Waste policies, including the recently introduced tax on incineration, are discussed further in Chapter 5.

Vollebergh (2014) also addresses the fiscal sustainability of current Dutch energy taxes. The increasing tax rates, combined with other policies aimed at curbing fossil fuel use, are leading to a decrease in fossil energy consumption and thus to tax-base erosion. Technological innovations are accelerating this trend. For example, vehicle fuel efficiencies are rapidly improving, and thanks to better insulation techniques and other innovations, it is no longer a given that new housing developments will be connected to the natural gas network. The Netherlands, therefore, needs to start thinking about an alternative design of its energy taxes. Reforms that merely build on the present energy system should be avoided because they are likely to result in decreasing tax revenues. According to

Figure 3.5. **Energy tax rates do not vary according to relevant environmental damages, 2013**

Direct and indirect damages caused by emissions of greenhouse gases and local air pollutants

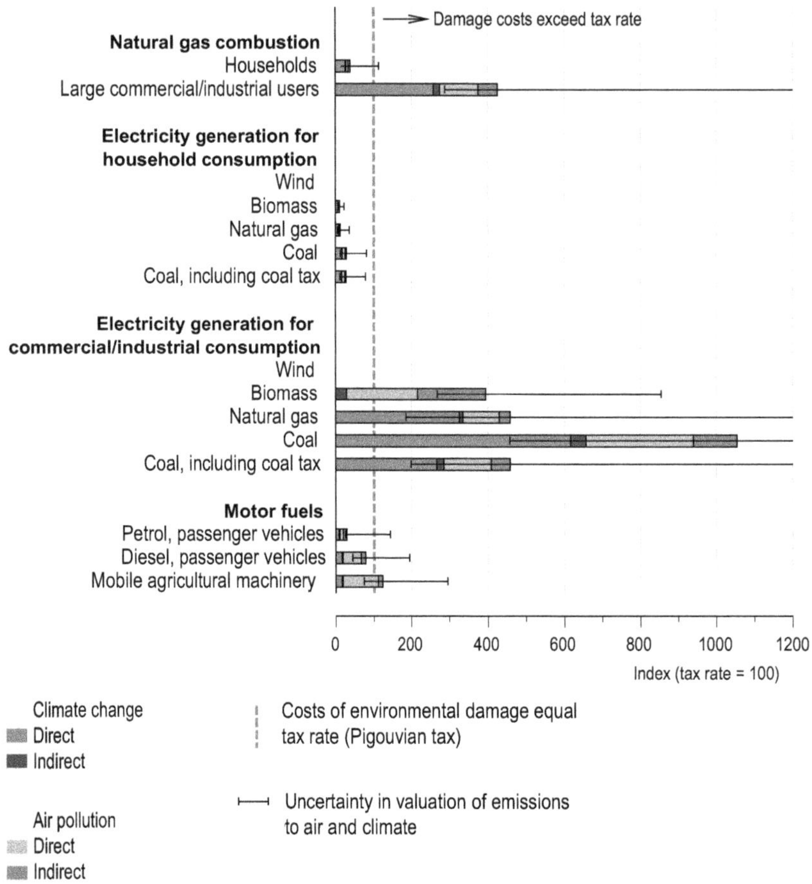

Source: Vollebergh, H. (2014), "Green Tax Reform: Energy Tax Challenges for the Netherlands", *PBL Policy Brief*, No.1501.

Note: The shaded bars reflect the estimated direct and indirect climate change and air pollution damages, respectively, whereas the continuous black lines represent the uncertainty in the estimates. The dotted vertical line reflects the tax rate that the different products and uses are facing at present, normalised in relation to the estimated damages.

Vollebergh (2014), a better strategy is to anticipate the technological changes that are already on the horizon, such as continued reductions in the CO_2 emissions per km driven by various vehicle types, and reduced heating needs of dwellings.

3.2. Taxes on motor vehicles

Taxes on motor vehicle fuels provide a direct incentive to limit CO_2 emissions (although often with tax rates not well-aligned with GHG emissions from different fuels). However, the Netherlands also (like a number of other countries) seeks to limit CO_2 emissions via the one-off tax on motor vehicle purchases. The higher the CO_2 emissions per km driven in a test cycle, the higher the purchase tax applied for that vehicle type. Such tax rate differentiation can, in principle, also be made in annual taxes on motor vehicle ownership, but the Netherlands does not do so. Figure 3.6 compares the incentives to abate emissions per tonne of CO_2 that a diesel vehicle will emit over its lifetime in countries that apply such

Figure 3.6. **CO_2 abatement incentives in motor vehicle taxes are very progressive**

EUR per tonne emitted by diesel vehicles over vehicle lifetime for selected emission levels per km driven

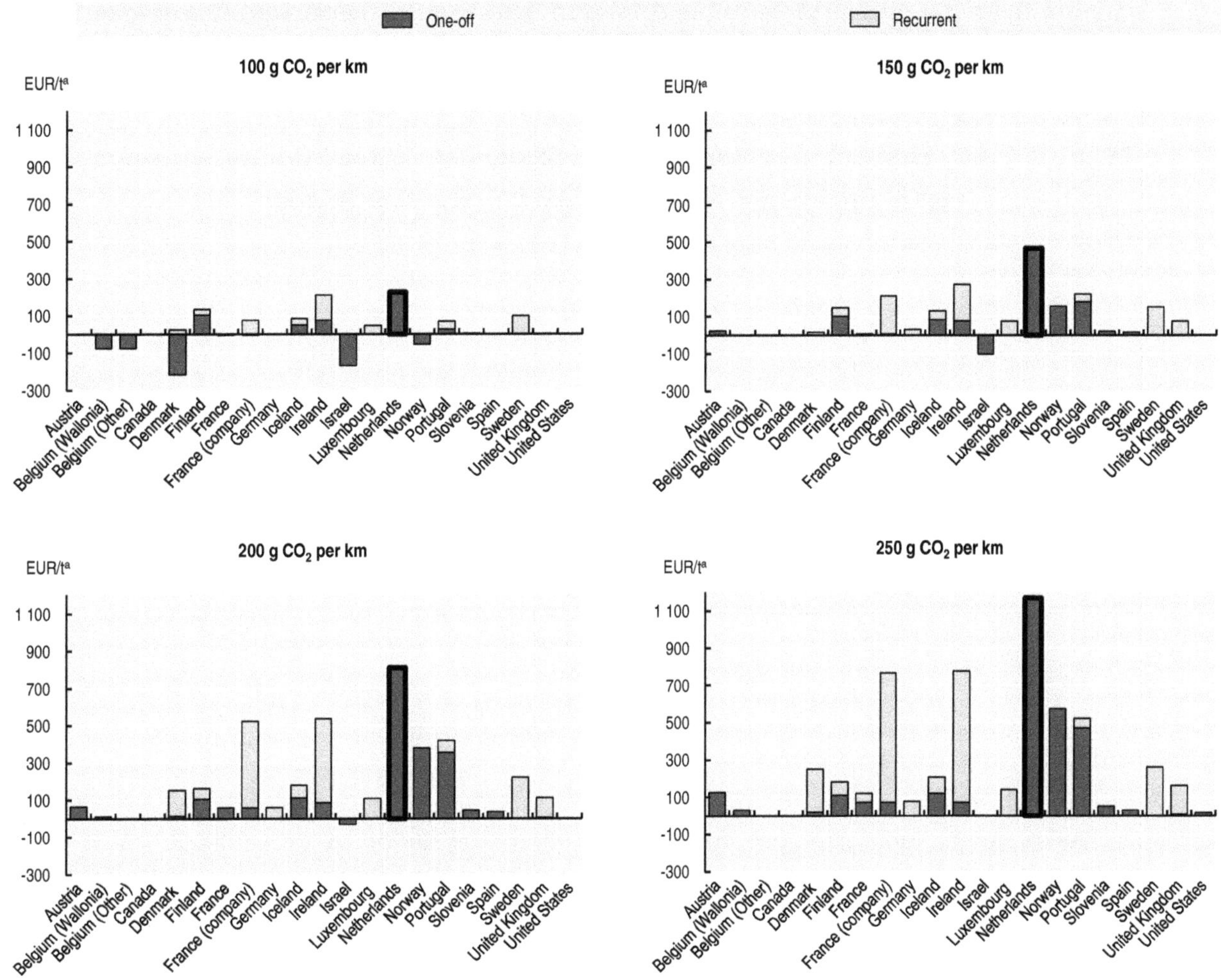

a) EUR per tonne emitted by diesel vehicles over vehicle lifetime of the vehicle, for selected emission levels per km driven. Tax rates as of 1 January 2015 for the Netherlands, 2014 or earlier for other countries.

Source: OECD (2015), *OECD Database on Instruments Used for Environmental Policy and Natural Resources Management.*

StatLink http://dx.doi.org/10.1787/888933280238

taxes, summed over any applicable one-off and recurrent taxes. The calculations assume that each vehicle is driven 200 000 km over its lifetime, which is assumed to be 15 years.

Figure 3.6 shows that the CO_2 element in the Dutch motor vehicle purchase tax is very progressive, and that the tax rate for high-emitting vehicles is indeed very high. For a diesel vehicle that on average emits 250 g CO_2 per km driven, the tax per tonne of CO_2 emitted over its lifetime exceeds EUR 1 150.[3] It should be noted that *each tonne* of CO_2 emitted causes exactly the same environmental damage, regardless of whether it is emitted from a high- or a low-emitting vehicle, or from a petrol or diesel vehicle. These abatement incentives are disproportionate to the drastically lower abatement incentives in other parts of the Dutch economy; an emission allowance in the EU ETS, for example, cost about EUR 7 in the beginning of 2015. The higher tax rate on diesel vehicles compared to petrol vehicles has, however, helped limit the share of diesel vehicles in the Netherlands compared to several neighbouring countries, in spite of the lower tax rate on diesel than on petrol.

The CO_2 element in the Dutch motor vehicle purchase tax has increased in recent years (Figure 3.7). This increase compensated for a reduction in an element of the tax that varied with vehicle price in place before 2013. From 2014 to 2015, the tax rate increased for vehicles with emissions between 167 and 300 g CO_2 per km, but was reduced for (the rather few) vehicles with even higher emissions.

Figure 3.7. **CO_2 element in motor vehicle purchase tax increased in recent years**

EUR per vehicle for petrol vehicles with different CO_2 emissions per km driven

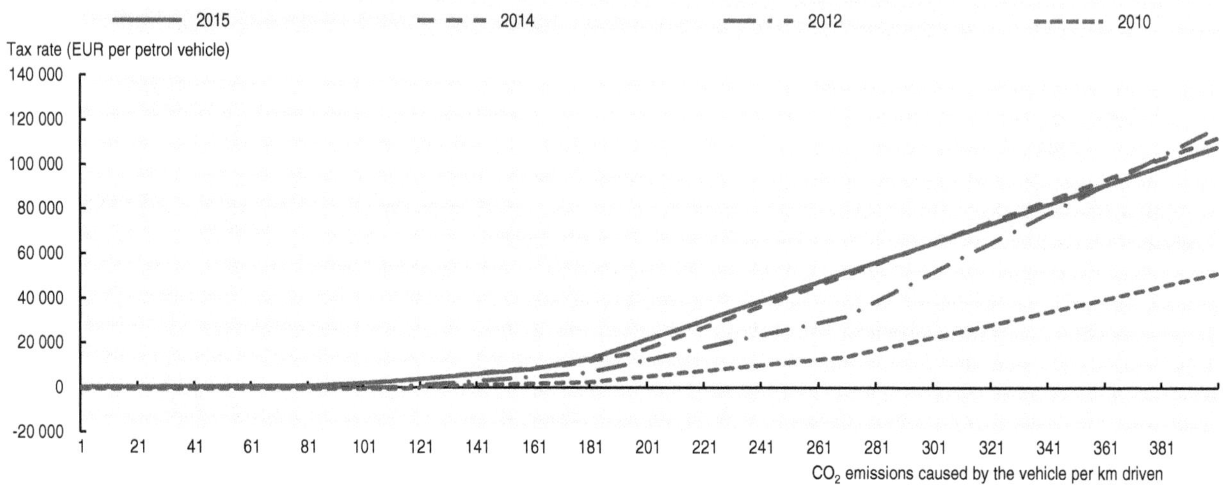

Source: Based on OECD (2015) *OECD Database on Instruments Used for Environmental Policy and Natural Resources Management.*

StatLink http://dx.doi.org/10.1787/888933280240

As shown in Table 3.1 above, there is also an annual tax on motor vehicles, which varies according to the type and the weight of the vehicle. If a vehicle weighs 1 300 kg, for example, the annual tax for a petrol version is EUR 364.68 and for a diesel version is EUR 984.76. A yearly tax difference of more than EUR 620 has also helped keep the share of diesel vehicles relatively low in the Netherlands.

The annual vehicle tax includes an exemption for "classic" cars (so-called old timers). While this might be justified from a "cultural heritage" point of view, it can be unfortunate from an environmental point of view, as many of these vehicles can be highly polluting. According to PBL (2011), the exemption concerned 300 000 vehicles older than 25 years until recently, but from 2012 onwards, only vehicles registered before the end of 1986 are exempt, which reduced the number of exempted vehicles considerably.

The annual tax on vehicle ownership also applies to buses, delivery vans and lorries, with tax rates depending on vehicle weight. Since the tax rates are relatively low, it is doubtful they have much environmental impact. In addition, the use of highways is also taxed (Eurovignette), with rates depending on the environmental standard of the vehicles. The rates range from EUR 750 for vehicles that conform with the EURO-2 or stricter standards to EUR 1 550 for vehicles that do not conform with any EU pollution standards. While such tax rate differentiation is positive from an environmental perspective, it is not likely these relatively modest tax rates have a strong environmental impact either.

Within the review period, there were plans to replace much of the current fuel and vehicle taxes with a GPS-based kilometre charge whereby drivers would pay a fee per kilometre, depending on time and place of car use (see discussion in Chapter 4). A proposal for such a scheme had been considered as early as 2005, but was set aside when the government resigned for unrelated reasons, resulting in a missed opportunity.

3.3. *Company car taxation*

In most OECD member countries, the benefits reaped by individuals who can use a company-owned car are taxed more leniently than other types of income. One recent OECD study suggests the foregone revenue related to such under-taxation is very substantial (Harding, 2014); another argues the related environmental and other social costs caused by increased air emissions, more traffic accidents and greater congestion are significantly higher than the estimated foregone revenue (Roy, 2014).

In the Netherlands, between 0 and 25% of the capital value of the company-owned vehicle that the employee may use for private purposes is considered a taxable benefit.[4] Harding (2014) developed a "benchmark" tax system that compares tax systems applied in the participating countries in 2012 using different assumptions. Drawing on this benchmark, Figure 3.8 indicates that in the mid-point estimate, the Dutch system captured about 70% of the taxable benefit, placing the Netherlands among the third of countries that captured the largest share of these benefits.

Figure 3.8. **Dutch system among the top third of countries in capturing the taxable benefit of company cars**

Assuming a three-year useful life of the company-owned cars

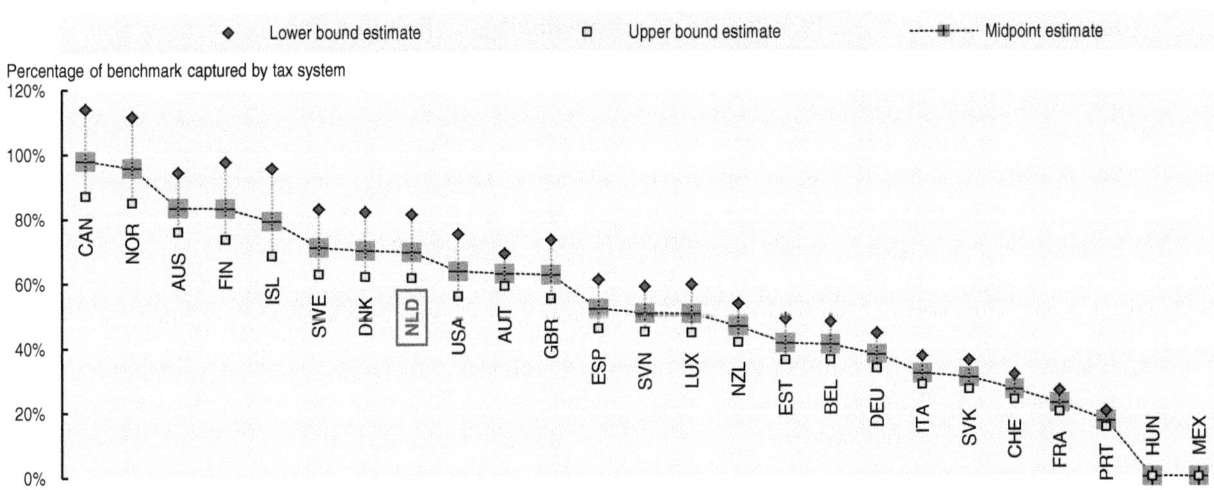

Source: Harding (2014), "Personal Tax Treatment of Company Cars and Commuting Expenses: Estimating the Fiscal and Environmental Costs", *OECD Taxation Working Papers*, No. 20

StatLink http://dx.doi.org/10.1787/888933280251

However, a disadvantage of the Dutch tax treatment of company-owned car fringe benefits is that there is no component that varies with the distance driven for private purposes.[5] If the employer also covers the operating costs of the vehicle, then, the employee can take personal trips at no cost. In terms of environmental and other social costs (congestion, accidents, etc.), such a feature of the tax system is particularly harmful (Roy, 2014).

3.4. Other environmentally related taxes, fees and charges

Water management

An elaborate financing structure has been established in the Netherlands to fund water management tasks, including flood protection, freshwater supply, water quality management and water supply and sanitation (OECD, 2014d). There are multiple taxes and levies in place to fund this expenditure. The central government's environmental tax on groundwater abstractions was abolished on 1 January 2012. The total amount raised from this tax was about EUR 180 million per year (OECD, 2014b). The government also planned to abolish the tap water tax as of 1 January 2013, but that legislation did not enter into force for budgetary reasons. Instead, the tap water tax was doubled as of 1 January 2014, from EUR 0.165 to EUR 0.33 per m^3. The tax is levied from water suppliers for up to 300 m^3 a year per connection to the water system. Above this ceiling, the tax is not levied. Large users of water are basically exempt from the tax, which from a water management point of view is highly regrettable. On 1 January 2015, the tax rate was raised to EUR 0.333 per m^3.

Provinces finance groundwater management by charging a groundwater levy for large groundwater abstractions, which applies mostly to industry and drinking water companies. The agricultural sector is typically not charged for groundwater abstractions (OECD, 2014d).

Regional water authorities finance their water management tasks using their own levies. There is a wastewater treatment levy to cover the costs of wastewater treatment (*Zuiveringsheffing*), a water systems levy to cover the costs of ensuring "dry feet" and providing sufficient and clean surface water (*Watersysteemheffing*) and a pollution levy for direct discharges into surface water (*Verontreigingingsheffing*). Levies for wastewater treatment and water system management differ greatly among the 24 regional water authorities (OECD, 2014d).

In 2001-13 there was a sharp rise in revenues from sewerage charges, increasing from EUR 665 million to nearly EUR 1.5 billion, a 110% increase. Statistics Netherlands indicates that due to this sharp rise in sewerage charges, total revenues from environmental fees increased by almost 40% between 2001 and 2013 (CBS, 2014a).

Run-off from agriculture is an important source of water pollution in the Netherlands. To address this pollution in a cost-effective way, the government introduced in 1998 an innovative "minerals accounting system" known as MINAS to manage the nutrient balance at farm level (OECD, 2007). In theory, such a system is the best instrument for decreasing total losses of nutrients, and hence nutrients pollution, from agriculture. Unfortunately, the European Court of Justice in 2003 ruled that the system did not comply with the EU's Nitrate Directive, and the system was replaced by a regulatory approach from 2005.

Waste, landfilling and incineration

A waste tax covering landfilling was abolished as of 1 January 2012, but reintroduced for budgetary reasons as of 1 April 2014. As of 1 January 2015, the coverage of this tax was extended to include the incineration of mixed waste, with a tax rate of EUR 13 per tonne of waste for both landfilling and incineration. There is a landfilling ban in place for several types of waste (Chapter 5), including biodegradable waste in line with EU rules. It is also notable that energy production in waste incineration plants is not covered by the EU ETS, which means there are no interactions between the incineration tax and the ETS "cap".

The environmental damage caused by landfilling and incineration varies with the quality of the facilities. While it can be complicated to measure (some of the) actual emissions from a landfill, this is relatively simple to do (and is actually done) at an incinerator. More than 10 years ago, for example, Norway introduced a tax on measured emissions of a number of pollutants from each incinerator.[6] Due to concerns about competition with Swedish incinerators, this tax has since been abolished. However, the Netherlands could consider such an emission-based tax as an alternative to the input-based tax now in place. This would provide a much more direct incentive to operators of incinerators to limit as much as possible environmental damages related to the combustion process. The coverage could also be extended to include emissions from the combustion of imported waste, which cause the same environmental harm as those from domestic waste.

In addition to taxes on landfilling and incineration (which are paid by the operators of the waste collection systems), municipalities use various economic instruments to make households and others pay for the collection services provided. According to Dijkgraaf and Gradus (2014), the share of Dutch municipalities using unit-based waste collection fees increased from 15% to 37% between 1998 and 2012. These unit-based fees can be related to the volume of bins picked up; the frequency of collection to which the households subscribe; the number of bags of unsorted waste collected; or to the weight of unsorted waste collected. Dijkgraaf and Gradus (2014) show that unit-based pricing systems are more important for reducing the operating costs of collection than the choice of institutional arrangement (private or public collection, etc.). In particular, the authors find that bag-based and frequency-based pricing systems contribute the most to reducing costs by reducing waste amounts and administrative costs. However, a disadvantage of a bag-based system is that it is not easy to price and, hence reduce, the amounts of compostable waste. Dutch waste policies are discussed in further detail in Chapter 5.

Aviation

An air passenger tax was levied from 1 July 2008 to 30 June 2009. It covered passengers aged two years and older starting their journey from an airport handling traffic for larger planes. The tax rate was EUR 11.25 for European destinations, destinations up to 2 500 km and destinations up to 3 500 km in countries with at least one airport within the boundary of 2 500 km. For other destinations, the tax rate was EUR 45 per passenger.

The tax was abolished largely due to concerns that it caused potential passengers to take their flights from neighbouring countries. Soon after the Dutch tax was abolished, a similar tax was introduced in neighbouring Germany. The air travel tax is applied to tickets for passenger flights departing from German airports, with rates depending on the flight distance (OECD, 2012a).

The inclusion of intra-EU aviation in the EU ETS weakens the argument for taxing passenger flights within the EU – as doing so would largely lead to higher GHG emissions somewhere else within the system. A tax on long-distance flights could help internalise some of the environmental damages caused by aviation, at least until a global system to address externalities is in place. Such a tax would need to be considered in the broader international context of the airline industry. The influence of a small country in this network is limited, as there are many alternative routes. Air transport is also briefly discussed in Chapter 4.

3.5. *Environmentally motivated tax preferences*

Energy Investment Tax Allowance

Since 1997, the Netherlands has had a tax allowance to promote investments in energy-saving technologies and sustainable energy production. This Energy Investment Tax Allowance reduces costs for firms investing in the newest energy-saving and sustainable energy technologies. Firms investing in technologies listed in the annually updated "Energy List" may deduct some of the investment costs from their taxable profits in the year of the investment. This decreases the payback period of the investment. The list contains generic technologies that meet a certain energy-saving standard, as well as a selection of novel, but proven, technologies with a higher energy-saving potential than conventional technologies, and may thus also reduce the costs for investors to find particular technologies.

Ruijs and Vollebergh (2013) found that in the first years of the scheme, a lack of accountability of the eligible tax expenditures contributed to larger than expected revenue losses in some years. Its main weakness is the difficulty to prevent firms that would have made these investments in any case from receiving subsidies.[7] More stringent eligibility rules and better evaluation processes to update the Energy List, together with reductions in the tax deduction percentage, have improved the effectiveness of the scheme over the years. Nevertheless, a substantial share of free riders appears to remain.

Using only the technology list – without the additional benefit of receiving a tax reduction – may not be sufficient for companies to switch to new energy-saving technologies. According to Ruijs and Vollebergh (2013), the tax preferences need not be large, however, as reductions in corporate tax rates or tax deduction percentages in recent years have not had a negative impact on the amount of energy-saving achieved through the scheme.

Commuting expenses

Opinions differ across the OECD on whether commuting expenses should be treated as private expenses or work-related expenses (Harding, 2014). If commuting is considered to be entirely the choice or responsibility of an individual, commuting expenses are generally treated the same way as other personal expenses. Therefore, reimbursement or subsidisation of commuting expenses by an employer is taxed; when an employee pays such costs, they are non-deductible. The second approach considers the cost of getting to work as an employment expense. In such cases, tax systems often allow deductions for expenditures paid by the employee, as well as exemptions for expenditures paid by the employer.

The Netherlands belongs to the first category, and does generally not allow deduction of commuting expenses when calculating the taxable income of employees. There is, however, one exception: some expenses related to travelling to work by means of public transport may be deducted if the distance between home and workplace is longer than 10 km. In addition, contrary to conventional practice for other benefits of this kind in the Netherlands, employer-paid public transport costs are not taxable.

Other environmentally motivated tax preferences

A reduced value-added tax (VAT) rate of 6% was applied in 2013 for the installation of double glazing windows. Other types of energy-efficiency measures in buildings, such as floor, roof and wall cavity insulation, were already eligible for the reduced tax rate (Ecologic

Institute and eclareon, 2014). The cost effectiveness of such subsidy measures should be carefully assessed, as experiences in other countries indicate that actual reductions in energy use are much lower than expected *ex ante*.[8]

Through the "Green Funds" scheme, consumers can receive a tax benefit if they invest in a green fund. In return, banks offer green loans at lower interest rates to so-called green projects, using the extra liquidity generated by consumers' investments. These projects address nature, bio-agriculture, agriculture, sustainable resource use, recycling, renewable energy, energy saving, sustainable construction, sustainable mobility or the sustainable water cycle. In 2012, loan applications amounting to EUR 95 million were approved (Ecologic Institute and eclareon, 2014).

4. The use of other market-based incentives for environmental policy

4.1. *The EU ETS*

One of the most important market-based environmental policy instruments applied in the Netherlands, in addition to environmentally related taxes, fees and charges, is the EU ETS for GHGs.[9] The ETS contributes to a cost-effective abatement of CO_2, nitrous oxide (N_2O) and perfluorocarbon (PFC) emissions[10] across more than 11 000 power stations, industrial plants and airlines in 31 European countries.[11] In 2013, about 450 Dutch entities were covered by the ETS.

At the outset, almost all emission allowances in this trading system were allocated for free. However, in the current phase, an increasing share of allowances is being auctioned. This is a positive development, both from an equity perspective – it is "fair" that polluters pay – and *indirectly* from an economic efficiency perspective, as the revenues raised through allowance auctioning make it possible to reduce distorting taxes. The allocation method does not, however, *directly* affect the economic efficiency of the scheme, as the system in any case contributes to equalising the costs of additional abatement across all the participants. Firms that can abate at low cost will do so, and avoid having to buy emission allowances; firms for which it is costly to abate will refrain from doing so, and buy allowances instead.

The total GHG emissions from sectors covered by the system are determined by the overall "cap" that has been fixed for each year up to 2020. Hence, it is *not* affected by whether one of the individual firms covered by the system is abating its emissions or not.

The total cap was fixed just prior to the outbreak of the recent economic crisis, which has reduced economic activity levels and related CO_2 emissions considerably, compared to what was assumed when the cap was set. The lower-than-expected "business-as-usual" emission levels have reduced demand for emission allowances, and hence lowered their price. In mid-April 2015, the price of an emission allowance for 1 tonne of CO_2 was about EUR 7; this was in spite of measures taken at the European level to lift the prices, particularly by holding back some allowances from current auctions. This price level is well below most available estimates of the future damages caused by each tonne – the "social costs of carbon". It is also below the price level expected to be necessary to reduce emissions enough to limit the increase in global average temperatures to 2°C, the target agreed by the Parties to the United Nations Framework Convention on Climate Change (UNFCCC). It would therefore be desirable if additional measures could be taken *at the European level* to underpin the price level in order to better stimulate the required transition to a low-carbon economy; an ETS-wide minimum price of allowances, for example, could be established.

It is also possible for individual countries to effectively make the ETS cap stricter by buying up emission allowances and then retiring them, making sure they will never be used. This could be a more cost-effective GHG abatement measure than many instruments currently in use, including various support measures for renewable energy and energy efficiency.

While measures at the European level to support allowance prices could be useful, any similar national measures, such as a national "price floor", would not cause any EU-wide emission reductions. Reduced emissions in one country would free up emission allowances only to lead to lower allowance prices and higher emissions somewhere else, possibly with higher tax revenue in the country that introduced the "price floor".

While measures to lift explicit carbon prices in the ETS sectors are rare, all EU countries apply additional policy measures to increase energy efficiency and reduce GHG emissions for sectors covered by the EU ETS. As indicated, such measures do not lead to lower EU-wide GHG emissions; they only shift emission reductions from one source to another, normally increasing abatement costs. In the Netherlands, the Renewable Energy Subsidy Scheme (discussed below) and the Energy Investment Tax Allowance (already presented) are examples of such policy measures. To the extent they address electricity use, for example, neither scheme will reduce EU-wide GHG emissions, as long as the overall "cap" of the ETS remains unchanged.

Such policy measures are sometimes justified due to other benefits they generate. Whereas technology spillovers represent a valid argument in such a context, Braathen (2011) indicates that arguments such as increased energy security or reduced emissions of local air pollutants are less likely to hold in practice. For example, an effective "cap" on CO_2 emissions determines the total amount of carbon that will be emitted across the countries covered by the ETS. If a subsidy scheme causes a number of wind turbines to replace a coal-fired power plant, the emissions of local pollutants from the coal-fired power plant would decrease. But as the total amount of carbon emitted will remain unchanged, emissions of local air pollutants will probably increase somewhere else within the system. Ultimately, it would need to be assessed whether the new sources of carbon emissions cause more or less local air pollution than the source that the wind turbines replaced.

4.2. *Renewable Energy Subsidy Scheme*

Renewable energy supply (RES) has increased significantly since 2000, but still accounted for only 4.2% of energy supply in 2013 (Chapter 1). The Netherlands has a feed-in-tariff system that subsidises renewable energy producers for the generation of such energy (SDE+) (see also the discussion in Section 6.4). The SDE+ compensates for the difference between the cost price of fossil energy sources and that of renewable energy, depending on the relevant technology (RVO, 2014a). The size of the subsidy depends on the technology used and the amount of renewable energy produced. The SDE+ contribution depends on the energy price at any given time. If the energy price is high, the renewable energy producers receive less SDE+, but more from their energy purchasers. With a lower energy price, they receive more SDE+, but less from their energy purchasers.[12] The subsidy applies to a maximum number of full-load hours and has a maximum period of 5, 12 or 15 years, depending on the technology (RVO, 2014a).

The SDE+ has one fixed annual budget for all categories of renewables. This means that all technologies compete against each other, and the support is allocated in six stages on a "first come, first served" basis. In each round, the support increases. However, late bidders run the risk of rejection due to lack of funds (Ecologic Institute and eclareon, 2014). The budget, which is EUR 3.5 billion in 2015, is scheduled to reach EUR 3.8 billion in 2020. Approximately 500 applications were accepted in 2013, according to Ecologic Institute and eclareon (2014).

Competition between the different renewable technologies should help limit the costs of the SDE+ scheme. Still, ECN (2011) suggested it would be more cost effective to transform the scheme to a hybrid renewable quota system, in co-operation with the joint Swedish and Norwegian renewable quota system. A renewable quota system could stimulate deployment of low-cost technologies for renewables (e.g. large-scale biomass digestion, biomass co-combustion) at the expense of high-cost, small-scale technologies. The report did, however, suggest that some elements of SDE+ subsidies could be maintained for selected renewable technologies that are promising, but currently expensive.

In addition to the SDE+ scheme, photovoltaic installations with a capacity of 0.601 kilowatt-peak (kWp) to 3.5 kWp are eligible for a 15% subsidy of investment cost. For installations with a capacity greater than 3.5 kWp, support is calculated by multiplying the 15% of investment costs by 3.5 and then dividing by the actual capacity in kWp. The maximum subsidy is EUR 650. The foreseen budget of EUR 50 million for 2012 and 2013 was exhausted in August 2013. In total, the installed capacity amounts to a yearly electricity production of 315 gigawatt hour (GWh).

4.3. *Support for energy-efficient passenger vehicles*

Since 2010, the most efficient passenger vehicles were for several years completely exempted from the one-off tax on motor vehicle purchases, as well as the annual vehicle tax. From 2015, the rules of the vehicle purchase tax changed somewhat; the purchase tax now applies to all vehicles causing CO_2 emissions in their use (see Figure 3.6).[13] The fiscal advantages have resulted in a rapid increase in the range of energy-efficient passenger vehicles on offer, as well as in high sales volumes. By the end of 2012, approximately 7 300 electrical vehicles were registered and 8 000 charging points were installed (Ecologic Institute and eclareon, 2014). As pointed out in PBL (2015), the Netherlands is one of the leading countries in Europe with respect to the sales of passenger vehicles with low test-cycle CO_2 emissions. However, the increase in the sales of tax-exempt vehicles (e.g. those with no CO_2 emissions) contributed to the tax-base erosion described in Section 3. In addition, the real-world reduction in CO_2 emissions has been much lower than predicted by test results, and the tax benefits also contributed to increased car sales and use, along with the related externalities.

Company car taxation rules discussed in Section 3.3 have also stimulated sales of electric and hybrid-electric vehicles. For example, vehicles with CO_2 emissions of up to 50 g per km have no additional tax liability; drivers who also use their company car privately do not pay any additional tax for five years. In addition, many hybrid-electric vehicles will be driven on either petrol or diesel much of the time, often with higher emissions per km driven than "normal" versions of similar vehicles.

PBL (2015) singles out several lessons regarding fiscal stimulation of environmentally friendly vehicles:[14]

- Tax deductions can encourage manufacturers to place new products on the market that meet the new environmental standards.

- A combination of tax measures can produce a large consumer response.
- Tax measures should take into account interactions with other policy instruments.[15] The car industry is subject to EU rules regarding the average CO_2 emissions from the total number of cars sold each year. As a result, the extra sales of cars with low CO_2 emissions triggered by the tax preferences applied in the Netherlands can lead to fewer sales of these cars in the rest of the EU. The effect on EU-wide CO_2 emissions is, therefore, probably very small.

As discussed further in Chapter 4, the tax preferences for electric vehicles are a very costly way to achieve reductions in emissions of CO_2 and local air pollutants.

4.4. *Other environmentally motivated subsidies*

The Ministry for Economy, Agriculture and Innovation offers subsidies for new energy-efficient installations and measures in the horticulture sector. The budget was EUR 2.3 million for 2013. Companies that received funding in prior years are not eligible for the subsidy (Ecologic Institute and eclareon, 2014).

A revolving fund for energy savings in buildings was established in 2013, with EUR 75 million being financed from the state budget and EUR 225 million co-financed by two private banks. The fund is directed towards landlords, owners and tenants to finance energy-saving technology and measures with the help of low-interest loans with a 12-year payback period (Ecologic Institute and eclareon, 2014).

By 2013, 14 projects in 13 provinces had been launched in the framework of the "Block for Block" pilot programme. Involving private actors, provinces, corporations and municipalities, the goal was to make at least 2 000 existing apartments highly energy efficient by 2014 (Ecologic Institute and eclareon, 2014).

5. Environmentally harmful subsidies

PBL (2011) indicates that environmentally harmful subsidies in the Netherlands amounted to between EUR 5-10 billion in 2010.[16] According to the study, it is difficult to derive a more precise number as any estimate will depend on varying criteria and methods of calculation. The same applies to determining the harmful effects on the environment; in many cases, it can be difficult to assess the exact impact on the environment if a given support scheme were abolished.

5.1. *The common agricultural policy of the EU*

One of the main environmental problems in the Netherlands is run-off of nutrients from the intensive livestock farming activity. According to OECD (2007), high minimum prices for grain introduced as part of the EU's Common Agricultural Policy (CAP) enabled Dutch livestock farmers to largely out-compete counterparts in other EU member states several decades ago; Dutch farmers had easier access to the Rotterdam harbour, allowing them to import alternative, less costly feeds (e.g. cassava) for their animals. This, in turn, partly explains the severe problems related to nutrients that gradually developed in the Netherlands.

In recent years, the introduction of various "cross-compliance requirements" has improved the environmental dimension of the CAP. They require farmers to comply with a number of environmental obligations in order to receive financial support. According to

PBL (2011), environmentally harmful subsidies in the agriculture sector have been greatly reduced over the past years. Due to the cross-compliance requirements, the system of direct production support has shifted to support per hectare. In the opinion of this report, the agricultural subsidies are no longer environmentally harmful or less harmful than they used to be.

However, many of the cross-compliance obligations should have been complied with in any case. Further, it is likely that without the CAP in place, or with much lower support rates than at present, livestock activity levels would have been significantly lower. After all, the Netherlands is one of the most densely populated countries in the world, where land has a high alternative value. Over time, lower livestock activity levels would most probably have helped significantly reduce nutrient run-off.

Van Grinsven et al. (2015, 2013) discuss the costs and benefits of nitrogen applications in agriculture in the Netherlands and in the EU as a whole. In their 2015 paper, a scenario that reduces the Dutch pig and poultry sector by 50%, the dairy sector by 20% and synthetic N-fertiliser use by 40% would lower annual N-pollution costs by EUR 0.2-2.2 billion (40%). The estimated benefit would be larger than the loss of GDP in the primary agriculture sector, but not enough to cover production loss in the supply and processing chain. However, these studies used a relatively low shadow-price on damages to human health.[17]

Decisions about the CAP are taken at a European level. Still, from an environmental point of view, the Netherlands has good reasons to argue at the EU level for significant reduction of these support measures, combined with stricter cross-compliance requirements.

Domestic Dutch policy measures regarding the agriculture sector also have negative environmental impacts. According to PBL (2011), a low VAT tax rate of 6% applies to all food products, instead of the general 19% tariff. Raising the tax rate to 19% for meat only would yield EUR 0.6 billion; this could reduce GHG emissions by 0.2 million tonnes (Mt), but largely in other countries. The same study indicates that ornamental plants benefit from a VAT rate of 6% because they are classified as agricultural products; raising the tax rate to 19% was estimated to raise some EUR 0.4 billion in additional revenue, while also reducing environmental impacts related to their cultivation.

5.2. Exemptions in energy taxes

There are a number of exemptions and refund mechanisms in Dutch energy taxes, mainly benefiting large-scale users (Section 3.1). These include a refund of the energy tax for large industrial electricity consumers if they enter into long-term agreements on energy efficiency with the government and pay on average more per kWh than the EU minimum tax rate; reduced natural gas tax rates for the horticulture sector if it participates in energy efficiency agreements; and rebates and subsidies for energy distribution firms to deploy combined heat and power, energy-saving technologies and renewable electricity.

A red colour is being added to diesel for use in activities such as construction, agriculture, coastal and inland shipping, and diesel locomotives. This makes it administratively possible to apply a lower tax rate or to exempt such uses completely from taxation. PBL (2011) indicates that an abolition of these tax preferences could increase government revenues by approximately EUR 235 million. However, some of these tax preferences (e.g. regarding coastal and inland shipping) result from international agreements that the Netherlands cannot change unilaterally. As of 1 January 2013, the red diesel tax preference was abandoned for leisure vessels.

PBL (2011) also referred to a study by De Visser et al. (2011), which estimated that end-use of fossil energy received government support of EUR 4.4 billion, mainly through tax reductions and exemptions. The study estimated the price that would have applied if all environmental costs had been internalised. The difference between this price and the one actually paid by large-scale users was counted as the environmentally harmful subsidy, representing a cost of about EUR 1.8 billion. However, while external costs ought to be internalised in fuel prices for all users, it is not common OECD practice to count non-internalised externalities as part of support estimates.

5.3. *Other environmentally harmful subsidies*

PBL (2011) indicates there is an agreement that the government accepts a lower-than-normal return on its shares in Amsterdam Airport Schiphol. To the extent that this contributes to higher activity levels at the airport, this could also be seen as an environmentally harmful subsidy.

6. Investing in the environment to promote green growth

6.1. *Environment-related components of the fiscal stimulus packages*

As in many OECD member countries, the Netherlands supported the economic recovery by introducing discretionary fiscal measures of above 2% of GDP over 2009-10 (OECD, 2010). Environment-related measures were estimated at 6% of the total package or 0.15% of 2009 GDP (Table 3.2). They included various instruments aiming to support the construction and car sectors, as well as renewable energy generation and energy saving. The fiscal stimulus turned the 2008 budget surplus of 0.7% into a deficit of over 5% of GDP in 2009, leading the government to adopt successive consolidation plans. Government spending was cut significantly, particularly on environmental protection. At the same time, some implicit subsidies increased, in particular the foregone revenue from tax reduction for low-emitting vehicles (Section 3.5).

Table 3.2. **Environment-related components of the fiscal stimulus package**

Measure	Description	Budget (EUR million)
Investments in innovation and sustainability	Subsidy to support investment in renewable energy, environmental technologies and infrastructure	232 (2009-10)
Energy saving in housing	Subsidy to support energy efficiency	320 (2009-10)
Car scrapping scheme	Subsidy to buy environmentally friendly vehicles	65 (2009-10)
Wind energy at sea	Subsidy to support investment in wind energy sector	175 (2010-11), then 160 million each year after 2011
Green tax allowances	Additional funding for existing tax allowances for companies investing in sustainable production facilities (VAMIL/MIA)	60 (2009-10)
Total		**852**

Source: Government of the Netherlands (2014).

6.2. *Expenditure for environmental protection*

Over the past decade, public and business environmental expenditure[18] increased broadly in line with economic growth before declining at the same pace in the aftermath of the global economic crisis. As a result, it remained at around 2% of GDP, a relatively high level compared with other European countries. The public and business sectors (including private specialised producers of environmental services) bear an almost equal share of environmental expenditure (Figure 3.9). As in other OECD member countries, waste and wastewater management are the main expenditure items, accounting for about 60% of the

Figure 3.9. **Reduced environmental expenditure in the wake of the economic crisis**

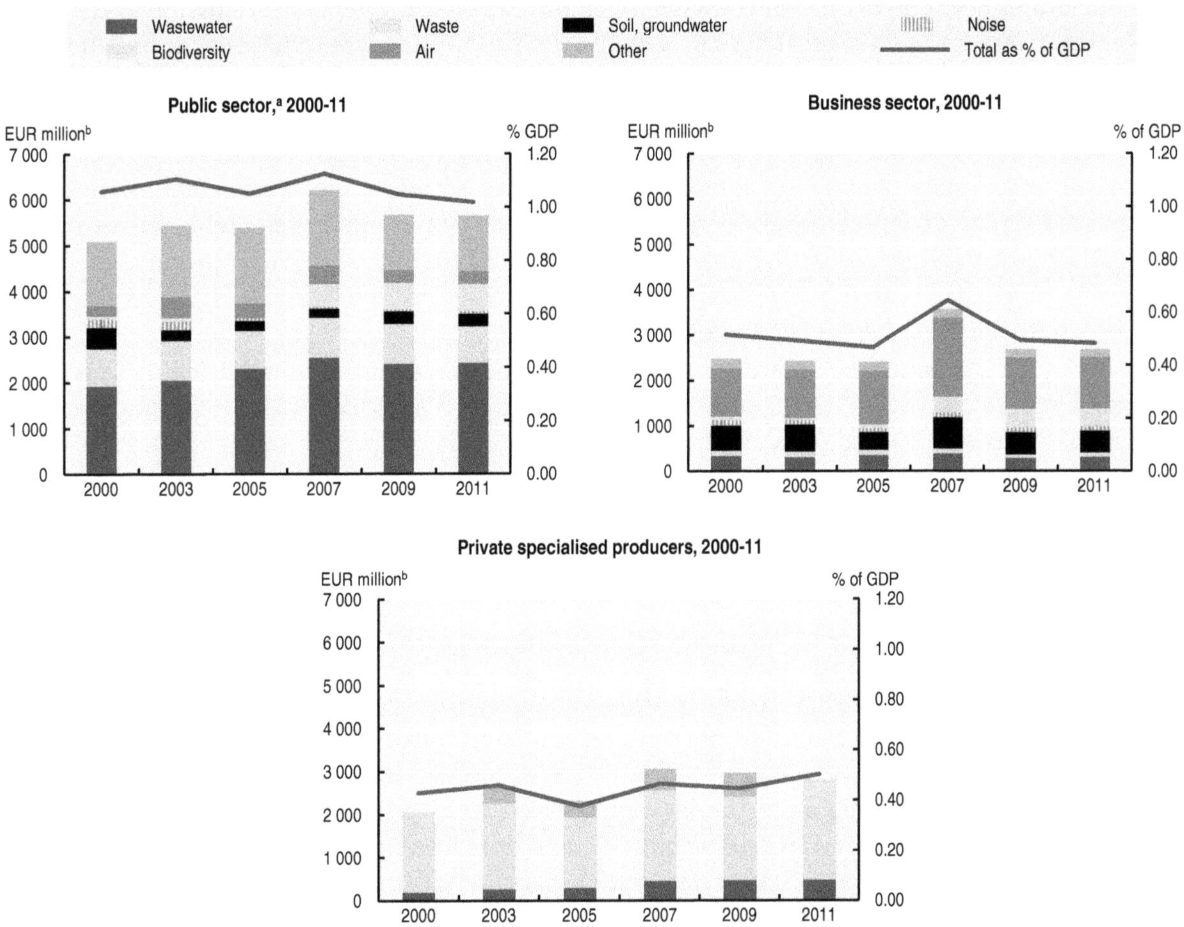

Note: Data refer to investment and internal current expenditure (excluding payments to specialised producers of environmental protection services) less receipts from by-products (e.g. material recovered as a result of waste treatment). Includes expenditure on i) pollution abatement and control covering air protection, waste and wastewater management, protection and remediation of soil and groundwater, and other environmental protection activities (R&D, administration, education); and ii) biodiversity and landscape protection. Excludes expenditure on water supply.

a) Including public specialised producers of environmental protection services.

b) At 2005 prices.

Source: OECD (2014), *OECD Environment Statistics* (database).

StatLink http://dx.doi.org/10.1787/888933280268

total. Spending on wastewater treatment is mostly incurred by municipalities and regional water authorities. Waste management activities have been increasingly contracted out to specialised operators, but a large part continues to be carried out by municipalities and through inter-municipal co-operation (CBS, 2012).

Between 2000 and 2011, investment in waste and wastewater management, as well as protection of air and climate, grew by more than 30%, although 2011 levels remained below their pre-crisis levels. Investment in wastewater treatment has grown faster than all other domains. This has allowed the Netherlands to comply with the Urban Wastewater Treatment Directive and to meet the highest treatment standards (OECD, 2014d). Despite irregular patterns linked to changes in incentive schemes, investment in air and climate protection has grown from 60% to about 75% of business environmental investment, which reflects the growth of renewable energy (CBS, 2011). The one-off increase in 2007 is explained by investment in environment-friendly livestock buildings to reduce ammonia emissions through improved manure discharge (CBS, 2010).

Statistics Netherlands also calculates environmental costs incurred by sector (including households) net of transfers from other sectors. Overall, net environmental costs decreased by 4% in real terms over 2001-11. In 2011, enterprises continued to bear the largest part (38%) of these costs. However, between 2001-11, there was a shift from business to households, whose share increased from 27% to 31%. This is explained by higher subsidies for renewables energy, which have reduced the cost to business for the protection of air and climate, and by rising household spending for waste and wastewater charges (CBS, 2011). In 2011, the government contributed 32% of net environmental costs, as in 2001, but with larger cost for air protection and reduced cost for waste management.

6.3. *Expenditure on water management*

In 2012, expenditure on water management by public institutions and drinking water companies totalled EUR 6.7 billion or 1.1% of GDP[19] (OECD, 2014d). Wastewater management accounted for about half of this total, water supply for one-third and flood management for the remainder. Regional water authorities incurred the largest share of expenditure by far (42%), followed by municipalities (20%), drinking water companies (21%) and the national government (15%). The provinces have a relatively small share (2%) of expenditures for water management tasks.

Regional transfers are limited. An estimated 80% of the total public budget for water resources is spent by regional and local-scale water institutions in their own territory, which finance their budgets mostly from local charges. However, part of the costs of water-related services (in particular for flood protection) are funded by the central government and financed from general tax revenues. There is significant variation in municipal sewerage levies, as well as in the levies for wastewater treatment and water system management of the 24 regional water authorities. Prices for drinking water varied between EUR 1.09-2.07 per m^3 in 2012. Dutch tariffs for water services appear in the upper end of tariffs monitored in OECD member countries. Overall, Dutch tap water quality is high.

Overall, the Netherlands has a robust financing system for water resources management based on the user pays and polluter pays principles. Nearly all financial costs[20] of service[21] provision are recovered through water charges and levies on discharges, water pollution and groundwater abstractions (European Commission, 2012a). However, the contribution from the various sectors (households, agriculture and industry) to cost recovery is unclear as is the extent to which price incentives stimulate efficient water use. Abstraction charges for bulk water supply are almost completely absent (OECD, 2014d). The recent abolition of the central government's groundwater tax also undermines the fuller application of the user pays principle. The polluter pays principle is not applied to diffuse sources of pollution, a main driver of inadequate water quality. The ecological quality of surface waters does not meet the objectives of the Water Framework Directive in part due to over-fertilisation in agricultural areas.

6.4. *Investment in renewables and energy efficiency*

In past years, the policy and investment framework for renewable energy and energy efficiency has been characterised by relative instability (IEA, 2014). After the ambitious energy and climate agenda[22] of 2007-08 was revised downwards, the Netherlands has been following the EU policy (IEA, 2009). The 2020 EU climate and energy package translates into the national targets of a 14% share of renewables in gross final energy consumption and a GHG emissions reduction (for the non-ETS sector) of 16% by 2020, below 2005 levels. The

2013 Energy Agreement for Sustainable Growth adopted between the Dutch government, businesses, trade unions and nongovernmental organisations (NGOs) set targets to i) save 1.5% in final energy consumption annually by 2020[23] and ii) raise the share of renewable energy in final energy consumption to 16% in 2023 (Box 3.1).

Box 3.1. **Main objectives of the 2013 Energy Agreement for Sustainable Growth**

- Achieve energy savings and energy efficiency in the buildings, industry, commercial, transport and agriculture sectors of around 100 petajoules (PJ) by 2020.
- Scale-up renewable energy generation, notably on- and offshore wind capacities, and stimulate biomass in coal-fired power stations up to a maximum of 25 PJ by 2020. Specific SDE+ funds to be dedicated to research, development and deployment (RD&D) support for renewable energy demonstration and deployment.
- Encourage locally generated renewable energy.
- Complete the energy transmission network.
- Encourage properly functioning EU ETS, ensuring international competitiveness of energy-intensive companies.
- Phase-out the least efficient coal-fired power stations and develop carbon capture and storage.
- Reduce CO_2 emissions of the transport sector by 17% by 2030 and by 60% by 2050 (below 1990 levels).
- Promote employment and training in the installation and construction sectors and, in the longer term, in the renewable energy sector (approximately 15 000 extra jobs from 2017 onwards).
- Encourage commercialisation of new technologies for growth and export to join the global Top 10 Cleantech rankings by 2030.
- Leverage financing of investments in renewable energy and energy-saving projects

Source: IEA (2014).

Renewable energy sources

The Netherlands has a complex system of incentives supporting investment in renewable energy. The main instruments are a subsidy scheme, the Energy Investment Tax Allowance (Section 3.5) and the biofuel blending requirement. In the past decade, budget concerns have led the government to introduce several changes in the subsidy system (IEA, 2014). A first feed-in premium scheme (MEP) was introduced in 2003. Domestic producers of electricity (and combined heat and power) from renewable sources that feed-in to the national grid were provided a fixed subsidy per kWh, depending on technology, on top of the price of wholesale electricity. In 2008, it was replaced by a modified feed-in tariff system (SDE) that guaranteed a fixed subsidy with an option for a higher price per kWh if the electricity price went above the feed-in tariff price (IEA, 2009). Unlike the MEP, SDE annual expenditures were capped per technology and excluded biomass co-firing with coal in power plants. MEP and SDE were financed through the government budget. About EUR 630 million was paid annually on average over 2005-13 (EEA, 2014a). Payments are still ongoing as the subsidies run for 10-15 years, although MEP payments were coming to an end in 2013 (RVO, 2014b).

In 2011, SDE was transformed into the SDE+, a floating feed-in premium system based on a competitive tendering process with a gradual shift of funding from the state budget to final consumers (Section 4.2) (Ecofys, 2014). Compared to the SDE, it covers renewable heat in addition to renewable electricity and gas, and has one overall annual budget for all technologies. SDE+ aims to provide incentives for the deployment of renewable energy at the lowest possible cost.

MEP and SDE have stimulated renewable energy deployment, mainly biomass co-firing (until 2013) and onshore wind energy. Electricity production from renewable energy has quadrupled since 2000 (Chapter 1). However, the schemes have not been sufficiently effective to achieve interim targets of the National Renewable Energy Action Plan adopted in 2010 under the EU's Renewable Energy Directive (2009/28/EC). With a 4.5% share of renewables in gross final energy consumption in 2012, the Netherlands is not on track to meet either its 2020 objective of 14% or its 2023 target of 16% (ECN, 2014; EEA, 2014b). The budget of the support schemes has been underspent due to several market barriers. These include relatively strong opposition to wind energy and subsidies considered too low to make biomass and solar electricity projects profitable (Van der Elst and Bosch, 2012).

With the implementation of SDE+, the share of renewable energy is expected to grow significantly from 2017 onwards (ECN, 2014). However, this positive forecast is subject to favourable development of uncertainties surrounding co-firing of biomass in coal-fired plants and operation of delayed large offshore wind projects. Under the 2013 Energy Agreement, government and industry agreed to open the scheme to offshore wind. The Offshore Wind Energy Act, expected to enter into force in 2015, should help expedite the permitting and subsidy process. It makes the government (instead of permit applicants) responsible for spatial planning arrangements, environmental impact assessment and connection to the grid of the proposed wind projects (RVO, 2014c). Regulations are being developed to support biomass in coal-fired power plants under SDE+, capped at a maximum of 25 PJ and under stringent Dutch sustainability criteria in line with the Energy Agreement (RVO, 2014b).

Energy efficiency

The Netherlands has implemented an extensive set of measures to promote energy efficiency across all economic sectors (Minister of Economic Affairs, Minister of the Interior and Kingdom Relations, 2014). In the building sector, minimum energy performance standards and performance certificates have been introduced. A reduced VAT rate applies to insulation works. Since 2013, a fund of EUR 300 million has been directed towards landlords and tenants to finance energy-saving technology and measures (Section 3.5) (EEA, 2014b). The programme "More with Less", combines customised advice for residential energy users with subsidies for undertaking energy saving measures.

The government has also entered into long-term agreements with companies in industry, agriculture and the service sector that have reportedly provided large savings. Under these voluntary agreements, companies commit to implement energy efficiency plans in return for an exemption from energy taxes (Section 5.2). Cogeneration of electricity and heat is also fostered by lowering investment costs. Support to combined heat and power, particularly in horticulture, has significantly contributed to energy savings. However, questions remain about whether taxing energy use in these sectors would have provided better environmental outcomes (PBL, 2011). In the transport sector, energy efficiency is promoted through European vehicle standards and fiscal preferences for the purchase of more efficient vehicles (Chapter 4, Section 4.3). In addition, all sectors can benefit from tax incentives for investment in energy-saving technologies and sustainable energy production under the Energy Investment Tax Allowance. Green investment schemes also provide for investment deductions and accelerated depreciation (VAMIL and MIA). These instruments have stimulated large investment in clean energy over the past decade (Figure 3.10). The large growth in 2013 was essentially due to investment in low-emitting vehicles. Questions remain about whether such investments would have been made without support, as well as the resulting windfall gains. The impact of individual measures is difficult to assess, as they sometimes overlap[24] and interact with other factors (e.g. energy prices) and policy instruments[25] (Ruijs and Vollebergh, 2013; Minister of Economic Affairs, Minister of the Interior and Kingdom Relations, 2014) (Section 4.3).

Figure 3.10. **Large investments in clean energy over the past decade**

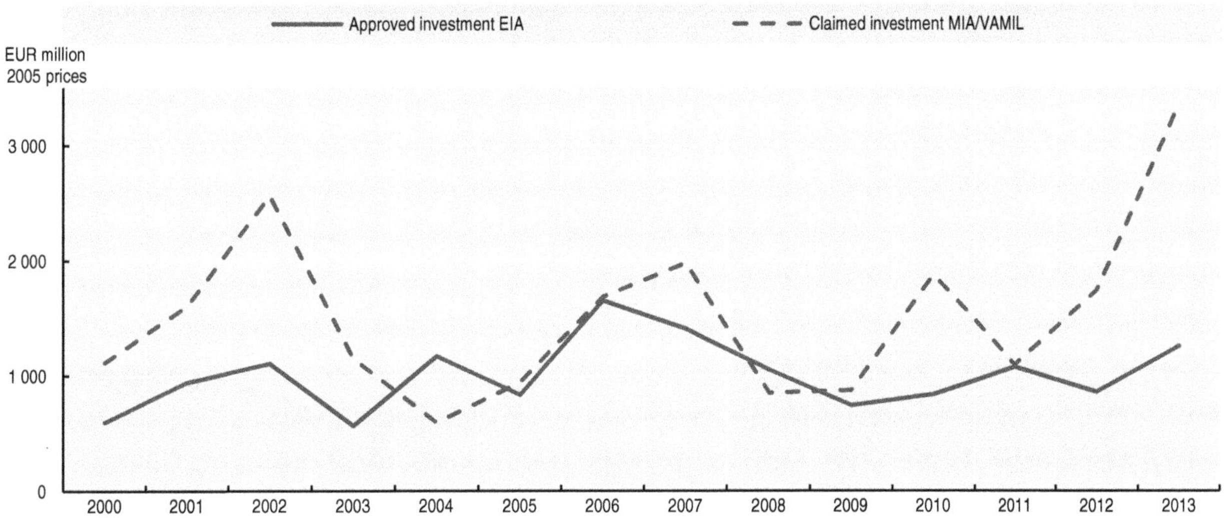

Note: EIA: Energy Investment Tax Allowance (tax incentives for investment in energy-saving technologies); MIA,VAMIL: investment deductions and accelerated depreciation for green investment.
Source: Netherlands Enterprise Energy (2014), *Energie Investeringsaftrek (EIA), Jaarverslag 2013;* Netherlands Enterprise Energy (2014), *MIA en Vamil Jaarverslag 2013*; NL Agency (2013), *MIA en Vamil Jaarverslag 2012*; SIS (2015), *ODYSSEE-MURE* (database).

StatLink http://dx.doi.org/10.1787/888933280275

The Netherlands has exceeded its 2010 intermediate target[26] under the Energy Service Directive (2006/32/EC). In the period to 2020, existing measures are expected to deliver an annual efficiency improvement rate of 0.7-1.2%. Additional measures from the Energy Agreement could raise this rate to 1.0-1.4%, keeping the Dutch objective under the European Energy Efficiency Directive (2012/27/EU) within reach. However, this will not be sufficient to achieve the Energy Agreement target of additional energy efficiency improvement of 100 PJ in 2020 (ECN, 2014). The evaluation of the 2013 Energy Agreement, planned in 2016, should provide the basis for reviewing the set of instruments.

7. The environmental goods and services sector

In 2012, the environmental goods and services sector (EGSS) accounted for 2.1% of GDP and 1.8% of employment (130 000 full-time equivalent) (Figure 3.11). This is broadly in line with the EU average considering the differences in coverage among countries (OECD, 2014e). As in other OECD member countries, waste[27] and wastewater management, renewable energy and energy saving (including insulation) are the most important activities,

Figure 3.11. **The environmental goods and services sector grew faster than the whole Dutch economy**

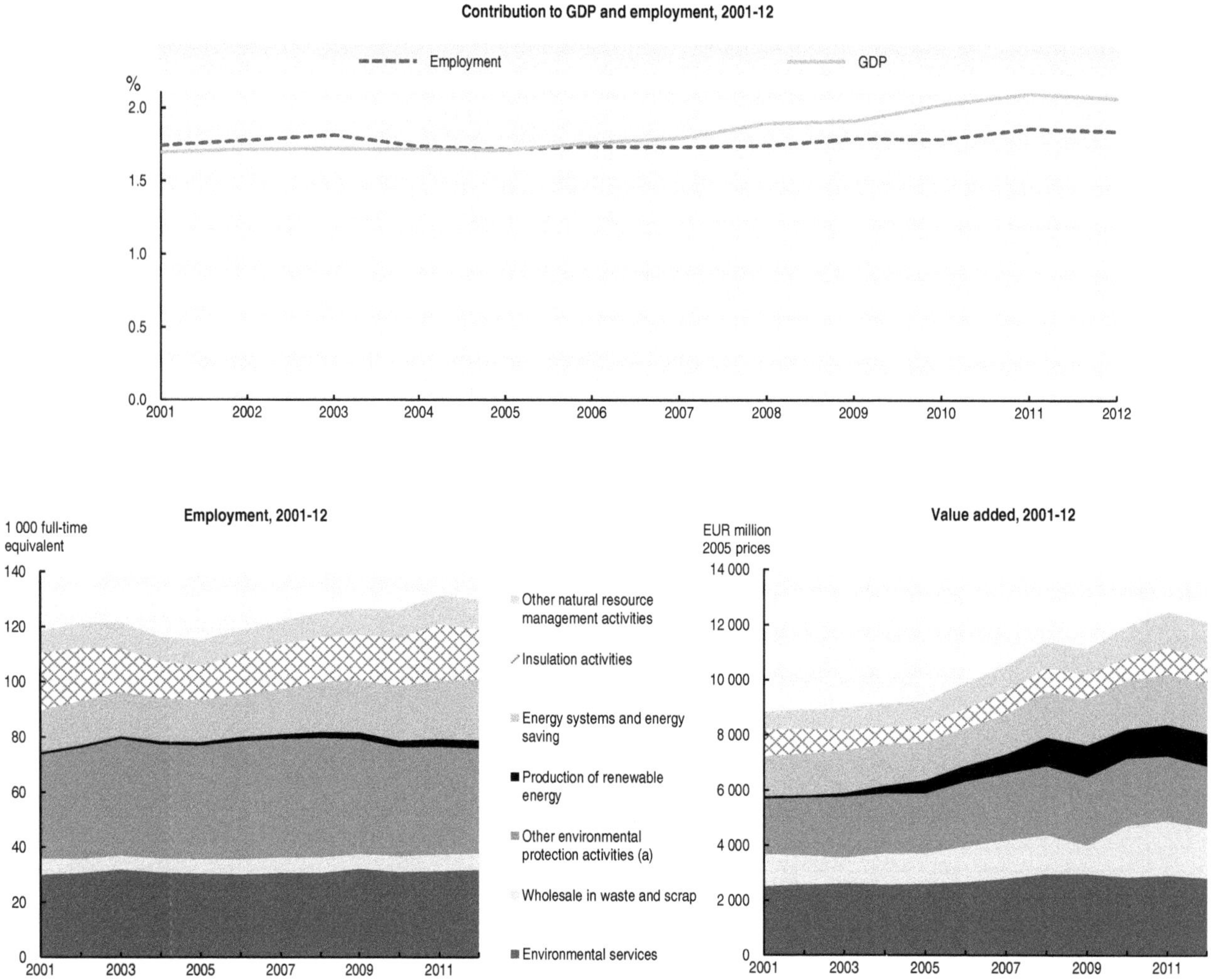

Note: The environmental goods and services sector (EGSS) consists of a group of companies and authorities involved in activities with respect to measuring, preventing, limiting, minimising or correcting environmental damage to water, air and soil, and problems related to waste, noise and ecosystems. This definition includes "cleaner technologies" and "cleaner goods and services" that reduce environmental risk and minimise the use of natural resources and pollution.

a) Other environmental protection includes activities related to: government administration, consultancy and engineering, construction, production of industrial equipments, organic agriculture, in-house activities, inspections and certifications, philanthropic organisations and education.

Source: CBS (2015), *StatLine* (database).

StatLink http://dx.doi.org/10.1787/888933280289

accounting together for 70% of value added and 60% of employment in the EGSS. Despite its relatively small size, the EGSS grew faster than the whole Dutch economy in the past decade, in particular since 2005.

The production of renewable energy has been the fastest growing activity both in terms of value added and employment, reflecting increased generation of heat, electricity and biogas from biomass and more wind and solar energy production (CBS, 2014a, 2013) (Figure 3.11). Activities in the renewable energy value chain[28] (energy systems and energy saving) have also benefited from this growth. Since the early 2000s, employment in waste and wastewater management services has remained relatively stable, while the increasing trend in related value added reversed with the economic downturn. By contrast, wholesale in waste and scrap, as well as recycling activities, quickly recovered from the crisis, driven by international demand for used metals and increased re-export of waste and scrap materials. Employment in other environmental protection activities remained steady overall, but government administration[29] of environmental protection lost 4 200 out of 13 000 full-time jobs between 2007-12. On the other hand, despite their relatively small contribution to the EGSS, employment and value added in environmental analysis and control, as well as organic agriculture, increased steadily.

8. Promoting environmental technology and eco-innovation

8.1. *General innovation performance*

The Netherlands is a strong performer in the area of innovation. It is among the world leaders in patenting activity, which is mostly performed by large companies. In 2012, gross domestic expenditure on research and development (R&D) accounted for 2.2% of GDP, which was above the EU average. Still, it was significantly below R&D intensities in other OECD member countries with advanced innovation systems such as Korea (4.4%), Finland (3.6%), Sweden (3.4%) and Japan (3.3%) (OECD, 2014f). While government spending on R&D as a share of GDP was on par with these other advanced systems, business expenditure was closer to the EU average. After a period of relative stability in 2000-10, projections for R&D intensity are uncertain: public expenditure on R&D is set to decrease over 2012-18[30] and the growth of business expenditure is yet to be confirmed[31] (van Steen, 2014).

Concerns over international competitiveness led the Dutch government to adopt the Top Sectors policy in 2011. It focuses public resources on nine sectors in which the Netherlands has a competitive advantage (agri-food, horticulture and propagation materials, high-tech systems and materials, energy, logistics, creative industry, life sciences, chemicals and water). The policy seeks to leverage business R&D, foster co-ordination of businesses, government and knowledge institutes and maximise economic impact (OECD, 2014f). However, achieving the R&D intensity target of 2.5% by 2020 will be challenging without sufficient public support.

8.2. *Performance on eco-innovation*

Public spending on environment-related R&D declined from more than 3% of the total government budget on R&D in the early 2000s to slightly less than 1% of the total in 2012-13, below the OECD average (Figure 3.12) (OECD, 2014e). This share is projected to decrease further to 0.5% in 2018, partly due to the budget cut of the Netherlands Environmental Assessment Agency (PBL) (van Steen, 2014). Public investment in energy RD&D rose between 2005-10, plummeted in 2011[32] and only partially recovered in 2012 (IEA, 2014) (Figure 3.12). The share of energy spending in the government's R&D budget, already lower than in most other OECD member countries, is planned to be halved from about 2% in 2012-13 to 1% in 2018. This is due in part to the reduced budget of the Energy Research Centre (ECN). There are doubts that private resources will compensate for the shortfall in public funding, as intended by the Top Sectors approach (van Steen, 2014; Korting, 2015). Over 2011-13, about EUR 300 million was allocated to the Energy Top Sector, out of which about 40% came from private funds. Bioenergy, natural and bio-based gas, and solar energy were the largest investment areas (ECN, 2014).

Over 2000-11, the Netherlands developed a comparative advantage[33] in technologies related to energy efficiency in lighting, energy generation from biofuels and waste and CO_2 capture and storage (CCS). In 2009-11, environment-related technologies accounted for 10%

Figure 3.12. **Public R&D spending on energy and environment rose then dropped sharply**

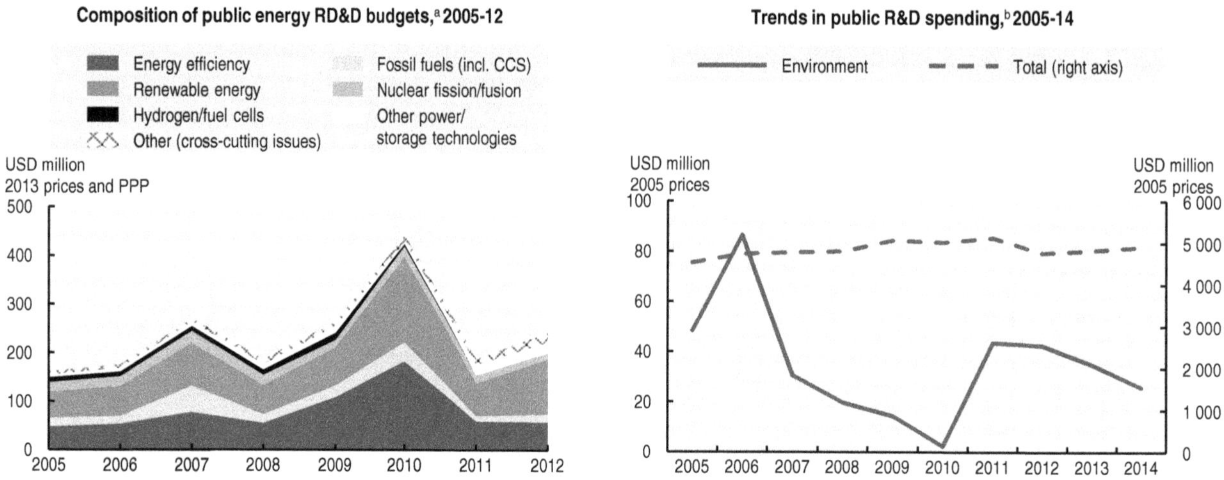

a) Government budgets for research, development and demonstration (RD&D).
b) Government budget appropriations or outlays for R&D; breakdown according to the NABS 2007 classification; environment: excluding R&D funded from General University Funds. 2014: Provisional data including estimates and projections.
Source: IEA(2015), *IEA Energy Technology and RD&D Statistics* (database); OECD (2015), *OECD Science, Technology and R&D Statistics* (database).

StatLink http://dx.doi.org/10.1787/888933280291

of overall patent applications associated with inventors located in the Netherlands, up from 6% in the early 2000s. Although an increasing number of patent applications have been filed for technologies related to water pollution abatement, there has been a shift in focus from general environmental management to climate- and energy-related technologies, as in other OECD member countries (Figure 3.13). In 2009-11, the Netherlands ranked fifteenth and fourteenth in the OECD in terms of patent applications in environment-related technologies per GDP and per capita, respectively. Despite this relatively good position, the Netherlands seems to have lost ground in recent years. Between 2010-13, it fell from seventh to thirteenth place in the EU Eco-Innovation Scoreboard,[34] below the EU average (EIO, 2014).

The Netherlands as a whole is lagging behind large innovative economies and close competitors in terms of green innovation (Dechezleprêtre et al., 2013) (Annex 3.A). It has a relatively small number of sectors with a rapid rate of green innovation and a relatively large number of sectors with a slow rate of green innovation. The sectors of food production and processing, and manufacturing of radio and television equipment, have a strong green competitive position, whereas the basic chemicals sector is putting its comparative advantage at risk by a sluggish green innovation activity.

8.3. The eco-innovation policy framework

A strong environmental regulatory and policy framework has been a major driver of Dutch eco-innovation policy. Tight regulations, combined with the introduction of a levy on water pollution in the 1970s, allowed the financing of large investments in water purification, sparked R&D and innovation, and created technical and technological capital in the area of water technology. The country is still one of the world leaders in this area (Van der Veen and Ploeg, 2013). However, more recently, the Netherlands abandoned its leadership role in environmental policy to follow EU policy. Changes in energy and climate policies, and the lack of long-term directions for the development of innovative energy options, reduce the chance of a successful energy transition (CBS, 2014b).

Figure 3.13. **Patent applications shift towards climate- and energy-related technologies**

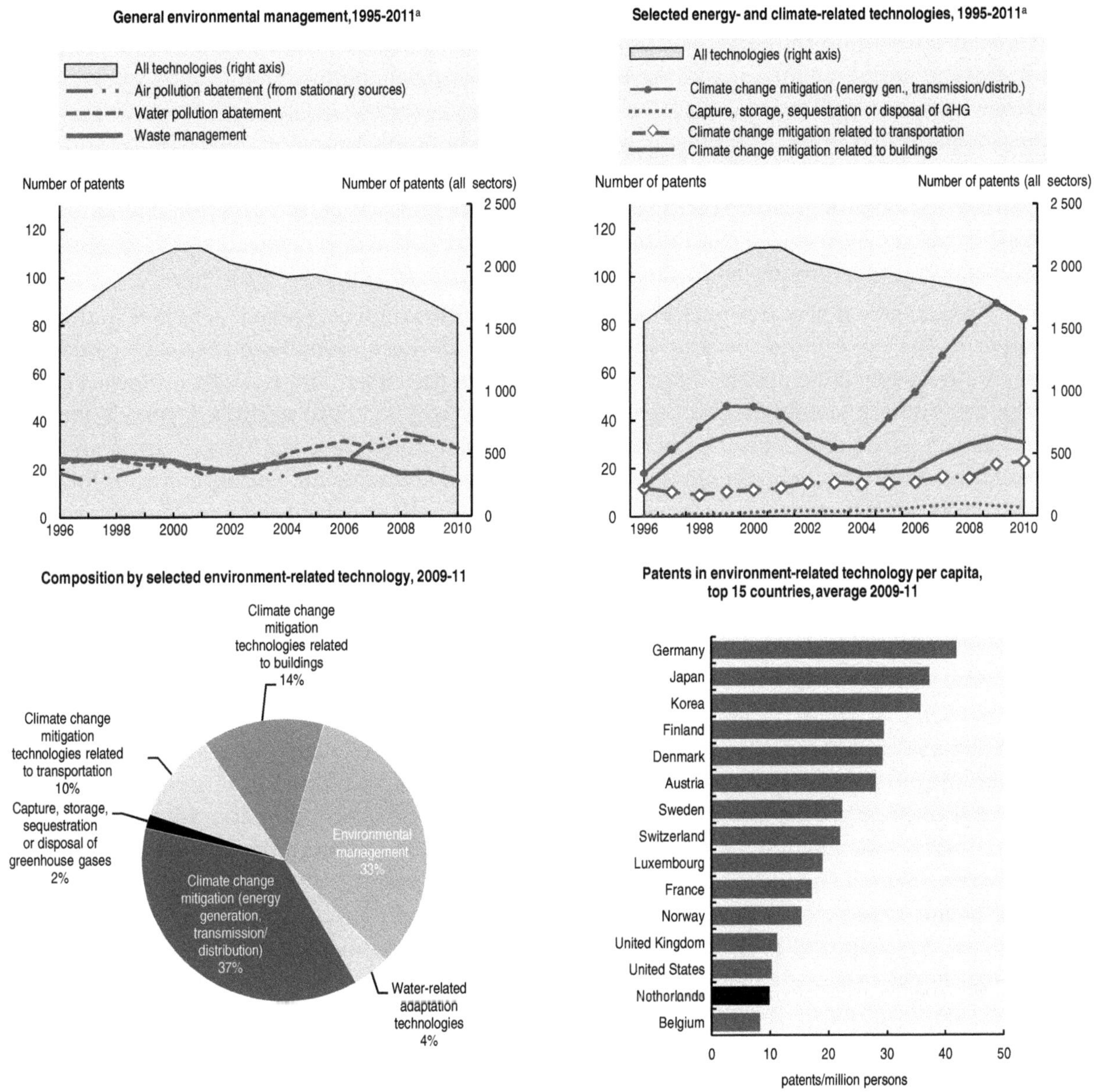

Note: Patent applications for environment-related technologies having sought protection in at least two jurisdictions. Data refer to fractional counts of patents based on the priority date and the inventor's country of residence.

a) Three-year moving average data.

Source: OECD (2015), "Patents in environment-related technologies : Technology development by inventor country", *OECD Environment Statistics* (database).

StatLink http://dx.doi.org/10.1787/888933280303

Since 2011, the Top Sectors policy has aimed to prioritise R&D in areas of Dutch expertise, and address market and government failures (Gerritsen and Høj, 2013). These failures include limited knowledge transfer from universities, lack of co-ordination among different branches of the government, overly detailed sector regulation and an insufficient supply of skilled workers. The selection criteria included sectors that are knowledge-intensive and export-oriented, and that could make an important contribution to solving societal issues. Research and innovation are to be strengthened via "innovation contracts" based on public-private partnership agreements at the sector level. There are no additional public resources available, but part of existing resources is explicitly allocated to the top sectors. Private sector demand is given a larger role in the work of the research institutions. In addition, long-term partnerships between industry and research bodies within top sectors is promoted via an additional tax credit for participation in Top Consortia for Knowledge and Innovation (TKIs). The Top Sector Energy consists of seven TKIs in offshore wind, gas, smart grids, energy consumption in the built environment, solar energy and, shared with the Chemicals Top Sector, bio-based economy and sustainable process technology. The water sector includes water and delta technology (eco-engineering, water safety, smart dykes and liveable Delta), maritime construction (clean and cleverly designed ships), water as a resource and water purification (OECD, 2014d).

In the context of scarce public resources, the prioritisation of research activities in the areas of the top sectors could be justified, insofar as these earmarked activities could create relatively large positive (knowledge) spillovers (Gerritsen and Høj, 2013). However, the government should ensure these earmarked activities do not become a vehicle for favouring particular industries or firms. A particular concern is that larger firms and existing industries are better organised than SMEs and emerging industries, and can thus gain from a "first-mover" advantage in dealing with public support schemes. These risks can be mitigated by having mechanisms in place to permit the withdrawal of support at the appropriate stage and to ensure accountability and transparency. An assessment of the Top Sectors initiative is scheduled for 2015 (Warwick and Nolan, 2014). In 2013, a specific scheme (MIT) was introduced to strengthen innovative SMEs in top sectors.

The Top Sector policy focuses strongly on innovation, but pays less attention to green innovation (PBL, 2014). Although many plans identify sustainability as important, they do not always result in concrete proposals. In only three of the nine top sectors, sustainability is an integral part of plans and innovation contracts. The combination of greening and competitiveness is even less often the focus. Top sectors are mainly demand-driven rather than based on a vision for the future, which might erode attention for more long-term oriented research (Van der Veen and Ploeg, 2013). As an example, over 2011-13, the Energy Top Sector gave priority to technology development and demonstration with reduced allocations to applied research. This creates a gap in the innovation chain and raises concerns about the adequacy of research funding for achieving the renewable energy targets of the Energy Agreement (Korting, 2015).

There is room for developing a more active eco-innovation policy that provides directions and helps target funding in areas where green innovation will support Dutch competitiveness (PBL, 2014). PBL identified the sustainable built environment and the circular economy as opportunities to seize on the model of the cross-sector bio-based agenda. The "Waste to Resource" programme being prepared by the Ministry of Infrastructure and the Environment lays the ground for a long-term strategy on the circular economy (Chapter 5). It aims to support sustainable design, new business models (Box 3.2) and the dissemination and structuring of innovation to make the Netherlands a hot spot of the circular economy in 2020 (Ministry of Infrastructure and the Environment, 2014). The Top Sectors policy does not emphasise service sectors, which account for a large part of the value added stemming from exports. They could be better supported by giving more attention to non-technological innovation. The OECD made this recommendation for the water sector where innovation has generated a certain degree of path-dependency based on conventional infrastructure approaches (OECD, 2014d).

Box 3.2. Turntoo: New business models for resource efficiency

Turntoo, a Dutch company, has based its business model on an alternative system in which products are not sold by the producer to the consumer, but remain the property of the producer throughout their life cycles. This approach has several environmental benefits. Because producers derive their profits from its use rather than its sale, they have an incentive to make the product as durable and efficient as possible. In addition, producer ownership means that once a product reaches the end of its life, the producer will collect and reuse it, preventing products from becoming waste. Finally, producers have an incentive to make them as reusable as possible.

For example, a German precision engineering company provides washing machines to a Dutch social housing provider, which will initially pay EUR 10 per month for the washing machine service (including energy and water). Later, tenants will pay per wash. Tenants will receive top-end washing machines with the highest energy efficiency ratings. The housing provider will be faced with fewer tenants who cannot pay their rent because of rising energy costs.

The full environmental benefits of the scheme have not been quantified. However, because the washing machines are high quality and result in energy and water savings, GHG emission reductions are expected (compared to the lower standard washing machines that tenants might otherwise have). The scheme is also resource efficient: the washing machine parts and embodied raw materials will ultimately be reused. For companies, a recurring business model with a constant revenue stream from machine use will smooth out the peaks and troughs of demand cycles that occur with the traditional "sale for ownership" business model. Companies can manage their resources better, because they will know how many washing machines have been leased and therefore which recyclable and reusable materials will come back to them.

Source: http://ec.europa.eu/environment/ecoap/about-eco-innovation/good-practices/netherlands/201211126-turnto-final_en.htm.

There is no specific eco-innovation plan. However, related activities have been supported through various generic measures (investment support for joint R&D projects within the top sectors; fiscal incentives for R&D) and specific instruments (direct support for sustainable energy; tax incentives for investment in energy-saving technologies and sustainable energy production; green investment; low-emitting vehicles and insulation works). In some cases, however, such as subsidies for renewable energy, their design has hindered the development of more innovative technologies (Section 4 and 6). Better reflecting environmental externalities in energy or water prices could help enhance efficiency in allocating resources. Since the beginning of this decade, there has been a shift from direct funding of research and innovation to indirect funding, through tax incentives. These instruments were found to have positive indirect effects on innovation and labour productivity (Warwick and Nolan, 2014). However, although such tax incentives ensure a more market-based selection of research projects, they leave little room for steering research resources into areas with (perceived) high social returns. In addition, they involve significant deadweight losses and tend to benefit incumbent firms more than young SMEs, which often lack taxable income to take advantages of tax reliefs (Gerritsen and Høj, 2013).

Green Deals were introduced in 2011 to remove regulatory barriers to green innovation (Chapter 2). These agreements between the government, companies, civil society organisations and sub-national governments (provinces and municipalities) help address the concrete problems faced by parties concerning legislation and licensing. They have been particularly successful in the energy sector (PBL, 2014). Close to 200 Green Deals have been concluded so far covering a broad spectrum of themes, including energy, climate, water resources, biodiversity, bio-based economy, food, construction and mobility. Involving the Ministry of Education, Culture and Science more closely in their development may make the Deals more conducive to innovation.

The Netherlands is among the most advanced EU countries in green public procurement (European Commission, 2012b). It has had a dedicated National Action Plan since 2003, revised in 2007. In 2005, the government resolved to achieve 100% sustainable procurement by 2010. A report showed that 99.8% of procurement by the central government was sustainable in 2010. Other authorities scored around 85%, exceeding their own objectives (municipalities 75%, provinces 50% in 2010) (Padding, 2012). A recent evaluation confirmed the criteria are used on a broad scale (RIVM, 2014). The criteria result in reduced environmental pressure for half of the product groups. For the other half, the criteria have no impact due to faster developments in EU regulation. The National Institute for Public Health and the Environment (RIVM) recommended setting relative minimum requirements for criteria to evolve with market development, moving towards rewarding criteria and using life-cycle costing. In recent years, public procurement of innovation is gaining interest as part of the shift towards circular procurement.

9. Environment, trade and development

9.1. *Official development assistance*

In 2013, the Netherlands was the sixth-largest donor of the OECD Development Assistance Committee (DAC) in terms of official development assistance (ODA) as a percentage of gross national income (GNI) (Annex 3.A). Between 2000 and 2013, the Netherlands' net ODA decreased from 0.84% to 0.67% of GNI, below the 0.7% target for the first time since 1975 (OECD, 2014g) (Figure 3.14). The government remains committed to the target.[35] As part of its fiscal consolidation efforts, however, the government will cut EUR 3.3 billion from ODA over 2014-17 compared with a budget of EUR 4.1 billion in 2013 (MFA, 2014a, 2013). In the long-run, these budget cuts may exert a negative effect on the Dutch economy. The Evaluation Department of the Ministry of Foreign Affairs (MFA) estimated that each euro of Dutch bilateral aid produces a EUR 0.70-0.90 return from increased exports, leading to a value added of about EUR 0.40-0.55 for each euro spent (MFA, 2014b). This positive relationship between aid and trade remains, while tied aid has diminished substantially.

Since 2010, the focus of Dutch aid has shifted from social development towards economic sectors. It supports the self-reliance of developing countries and promotes relationships among development objectives, global public goods (such as climate) and Dutch national interests (OECD, 2011). In 2012, trade and aid were combined in one ministerial portfolio, namely Foreign Trade and Development. The priorities of the government are i) to eradicate extreme poverty in a single generation; ii) sustainable, inclusive growth all over the world; and iii) success for Dutch companies abroad (MFA, 2013).

The Netherlands has reduced the number of its partner countries from 33 to 15, and narrowed its thematic focus to four areas: i) security and the rule of law; ii) water; iii) food security; and iv) women's rights, and sexual and reproductive health and rights. The MFA delivers most of Dutch ODA. In 2014, its Climate, Energy, Environment and Water Department was transformed into the Global Public Goods Department with a view to

Figure 3.14. **Decrease in Dutch official development assistance as a share of GNI**

Net ODA disbursements, 2000-13

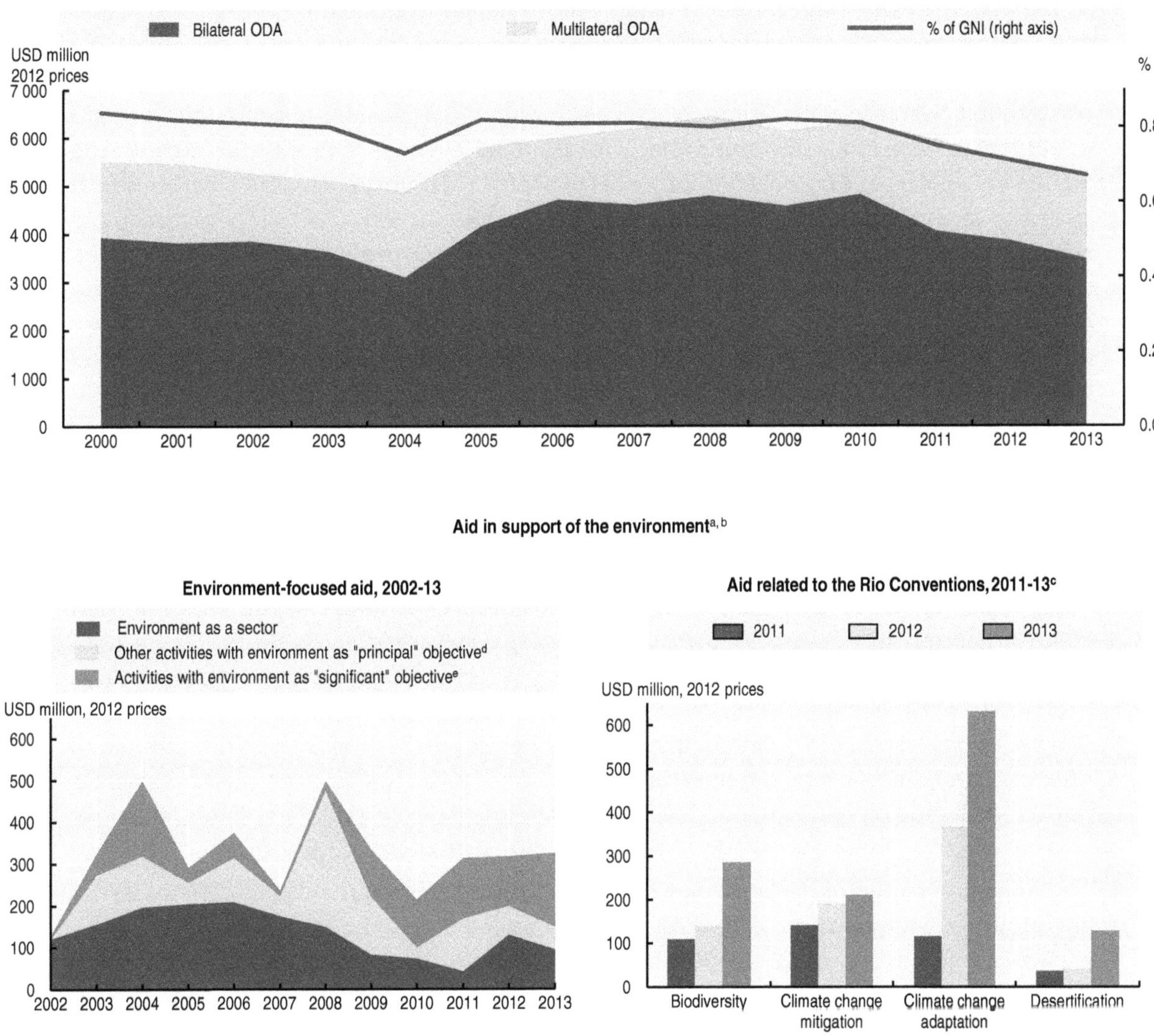

a) Commitments of total sector-allocable bilateral ODA.
b) The marker data do not allow exact quantification of amounts allocated or spent in support of the environment. They give an indication of such aid flows and describe the extent to which donors address these objectives in their aid programmes. The coverage ratio for activities screened against the environment policy marker is 100% of total sector-allocable aid.
c) Most activities targeting the objectives of the Rio Conventions fall under the definition of "environment-focused aid" but there is no exact match of the respective coverages. An activity can target the objectives of more than one of the conventions, thus respective ODA flows should not be added.
d) Activities where environment is an explicit objective of the activity and fundamental in its design.
e) Activities where environment is an important, but secondary, objective of the activity.
Source: OECD (2015), *OECD International Development Statistics* (database); OECD calculations.

StatLink http://dx.doi.org/10.1787/888933280317

adopt more integrated approaches and to make the water, energy, food, climate nexus operational. It was renamed as the Inclusive Green Growth Department. The department is responsible for the international sustainability agenda, including climate change. It co-operates with national and international partners such as the Netherlands Environmental Assessment Agency (NEA), the Netherlands Commission for Environmental Assessment (NCEA), the UNESCO-IHE Institute for Water Education, the Climate Development and Knowledge Network (CDKN), the World Resources Institute (WRI) and Dutch universities.

Aid to the environment sector accounted for 6-7% of sector-allocable bilateral ODA in the first half of the 2000s then fell to less than 2% in the aftermath of the crisis before rebounding to nearly 4% in 2012-13.[36] Since 2000, the drop in aid to the environment sector was only partially offset by bilateral aid for programmes with environmental objectives outside of the environment sector (in the energy, water and agriculture sectors). This has resulted in a decrease of environment-focused aid[37] to 10% of sector-allocable bilateral aid in 2012-13, a very low share compared with the DAC average of more than 30%. In the planned budget, spending on environment is expected to be further cut and environmental issues to be integrated into other priorities where relevant (MFA, 2013). By contrast, aid related to climate change has risen in the framework of the Copenhagen pledges to scale-up climate financing (Figure 3.14). Compared with other DAC donors, Dutch bilateral climate-related aid has a very strong focus on adaptation, rather than mitigation, notably for water management, climate-smart agriculture and emergency preparedness in least developed countries (OECD, 2014g). On average, over 2012-13, 18% of Netherlands' bilateral aid focused on climate change,[38] below the DAC average of 23%.

The Netherlands is regarded as an international leader on environment and climate change issues, particularly their impact on poor countries (OECD, 2011). Dutch climate funds have supported innovative schemes for capacity building in developing countries to enhance their access to carbon markets and also increase sustainable access to modern energy services for energy-poor people (OECD, 2011). Over 2008-14, the MFA invested EUR 500 million in renewable energy in developing countries, through a variety of channels, under the Promoting Renewable Energy Program. Although the programme had been effective in providing access to electricity, it resulted in only a modest reduction of CO_2 emissions (MFA, 2014c). Dutch private sector development programmes contributed to finance water, energy and transport infrastructures in low-income countries, but their impact, including on environment, is difficult to assess (MFA, 2014d). The Netherlands has also been leading innovative work on water and climate change adaptation.

All Dutch-supported interventions are screened for environment and climate issues during project preparation. The OECD recommended strengthening related expertise, particularly in partner countries (OECD, 2011). Although this capacity remains limited in Dutch embassies, three services were organised to provide technical assistance to the aid programmes: the Netherlands Water Partnership together with UNESCO-IHE for water; the Centre for Development Innovation of the Wageningen University for food security; and the Dutch Sustainability Unit (DSU) for environment and climate change. In addition, WRI seconded a staff member to the Dutch embassy in Uganda to provide technical assistance for integrating water, food security and climate change into partner countries in East and southern Africa. DSU was established in 2013 within the NCEA to provide, on request, support to both the MFA and the Dutch embassies. It is the key organisation in co-ordinating technical support on environment and climate change issues. The NCEA has also become a crucial support on strategic environmental assessment (SEA). Between 2000 and 2012, the NCEA assisted around 15 partner countries with the introduction of SEAs (OECD, 2012b).

9.2. Corporate social responsibility

The Netherlands actively promotes the OECD Guidelines for Multinational Enterprises.[39] The Dutch national contact point (NCP) has an allocated budget and four dedicated staff housed in the Ministry of Foreign Affairs[40] (OECD, 2014h). The NCP consists of four independent experts and, since 2013, of four advisory members from the Ministries of Economic Affairs; Foreign Affairs; Social Affairs and Employment; and Infrastructure and Environment. The NCP holds an advisory meeting four times a year with representatives from the most important civil society stakeholders. As part of the 2011 update of the guidelines, the role of the NCP was further strengthened. A 2014 decree entitled the government to ask the NCP to undertake cross-company research in serious circumstances and formalised stakeholder consultation. It also gave the NCP room to lead dialogues on CSR issues without formal notification about an alleged breach of the guidelines.

The Netherlands is among the OECD member countries with the largest number of specific instances reported to the NCP (OECD, 2014h). Since the establishment of a complaints procedure in 2001, the NCP has concluded 23 complaints out of which 4 cases related to the environment. In 2011, two complaints against Royal Dutch Shell Group alleged it had breached the disclosure, environment and consumer interests' provisions of the guidelines with respect to its operations in Nigeria. In this case, two major oil spills from abandoned oil facilities contaminated large areas, threatening the health and livelihood of thousands of people[41] (UNEP, 2011). The specific instance process, led by the Dutch NCP with the support of the UK NCP, involved a dialogue between the parties involved, but no agreement was reached. In concluding the specific instance, the NCP released a public statement urging both parties to continue the discussion and offering to play a facilitating role (MFA, 2014e).

Although evaluations of the effects of the Dutch CSR policy are scarce, there are examples of interventions that led to positive environmental impacts, such as the Sustainable Trade Initiative. Other examples include the standards on soy and palm oil developed by the Round Table on Responsible Soy and the Roundtable on Sustainable Palm Oil, respectively. The standards include criteria to halt further deforestation, but there is no evidence yet that this works beyond the certified production unit (MFA, 2014f).

The Netherlands has implemented the 2012 OECD Recommendation on Common Approaches for Officially Supported Export Credits and Environmental and Social Due Diligence to minimise the adverse impacts of Dutch investments abroad. Atradius Dutch State Business, which manages the Dutch state's export credit insurance programme and foreign investment scheme, screens all applications to determine whether an environmental and social review is required. Companies applying for financial government support must state they are aware of the guidelines and endeavour to comply with them to the best of their ability. Applicants have to prepare a CSR policy plan based on the guidelines (OECD, 2014i).

Recommendations on green growth

- Ensure the assessment of the 2013 Energy Agreement planned for 2016 is carried out in a thorough, independent and transparent manner. If this assessment indicates that it is unlikely that the agreed objectives will be met, or if the cost effectiveness of certain instruments is low, changes should be made to increase the environmental effectiveness and economic efficiency of Dutch climate and energy policy.
- Consider a partial switch from taxation of electricity towards taxation of natural gas use in households. As natural gas use is not covered by the EU ETS, this would lead to lower

Recommendations on green growth *(cont.)*

EU-wide GHG emissions. Consider contributing to effectively making the "cap" of the ETS stricter by buying and retiring some emission allowances. Reconsider the planned tax exemption for coal used in electricity generation, taking into account the impact of such a tax on local air pollution. Carefully consider the long-term fiscal sustainability of the current vehicle taxes.

- When assessing the introduction – or reintroduction – of environmentally related taxes, the environmental benefits that these taxes can stimulate should be considered on par with their administrative cost and their revenue generation potential. Even if the revenue generation potential of some taxes may be small, the environmental advantages they might contribute to could justify their implementation.
- Develop an ambitious framework for promoting eco-innovation that includes a balanced and consistent mix of increased public support for R&D, demand-side measures and partnerships with the private sector, with a focus on frontrunner SMEs; maintain a stable and clear policy and investment framework for innovation to support policy objectives, such as those for the circular economy and renewable energy; continue to refine criteria for public procurement to reap greater environmental gains and encourage green procurement approaches in the private sector.
- Ensure a strong and balanced commitment to the environment and climate within an increased volume of official development assistance, in line with international commitments.

Notes

1. When people travel across the border to buy fuel, they also frequently buy other products that are cheaper in the other country.
2. Figure 3.4 illustrates that the comparatively low fuel tax rates applied in Luxembourg make its composition of energy-related CO_2 emissions very different from other countries. While use of petrol and diesel represents some 15-25% of emissions in the other countries, the share of these fuels in total registered CO_2 emissions is above 65% in Luxembourg. Much of these emissions will, however, physically take place in other countries, where the imported fuel is being used.
3. The Dutch tax rates for petrol vehicles are lower than the ones for diesel vehicles, but the rate per tonne of a petrol vehicle emitting 250 g per km is still higher than EUR 850.
4. The share depends on the CO_2 emitted by vehicle per km driven. For vehicles with emissions below 50 g per km driven, a rate of zero is applied (e.g. there is no taxation of this benefit). For vehicles with larger emissions, a rate between 14% and 25% is applied. The amount of taxable benefit is also reduced for old vehicles (Harding, 2014).
5. Except that no benefit is deemed to occur if the personal use is less than 500 km per year.
6. For a description of the Norwegian tax on waste incineration, see OECD (2004).
7. Ruijs and Vollebergh (2013) indicate that Aalbers et al. (2007) found an average free-rider share of 47% for the year 2005.
8. Three recent studies assessing policies meant to stimulate the energy efficiency of buildings are Alberini and Bigano (2014); Levinson (2014); and Alberini, Gans and Towe (2013).
9. See *www.eea.europa.eu/data-and-maps/data/data-viewers/emissions-trading-viewer*.
10. At the outset, the ETS covered only CO_2 emissions. Since 2013, N_2O from the production of nitric, adipic and glyoxylic acid and PFC emissions from aluminium production are also included (*www.eea.europa.eu/data-and-maps/data/data-viewers/emissions-trading-viewer*).
11. This refers to the 28 EU member states plus Iceland, Norway and Lichtenstein.

12. From 2014, projects that apply for the SDE+ subsidy are no longer eligible for the Energy Investment Tax Allowance. See Section 3.5.
13. Each additional gramme of CO_2 emitted per km driven, according to the test cycle, is taxed at EUR 6.
14. Greene and Braathen (2014) give a general discussion of tax preferences for environmental goals.
15. Braathen (2011) gives a more general discussion of such interactions.
16. This is clearly an underestimate, as it includes only subsidies that are larger than EUR 100 million.
17. A "value-of-a-life-year" (VOLY) of EUR 40 000 was used across all EU countries to assess the costs of a premature mortality. As a comparison, OECD (2014c) used a "value-of-a-statistical-life" (VSL) of close to USD 3.8 million (approximately EUR 2.9 million) for the Netherlands in 2010. OECD (2014c) also argues in general for the use of VSL values, rather than VOLY values, because the latter places a lower value on the life of the elderly than younger people, among other reasons. A "conversion" between VOLY and VSL would depend on the number of life years assumed to be lost for persons affected by environmental damage. However, if one assumed that each mortality caused a loss of 20 life-years, a VOLY of EUR 40 000 would roughly translate into a VSL figure of EUR 800 000; less than one-third of the value used for the Netherlands in OECD (2014c).
18. Investment and internal current expenditure (excluding payments to specialised producers of environmental protection services) less receipts from by-products (e.g. material recovered as a result of waste treatment). Includes expenditure on i) pollution abatement and control covering air protection, waste and wastewater management, protection and remediation of soil and groundwater, and other environmental protection activities (R&D, administration, education); and ii) biodiversity and landscape protection. Excludes expenditure on water supply.
19. When including expenditure by industry and agriculture (e.g. for water production, water treatment, drainage and water storage), this total rises to about 1.26% of GDP.
20. Including investment, operating and maintenance costs, costs for research and implementation of groundwater measures.
21. Production and supply of water, including self-service, collecting and discharging of rain and wastewater, wastewater treatment, groundwater management and regional water management.
22. The 2007 Clean & Efficient programme and the Energy Report 2008 strategy called for a 30% reduction in GHG emissions from 1990 levels, 20% renewables in the energy mix and annual energy efficiency improvements of 2% by 2020.
23. Dutch target under the EU Directive (2012/27/EU) on Energy Efficiency.
24. It is not possible to apply for support for the same investment under both the Energy Investment Tax Allowance and MIA, but it is possible to combine the tax allowance or MIA with VAMIL.
25. In 2006, the Energy Investment Tax Allowance was used to bridge the gap between the closure of MEP and the take-off of SDE. From 2014, projects that apply for the SDE+ subsidy are no longer eligible for the tax allowance.
26. 2% reduction in final energy consumption compared with 2001-05 average.
27. Statistics Netherlands includes wholesale in waste and scrap in waste management activities.
28. Including, for example, the construction of wind farms, the manufacturing of solar panels, and the manufacturing and installation of insulation materials for buildings.
29. Including administrative activities of central government, provinces, municipalities and joint arrangements.
30. By a 0.13 percentage point over 2012-18 and a 0.14 percentage point when considering indirect funding through tax incentives.
31. The increase in business expenditure on R&D in 2011 is mostly due to a change in the statistical measurement.
32. Also due to the move from the Energy Transition Framework to the Top Sectors approach.
33. As measured by the revealed technology advantage, i.e. the Netherlands' share of world patents in these technologies is higher than its share in all fields.
34. The Eco-Innovation Scoreboard is an index based on indicators in five areas: eco-innovation inputs, eco-innovation activities, eco-innovation outputs, resource efficiency outcomes and socio-economic outcomes.

35. "The Netherlands will continue to uphold the accepted 0.7% international standard, even though it is not itself currently meeting that target" (MFA, 2014a).
36. 75% of Dutch bilateral ODA was allocable by sector in 2012-13 compared with 50% in the first half of the 2000s.
37. Includes activities where environment is a principal or significant objective.
38. Includes overlapping amounts between mitigation and adaptation activities.
39. The OECD Guidelines for Multinational Enterprises provide a global framework for responsible business conduct covering all areas of business ethics, including tax, competition, disclosure, anti-corruption, labour and human rights, and environment. While observance of the guidelines by enterprises is voluntary and not legally enforceable, 46 adhering governments are committed to promoting them and making them influential among companies operating in or from their territories.
40. In 2012, the political responsibility for the NCP was transferred from the Ministry of Economy to the Ministry of Foreign Affairs.
41. UNEP estimated that full environmental restoration of Ogoniland may take up to 30 years. It called for an initial capital injection of USD 1 billion from the oil industry and the Nigerian government to cover the first five years of the clean-up project.

References

Aalbers, R.F.T. et al. (2007), "Ex-post evaluatie Energie Investeringsaftrek" [Ex-Post Evaluation Energy Investment], SEO Amsterdam, *Odracht van het Ministerie van Economische Zaken*, SEO-rapport nr. 999, Amsterdam.

Alberini, A. and A. Bigano (2014), "How effective are energy-efficiency incentive programs? Evidence from Italian homeowners", *Nota di Lavoro*, No. 97, Fondazione Eni Enrico Mattei, Milano, *www.feem.it/getpage.aspx?id=6942&sez=Publications&padre=73*.

Alberini, A., W. Gans and C. Towe (2013), "Free riding, upsizing, and energy efficiency incentives in Maryland homes", *Nota di Lavoro*, No. 82, Fondazione Eni Enrico Mattei, Milano, *www.feem.it/getpage.aspx?id=5808&sez=Publications&padre=73*.

Braathen, N.A. (2011), "Interactions between emission trading systems and other overlapping policy instruments", *OECD Green Growth Papers*, No. 02, OECD Publishing, Paris, *http://dx.doi.org/10.1787/5k97gk44c6vf-en*.

CBS (2014a), *Environmental Accounts of the Netherlands 2013*, Statistics Netherlands, The Hague, *www.cbs.nl/NR/rdonlyres/6293456F-8E61-4821-964D-17C7D67416B8/0/environmentalaccountsofthenetherlands2013.pdf*.

CBS (2014b), "Dutch quality of life is high, but not sustainable", *Press release*, 25 November, Statistics Netherlands, The Hague, *www.cbs.nl/NR/rdonlyres/00FC1466-71BE-46D4-B33F-4B56AE138A97/0/pb14e074.pdf*.

CBS (2013), *Environmental Accounts of the Netherlands 2012*, Statistics Netherlands, The Hague, *www.cbs.nl/NR/rdonlyres/090445AD-E1CB-4147-A404-0C36F02DF112/0/2013c174pub.pdf*.

CBS (2012), *Environmental Accounts of the Netherlands 2011*, Statistics Netherlands, The Hague, *www.cbs.nl/NR/rdonlyres/3F5F2C12-CB59-4C59-AE1A-FD46AF6D4DAD/0/2011c174pub.pdf*.

CBS (2011), *Environmental Accounts of the Netherlands 2010*, Statistics Netherlands, The Hague, *www.cbs.nl/NR/rdonlyres/A3AF6855-3FF1-4344-8699-7C181A293979/0/2010c174pub.pdf*.

CBS (2010), *Environmental Accounts of the Netherlands 2009*, Statistics Netherlands, The Hague, *www.cbs.nl/NR/rdonlyres/68DCDF0D-76C6-458F-B3EC-073E8447DF13/0/2009c174pub.pdf*.

Dechezleprêtre, A. et al. (2013), *Position of the Netherlands in the Emerging Green Economy*, Netherlands Environmental Assessment Agency, The Hague.

De Visser, E. et al. (2011), *Overheidsingrepen in de Energiemarkt: Onderzoek naar het Nederlandse Speelveld voor Fossiele Brandstoffen, Hernieuwbare Bronnen, Kernenergie en Energiebesparing* [Government Interference in the Energy Market: Investigation of the Dutch Support to Fossil Fuels, Renewables, Nuclear Energy and Energy Efficiency], Ecofys and CE, Utrecht, *www.ce.nl/publicatie/overheidsingrepen_in_de_energiemarkt/1159*.

Dijkgraaf, E. and R. Gradus (2014), "Efficiency effects of unit-based pricing systems and institutional choices of waste collection", *Tinbergen Institute Discussion Paper*, TI 2014-003/VI, Tinbergen Institute, Amsterdam/Rotterdam, *www.tinbergen.nl/discussionpaper/?paper=2258*.

ECN (2014), *Nationale Energieverkenning 2014* [National Energy Outlook 2014], Energy Research Centre of the Netherlands, Petten, *www.ecn.nl/publicaties/ECN-O--14-036*.

ECN (2011), *Cost-Benefit Analysis of Alternative Support Schemes for Renewable Electricity in the Netherlands*, Energy Research Centre of the Netherlands, Petten, *www.energie-nederland.nl/wp-content/uploads/docs/E11002.pdf*.

Ecofys (2014), "Design features of support schemes for renewable electricity", *Task 2 Report*, for the European Commission, DG ENER, Utrecht, *www.ecofys.com/files/files/ec-fraunhofer-isi-ecofys-2014-design-features-of-support-schemes.pdf*.

Ecologic Institute and eclareon (2014), *Assessment of Climate Change Policies in the Context of the European Semester. Country Report: The Netherlands*, Ecologic Institute and eclareon GmbH, Berlin, *www.ecologic.eu/sites/files/publication/2014/countryreport_nl_ecologiceclareon_jan2014_0.pdf*.

EEA (2014a), *Energy Support Measures and their Impact on Innovation in the Renewable Energy Sector in Europe*, European Environment Agency, Copenhagen.

EEA (2014b), *Trends and Projections in Europe 2014, Tracking Progress towards Europe's Climate and Energy Targets for 2020*, European Environment Agency, Copenhagen.

EIO (2014), *Eco-Innovation Scoreboard* (database), *http://database.eco-innovation.eu/* (accessed 22 March 2015).

European Commission (2012a), *Commission Staff Working Document, Member State: Netherlands, Accompanying the document: Report from the Commission to the European Parliament and the Council on the Implementation of the Water Framework Directive (2000/60/EC): River Basin Management Plan*, COM (2012) 670 final, SWD (2012) 379 final, European Commission, Brussels, *http://ec.europa.eu/environment/water/water-framework/pdf/3rd_report/CWD-2012-379_EN-Vol3_NL.pdf*.

European Commission (2012b), *The Uptake of Green Public Procurement in the EU27*, prepared by the Centre for European Policy Studies and the College of Europe for the European Commission, European Commission, Brussels, *http://ec.europa.eu/environment/gpp/pdf/CEPS-CoE-GPP%20MAIN%20REPORT.pdf*.

Gerritsen, M. and J. Høj (2013), "Reforming policies for the business sector to harvest the benefits of globalisation in the Netherlands", *OECD Economics Department Working Papers*, No. 1011, OECD Publishing, Paris, *http://dx.doi.org/10.1787/5k4dlffl1kkk-en*.

Government of the Netherlands (2015), "Tussenbalans Groene Groei" [Balance between Green Growth], Parliamentary document: Letter to the House of Representatives, 18 June 2015, Minister of Economic Affairs, State Secretary for Infrastructure and the Environment, Minister for Foreign Trade and Development, and Minister of Housing and National Service.

Government of the Netherlands (2014), "Answers to OECD Environmental Performance Review Questionnaire" (internal document).

Government of the Netherlands (2013), "Green Growth: for a strong, sustainable economy", Parliamentary document: Letter to the House of Representatives, 28 March 2013, Minister of Economic Affairs and the State Secretary for Infrastructure and the Environment.

Greene, J. and N.A. Braathen (2014), "Tax preferences for environmental goals: Use, limitations and preferred practices", *OECD Environment Working Papers*, No. 71, OECD Publishing, Paris, *http://dx.doi.org/10.1787/5jxwrr4hkd6l-en*.

Harding, M. (2014), "Personal tax treatment of company cars and commuting expenses: Estimating the fiscal and environmental costs", *OECD Taxation Working Papers*, No. 20, OECD Publishing, Paris, *http://dx.doi.org/10.1787/5jz14cg1s7vl-en*.

IEA (2014), *Energy Policies of IEA Countries, The Netherlands, 2014 Review*, IEA/OECD Publishing, Paris, *http://dx.doi.org/10.1787/9789264210462-en*.

IEA (2009), *Energy Policies of IEA Countries: Netherlands 2008*, IEA/OECD Publishing, Paris, *www.oecd.org/bookshop?lang=en&pub=9789264043398*.

Korting (2015), "Applied research is essential for the Energy Agreement", *www.ecn.nl/news/item/applied-research-is-essential-for-the-energy-agreement/* (accessed 29 January 2015).

Levinson, A. (2014) "How much energy do building energy codes really save? Evidence from California", *NBER Working Paper*, No. 20797, National Bureau of Economic Research, Cambridge, US, *www.nber.org/papers/w20797*.

MFA (2014a), "Response to the AIV advisory letter 'Development cooperation: Beyond a Definition'", Ministry of Foreign Affairs of the Netherlands, The Hague, *http://aiv-advice.nl/6fx/publications/advisory-letters/development-cooperation-beyond-a-definition#government-responses*.

MFA (2014b), "Good things come to those who make them happen", *IOB Study*, No. 392, Ministry of Foreign Affairs of the Netherlands, The Hague.

MFA (2014c), "Access to energy in Rwanda, impact evaluation of activities supported by the Dutch Promoting Renewable Energy Programme", *IOB Evaluation*, No. 396, Ministry of Foreign Affairs of the Netherlands, The Hague.

MFA (2014d), "In search of focus and effectiveness", *IOB Evaluation*, No. 389, Ministry of Foreign Affairs of the Netherlands, The Hague.

MFA (2014e), *NCP Final Statement Shell in the Niger Delta II*, Ministry of Foreign Affairs of the Netherlands, The Hague.

MFA (2014f), "Riding the wave of sustainable commodity sourcing", *IOB Review*, No. 397, Ministry of Foreign Affairs of the Netherlands, The Hague.

MFA (2013), *A World to Gain, A New Agenda for Aid, Trade and Investment*, Ministry of Foreign Affairs of the Netherlands, The Hague, *www.government.nl/government/documents-and-publications/reports/2013/04/30/a-world-to-gain.html*.

Ministry of Economic Affairs, Ministry of the Interior and Kingdom Relations (2014), *Third National Energy Efficiency Action Plan for the Netherlands*, The Hague.

Ministry of Infrastructure and the Environment (2014), "Implementation of the Waste to Resource programme", Letter to the House of Representatives, *www.government.nl/government/documents-and-publications/parliamentary-documents/2014/01/28/implementation-of-the-waste-to-resource-programme.html*.

OECD (2014a), *OECD Economic Surveys: Netherlands 2014*, OECD Publishing, Paris, *http://dx.doi.org/10.1787/eco_surveys-nld-2014-en*.

OECD (2014b), *OECD Database on Instruments used for Environmental Policy and Natural Resources Management*, *www.oecd.org/env/policies/database* (accessed 30 March 2015).

OECD (2014c), *The Cost of Air Pollution: Health Impacts of Road Transport*, OECD Publishing, Paris, *http://dx.doi.org/10.1787/9789264210448-en*.

OECD (2014d), *Water Governance in the Netherlands, Fit for the Future?*, OECD Publishing, Paris, *www.oecd.org/bookshop?lang=en&pub=9789264208940*.

OECD (2014e), *Green Growth Indicators 2014*, OECD Publishing, Paris, *www.oecd.org/bookshop?lang=en&pub=9789264202023*.

OECD (2014f), *OECD Reviews of Innovation Policy: Netherlands 2014*, OECD Publishing, Paris, *www.oecd.org/bookshop?lang=en&pub=9789264213098*.

OECD (2014g), *Development Co-operation Report 2014: Mobilising Resources for Sustainable Development*, OECD Publishing, Paris, *http://dx.doi.org/10.1787/dcr-2014-en*.

OECD (2014h), *Database of Specific Instances*, *http://mneguidelines.oecd.org/database/* (accessed 20 October 2014).

OECD (2014i), *Annual Report on the OECD Guidelines for Multinational Enterprises 2014, Responsible Business Conduct by Sector*, OECD Publishing, Paris, *www.oecd.org/bookshop?lang=en&pub=9789264220898*.

OECD (2013a), *Taxing Energy Use: A Graphical Analysis*, OECD Publishing, Paris, *www.oecd.org/tax/tax-policy/taxingenergyuse.htm*.

OECD (2012a), *OECD Environmental Performance Reviews: Germany 2012*, OECD Publishing, Paris, *http://dx.doi.org/10.1787/9789264169302-en*.

OECD (2012b), *Strategic Environmental Assessment in Development Practice: A Review of Recent Experience*, OECD Publishing, Paris, *http://dx.doi.org/10.1787/9789264166745-en*.

OECD (2011), *DAC Peer Review of the Netherlands*, OECD Publishing, Paris, *www.oecd.org/dac/peer-reviews/49011988.pdf*.

OECD (2010), *OECD Economic Surveys: Netherlands 2010*, OECD Publishing, Paris, *www.oecd.org/bookshop?lang=en&pub=9789264083141*.

OECD (2007), *Instrument Mixes Addressing Non-point Sources of Water Pollution*, OECD Publishing, Paris, *www.oecd.org/officialdocuments/publicdisplaydocumentpdf/?doclanguage=en&cote=com/env/epoc/agr/ca(2004)90/final*

OECD (2004), *Addressing the Economics of Waste*, OECD Publishing, Paris, *http://dx.doi.org/10.1787/9789264106192-en*.

Padding, T. (2012), *100%? Six years of Sustainable Procurement in the Netherlands*, *www.pianoo.nl/sites/default/files/documents/documents/sixyearsofsustainableprocurementinthenetherlands.pdf* (accessed 15 May 2015).

PBL (2015), *Assessment of the Dutch Human Environment 2014 – The Future is Now*, PBL Netherlands Environmental Assessment Agency, The Hague.

PBL (2014), *Green Gains – In Search of Opportunities for the Dutch Economy*, Netherlands Environmental Assessment Agency, The Hague.

PBL (2011), *Environmentally Harmful Subsidies*, Netherlands Environmental Assessment Agency, The Hague, *www.pbl.nl/sites/default/files/cms/publicaties/PBL_2011_Environmentally%20Harmful%20Subsidies_500209002.pdf*.

RIVM (2014), *Environmental Profit of Sustainable Procurement: A Quick-Scan of the Minimum Criteria*, National Institute for Public Health and the Environment, Bilthoven.

Roy, R. (2014), "Environmental and related social costs of the tax treatment of company cars and commuting expenses", *OECD Environment Working Papers*, No. 70, OECD Publishing, Paris, *http://dx.doi.org/10.1787/5jxwrr5163zp-en*.

Ruijs, A. and H.R. Vollebergh (2013), "Lessons from 15 years of experience with the Dutch tax allowance for energy investments for firms", *OECD Environment Working Papers*, No. 55, OECD Publishing, Paris, http://dx.doi.org/10.1787/5k47zw350q8v-en.

RVO (2015), "MIA, Vamil en Green Deals" [MIA, Vamil in Green Deals], Netherlands Enterprise Agency, The Hague, *www.rvo.nl/subsidies-regelingen/mia-vamil-en-green-deals* (accessed 25 March 2015).

RVO (2014a), *SDE+ 2014. Instructions on How to Apply for a Subsidy for the Production of Renewable Energy*, Netherlands Enterprise Agency, The Hague, *http://english.rvo.nl/sites/default/files/2014/04/Brochure%20SDE%2B%202014.pdf*.

RVO (2014b), *Renewable Energy Report, Part 1 Implementation 2003-2013, + SDE+, SDE, OV-MEP & MEP Annual Report 2013*, Netherlands Enterprise Agency, Utrecht, *http://english.rvo.nl/sites/default/files/2014/09/Renewable%20energy%20report.pdf*.

RVO (2014c), *Borssele Wind Farm Zone, Project and Site Description*, Netherlands Enterprise Agency, Utrecht, *https://rvothema4.pleio.nl/file/download/30981302*.

UNEP (2011), *Environmental Assessment of Ogoniland*, United Nations Environment Programme, Nairobi, *http://postconflict.unep.ch/publications/OEA/UNEP_OEA.pdf*.

Van der Elst, C. and P. Bosch (2012), *An Outlook for Renewable Energy in The Netherlands*, Rabobank Industry Note #320, Rabobank International, Utrecht.

Van der Veen, G. and M. Ploeg (2013), *Eco-Innovation in the Netherlands, EIO Country Profile 2013*, Eco-Innovation Observatory, *www.eco-innovation.eu/images/stories/Reports/EIO_Country_Brief_2013_Netherlands.pdf*.

Van Grinsven, H.J.M et al. (2015), "Potential of extensification of European agriculture for a more sustainable food system, focusing on nitrogen", *Environmental Research Letters*, Vol. 10, *http://dx.doi.org/10.1088/1748-9326/10/2/025002*.

Van Grinsven, H.J.M et al. (2013), "Costs and benefits of nitrogen for Europe and implications for mitigation", *Environmental Science & Technology*, Vol. 47, pp. 3571-3579, *http://dx.doi.org/dx.doi.org/10.1021/es303804g*.

van Steen, J. (2014), *Total Investment in Research and Innovation (TWIN) 2012-2018, Facts & Figures*, Rathenau Institute, The Hague, *www.rathenau.nl/uploads/tx_tferathenau/Total_Investment_in_Research_and_Innovation__TWIN__2012-2018_-_Rathenau_Instituut_.pdf*.

Vollebergh, H. (2014), *Green Tax Reform: Energy Tax Challenges for the Netherlands*, Netherlands Environmental Assessment Agency, PBL Publication number 1501, The Hague.

Warwick, K. and A. Nolan (2014), "Evaluation of industrial policy: Methodological issues and policy lessons", *OECD Science, Technology and Industry Policy Papers*, No. 16, OECD Publishing, Paris, *http://dx.doi.org/10.1787/5jz181jh0j5k-en*.

ANNEX 3.A

Data on green growth performance

Figure 3.A1. **Environmentally related taxes**

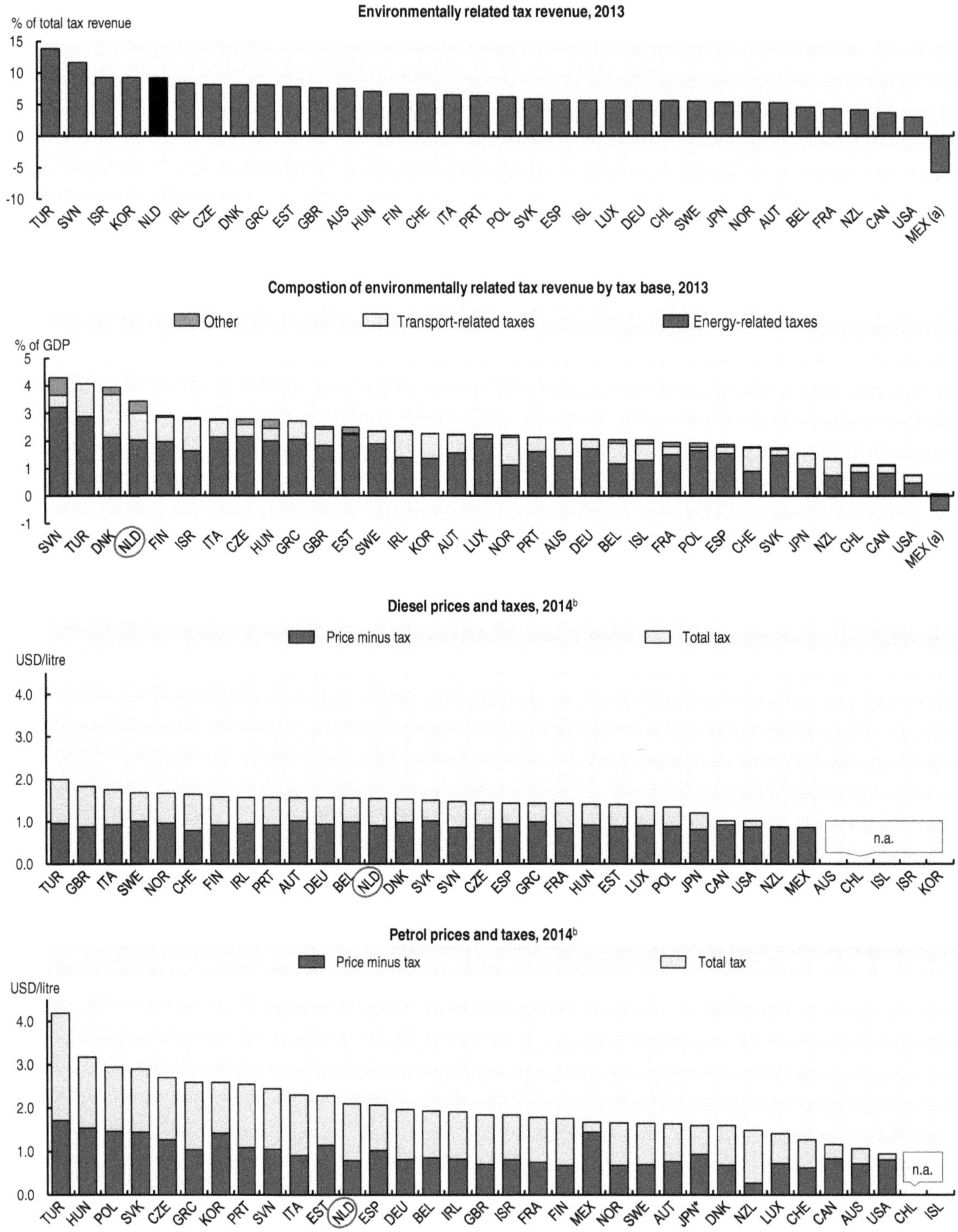

Notes: Data refer to the indicated year or to the latest available year. They may include provisional figures and estimates.

a) Until 2014, the system used to stabilise end-use prices of motor fuels caused tax revenue to turn negative (i.e. become a subsidy) in years when the international oil price was high. Mexico's 2013 Tax Reform corrected this mechanism and introduced a tax on fossil fuels based on their carbon content, which will yield positive revenue.

b) Diesel: automotive diesel for commercial use, current USD; petrol: unleaded premium (RON 95), except Japan (unleaded regular), USD at current prices and purchasing power parities.

Source: IEA (2015), *IEA Energy Prices and Taxes Statistics* (database); OECD (2015), *OECD Database on Instruments Used for Environmental Policies and Natural Resources Management* (database).

StatLink http://dx.doi.org/10.1787/888933280590

Figure 3.A2. **Green innovation**

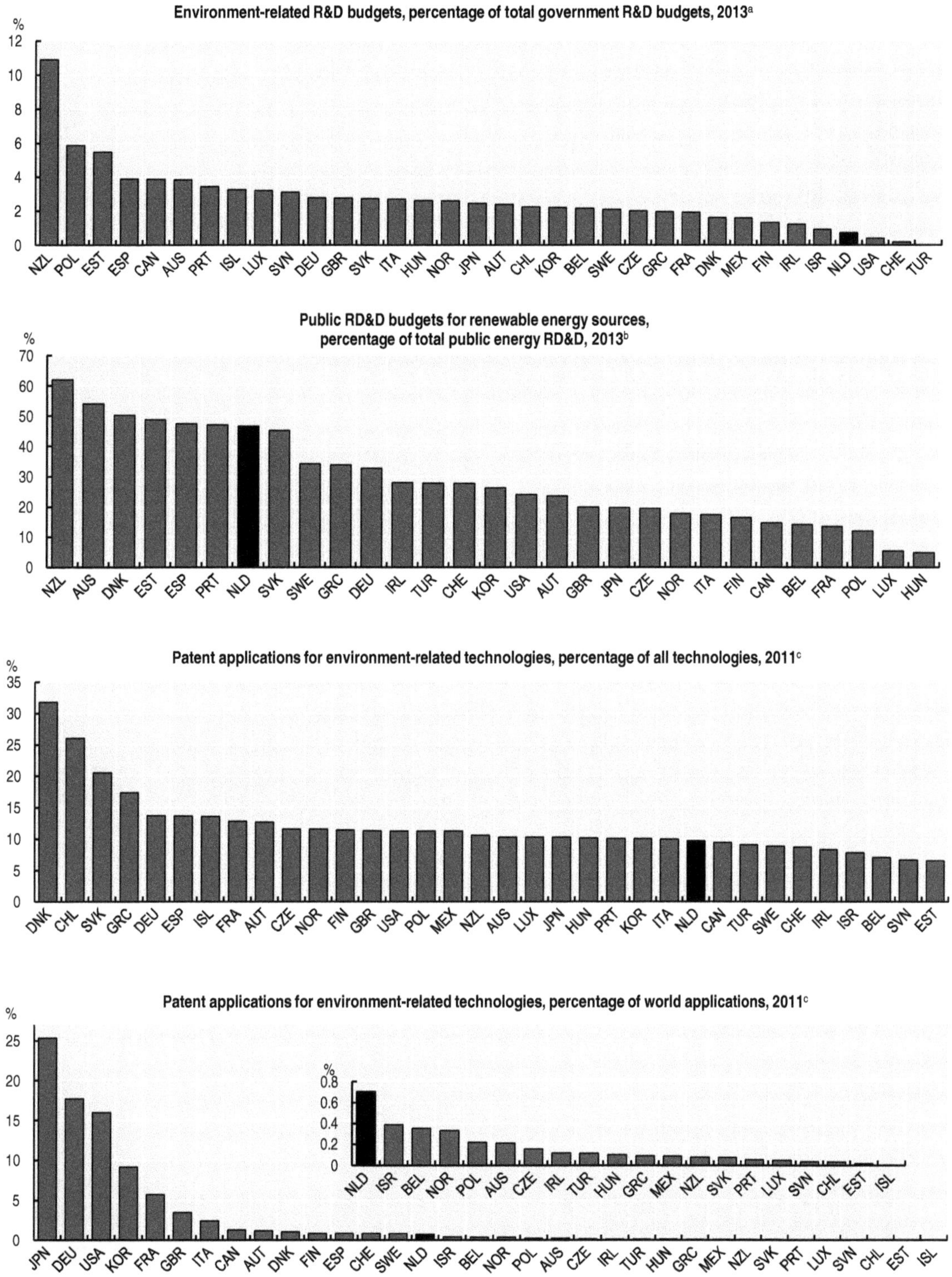

Notes: Data refer to the indicated year or to the latest available year. They may include provisional figures and estimates.

a) Government budget appropriations or outlays for research and development (R&D); breakdown according to the NABS 2007 classification.

b) Public energy technology budgets for research, development and demonstration (RD&D).

c) Higher values inventions that have sought patent protection in at least two jurisdictions . Data are based on patents applications filed under the Worldwide Patent Statistical Database (PATSTAT) of the European Patent Office (EPO) and refer to fractional counts of patents by inventor's country of residence and priority date.

Source: IEA (2015), *IEA Energy Technology RD&D Statistics* (database); OECD (2015), "Patents in environment-related technologies: Technology development by inventor country", *OECD Environment Statistics* (database).

StatLink http://dx.doi.org/10.1787/888933280607

Figure 3.A3. **International development co-operation**

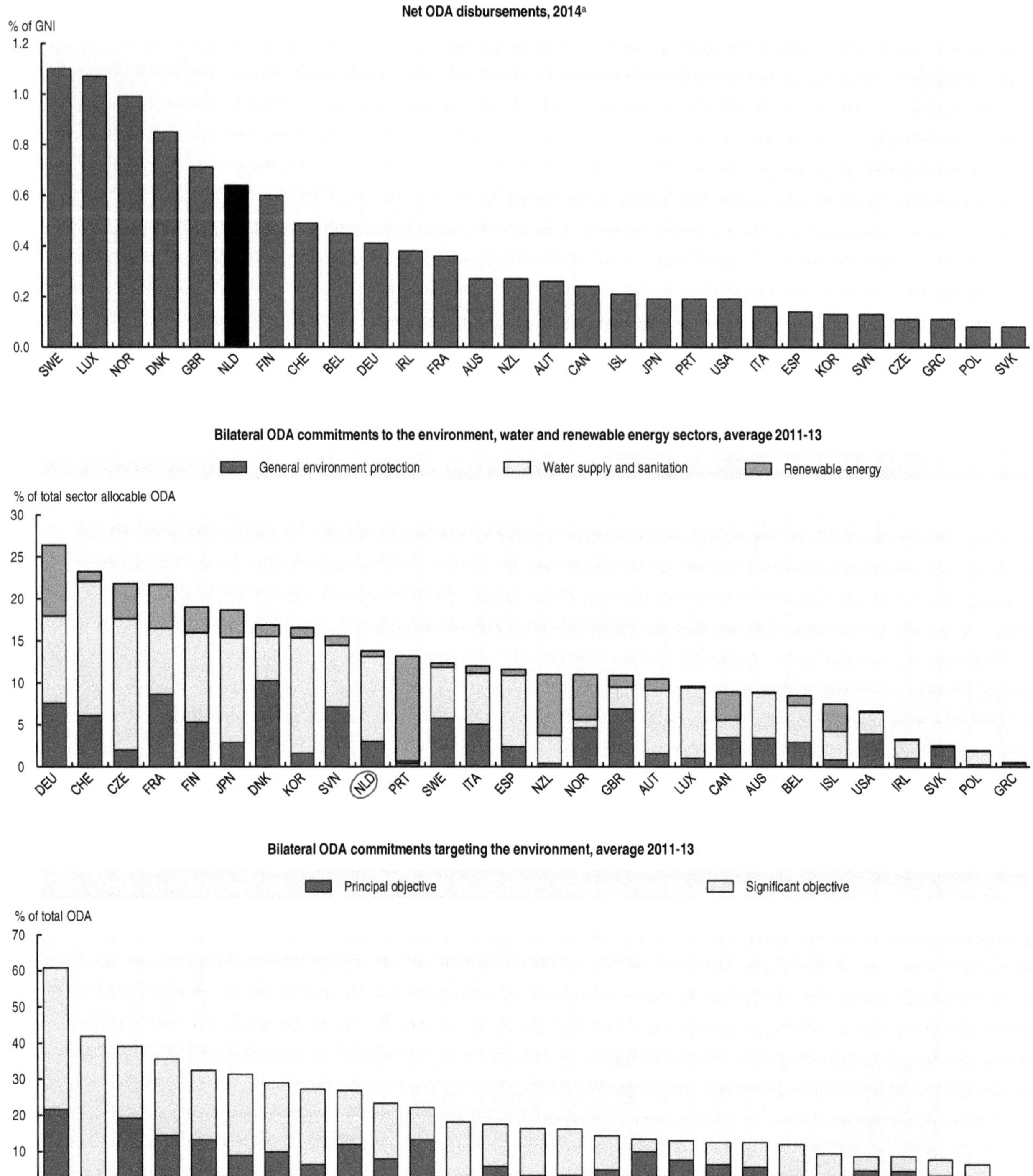

Notes: Data refer to the indicated year or to the latest available year. They may include provisional figures and estimates. 2014 data re preliminary.
Official development assistance by member countries of the OECD Development Assistance Committee (the Czeck Republic, Iceland, Korea, Poland, the Slovak Republic and Slovenia became DAC members after 2005). In comparing data across countries it should be noted that the coverage ratio of the environmental policy objective (ie. the proportion of aid which is screened against the policy markers) varies considerably among countries; low coverage rates can increase significantly the shares of environmental-focused aid.
Source: OECD (2015), *OECD International Development Statistics* (database).

StatLink http://dx.doi.org/10.1787/888933280618

PART II

Progress towards selected environmental objectives

PART II

Chapter 4

Sustainable mobility

This chapter reviews the Netherlands' progress in promoting sustainable mobility. It discusses mobility trends in freight and passenger transport and examines their impact on air pollution, greenhouse gas emissions, noise, congestion and traffic safety. The chapter provides an overview of the country's various policy visions for sustainable mobility over the review period, as well as governance arrangements. Finally, it assesses the policy instruments in place to promote sustainable mobility and examines their performance in achieving the country's objectives. The recommendations on sustainable mobility are summarised in a box at the end of the chapter.

The statistical data for Israel are supplied by and under the responsibility of the relevant Israeli authorities. The use of such data by the OECD is without prejudice to the status of the Golan Heights, East Jerusalem and Israeli settlements in the West Bank under the terms of international law.

1. Introduction

Mobility is an important ingredient of a well-functioning society. Mobility of workers and goods makes the economy more productive, mobility of children and students helps build better human capital and other forms of mobility help sustain the social and cultural network. How to organise this mobility most effectively, however, is not obvious. Individual mobility decisions of firms and households create negative, as well as positive externalities, which are not considered in individual decisions. This is the main challenge of sustainable mobility: how to make sure that a country organises its mobility systems so that individual decisions contribute to the best for society as a whole.

The Netherlands is a small, densely populated country with significant transit activity to and from Rotterdam, the largest port in Europe. As in any densely populated country, this implies a constant tension between the available transport capacities and the demand for transport, as well as a constant pressure on the environment. The Netherlands has two additional features: its housing market policies favour home ownership, which makes people choose to commute rather than to relocate; and its location as a literally "low" country. Its geography is a challenge in terms of flood protection, but also an opportunity for cheap and environmentally friendly freight transport on inland waterways.

2. Mobility trends

As in many high-income countries, overall freight and passenger transport volumes in the Netherlands have been relatively stable since 2000 (except for rail freight, which is only a small share of total). Figure 4.1 illustrates these trends. Growth in gross domestic product (GDP) has been modest, the share of transport-intensive manufacturing sectors is declining and car ownership is saturated.

2.1. Trends in passenger transport

Total mobility in terms of billion passenger kilometres (km) has been stable since 2000 (Figure 4.2). The total passenger km (pkm) travelled by car has been stable, but solo drivers are responsible for more and more pkm. Rail use represents only 10% of total distance travelled, but grew by 25% over 2004-13. The Netherlands is remarkable in that 10% of total distance travelled is by bicycle.[1] The Netherlands, along with Denmark, has achieved an exceptionally high share of bicycle use compared to other OECD member countries. This is due to relatively flat geography, but also to its policy of separate bike paths that minimise interference with cars (Pucher and Buehler, 2007).

The motives for passenger trips have been changing over the last 20 years, driven by changes in the age structure of the population and lifestyles. Trips related to work (22%) and education (10%) account for less than one-third of all trips. The number of work-related trips grew up to 2008, driven by the increased participation of people 40 years-old and older (mainly women) in the labour force (KiM, 2014). The economic recession caused this growth to slow, and is also partly responsible for a 6% decrease in shopping trips.

Figure 4.1. **Trends in freight and passenger transport relatively stable since 2000**

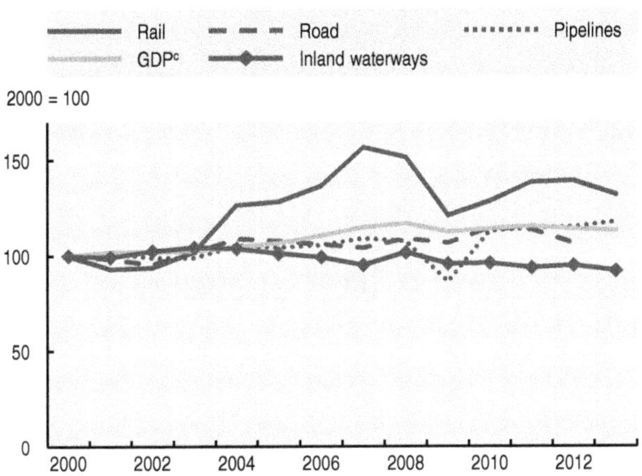

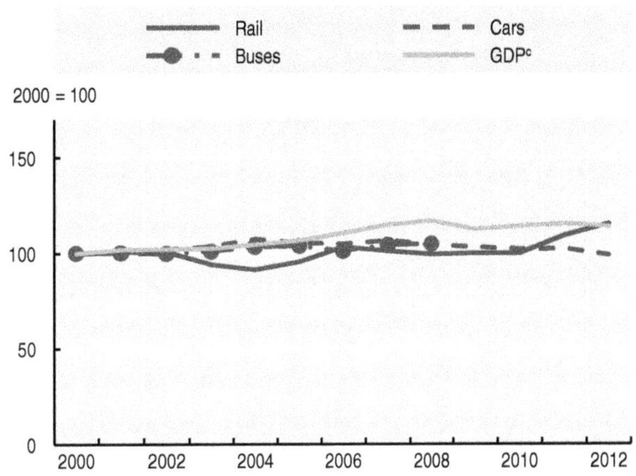

a) Based on values expressed in tonne-km.
b) Based on values expressed in passenger-km.
c) GDP at 2005 prices and purchasing power parities.
Source: ITF (2015), *Trends in the Transport Sector* (database); OECD (2014), "OECD Economic Outlook No. 95", *OECD Economic Outlook: Statistics and Projections*(database).

StatLink http://dx.doi.org/10.1787/888933280326

Figure 4.2. **Total passenger mobility stable since 2000**

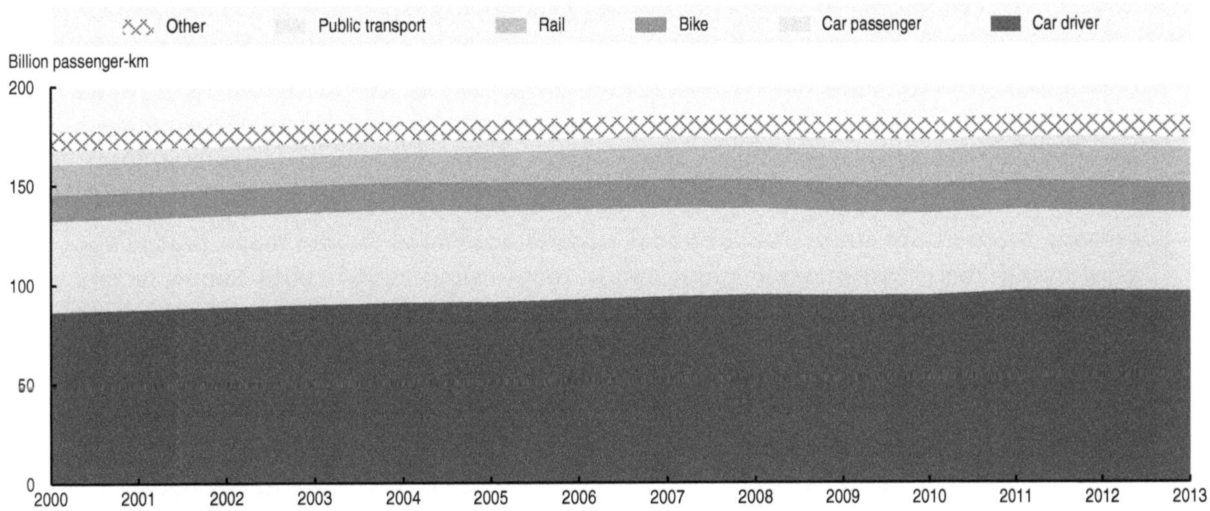

Source: KiM (2014), *Mobiliteitsbeeld 2014 [Mobility Picture 2014]*.

StatLink http://dx.doi.org/10.1787/888933280338

According to KiM (2014), it is not yet clear whether online shopping leads to a net decrease of shopping trips.

The evolution of car use by age, motive and gender for 1995-2012 is shown in Figure 4.3. Car use by people under 35 years has notably decreased, while trips for shopping and leisure have also both declined in recent years. Car use by women and older people has been increasing. Car ownership in the Netherlands is stable, and comparable to other European countries with the same level of income per capita, but on the lower end.

Bicycle use has always been strong in the Netherlands. In recent years, a major change has been increased use of e-bikes by people older than 50 years. With an e-bike, trips are

Figure 4.3. **Shifting trends in car use since 1995**

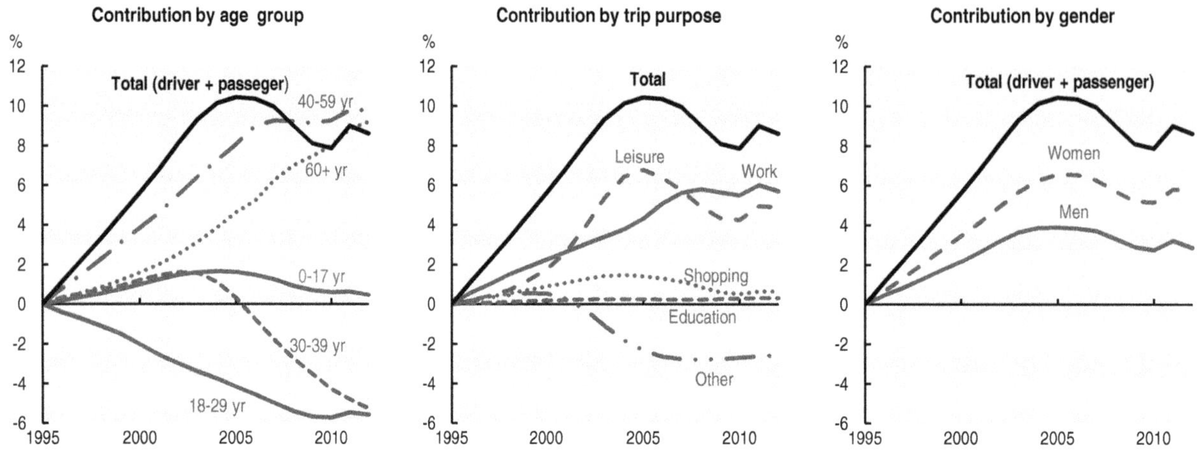

Source: KiM (2013), *Mobiliteitsbeeld 2013 [Mobility Picture 2013].*

StatLink http://dx.doi.org/10.1787/888933280341

almost twice as long as with a normal bike. About 10% of the population has an e-bike, and the Dutch are the frontrunner in e-bike use in Europe (KiM, 2014).

Rail use has increased by 24% and local public transport use (bus, tram, metro) has increased by 11% over 2004-13. The main increase in rail use has occurred in the Randstad where some lines increased in use by 75%, while use has decreased on other lines. Almost half of all morning commuters who use a train reach the station by bicycle (KiM, 2014). In aggregate terms, the supply of rail km has followed total passenger km. However, since 2009, passengers are reportedly less satisfied with the quality of service, mainly due to train delays (KiM, 2014).

Air transport has had the strongest increase of all modes of passenger mobility, growing by one-third since 2004. Regional airports accounted for the major part of the growth, with their share increasing from 13% in 2004 to almost 25% in 2013. Supply factors such as the development of low-cost airlines drive the increase, but the trend is also apparent in other high-income countries. The main motives for air transportation are holidays (54%) and business (24%).

2.2. Trends in freight transport

The overall volume of freight transport has been relatively stable over the last ten years. The increase of incoming transit via sea and air has more or less compensated for the decline of freight with an origin and destination in the Netherlands (inland transport flows were 524 million tonnes [Mt] in 2013). Table 4.1 shows the importance of national freight flows versus import and export movements via sea and air. As the Netherlands has the largest port in Europe, a lot of freight arrives via the sea (407 Mt in 2013); a large part (340 Mt)

Table 4.1. **Volume of freight transport, 2004-13**

Mt-km	Import via sea and air	Export via sea and air	Inland transport flows	Export over land	Import over land	Transit over land
2004	352	113	575	344	175	80
2013	407	174	524	340	159	98

Source: KiM (2014), *Mobiliteitsbeeld 2014 [Mobility Picture 2014], Kennisinstituut voor Mobiliteitsbeleid [Netherlands Institute for Transport Policy]*, KIM-14-R01, ISBN: 978-90-8902-124-3.

is transferred to the hinterland (Ruhr area and beyond) or transhipped (174 Mt). More goods arrive in the port than leave (174 Mt exported via sea and air, versus 407 Mt imported). The growth of freight transit traffic is directly related to the growing internationalisation of economic activity; the decline of national freight traffic has more to do with the stronger service orientation of the economic activity. Dutch ports are responsible for close to half of total freight volume of all ports in the Le Havre-Hamburg area.

Two main trends are apparent in terms of the mode used to transport freight between the Port of Rotterdam and the hinterland: more short sea shipping (sea to sea) and less road transportation. With respect to freight volume, inland waterways are notably three times more important than rail (Figure 4.4).

Figure 4.4. **More short sea shipping and less road transport in moving containers to and from the Port of Rotterdam, 2004-13**

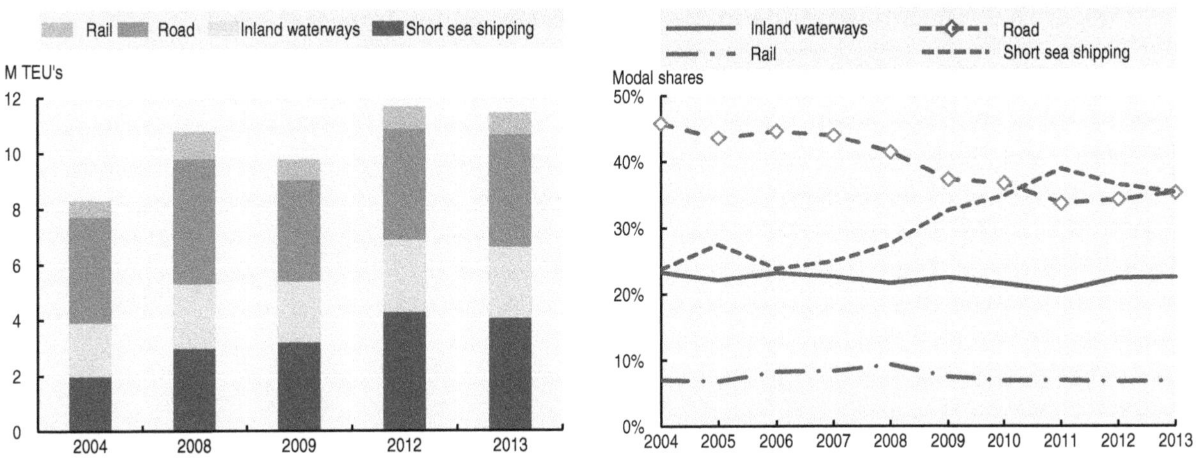

Source: KiM (2014), *Mobiliteitsbeeld 2014 [Mobility Picture 2014].*

StatLink http://dx.doi.org/10.1787/888933280357

Government investment in infrastructure (land, transport and water) increased between 2004-09 from 1.6% of GDP to 1.9%, then decreased to 1.5% in 2013 (KiM, 2014, 2013). In 2013, the Dutch government spent around EUR 6 billion on transport infrastructure, split between investment and maintenance. Roads and railways each received about 40% of total transport expenditure.

3. Trends in environmental, congestion and safety impacts of mobility

Mobility gives rise to negative effects on the environment (air pollution and noise), as well as congestion and safety externalities. Over the review period, the performance of the Netherlands in reducing these negative impacts has been very good. Air pollution emissions have declined significantly since 2004, except for CO_2 emissions, which have declined only slightly since 2008. Noise levels from transport, and hours lost from congestion (congestion losses), have also declined. Traffic safety has significantly improved. This section discusses each of these in turn.

3.1. Air pollution and greenhouse gas emissions from transport

All air pollution emissions from transport have declined significantly since 2004, with the exception of CO_2 emissions for which there has only been a small decrease since 2008

(Figure 4.5). The bulk of air pollution emissions originate from road transport. CO_2 emissions have decreased only slightly since 2008, driven by the economic recession and subsidies for cleaner cars. NMVOC emissions have declined significantly due to stricter emission standards for cars. NO_x and PM_{10} emissions from gasoline cars declined strongly as a result of better abatement equipment and better fuels. This was not the case for NO_x from diesel cars. According to the European test cycle, NO_x emissions should have gone down for diesel cars, but there seems to be a strong difference between actual emissions and test cycle emissions (Ligterink et al., 2013). Further, monitoring studies have revealed a significant and growing discrepancy between actual CO_2 emission reductions and those calculated on the basis of emission data from the European test cycle results; actual emission reductions turned out to be only half of what was estimated by test values (PBL, 2015).

Figure 4.5. **Declining trends in air pollution emissions from transport, 2004-13**

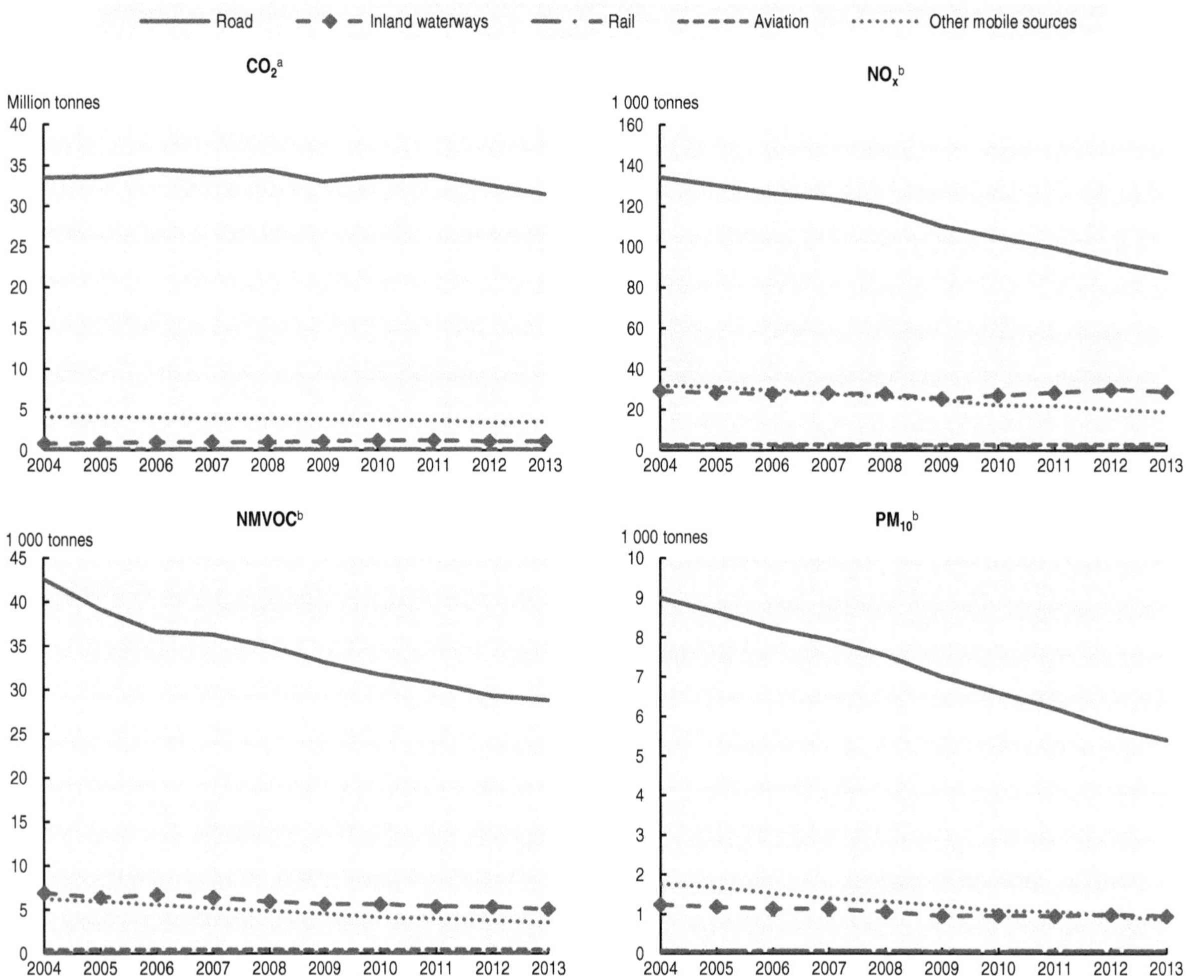

a) Emissions from road, water, rail and air transport reported according to the IPCC guidelines and calculated on the basis of motor fuel sales in the Netherlands.
b) Emissions from mobile sources, excluding emissions from mobile machinery, fishery and seagoing shipping.
Source: CBS (2015), *StatLine* (database).

StatLink http://dx.doi.org/10.1787/888933280360

The decline in conventional emissions (NMVOC, NO_x and PM_{10}) has allowed the Netherlands to improve overall air quality, limit average concentrations of pollutants and the number of hot spots that exceed limit concentrations. The spatial variation in average (yearly) concentration is shown in Figure 4.6.

Figure 4.6. **Improvements in average concentrations of PM_{10} and NO_x, while some hot spots remain, 2013**

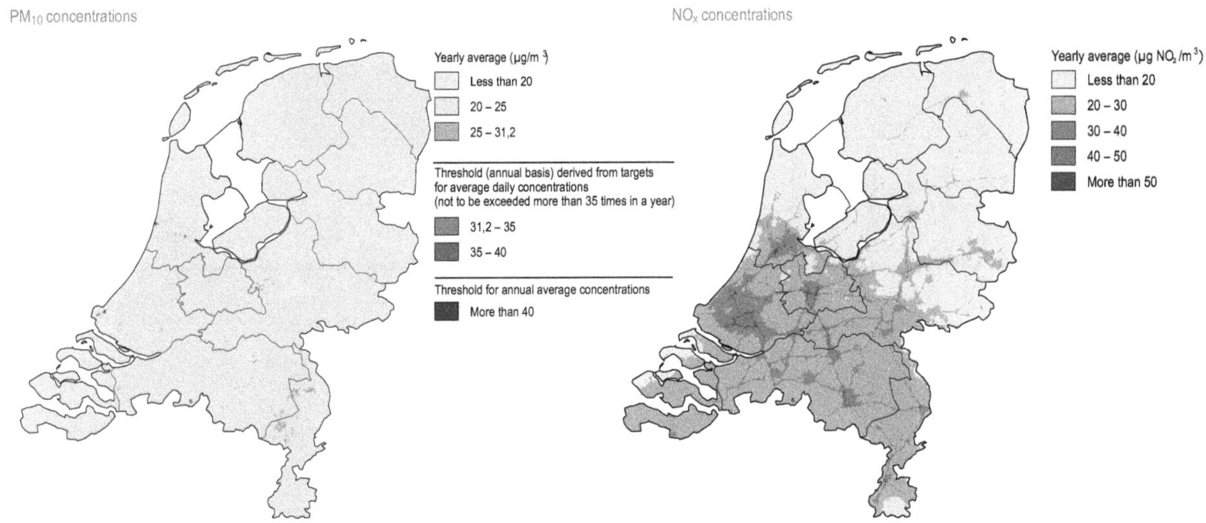

Source: CBS (2014), *Environmental Data Compendium* (website) based on PBL data.

The yearly limit concentrations of PM_{10} and nitrogen dioxide (NO_2) set by the EU are exceeded along a limited number of roads, a clear improvement compared to 2004. The growth of car kilometres of 5% has been largely compensated by the introduction of cleaner cars that satisfy the Euro 4 standard (2005) and the Euro 5 standard (2009/2011). To interpret these data, four points are important. First, some of the emissions responsible for the concentrations originate abroad and, within the Netherlands, from sectors other than transport (industry, agriculture; see Chapter 1). Second, the concentrations depend on weather conditions (wind, inversion, etc.). Third, damage from the concentrations depends strongly on the population density in the high-concentration areas. Finally, even when concentrations remain under the limit, further reductions in densely populated areas may still be valuable in cost-benefit terms.

3.2. *Noise levels from transport*

The absolute noise levels from transport are decreasing in the Netherlands, while the sensitivity and attention of the population to noise issues is increasing. Sensitivity is rising because low noise hindrance is an income elastic good and well-publicised medical research points to higher than expected damages from exposure to traffic noise, including to cardiovascular health and cognitive function (EEA, 2010). Figure 4.7 shows that many more households suffer from excessive road transport noise than from excessive rail or air transport noise. Along national roads in 2006, 6 300 houses suffered from noise levels that exceeded 65 decibels (dB [A]) (the target for the maximum level of exposure for houses along roads). In 2011, this number was reduced to 4 000 due to changes in infrastructure

Figure 4.7. **Households suffer more from road noise than from noise due to rail or air transport, 2010**

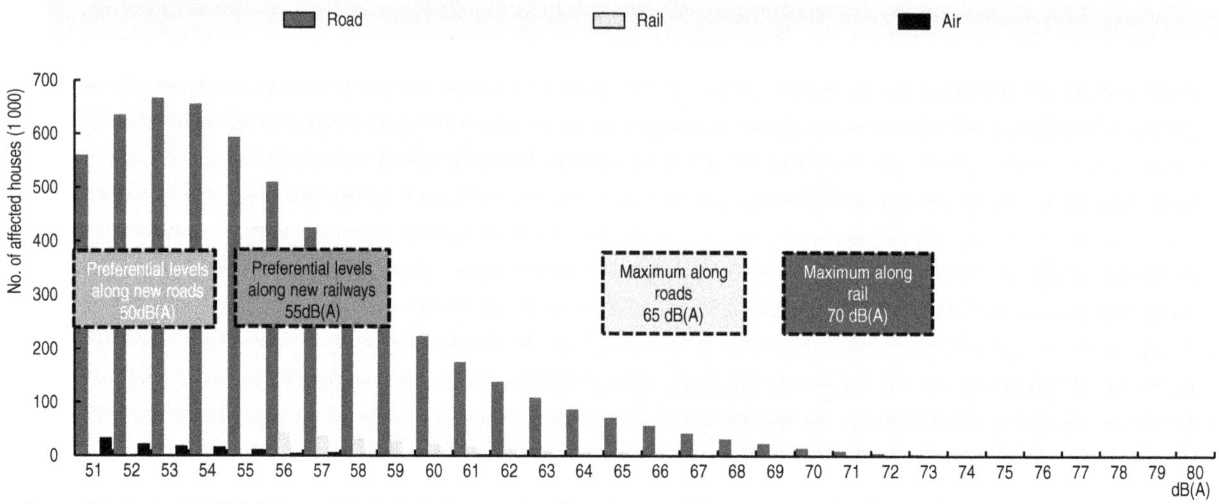

Source: Schroten A. et al (2014), *Externe en infrastructuurkosten van* verkeer [External costs and infrastructure costs of road transport].

StatLink http://dx.doi.org/10.1787/888933280375

such as noise barriers, better road pavement and insulation of houses (Government of the Netherlands, 2014; KiM, 2014).

The noise caused by the Schiphol airport decreased between 2005 and 2013 due in part to fewer very noisy freight flights in the early morning and at night.

3.3. *Traffic congestion*

All modes of transport suffer from congestion, but congestion is most prominent for road transportation. Congestion losses (measured as number of hours lost) have been declining in all congestion-prone regions in the last three years (with the exception of the provincial roads in Noord-Brabant where the number of lost hours was stable) due primarily to additional lanes on the main roads (KiM, 2014). Since 2004, there has been a 42% decrease of travel time losses due to more road capacity in heavily congested areas along with a 30% increase of travel time losses due to an increase in traffic volumes. The latter was caused by growth in population, employment and car ownership. Peak hour congestion on rail lines reduces the likelihood of all users getting a seat, and thus decreases comfort levels. It also potentially lowers the reliability of the rail system.

3.4. *Traffic safety*

The Dutch road system performs rather well in international comparisons of traffic safety (OECD/ITF, 2014), (Table 4.2). In 85% of accidents, a car was involved. However, over the last 12 to 15 years, the number of people killed in car accidents has been reduced by 57%. This is due to better car technologies, better road design (the building of roundabouts) and improved traffic regulation (KiM, 2013). Bicyclists are the group with the slowest progress in terms of reduced accidents. The risk for bicyclists per kilometre travelled has decreased, but much less than for car passengers; bicyclists are still 11 times more likely to be killed. Each year, about 200 cyclists are killed. In addition, 11 000 bicyclists are seriously injured each year; a car was involved in only 15% of these accidents. This type of accident is not decreasing partly because of increased cycling by people over 70 years of age.

Table 4.2. **Declines in road fatalities by user group since 1990**

	1990 (reported)	2000	2010	2011	2012	2012 Percentage change from 2011 %	2000 %	1990 %
Bicyclists	304	233	162	200	200	0.0	-14.2	-34.2
Mopeds	95	104	43	43	44	2.3	-57.7	53.7
Motorcycles	72	95	63	52	54	3.8	-43.2	-25.0
Passenger car occupants	702	543	246	231	232	0.4	-57.3	-67.0
Pedestrians	144	114	72	74	68	-8.1	-40.4	-52.8
Others incl. unknown	59	77	54	61	52	-14.8	-32.5	-11.9
Total	1 376	1 166	640	661	650	-1.7	-44.3	-52.8

Source: OECD/ITF, (2014).

4. Overall objectives of sustainable mobility policy

Successive governments have put forward many different policy visions for sustainable mobility over the last ten years. Over this period, six policy documents have shaped Dutch policy orientations with respect to mobility. The frequent shifts in policy vision are related to the country's many coalition governments over the review period. Changes in policy are typically necessary when external conditions change dramatically. The economic recession, for example, required a revision of tax and subsidy programmes. Other issues, however, such as addressing climate change and road and congestion management, have been constant challenges; this makes it more difficult to understand why so many major policy shifts have occurred. The remainder of this chapter will focus on a few key objectives and policy orientations.

In 2005, there was an emphasis on acceptability, reliability and decentralisation of policies. One of the most daring initiatives was a proposal for a national road pricing system called "Paying Differently for Mobility". This system aimed to reform the high vehicle purchase and registration taxes into a system where car users would pay a kilometre fee that varied according to the time and place of car use. However, before the draft bill could be officially discussed in Parliament in 2010, the government resigned and the whole project was put on hold.

In 2008, the new government prioritised reform of car purchase taxes as part of the project "Paying Differently for Mobility". The introduction of a CO_2-based charge in the vehicle purchase tax aimed to encourage the purchase of cleaner and more fuel-efficient vehicles. The tax sought primarily to achieve the medium-term (2012) EU emission targets in the framework of the Kyoto Protocol. The EU translated the objective into an overall country objective for sectors not covered by the EU emissions trading system (ETS) (building, service, transport and agriculture), as well as a set of fuel-efficiency standards for cars and the promotion of non-fossil fuel use. The Dutch government translated the objective into a reduction of CO_2 emissions for the transport sector from 39 Mt to 30-34 Mt in 2005-20. Hekkenberg and Verdonk (2014) expect that CO_2 emissions in 2020 will be in the range of 30-37 million tonnes. For cars, the plan was to introduce very strong incentives to buy more fuel-efficient vehicles, as well as more hybrid and electric vehicles. But the realised emission reduction is smaller than expected (see discussion below).

In 2008, a broad sectorial agreement on mobility, logistics and infrastructure complemented actions at the level of car purchases. It covered a large variety of actions addressing road freight, inland waterways, rail and air transport, as well as supplementary actions to promote new vehicle technologies and biofuels. As these actions are bottom-up efforts and have complex interactions, their overall impact is not easy to assess. Nevertheless, some measures have been assessed. For example, Goudappel-Goffeng (2013) assessed the programme "*Beter Benutten*" (Better Use of Existing Infrastructure), which contained 300 measures, including stimulation of bicycle use and off-peak driving, as well as better road management. They found the measures contributed to an overall reduction of emissions of the order of 1% for CO_2, NO_X and PM_{10}. The most effective measures were those that reduced peak travel and decreased overall demand.

In 2012, a new vision on infrastructure and spatial planning was set out. The National Policy Strategy for Infrastructure and Spatial Planning priorities are: safe, competitive, accessible and liveable. This vision defined plans with a 2040 horizon and strongly decentralised land-use decisions to the regional and municipal governments. The overarching objectives for the medium term (2028) are to improve competitiveness by strengthening the country's spatial and economic structure, to improve accessibility and to aim for a liveable and safe environment (Government of the Netherlands, 2012).

Also in 2012, the new government affirmed it does not plan to reconsider road pricing for cars, but will instead rely on more efficient management of road infrastructure. For trucks, there are no plans to implement kilometre charging before 2020, but the current Eurovignette (a road user charge) for trucks above 12 tonnes will focus more on cleaner trucks as they will have to pay a lower price for the vignette. The aim is to reduce congestion through better road management and additional lanes on existing motorways in high congestion locations.

In 2013, the 2008 sectorial agreements were reformulated and strengthened by the Energy Agreement for Sustainable Growth of the Netherlands Social Economic Council (Chapters 2 and 3). The council, an important advisory body to Parliament and the government, represents the interests of trade unions and industry on all major economic and social issues. Parliament mandated the council to produce an agreement between the different sector-based organisations, government and civil society on environmental policy initiatives for different sectors, including transport. The resulting agreement contains an ambitious plan to reduce GHG emissions through mainly voluntary actions. For the longer term (2035) the aim is to have all new cars driving free of carbon emissions and an overall reduction of CO_2 emissions by at least 60% for the transport sector in 2050 (SER, 2014).

5. Governance for sustainable mobility

In recent years, the government merged different ministries into the Ministry of Infrastructure and Environment to integrate various policy domains that deal with infrastructure, transport, housing and the environment. In addition, the government improved consultation and co-decision with regional authorities through a multi-annual programme for infrastructure, spatial planning and transport ("MIRT") (Government of the Netherlands, 2014).

The Netherlands has a tradition of long-term planning and consensus-based decision making, known as the "polder approach" (Chapter 2). Long-term planning is informed by specialised public research institutions, then discussed in different councils and finally approved by Parliament. There is also a strong tradition of public debate.

The Netherlands was a forerunner in terms of long-term planning and long-term policy visions. It has good public research institutes that can help prepare and assess mobility policies, including the Netherlands Bureau for Economic Policy Analysis (CPB), the Netherlands Environmental Agency (PBL) and the Institute for Transport Policy Analysis (KiM). These institutes have a worldwide reputation for scientific excellence and have kept their independence, which is crucial for good policy making on matters that are inherently complex and technical.

The Netherlands also has a strong tradition of second opinion for large infrastructure projects that has improved policy making. In a second opinion, a different team of experts checks the methodology and calculations of the project assessment using the same basic data. This tradition exists for infrastructure projects, but could be implemented more actively for other important policy interventions related to sustainable mobility. For example, a coherent assessment of climate policy in transport is lacking and the rules for valuing CO_2 emission reductions are not clear (OECD, 2014). In addition, according to Koopmans (2010), an important part of waterway and rail infrastructure projects do not pass the cost-benefit test. Moreover, public transport projects that are decentralised to local authorities, but co-financed by the central government, escape a rigorous cost-benefit test. This is particularly worrisome in the context of the trend to decentralise decision making for infrastructure planning (Chapter 2). According to Wouter (2014), cost-benefit analysis is a guarantee for better decision making if it is based on model analysis, reasonable exogenous inputs and a standard methodology.

There is traditionally strong co-operation and co-ordination between local, provincial and national authorities in addition to co-operation with a broad range of stakeholders. One example is the Sustainable Infrastructure Corporation, a joint initiative of governments, market players and knowledge institutions. It aims to incorporate sustainability into infrastructure projects, as well as to integrate sustainability into all phases of public procurement.

In 2011, the Netherlands launched the Green Deals programme to remove barriers, such as lack of funds and unnecessary legislation that hamper initiatives to "green" the economy" (Chapter 2). By formalising co-operation between interested partners and the government and helping parties overcome barriers, the hope is to realise quick wins. Green Deals cover a large number of initiatives, including some related to transport (such as R&D for new fuels). On the one hand, Green Deals can work quickly by avoiding a long legislative process. On the other, they may end up supporting the wrong projects as the government may not be the best judge of what will likely succeed. There is a risk of a "winners' curse" for the most rosy R&D project proposals: governments want to support those projects that promise the largest benefits. But, when the ultimate effect of the proposed action is highly uncertain, the proposal that is most optimistic is likely to be the one supported. It may be wise to organise systematically a cost-benefit analysis for each of these initiatives, as well as for combinations of initiatives.

6. Policy instruments for sustainable mobility: An assessment

The Netherlands has a strong record in sustainable mobility policy. In particular, it has a well-developed planning and policy process, a high-quality network of policy research institutes, a relatively high share of environmentally friendly modes of transport (such as biking), a relatively low share of diesel cars and a high share of inland waterways for freight transportation. This section examines policy for road transport, rail, inland waterways and air, as well as local initiatives.

6.1. Road transport policy

The government has several policy levers to address the main externalities related to road transport, which are congestion, climate impacts, air pollution, noise and accidents. It can tax and subsidise the use and purchase of particular types of cars and trucks, regulate the use of roads and increase the capacity of the road network. Table 4.3 lists the main economic instruments available to address externalities from road transport and indicates whether they are implemented in the Netherlands.

Table 4.3. **Main economic instruments for addressing externalities from road transport**

Policy instrument	Cars	Trucks
Gasoline excise tax	Yes	n/a
Diesel excise tax	Yes	Yes
Taxes and subsidies for other fuels	Lower tax (LPG) or subsidy (electricity)	n/a
Vehicle purchase and ownership taxes	Progressive in function of carbon emissions + surcharge on diesel cars	Eurovignette is a fixed sum per year that is a function of axle weight and European norm
Parking charges	In most cities	n/a
Distance charging	No	No
Road pricing by time of day and by place	No	No

Failure to introduce road pricing as a missed opportunity

From an economic point of view, the optimal instrument to regulate congestion is road pricing (or tolling). Road pricing can be restricted to a city or implemented nationally. Such systems are implemented in several cities in Europe, such as London and Stockholm (Anas et al., 2011), as well as in Singapore. In the Netherlands, the cabinet had approved a national road pricing scheme that was to be decided in 2009-10 and would have become fully operational in 2017. Before Parliament could officially discuss the scheme, the government resigned for unrelated reasons. Evaluations of the proposal at the time indicated the cost of implementation, as well as a lack of public acceptance in the media and political support, posed significant barriers. Since then, the new government has affirmed it does not plan to reconsider road pricing for cars through 2017. Instead, recent governments have rolled out very high subsidy schemes for cleaner cars and addressed congestion through better use of road capacity. The 2013 Energy Agreement includes plans to begin studying road pricing again as of June 2016.

The main idea behind the proposed road pricing scheme was to substitute the high fixed charges on cars (high purchase and vehicle ownership taxes) with a variable charge per kilometre. Charges would be based on time of travel (peak versus off peak), location (congested versus non-congested areas) and the pollution characteristics of vehicles. For trucks, the charges would have replaced the Eurovignette. The scheme was expected to decrease the volume of car use, mainly in the congested areas. Koźluk (2010) summarises the Dutch plan and possible alternatives (see Besseling et al., 2005 for more details). The congestion pricing scheme would have cut congestion levels on all roads more or less in half. The reduction of CO_2 and NO_x emissions would have been more or less in line with the reduction of overall traffic volumes (5-10%).

Experience in London and Stockholm (Anas et al., 2011) has shown that implementing road pricing by setting up a cordon around the city can reduce congestion levels in and around cities very sharply through a small reduction of traffic in the peak hours (10% to

20%). Experience in Stockholm has also shown there is less than a one-to-one substitution of road use by public transport. Only one out of five passengers who disappeared from the road at peak times would end up in public transport (Eliasson et al., 2009). This implies that road pricing does not require a massive expansion of public transport capacity. Peak load pricing for public transport can also be an important complement for road pricing (Kilani et al., forthcoming).

The reasons why the proposed road pricing scheme was not accepted in the Netherlands is a challenging question that merits further research. Building on a model of policy reform, De Borger and Proost (2012) identify a number of potential barriers to such a scheme, including the cost uncertainty faced by road users. *Ex ante,* road users are unsure about the individual costs of switching from car use to public transportation. When non-drivers share in the benefit from collected toll revenues, the marginal car driver perceives high expected substitution costs and a low share of revenues from toll charges. After implementation, uncertainty is resolved. As a consequence, the marginal car user will typically enjoy lower-than-expected substitution costs, and thus may support congestion pricing *ex post*. Hence, a majority of drivers may vote against road pricing *ex ante*, or even vote against a pilot project, because their expected gain is negative. But they may support the scheme once it has been implemented. This observation is consistent with evidence from road pricing schemes in London and Stockholm.

Moreover, the Netherlands proposed a nation-wide scheme with strong regional variation, rather than a scheme for one city. This may have been an extra handicap to build consensus as each region may have started negotiating for its own (low) rate. In addition to the perceived effects on drivers, the cost of implementing the scheme and the transaction costs associated with operation can eat away 10-20% of the toll revenues. Technology, however, is making significant progress on this front.

Fuel taxes and parking charges as the main variable charges on road use for cars

In the absence of road pricing, fuel taxes and parking charges remain the main variable charges on road use for cars. Since fuel taxes are uniform over time and place, they cannot really address congestion. At best, they can only charge for CO_2 damage and charge in an imperfect way for the other mileage-related externalities (Box 4.1).

In addition to fuel taxes, high parking charges continue to be an important second-best instrument. These are used intensively in major Dutch cities and have increased over time (KiM, 2014). Good parking policies achieve two objectives. First, they reduce cruising for parking that occurs when on-street parking is too cheap compared to off-street parking (Calthrop and Proost, 2005). Van Ommeren et al. (2012) analysed empirically parking prices in the Netherlands. Using a sample of the National Traffic Survey (2005-07), they found that on-street prices are more or less equal to off-street prices. Amsterdam has one of the highest on-street parking prices (EUR 5 per hour in the centre) in the country. Most other Dutch cities have implemented parking pricing. The average on-street and off-street parking fee is about EUR 1.5 per hour and total parking revenues are about EUR 1 billion (about EUR 125 per car per year). As on- and off-street prices are very close, the assessment found very limited time spent cruising for parking (some 36 seconds per trip). In addition to reducing cruising, an extra levy on all parking (on- as well as off-street) can be a third-best way to limit car use in the city. It is not clear to what extent Dutch cities have used this option or its effectiveness. Finally, parking charges could become even more effective if employer-paid parking was eliminated (Van Ommeren and Wentinck, 2012).

Box 4.1. A second-best approach to road use externalities

As fuel taxes are uniform over time and place, they cannot really address congestion. At best, they can charge for CO_2 damage and charge in an imperfect way for the other mileage-related externalities. According to Parry et al. (2014a), the "ideal second best" gasoline tax equals the sum of two terms[a] described in Table 4.4. The first component, climate damage, is directly proportional to gasoline consumption. Climate damage estimated at EUR 25 per tonne of CO_2 equals approximately EUR 0.1 per litre (L).

The second component consists of other external costs associated with driving a particular vehicle 1 km in the Netherlands, including external congestion, air pollution, noise and external accidents. External congestion cost is the additional time and schedule delay one more car adds for all other car users that use the same road. The external accident cost is the increase in accident costs caused by one additional car for all other road users. Estimates of these costs vary strongly (see European Commission, 2014; Parry et al., 2014b). For the sake of illustration, assume these costs equal EUR 0.09 per km, that a car consumes 5 L per 100 km (and drives 20 km with each litre) and that, whenever the gasoline tax increases, half of the reduced gasoline consumption comes from less mileage (the Ω parameter in Table 4.4).

Table 4.4. Example of calculating an ideal level of a gasoline tax to correct for external costs

Gasoline tax (Euro/L) =	1
Climate damage per litre of gasoline (Euro/L)	0.10
Mileage-related external costs (Euro/km) x fuel efficiency (km/L) Ω	(0.09)(20)(0.5)

Note: Ω represents the share of the reduction of gasoline that comes from reduced mileage.

This example illustrates two important points. First, when the climate damage associated with the consumption of gasoline is around EUR 0.10 per L, this means that a gasoline tax of EUR 1 per L acts as a EUR 250 tax per tonne of CO_2. It is not called a carbon tax, but it acts as a carbon tax. Second, any gains in fuel efficiency reduce the "power" of a gasoline tax to make drivers pay for externalities: a larger km/litre in Table 4.4 requires a larger gasoline tax to generate the same effect.[c] So the shift to more fuel-efficient vehicles requires an increase in the gasoline tax if this tax is meant to make drivers pay for externalities. Furthermore, if an increase of gasoline taxes is impossible, the introduction of more fuel-efficient vehicles is counterproductive to tackle the other externalities.

Finally, a government will also raise tax revenues from the gasoline tax. From this perspective, the fuel-efficiency reactions and mileage reduction are inefficient as they reduce the revenue base.

a) Parry et al. (2014b) add a third component: the correction of myopic behaviour of car consumers that undervalue the gasoline savings of a more fuel-efficient car or of less driving. It is not considered here because empirical evidence for the EU car market (Grignolon et al., 2014) shows convincingly that consumers take into account on average 87% of the future fuel expenditures when they buy a car. So, the undervaluation is at best very limited.

b) Part of the external accident costs is internalised by drivers themselves via experience-rated insurance premiums.

c) For example, improving fuel efficiency from 5 to 4 L per 100 km means that 25 km can be driven per litre and the gasoline tax should increase to 0.1 + (0.09)(25)(0.5) = 1.225 EUR per L rather than EUR 1 per L.

Source: Based on Parry et al. (2014a).

Pricing of road use by trucks

Road use by trucks, priced by diesel excises and the fixed Eurovignette[2] charge, continues to be inefficiently priced in the Netherlands. The Eurovignette charge varies according to the truck's emission characteristics. The Netherlands will soon be surrounded by countries that apply kilometre charging, once Belgium implements such a scheme in 2016; this can threaten the revenue basis of Dutch truck taxes. Distance charges in neighbouring countries tend to generate much more revenue than the Eurovignette. Driving through the Netherlands is much cheaper per kilometre than in Germany (Figure 4.8). The figure shows that countries with distance charges (or tolls on motorways) make trucks pay much more than those that do not. The practice of implementing distance charging is spreading in European countries.

Figure 4.8. **Driving through the Netherlands is much cheaper per kilometre than in Germany**

Total charges for a standard domestic haul of 400 km by a 40-tonne truck

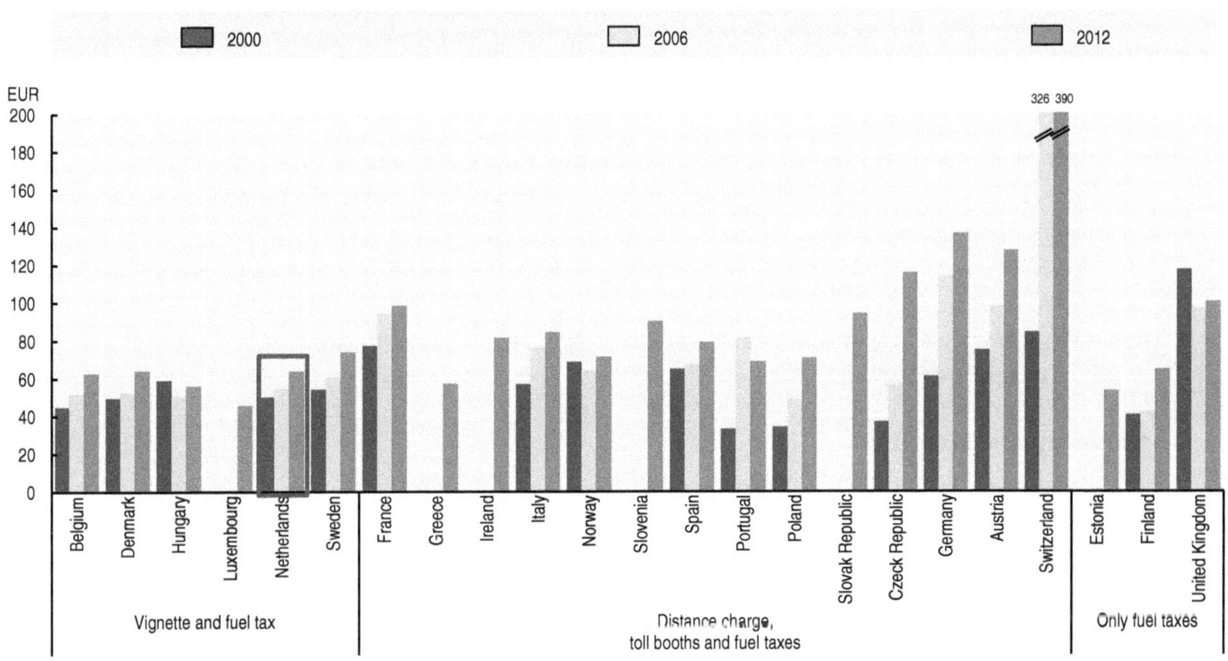

Note: Charging policy as of 2012.

Source: Based on data fom Hylén, B., J. Kauppila and E. Chong, 2013, "Road Haulage Charges and Taxes: Summary Analysis and Data Tables 1998-2012", *International Transport Forum Discussion Papers*, No. 2013/08; analysis by Mandell S. and S. Proost (2015) "Why truck distance charges are contagious and drive fuel taxes to the bottom", *Discussion Paper Series*, March DPS 15.04, KU Leuven, Center for Economic Studies.

StatLink http://dx.doi.org/10.1787/888933280387

A recent study by Mandell and Proost (2015) suggests that countries that do not implement distance charges, like the Netherlands, could risk losing significant amounts of their excise tax revenues. As international trucks can decide where to take fuel, countries with a distance charge can increase slightly their distance charge and lower their diesel excise to encourage fuelling in their country. In this way, they can undercut the diesel excise of neighbours without distance charges. The study concludes that based on geographical developments, the implementation of distance charges appears to follow a sequential pattern: distance charges are contagious. The central EU states already have a distance-based charge and several states bordering them are currently working towards implementing such a charge. The spread of distance charging for trucks in neighbouring countries makes the Netherlands vulnerable as probably at least half of the road freight can fuel abroad.

The reform of the purchase and ownership taxes on vehicles into a progressive carbon tax

Reform of the purchase and ownership taxes on vehicles into a progressive carbon tax was costly and is expected to have only a minimal effect on reducing overall emissions. Purchase and ownership taxes have different effects. Strong evidence suggests that high purchase taxes may encourage consumers to postpone replacing their cars, leading to rather old fleets and high pollution. This was the case in the Netherlands until 2005. In 2006-10, the country restructured vehicle purchase taxes (based on the value of the car) into a progressive CO_2 tax. The new tax implied a significant cost – thousands of euros per tonne of CO_2 abated.[3] Moreover, according to Geilenkirchen et al. (2014), a rebound effect makes the net saving of CO_2 emissions much smaller than expected: when the cost of driving decreases, vehicles are driven more. The net cost for the government budget in terms of base erosion remains to be estimated, but is substantial (EUR 1 to 2 billion in the first years of the reform).[4]

Compared to other countries, such as Denmark (Munk-Nielsen, 2014), the Dutch tax reform avoided the mistake of inadvertently promoting the purchase of diesel cars. The Netherlands has always maintained a specific annual vehicle tax for diesel cars that strongly discourages a shift to these vehicles. Diesel cars generate less tax revenue per kilometre (Harding, 2014) and have a small carbon emission advantage per kilometre driven in test cycles. In the real world, however, their NO_x emissions are clearly higher than those of gasoline cars (TNO, 2013).

Car scrapping subsidies

For a short period (May 2009 to April 2010), a scrapping scheme was implemented to reduce the number of older cars and delivery vans in the Dutch car stock. The objective was to increase car sales and reduce pollution by old cars. The scheme cost EUR 80 million and 80 000 car purchasers benefited from the subsidy. There was no cost-efficiency or cost-benefit assessment of the measure. The Netherlands was not alone in implementing tax incentives aimed at decreasing the share of older fuel-inefficient cars. Several other countries including, France and Germany, also used a scrapping scheme in 2008-10 (ITF, 2011). The net effect on CO_2 of such schemes was low or even negative (D'Haultfoeuille et al., 2014). Moreover, if one does not account for the macroeconomic stimulus (which could have been obtained in many other ways with larger social net benefits), these programmes were also very costly.

Plans for electric vehicle expansion

The Netherlands has strongly encouraged the expansion of electric vehicle use and has achieved the highest penetration of electric cars in the EU. There are diverse motivations for these efforts: to contribute to climate objectives, to reduce air pollution (NO_x, fine particulates) and noise in city centres, and to reinforce the country's economic position. The Netherlands set objectives to put 15-20 000 electric vehicles on the road by the end of 2015 and 1 million by the end of 2025. In 2014, more than 31 000 electric and plug-in electric hybrid vehicles were already on the road. For 2011-15, EUR 59 million was set aside to stimulate demonstration projects and to put the necessary infrastructure in place. Compared to many other countries, the Netherlands has already strongly promoted the purchase of electric hybrid cars: in 2014, it had captured 4% of the market of new car sales (ICCT, 2014). The aim of reinforcing the economic position by promoting the development and use of electric cars is a long shot as many countries with national car manufacturers (France, Germany, Japan) probably have a comparative advantage.

Because the electricity for electric vehicle charging is covered by the EU ETS cap, when driven electrically, they do not contribute to additional carbon emissions (outside of the cap). This is an absolute cap on carbon emissions, so replacing a fossil fuel car with an electric car effectively decreases carbon emissions, provided the cap is strict enough. Electric cars also do not emit almost any conventional air pollution. The EU strongly encourages the adoption of electric vehicles. But while electric vehicles may be a technology of the future, any cost-benefit analysis shows it is still a very costly approach to reduce CO_2 emissions (Proost and Van Dender, 2012).[5] PBL (2012) also finds that reaching the electrification objective is very costly, but recognises it is the only way to achieve the EU objective of decarbonising urban transport at present. There is a need for a thorough cost-benefit assessment of this programme at country level and an assessment of the decarbonisation objective at the EU level (Eliasson et al., 2014).

Stimulation of biofuel use in cars

EU regulations[6] oblige the Netherlands to introduce a minimum share of biofuels in automotive fuels of 5.5% in 2014. This can be achieved by blending biofuels and regular fossil fuels. Under the national subsidy programme for innovative biofuels for transport, the government has awarded support via a tendering process for four projects that produce biodiesel with waste and residues (Government of the Netherlands, 2014). Even if tendering procedures help keep costs down, there is a need to assess the biofuel objective at both the country and EU level; costs are high compared to other ways to reduce carbon emissions and the production of some biofuels has other negative side effects (food supply markets, deforestation, etc.)

Better use of road infrastructure

With one of the most dense and congested road networks in Europe, the Netherlands has everything to gain by capacity-enhancing measures. Small measures can improve the effective capacity of the road system. According to KiM (2014), many different factors explain the evolution of congestion levels on the main roads over the last ten years (Table 4.5).

Table 4.5. **Main factors driving time losses due to congestion on main Dutch roads, 2004-13**

Time losses in 2013 compared to 2004	
Population, employment, car ownership	+30%
Telework	-4%
Fuel price	-9%
Decrease of taxes on commuting trips	+8%
Decrease of speed and speed control	+3%
Other factors	-3%
Additional lanes on roads	-42%
Traffic management	-3%

Source: Kim (2014).

The increase of population, employment and car ownership (time losses +30%) has been, and will remain, the main factor contributing to congestion. The share of teleworkers (part-time) increased from 1-18% in 2000-13, contributing to a decrease of time losses of 4%.[7] The increase in real fuel costs (higher taxes partly compensated by better efficiency) has decreased traffic flows and has therefore decreased time losses (-9%). The tax-free allowance for commuting by car introduced in 2004 (EUR 0.18 per car km and EUR 0.15 per car km for distances longer than 10 km) led to an increase of peak traffic of 8% (van der Loop, 2012).

The main decrease in congestion has come from additional lanes to existing motorways (time losses -42%). Better road management has also contributed (time losses -3%). Adding capacity also attracts new traffic, part of it coming from secondary roads. According to KiM (2012), the additional traffic generated by the new capacity is smaller than the increase in capacity suggesting an increase in capacity of 10% would only generate a maximum increase of traffic of 5% over a few years. Other sources in the international literature (Duranton and Turner, 2011), which take a longer term into account, point to a much larger effect: the latent traffic generated would fully annihilate the gains in capacity. As the easy wins in terms of better road management have likely been exhausted, a further increase of road traffic can no longer be solved by additional road capacity. This leaves road pricing as a principal policy option to address congestion.

The 2013 Energy Agreement has a long list of mostly voluntary measures to reduce congestion. An example of a voluntary measure agreed under a previous programme is the system of 16 regional covenants where regional governments, large companies and regional employer organisations agreed to reduce the number of car trips by 5%. The number of trips was reduced by 1.5% instead of 5% in a period of a few years. This could be expected: when there is congestion, the efforts of a few companies to reduce work trips can be completely eroded by increased driving of non-participants. Goudappel-Goffeng (2013) assessed the environmental performance of most of these measures. The results indicate they have beneficial effects on conventional emissions, but are extremely costly in terms of CO_2 emissions (EUR 1 000-5 000 per tonne of CO_2).[8]

Road infrastructure investments

Over the last ten years, the Netherlands has mostly invested in additional lanes on existing major roads, as the road network was already complete. The country has a strong tradition in the assessment of these types of public investments. Since 2000, there has been a commitment to use CBA for all large infrastructure projects (De Jong, 2013). There is a common methodology ("OEI guideline" published by CPB and the Netherlands Economic Institute, NEI) and a second opinion ensures a thorough check of all major investments. The CBA outcome is not binding for the government, but most of it is public, enhancing transparency. Some projects with poor benefit-cost ratios have gone forward, but the CBA has often improved the quality of investment in the planning phase.

One missing dimension in most CBAs of transport projects is land use. A major investment in transportation infrastructure will change the choice of residences, workplaces and the associated agglomeration and environment effects. These second-round effects have been largely neglected due to the lack of a good spatial general equilibrium model. However, CPB has recently proposed such a new model that allows for estimating these spatial effects (Teulings, Ossokina, de Groot, 2014; Box 4.2). Their analysis

Box 4.2. Assessing transport projects remains a challenging task: An example from Amsterdam

One of the most difficult assessments in agglomerations is determining how new infrastructure will affect the job and housing market. According to the New Economic Geography theory, a better connection to more peripheral areas may actually harm an area instead of helping it, as most jobs would relocate to the centre. CPB has a new integrated land-use model that represents the land and job markets, as well as all commuting patterns. Teulings et al. (2014) used the model to show the effects of a policy experiment involving commuting patterns to Amsterdam, which is separated from the area north of the city by an important canal. Many people commute from the north to Amsterdam via five highway tunnels and two rail tunnels. In a theoretical closing of the two rail tunnels, the experiment suggested that a new transportation link (the two rail tunnels) may indeed lead to a higher concentration of jobs in the centre (Amsterdam). But while jobs move south, the north becomes a more attractive area to live in. As the more highly skilled people are more mobile and prefer to travel by train, they will benefit most from the new infrastructure. Table 4.6 shows the breakdown of the welfare effects by education level and land ownership.

Table 4.6. Welfare effects of new transport infrastructure by education level and land ownership

Welfare effect (EUR mln)	Education level			Land ownership			Total
	Low	Middle	High	North	South	Else	
Modal split	203	584	1 133				1920
Job relocation	66	191	461				718
Wage effect	0	19	23				42
Home relocation	-83	-149	-99				-331
Land owners				1 638	51	-1 335	354
Total	186	645	1 518	1 638	51	-1 335	2 703

Modal split (indicated in the first line of the table) is an important benefit because an additional rail connection improves the speed of commuting trips (time and comfort gains). It is remarkable that job relocation (from north to south) adds another 40% to the modal split gain. As the north and south of Amsterdam become more interesting for housing and jobs, land owners in these regions gain, while those in the rest of the country lose as total population remains constant. The results also show that only a small part of the total gains of a rail project (354 of 2 703, in EUR mln) is captured by the land owners. The policy experiment shows that planning and assessing new transport projects remains a challenging task.

Source: Teulings, Ossokina, de Groot (2014).

found that positive indirect effects can represent up to 30% of the direct effects and affect people very differently depending on their education level. Higher skilled people, for example, are more mobile and benefit more from rail passenger transport improvements.

6.2. Rail

Compared to other EU countries, the Dutch rail network is relatively small (Figure 4.9). It remains important, however, for commuting to the big cities.

Over the last ten years, rail use in terms of passenger kilometre has grown by 24%. According to KiM (2014), this growth cannot really be explained by substituting car for rail

Figure 4.9. **Compared to other EU countries, the Dutch rail network is relatively small**

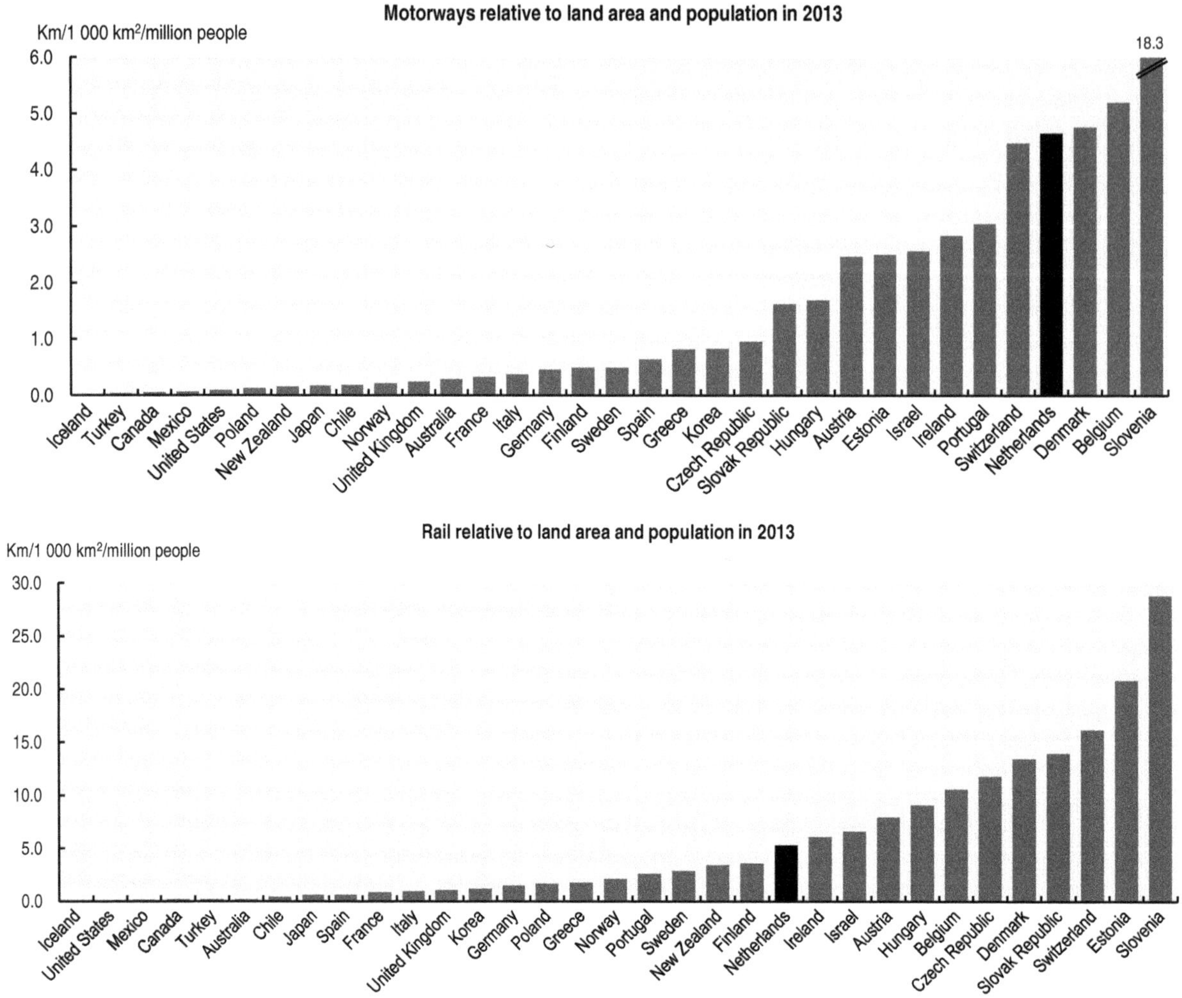

Source: Based on International Transport Forum (2015), Infrastructure Investment and Maintenance (website); OECD (2015), *OECD Environment Statistics* (database).

StatLink http://dx.doi.org/10.1787/888933280398

use, but is mainly due to population growth, an increase in the number of students, increases in car fuel prices, as well as increased supply of trains. The supply of more train kilometres compensates for the effect of higher prices for rail. During peak periods, and in the direction of the major cities, the rail network is crowded, which means there is less chance to find a seat and a possible increase in unreliability. The Dutch government expects a strong increase in ridership for lines connecting the big cities in 2011-30. In the Randstad, growth rates can be between 5-76% in total over this timeframe, depending on the particular line (Ministry of Infrastructure and Environment, 2014a). Extending the rail capacity in the peak period is costly. From an economic point of view, the right response is to differentiate prices between peak and off-peak times, and between congested and non-congested lines. This holds as much for rail as for car networks.

In the framework of their sustainability objective, the Dutch railways plan to electrify more regional lines, like the line in Limburg province, through a EUR 30 million project. This may not be a cost-effective climate policy action as the other benefits (time gains) are likely to be small. The Dutch railways also aim to increase their use of green electricity produced in the Netherlands from 50-100% over 2015-18 (Government of the Netherlands, 2014). This may be good marketing for the Dutch railways, but given the total cap on carbon emissions for electricity generation under the EU ETS, more green electricity in the Netherlands comes down to shifting emissions to another country within the system.

6.3. Inland waterways and air transport

The Netherlands is a transit country, but has succeeded in transporting a large share of its transit freight via relatively environmentally friendly means of transport like inland waterways and rail. The Dutch inland waterways and short sea shipping are the main modes of transport to transport goods in and out of the Port of Rotterdam. Dutch authorities have developed a system of green award certificates to stimulate environmentally friendly shipping and are also implementing a River Information System that allows for close monitoring of all ship movements, including their cargo. This is important for safety and also allows for optimisation of logistics (Government of the Netherlands, 2015a). Similar technological developments and co-ordination are needed in the road freight sector.

The airline industry is organised internationally via a system of hubs and spokes. The influence of a small country in this network is limited, as there are many alternative routes. The number of passengers in Dutch airports has grown by 33% since 2004; if real incomes increase, this growth will likely continue. Recently, regional airports have grown more than the international airport, Schiphol, due to the growth of low-cost carriers that use these airports.

An air passenger tax[9] was levied from 1 July 2008 up to 30 June 2009 (Chapter 3). The tax was abolished largely due to concerns that it caused potential passengers to fly from neighbouring countries. Soon after the Dutch tax was abolished, a similar tax was introduced in neighbouring Germany.

As long as CO_2 emissions are not regulated internationally, it is difficult for one country in isolation to address GHG emissions by air transport. However, the Netherlands could consider a passenger tax on extra-European aviation that takes into account associated CO_2 emissions, together with neighbouring countries. Such a tax would need to be considered taking into account potential competitiveness impacts in the broader international context of the airline industry.

The fact that intra-EU aviation is now included in the EU ETS weakens the argument for taxing passenger flights within the EU. But a tax on long-distance flights could help internalise some of the externalities caused by aviation, at least until a global system to address such externalities is agreed upon. To this end, member states of the International Civil Aviation Organization (ICAO) are currently working on the design and implementation of a global market-based measure for the reduction of CO_2-emissions by the aviation sector. A decision on this system will be taken at the ICAO Assembly in September 2016.

A key environmental issue around airports that national governments can tackle is noise. In Schiphol, noise has been regulated principally by limiting the total number of flights. Further refinement of the noise regulation by a system of ambient noise maxima is expected. As airplanes get quieter, and land-use planning and isolation programmes reduce noise impacts on residents, an absolute cap on flight movements or on noise levels becomes suboptimal. A finer instrument is needed to measure real noise damage (residents x scaled noise damage). An ambient noise tax or an ambient tradable noise scheme can be a more efficient solution. An ambient noise tax would charge airplanes based on noise emission, but also on local impact of the noise (which depends on time and place). A tradable ambient noise scheme achieves the same objective, but gives property rights for noise emissions to the existing carriers. This would allow a more balanced approach to the airport noise problem in Schiphol as the most valuable flights can buy rights to fly at certain times and in certain places. This system would make airlines account for the real noise costs associated with their activity.

6.4. *Noise reduction plans*

In 2012, new legislation came into force (SWUNG) that limits the growth in noise emissions on national road and rail infrastructure. Noise is measured at 60 000 locations along national roads. Between 2006-11, the number of houses with a noise level above 65 decibels along national roads was reduced from 6 300 to 4 000, due to measures like noise barriers and insulation of houses (Ministry of Infrastructure and Environment, 2014b). In the next five years, an additional decrease of 20% is planned. A noise innovation programme (IPG) resulted in cheaper solutions, such as quieter asphalt, to reduce noise at the source. Another programme helps municipal and provincial authorities to reduce nuisance noise.

Generally, there is increasing attention to noise problems created by traffic. Although the measured noise levels have decreased, there is increased sensitivity by the population because of possible health impacts, as well as loss of property values. In a study of the impact of a new bypass in The Hague on property values, Ossokina and Verweij (2014) showed that reducing traffic density by 50% induces, on average, a 1% increase in housing prices.

Reductions in traffic nuisance are valued much more positively when traffic density is already high. A high-density street sees its value increase five times more than a medium-density street. This finding highlights the need to concentrate efforts on the most critical points. It also helps identify a justifiable level of abatement. Currently, the trade-off between costs and benefits of noise reduction programmes is unclear.

6.5. *Local initiatives*

Many congestion, air pollution and noise problems are situated at the level of a city or conurbation. Municipalities are responsible for local roads and local public transport. This has led to very different modal shares of transport across cities (Figure 4.10).

Figure 4.10 shows the role of walking is more or less equal in all major cities. The major differences in modes are in the share of cycling, which varies between 20% in Rotterdam to more than 30% in Amsterdam and Utrecht. This shows that cycling has a substantial share of movement, and especially so for movements within 15 km. The role of public transport is limited in urban areas as biking is a cheap and safe alternative.

Provinces and urban conurbations receive a grant for public transport and can choose a private operator for its operations. If contracts choose the right output to reward and leave enough flexibility to the operator, French cities have shown this can be a source of efficiency gains (Gagnepain et al., 2011). According to the Dutch government, tendering allows cost savings of some 10-15% (Government of the Netherlands, 2015b).

Figure 4.10. **Share of cycling varies among major Dutch cities, 2011-13**

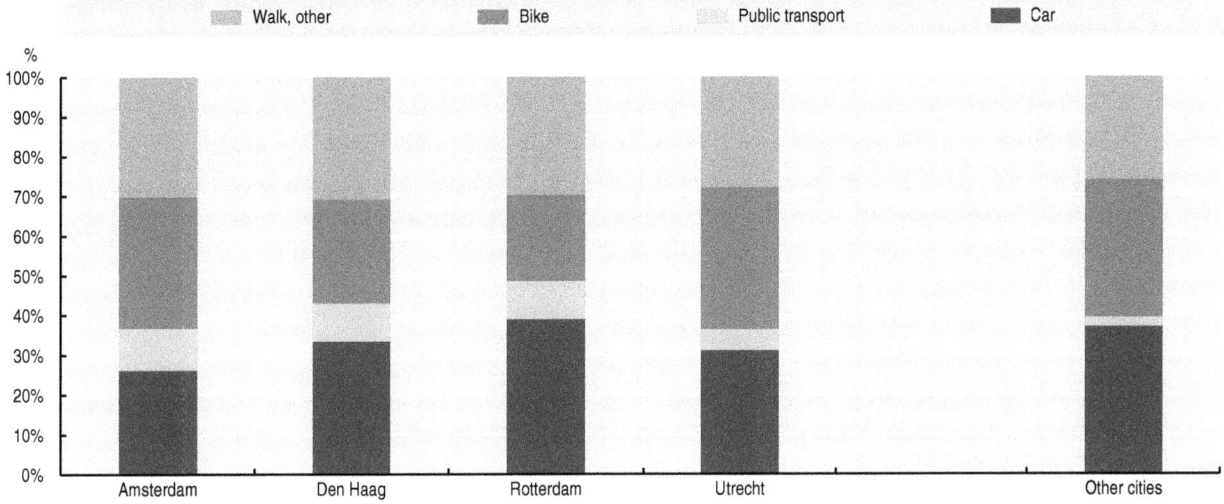

Source: KiM (2014), *Mobiliteitsbeeld 2014 [Mobility Picture 2014].*

StatLink http://dx.doi.org/10.1787/888933280403

Recommendations on sustainable mobility

- Allocate efforts to reduce carbon emissions across sectors based on a cost-efficiency analysis. For example, consider reducing the progressive CO_2 emission differentiation in the motor vehicle purchase tax; this would bring the abatement incentives per tonne of CO_2 emitted from high-emission vehicles more in line with the marginal abatement cost found in other parts of the economy.
- Reconsider the introduction of road pricing for cars, differentiated across place and time, possibly limited to the most congested zone of the country (Randstad). This can be done in a revenue-neutral way by substituting the vehicle purchase and ownership taxes and reducing motor fuel taxes.
- As long as road pricing is not introduced, the second-best option is to continue discouraging car use in urban areas through very high parking charges.
- Reconsider the pricing of public transport (local and rail) so it can cope with growing demand in the peak periods in the Randstad.
- Consider the introduction of distance-based road charging for trucks, as all neighbouring countries have already done or are doing. Trucks have become more fuel efficient and their options to fuel abroad limits the regulating and financing function of diesel charges.
- Consider the introduction of a passenger tax on extra-European aviation, together with neighbouring countries that have not already done so, taking into account potential competitiveness impacts in the broader international context of the airline industry.
- Continue efforts to reduce negative environmental impacts of transport, including through the ambitious plan for noise reduction. Evaluate the potential net benefits of further emission reductions in remaining air pollution hot spots.

Notes

1. International comparisons of modal shares are difficult when a mode with a share of 10% is not reported: the EU Statistical Booklet for Transport does not report the share of bicycling.
2. The Eurovignette is currently levied with Belgium, Sweden, Luxemburg and Denmark. Belgium will leave the Eurovignette system when it introduces the road pricing scheme in 2016.
3. Consider the substitution of a 13.3 L per 100 km car by a car consuming 10 L per 100 km. This provided for a reduction of the purchase tax of EUR 12 500 (based on data in van Meerkerk et al., 2014). Using a purely mechanical calculation, it implies a saving of 5.2 tonne of CO_2 at a cost of EUR 2 403 per tonne. For more fuel-efficient vehicles, the progressive tax will be smaller, but the abatement cost is still some EUR 1 000 per tonne of CO_2. A detailed assessment of this CO_2 tax component can be found in Chapter 3.
4. The greening of purchase tax on new vehicles has resulted in EUR 1.5 billion less in annual tax revenues from the annual vehicle taxes alone since 2007 (PBL, 2015).
5. A modern gasoline car emits some 2 tonnes of CO_2 per year (for 15 000 km) and some 10-15 tonnes over its lifetime. An electric car costs some EUR 10 000 more to produce and pays no usage taxes. This means that the CO_2 savings still come at a very high cost (EUR 666 to 1 000/tonne of CO_2, without discounting).
6. EU Renewable Energy Directive (2009/28/EC) of 23 April 2009.
7. KiM (2014) makes a different assessment than the Platform Smart Work Smart Travel, which claims a reduction of congestion by 40% (Government of the Netherlands, 2014).
8. It is not clear exactly which costs are included.
9. The air passenger tax was levied on passengers two years and older starting their journey from an airport for bigger planes. The tax rate was EUR 11.25 for European destinations and destinations up to 2 500 km (including destinations up to 3 500 km in countries with at least one airport within the boundary of 2 500 km). For other destinations, the tax rate was EUR 45 per passenger.

References

Anas, A. and R. Lindsey (2011), "Reducing urban road transportation externalities: Road pricing in theory and in practice", *Review of Environmental Economics and Policy*, Vol. 5/1, pp. 66-88.

Besseling, P., W. Groot and R. Lebouille (2005), Economische analyse van verschillende vormen van prijsbeleid voor het wegverkeer [Economic Analysis of Different Forms of Pricing for Traffic], *CPB Document* 87, CPB Netherlands Bureau for Economic Policy Analysis, The Hague.

Calthrop, E. and S. Proost (2005), "Regulating on-street parking", *Regional Science and Urban Economics*, Vol. 36, pp. 29-48.

CPB and NEI (2000), Evaluatie van infrastructuurprojecten: leidraad voor kosten-batenanalyse [Evaluation of Infrastructural Projects: Guide for Cost-Benefit Analysis], CPB Netherlands Bureau for Economic Policy Analysis/Nederlands Economisch Instituut, The Hague/Rotterdam.

D'Haultfoeuille, X., P. Givord and X. Boutin (2014), "The environmental effect of green taxation: The case of the French "Bonus/Malus", *Economic Journal*, Vol. 124/578, August, pp. F444-F480.

De Borger, B. and S. Proost (2012), "A political economy model of road pricing", *Journal of Urban Economics*, Vol. 71/1, pp. 79-92.

De Jong, G. (2013), *International Comparison of Transport Appraisal Practice, Annex 3, The Netherlands Country Report*, University of Leeds.

Duranton, G. and M. Turner (2011), "The fundamental law of road congestion: Evidence from the US", *American Economic Review*, Vol. 101/6, pp. 2616-2652.

EEA (2010), "Good practice guide on noise exposure and potential health effects", *Technical Report*, No. 11/2010, European Environment Agency, Copenhagen.

Eliasson, J. and S. Proost (forthcoming), "How sustainable is sustainable transport?" *Transport Policy*.

Eliasson, J. et al. (2009), "The Stockholm congestion charging trial 2006: Overview of effects", *Transportation Research Part A: Policy and Practice*, Vol. 43/3, pp. 240-250.

European Commission (2014), "Update of the handbook on external costs of transport", Ricardo-AEA/R/ED57769, Issue No. 1, 8 January 2014, *http://ec.europa.eu/transport/themes/sustainable/studies/doc/2014-handbook-external-costs-transport.pdf* (accessed 16 May 2015).

Gagnepain, P., M. Ivaldi and C. Vibes (2011), "The industrial organization of competition in local bus services", in De Palma, Lindsey, Quinet and Vickerman (eds.), *A Handbook of Transport Economics*, Edgar Elgar, pp. 744-762.

Geilenkirchen, G., G. Renes and J. van Meerkerk (2014), Vergroening van de aanschafbelasting voor personenauto's. Effecten op de verkoop van zuinige auto's en de CO_2-uitstoot [Greening the Purchase Tax for Passenger Cars. Effects on the Sale of Fuel-efficient Cars and CO_2 Emissions], *PBL Report*, No. 970, Netherlands Environmental Assessment Agency, The Hague.

Goudappel-Goffeng (2013), Inschatting duurzaamheidseffecten programma Beter Benutten [Sustainability Impact Assessment of the Better Utilisation Programme], *www.beterbenutten.nl/assets/upload/files/Eindrapportage%20Inschatting%20Duurzaamheidseffecten%20Beter%20Benutten.pdf* (accessed 29 April 2015).

Government of the Netherlands, (2015a), Ministry of Infrastructure and the Environment website, *www.government.nl/issues/freight-transportation/inland-shipping* (accessed 25 March 2015).

Government of the Netherlands (2015b), "Role of provinces and municipalities in public transportation", *www.rijksoverheid.nl/onderwerpen/openbaar-vervoer/rol-provincies-en-gemeenten-bij-ov* (accessed 18 March 2015).

Government of the Netherlands (2014), "Answers to OECD Environmental Performance Review Questionnaire" (internal document).

Government of the Netherlands (2012), De Structuurvisie Infrastructuur en Ruimte (SVIR) – [Spatial Planning and Mobility Vision], *www.rijksoverheid.nl/onderwerpen/ruimtelijke-ordening-en-gebiedsontwikkeling/vraag-en-antwoord/wat-is-de-structuurvisie-infrastructuur-en-ruimte-svir.html* (accessed 29 April 2015).

Harding, M. (2014), "The diesel differential: Differences in the tax treatment of gasoline and diesel for road use", *OECD Taxation Working Papers*, No. 21, OECD Publishing, Paris, *http://dx.doi.org/10.1787/5jz14cd7hk6b-en*.

Hekkenberg, M. and M. Verdonk (2014), Nationale Energieverkenning 2014, [National Energy Exploration 2014], ECN-O-14-036. Petten: Energieonderzoek Centrum Nederland, *www.pbl.nl/sites/default/files/cms/publicaties/pbl-2014-nationale-energieverkenning-2014_01364.pdf*.

ICCT (2014), *European Vehicle Market Statistics – Pocketbook*, International Council on Clean Transportation, Berlin, *www.theicct.org/sites/default/files/publications/EU_pocketbook_2014.pdf*.

Hylén, B., J. Kauppila and E. Chong (2013), "Road haulage charges and taxes: Summary analysis and data tables 1998-2012", *International Transport Forum Discussion Papers*, No. 2013/08, OECD Publishing, Paris, *http://dx.doi.org/10.1787/5k46n41ck5kk-en*.

ITF (2011), *Car Fleet Renewal Schemes: Environmental and Safety Impacts*, International Transport Forum, Paris, *www.internationaltransportforum.org/Pub/pdf/11Fleet.pdf*.

Kilani, M., S. Proost and S. van der Loo (forthcoming). "Road pricing and public transport pricing reform in Paris: Complements or substitutes? *Economics of Transportation*.

KiM (2014), Mobiliteitsbeeld 2014 [Mobility Picture 2014], Kennisinstituut voor Mobiliteitsbeleid [Netherlands Institute for Transport Policy Analysis], The Hague, KIM-14-R01, ISBN:978-90-8902-124-3.

KiM (2013), Mobiliteitsbalans 2013 [Mobility Picture 2013], Kennisinstituut voor Mobiliteitsbeleid [Netherlands Institute for Transport Policy Analysis], The Hague, KIM-13-R01, ISBN: 978-90-8902-113-7.

KiM (2012), De latente vraag in het wegverkeer [Latent Demand for Road Transport] Kennisinstituut voor Mobiliteitsbeleid [Netherlands Institute for Transport Policy Analysis], The Hague, KIM-14-A06, ISBN: 978-90-8902-123-6.

Koopmans, C. (2010), Zonder prijs geen kwaliteit: de heroverwegingen bij mobiliteit en leefomgeving [Without Price, not Quality: Reconsiderations of Mobility and the Environment], Journal of Public Finance, 42, 2.

Koźluk, T. (2010), "How the transport system can contribute to better economic and environmental outcomes in the Netherlands", *OECD Economics Department Working Papers*, No. 804, OECD Publishing, Paris, *http://dx.doi.org/10.1787/5km68g0zh7ls-en*.

Ligterink N.E., J.S. Spreen and P. van Mensch (2013), "NOx emissions of modern diesel vehicles: The last mile? A summary", TNO, Research Group, Sustainable Transport and Logistics, Delft, The Netherlands.

Mandell S. and S. Proost (2015), "Why truck distance charges are contagious and drive fuel taxes to the bottom", *Discussion Paper Series*, March DPS 15.04, KU Leuven, Center for Economic Studies, Leuven, Belgium.

Ministry of Infrastructure and Environment (2014a), Netwerk Nederland – OV op het goede spoor – Lange termijn spooragenda deel 2 [Network Netherlands – OV on Track – Long term Tracking Part 2], Ministry of Infrastructure and Environment, The Hague.

Ministry of Infrastructure and Environment (2014b), Actieplan omgevingslawaai van rijkswegen: periode 2013-18 [Action Plan for Ambient Noise from Highways 2013-18], Ministry of Infrastructure and Environment, The Hague, 14 January 2014.

Munk-Nielsen, A. (2014), "Diesel cars and environmental policy", presented to the conference on the future of fuel taxes, Center for Transport Studies-KTH Royal Institute of Technology, Stockholm, 18 September 2014.

OECD (2014), "Questionnaire on the use of monetary values of carbon in public policy assessments", ENV/EPOC/WPIEEP (2014)7, OECD Publishing, Paris.

OECD/ITF (2014), *Road Safety Annual Report 2014*, OECD Publishing, Paris, *http://dx.doi.org/10.1787/irtad-2014-en*.

Ossokina, I. and G. Verweij (2014), "Urban traffic externalities: Quasi-experimental evidence from housing prices", *CPB Discussion Paper*, No. 267, 09-02-2014, CPB Netherlands Bureau for Economic Policy Analysis, The Hague.

Parry, I.W.H. et al. (2014a), "Are energy efficiency standards justified?", *Journal of Environmental Economics and Management*, Vol. 67, pp. 104-125, *http://dx.doi.org/10.1016/j.jeem.2013.11.003*.

Parry, I.W.H. et al. (2014b), *Getting Energy Prices Right – From Principle to Practice*, International Monetary Fund, Washington, DC.

PBL (2015), *Assessment of the Dutch Human Environment 2014 – The Future is Now*, PBL Netherlands Environmental Assessment Agency, The Hague.

PBL (2012), Elektrisch rijden in 2050: gevolgen voor de leefomgeving [Electric vehicles in 2050: Consequences for the Environment], Netherlands Environmental Assessment Agency, The Hague.

Proost, S. and K. Van Dender (2012), "Energy and environment challenges in the transport sector", *Economics of Transportation*, Vol. 1/1-2, December, pp. 77-87.

Pucher, J. and R. Buehler (2007), "At the frontiers of cycling: Policy innovations in the Netherlands, Denmark and Germany", *World Transport Policy and Practice*, Vol. 13/3, pp. 8-57.

Schroten et al. (2014), Externe en infrastructuurkosten van verkeer [External costs and infrastructure costs of road transport], CE Delft, Delft, The Netherlands, *www.rijkswaterstaat.nl/images/Externe%20en%20infrastructuurkosten%20verkeer%202014_tcm174-367881.pdf* (accessed 21 July 2015).

SER (2014), *Monitoring Energy Agreement*, Social and Economic Council of the Netherlands, The Hague, *www.energieakkoordser.nl/~/media/files/internet/publicaties/overige/2010_2019/2013/energieakkoord-duurzame-groei/energieakkoord-duurzame-groei-9.ashx*.

Teulings, C., I.V Ossokina and H.L.F. de Groot, H. (2014), "Welfare benefits of agglomeration and worker heterogeneity", *CESifo Working Paper,* No. 4939, Center for Economic Studies and Ifo Institute, Munich.

TNO (2013), "Investigations and real world emission performance of EURO-6 light duty vehicles", *TNO Report* R11891, TNO, The Hague.

van der Loop, H. (2012), Verklaring reistijdverlies en betrouwbaarheid op hoofdwegen 2000-2010 empirisch onderzoek [Travelling Time and Reliability on Main Roads 2000-2010 Empirical Research], Netherlands Institute for Transport Policy Analysis, The Hague, KIM-12-A02, ISBN: 978-90-8902-096-3.

van Meerkerk, J., G. Renes and G. Ridder (2014), "Greening the Dutch car fleet: The role of differentiated sales taxes", *PBL Working Paper,* No. 18, January, Netherlands Environmental Assessment Agency, The Hague.

Van Ommeren, J.O. and D. Wentinck (2012), "The (hidden) cost of employer parking policies", *International Economic Review*, Vol. 53/3, August, pp. 965-978.

Van Ommeren, J.O. et al. (2012), "Empirical evidence on cruising for parking", *Transportation Research Part A*, Vol. 46/1, pp. 123-130.

Wouter, M. (2014), De donkere kant van het gebruik van kennis, modellen en de MKBA in de besluitvorming, Tijdschrift Vervoerswetenschap [The Dark Side of the Use of Knowledge, Models, and SCBA in Decision Making, Transportation Science Magazine], Vol 50/3, September, pp. 37-56, ISSN: 1571-9227.

PART II

Chapter 5

Waste and materials management

This chapter examines the Netherlands' track record in the area of waste prevention and management and recent efforts to stimulate the transition towards a circular economy. It provides an overview of trends in material consumption and waste management, as well as related policy and institutional frameworks. The chapter discusses the main objectives for waste management over the review period and assesses performance. Finally, the chapter examines the efforts to promote a circular economy and reviews the next steps that can encourage further progress. The recommendations on waste and materials management are summarised in a box at the end of the chapter.

The statistical data for Israel are supplied by and under the responsibility of the relevant Israeli authorities. The use of such data by the OECD is without prejudice to the status of the Golan Heights, East Jerusalem and Israeli settlements in the West Bank under the terms of international law.

1. Introduction

Sustainable waste management has been one of the Netherlands' strengths in environmental policy for many years. More recently, building on its well-established track record in waste management, the government has been laying the groundwork to stimulate the transition towards a circular economy. This is defined as "an economic system that is predicated on the reusability of products and raw materials and the conservation of natural resources and that pursues the creation of value in each link in the system" (Ministry of Infrastructure and Environment, 2014a). The circular economy requires going beyond the domain of traditional waste management into less well-developed terrain. With ambitious targets for the circular economy, the country faces new challenges in terms of developing new policies, encouraging new business models and finding new ways of working with businesses and society.

This chapter provides an overview of the main objectives, policies and institutions for waste management and the circular economy. It reviews trends in waste management and material consumption over the review period and assesses performance against the country's objectives. Finally, the chapter examines the efforts to date to promote the circular economy and the challenges that lie ahead.

2. Objectives, policies and institutions for waste management and the circular economy

2.1. *Waste management policy framework*

The Netherlands was one of the pioneers of sustainable waste management planning in the OECD. The first National Waste Management Plan (NWMP) (*Landelijk Afvalbeheer Plan*, LAP), which covered the period 2003-09, set targets to be achieved by 2012. It was subsequently updated by the second NWMP of 2009, which covers the period from late 2009 to 2015 and sets targets for 2015 and 2021. These plans built on policies put in place in the 1990s to reduce landfilling and improve recycling and recovery. Each plan has been updated over the period of its implementation to reflect significant changes in the sector. A new NWMP is prepared every five to six years. A third NWMP, expected in late 2016, will cover the period until 2022.

Each NWMP covers extensively the key issues for waste management and sets policy objectives, targets and actions. The plans cover the overall policy framework, as well as specific sectors.[1] The first plan also covered capacity planning for waste disposal facilities. In addition, the plans set out the roles and responsibilities of various actors and include provisions for monitoring and evaluation. The overarching objectives of the plans are as follows:

- continue the decoupling between waste production and GDP growth
- increase levels of recovery, including energy recovery and recycling
- reduce quantities of waste sent to landfill
- decrease overall environmental impact of waste management.

The Netherlands reached most of the quantitative targets in the first NWMP ahead of schedule. The second plan built on these achievements by setting more ambitious and refined targets (Table 5.1). The plans incorporate, and in many areas go beyond, targets set in EU legislation. Both plans have been independently evaluated. The European Commission has also reviewed these plans in recent projects, along with those of other member states (European Commission, 2013).

Table 5.1. **Towards achieving key targets from the National Waste Management Plans**

	Objectives, targets and performance[a]			
	1st NWMP (2003)		2nd NWMP (2009)	
	Target	Performance	Target	Performance
Waste production	66 million tonnes (Mt) in 2012 (from a base of 63 Mt in 2000).	By 2010, waste generation was down 5% from 2000.	68 Mt in 2015 and 73 Mt in 2021.	Waste generation still below 2000 levels.
Waste recovery/Reuse[b]	Increase total waste recovery rate from 77% to more than 83% between in 2000-12.	Achieved by 2005.	Increase total waste recovery rate from 83% to 85% between 2006-15.	Achieved by 2010.
Household	---		Increase waste recovery/reuse of household waste from 51% to 60% between 2006-15.	78% by 2010.
Small business/trade/ government (HDO)	---		Increase recovery/reuse of waste from business, government and services from 46% to 60% between 2006-15.	78% by 2010.
Industry	---		Maintain the level of recovery/reuse rate for industrial waste at 90%.	88% in 2010.
Construction and Demolition (C&D)	---		Maintain the level of recovery/reuse rate for construction and demolition waste at 95%.	At least 95% reached in 2010.
Disposal/Landfill	Limit the quantity of waste to be disposed of in 2012 to a maximum of 9.5 Mt, comprised of: 2 Mt of landfilled non-combustible waste 5.1 Mt of non-hazardous waste incinerated 0.1 Mt of hazardous waste incinerated in rotary furnaces and waste incinerators 2.3 Mt of sewage sludge.	Achieved by 2010	Reduce the landfilling of "combustible" waste originating in the Netherlands from 1.7 Mt to 0 Mt between 2007-12 (non-combustible waste is not included in this target).	By 2012, only 1% of all MSW generated was landfilled.
Material efficiency	No specific quantitative target set in objectives.		Using the cradle to cradle concept as inspiration, reduce the environmental impacts of seven material streams by 20% by 2015.	Not achieved.
Energy content of waste	---		Increase the energy output (electricity and heat) of incineration plant by 10% by 2012.	Achieved.
Emissions from waste treatment	---		Reduce CO_2 emissions from waste treatment facilities by 30% by 2020 compared with 1990. Remove any danger to humans and the environment from hazardous materials.	Achieved.

Source: CE Delft (2014a).

a) There are significant differences between the two NWMPs, which impact on their comparability. For example, the targets have different base years (2000 for the first plan and 2006 for the second). The second NWMP is broader in scope and covers additional areas such as material efficiency, the energy content of waste and emissions from waste treatment operations.

b) The targets for "useful recovery" include incineration for energy recovery, as well as reuse and recycling.

In addition to the targets above, other objectives of the NWMPs include the liberalisation of the waste market and the harmonisation of waste policies throughout the country. The promotion of market forces in waste management seeks to provide greater entrepreneurial freedom to waste management firms, reduce central planning of incineration capacity and encourage trade through open borders for import and export of non-hazardous combustible waste for incineration. The push to harmonise waste policies throughout the country aimed to reduce regional differences, while still allowing discretion for provinces and municipalities in policy implementation.

2.2. Legal framework for waste management

The Netherlands was one of the first European countries to develop comprehensive national waste management planning systems and reporting. The Environmental Management Act (EMA) of 2002 provides the main legal basis for waste management[2] in the Netherlands and introduced the legal requirement to develop NWMPs. This act preceded EU legislation setting out such a requirement (Article 28 of the 2008 EU Waste Framework Directive). While EU legislation now sets the general framework for waste management policy and legislation, the Dutch played a central and pioneering role in shaping EU waste legislation, in particular the use of core principles such as the "waste hierarchy". Further, the targets and policies put in place in the country are often more ambitious than those set out by the EU.

2.3. From waste policy towards a circular economy

In order to promote material efficiency and the transition towards a circular economy, the Netherlands has taken important steps in recent years to lay the groundwork for further progress. The second NWMP represented one of the first steps to look beyond traditional waste management and examine how to move towards greater resource efficiency. In a circular economy, the aim is to broaden the focus from strictly managing waste to minimising the environmental impact of materials across entire product chains from "cradle to cradle", covering raw material extraction, production, use and waste management, including reuse.

In 2014, the government set out an ambitious "Waste to Resource" programme. The programme built on the "More Value from Waste" programme outlined in 2011 and the first Waste Prevention Plan in 2013. Among the main objectives of the Waste to Resource programme is to halve the volume of material that "leaves" the economy within a span of ten years. In 2012, an estimated 10 million tonnes of waste went to incineration or landfill. The Waste to Resource programme seeks to drastically cut the resources "lost" in this way, through increased recycling and more sustainable production and consumption. The broad objectives and lines of action for the programme are summarised in Table 5.2. In addition to domestic efforts, the Netherlands has actively contributed to the development of a common policy on resource efficiency at EU level.

The government is exploring which specific measures or actions can and should be taken to achieve these broad objectives as well as determining priority areas and specific targets. It is also considering potential roles and responsibilities of the various actors involved, including the government. Given this exploratory process is ongoing at both the national and EU levels, the Netherlands has not yet outlined a detailed roadmap for achieving the transition to a circular economy. Ultimately, objectives and ambitions for the circular economy should feed into the third NWMP, expected in late 2016.

2.4. Institutional arrangements

The Ministry for Infrastructure and Environment is responsible for the policy and regulatory framework for waste management at the central government level. The ministry develops, co-ordinates, enforces and monitors the NWMPs. It ensures implementation of EU

Table 5.2. **Objectives and lines of action for the Waste to Resource programme**

High-level objectives	Actions
1. Promoting sustainability at the front of the chain	• ensuring the circular design of products • closing local and global cycles
2. Making consumption patterns more sustainable	• developing an approach to sustainable consumption patterns based on behavioural knowledge • strengthening the role of the retail sector, thrift stores and repair companies • using the purchasing power of the government to create a circular economy
3. Improving waste separation and collection	• minimising the quantity of residual Dutch waste in incineration plants • facilitating municipalities in improving waste separation and collection • inspiring households to improve their separation of waste • separating waste from offices, shops and public spaces
4. Focusing existing waste policy on a circular economy	• identifying and eliminating unnecessary obstacles in legislation • stimulating the application of end-of-waste status • promoting recycling through a level European playing field for waste • creating scope for innovation in legislation and in standards
5. Adopting an approach to specific material chains and waste streams	• setting up a support desk for a material chain approach • accelerating specific material chains such as the one for plastics • stimulating high-quality recycling in each material chain • using residual biotic streams in a high-quality way
6. Developing financial and other market incentives	• stimulating the use of new business models • driving the dissemination of knowledge and widespread use of innovative solutions • adapting landfill tax rules to ensure they tie in with promoting the circular economy
7. Connecting knowledge and education to the circular economy	• setting up knowledge and education programmes for Waste to Resource • focusing European research programmes on the circular economy • making the Netherlands a circular hot spot
8. Simplifying measurement methods, indicators and certification labels	• harmonising and standardising methods and indicators • improving information about waste streams.

Source: Ministry of Infrastructure and Environment (2014b).

directives and international obligations, as well as establishes detailed rules for the implementation of waste legislation. It also authorises collection of several specific waste streams, manages exemptions and enforces the landfill ban. The ministry's executive arm, the Rijkswaterstaat, develops and evaluates waste policies and regulations, and supports policy implementation.

Provincial authorities are primarily responsible for the licensing and enforcement of waste management activities (based on minimum standards established in the NWMPs). They are also responsible for the long-term closure and aftercare of landfills. To carry out these functions, they can charge a levy on landfilled waste. Revenues from this levy are put in a fund to cover post-closure landfill stewardship costs.

Municipal authorities are responsible for the collection of municipal waste, including promotion of separate collection of certain waste streams, as well as the stimulation of waste prevention. Their bylaws specify which types of household waste have to be separated and the frequency of collection. More than 400 municipalities in the Netherlands are in charge of waste collection and separation. They can collect waste themselves or outsource collection to a private party. Municipalities also set tariffs for waste collection, issue permits for some waste processing companies and monitor their actions.

Along with various levels of government, the waste management industry and civil society also play a role in waste management. Both industry and the public are involved in the development of the NWMPs and have legal obligations for responsible waste management. For instance, Dutch environmental legislation establishes a duty-of-care related to waste for the private sector (including both companies and citizens). Companies are required to contract an authorised party to collect their waste. In addition, extended producer responsibility (EPR) rules apply for several product streams (e.g. electrical and electronic equipment, packaging and "end-of-life" vehicles). Citizens are responsible for waste prevention and responsible waste management, for instance, by separating waste for collection according to municipal rules.

In the area of materials efficiency and the circular economy, the Ministry for Infrastructure and the Environment works with other key ministries, including the Ministry of Economic Affairs and the Ministry of Foreign Affairs. Consumer associations, industry and other private parties are also actively involved in shaping policy initiatives in this domain. In contrast to traditional waste management, roles and responsibilities of different actors for the circular economy are still under consideration.

3. Trends in waste management and material consumption

This section summarises key trends in waste generation, treatment and trade, as well as material consumption in the Netherlands over the review period. There are significant differences in how total waste is measured by Dutch national statistics and how it is measured by OECD and Eurostat statistics (Box 5.1). This section relies on national data when discussing progress towards national goals; it uses OECD or Eurostat data when comparing the country's performance with others.

Box 5.1. **Waste definitions**

As defined in the EU Waste Framework Directive, waste is "any substance or object which the holder discards or intends or is required to discard". As noted in the first NWMP, the interpretation of this definition sometimes leads to debate about whether a substance constitutes waste.

For *total waste*, Dutch national statistics exclude several types of waste that are included in OECD and Eurostat definitions: dredging spoils, animal manure, soils (including contaminated soils) and secondary wastes generated by waste treatment and recycling facilities. For *municipal solid waste* (MSW), certain building and demolition waste, some used paper and cardboard, as well as waste electrical and electronic equipment (WEEE) are included in national statistics, but not in OECD and Eurostat statistics.

These distinct definitions lead to very large differences. In particular, OECD and Eurostat data puts total waste produced in the Netherlands at around 120 Mt per year; approximately double the amount calculated by national waste statistics (around 60 Mt per year). The difference is much less pronounced (around 5%) with regards to municipal solid waste.

In this chapter, the assessment of national performance against goals set in the NWMPs draws on national statistics. In contrast, comparing the performance of the Netherlands with OECD and EU peers requires OECD and Eurostat data.

3.1. *Waste trends*

Waste generation

The Netherlands has reduced the amount of waste produced over the past decade, achieving an absolute decoupling of waste generation from gross domestic product (GDP). According to Dutch waste statistics, total waste generation in 2012 was 4% less than in 2000. This was driven by waste prevention and management policies, as well as macroeconomic factors, including the impact of the global economic crisis, which dampened overall consumption (CE Delft, 2014a). Nevertheless, in the context of modest GDP growth over the period, the fall in waste production is an important achievement. This is especially significant in light of the substantial increase in waste generation between 1985 and 2000 (from 45 Mt to 61 Mt).

According to Dutch statistics, the building industry (construction and demolition waste) produces the most waste (41%), followed by manufacturing (24%), and "consumers" (14%). Together, these three groups accounted for approximately 80% of all waste generated in 2012. Figure 5.1 shows the trends in waste generation for construction and manufacturing for 2002-10, along with the trend in value-added of these sectors.

Figure 5.1. **Waste generation declined while value added rose, 2002-10**

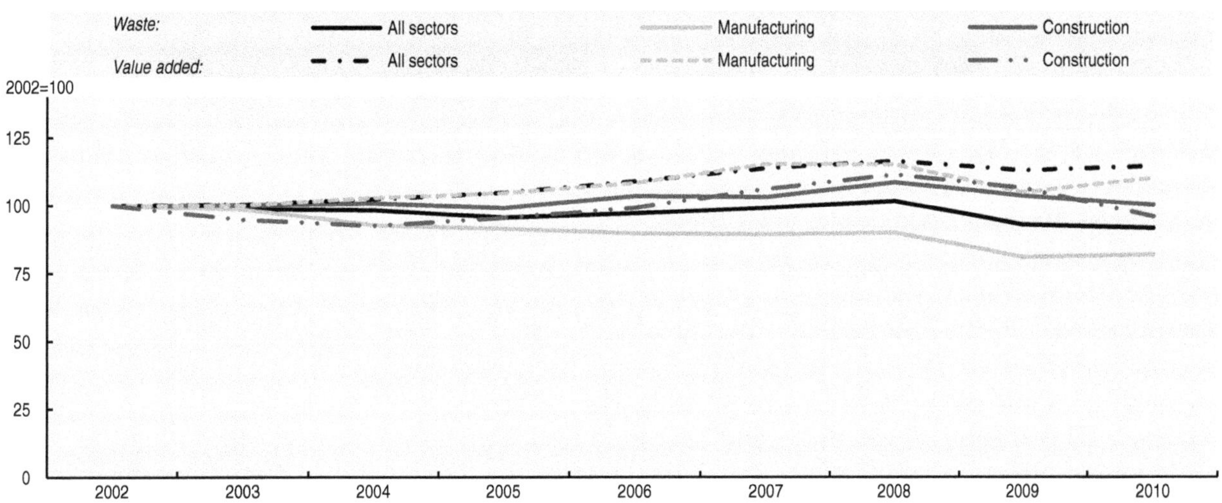

Source: CBS (2015), *StatLine* (database).

StatLink http://dx.doi.org/10.1787/888933280416

As with the trend for total waste, there was an absolute decoupling of MSW[3] generation from GDP. Household waste accounts for the large majority (nearly 90%) of MSW. While GDP increased, the amount of MSW produced dropped slightly from 9.5 Mt to 8.8 Mt in 2000 13 (CBS, 2014) to just under one-sixth of total waste produced, according to Dutch statistics.

According to OECD statistics, MSW on a per capita basis showed a significant decline, falling from 598 kg to 525 kg between 2000 and 2013; this is slightly above the OECD and OECD Europe averages of 520 kg and 480 kg respectively in 2013 (OECD, 2015) (Figure 5.2).

While the vast majority of waste produced is non-hazardous, the Netherlands generates a substantial amount of hazardous waste, nearly 4.9 Mt in 2012 (Eurostat, 2015). It is among the top ten OECD countries in terms of production of hazardous waste, according to 2010 data (Figure 5.3).

Waste treatment and trade

In terms of waste treatment, there has been a marked shift from landfilling to incineration, and within incineration, a shift from disposal to energy recovery. This shift was especially prominent for the treatment of household MSW. Landfilling of MSW declined from about 11% to 1.5% between 2000 and 2013. In 2012, almost half (48%) of household MSW was incinerated for energy recovery (Figure 5.4). Both industrial waste and

Figure 5.2. **Municipal solid waste per capita declined yet remains slightly higher than OECD average**

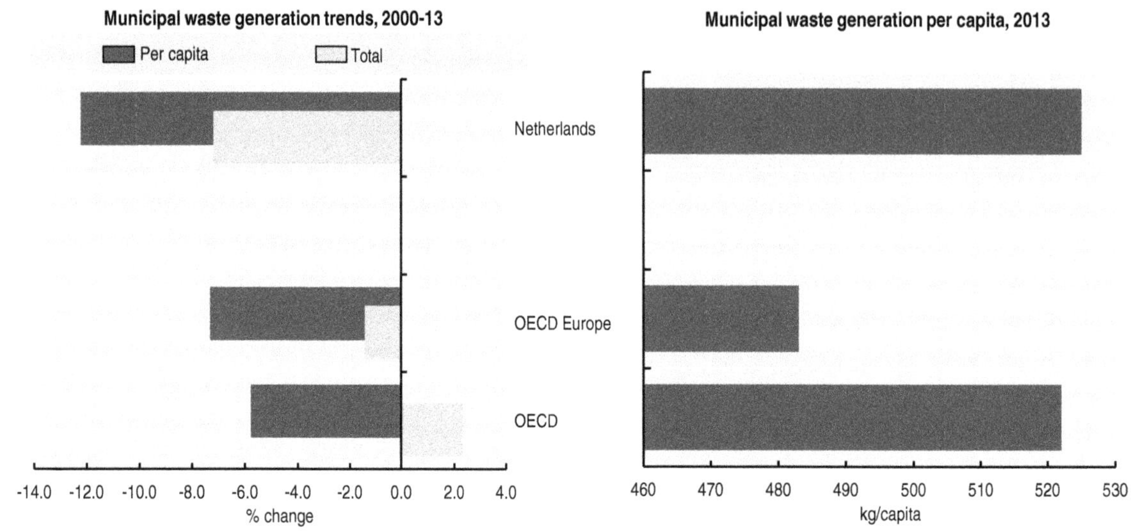

Source: OECD (2015), "Municipal waste", *OECD Environment Statistics* (database).

StatLink http://dx.doi.org/10.1787/888933280422

construction and demolition (C&D) waste already had very high rates of "useful recovery" (including incineration for energy recovery, as well as reuse and recycling) at the beginning of the review period and stood at 88% and 90% respectively in 2010.

The amount of electricity and heat produced from waste incineration during the period increased substantially. For example, gross production of electricity from waste increased from 2.5 GWh in 2000 to 3.4 GWh in 2010 (CBS, 2012). Approximately half of this is classified as renewable energy.

Material recycling rates (including recycling and composting) remained generally stable, showing some improvement, over the review period. Material recycling of household MSW increased slowly with rates growing from 50% to 56% in 2000-12 (CBS, 2014). Composted waste represented about one half of this total. Overall, the amount of waste separately collected from households had a modest increase from 45% to 51% over 2002-12.

The Netherlands' status as a major importer and exporter of waste expanded considerably during the review period. According to Dutch statistics from CBS, the amount of waste exported rose from 6.7 Mt to 12 Mt in 2000-10, reaching 20% of total waste generated. In a similar vein, the amount of waste imported nearly doubled, increasing from 6.6 Mt to 13 Mt. The vast majority of this waste was non-hazardous and traded among neighbouring countries, especially Germany and Belgium. In 2013, between 1.6-1.7 Mt of waste was imported for incineration, most of it coming from the United Kingdom.

3.2. Emissions from waste

Greenhouse gas (GHG) emissions from the waste sector dropped by over 60% between 2000 and 2012. This huge drop can be explained in part by the marked shift from landfilling towards incineration for energy recovery; since the country's waste incineration facilities also produce electricity or heat for energy purposes, their GHG emissions are attributed to

Figure 5.3. The Netherlands is among the top ten OECD member countries in production of hazardous waste

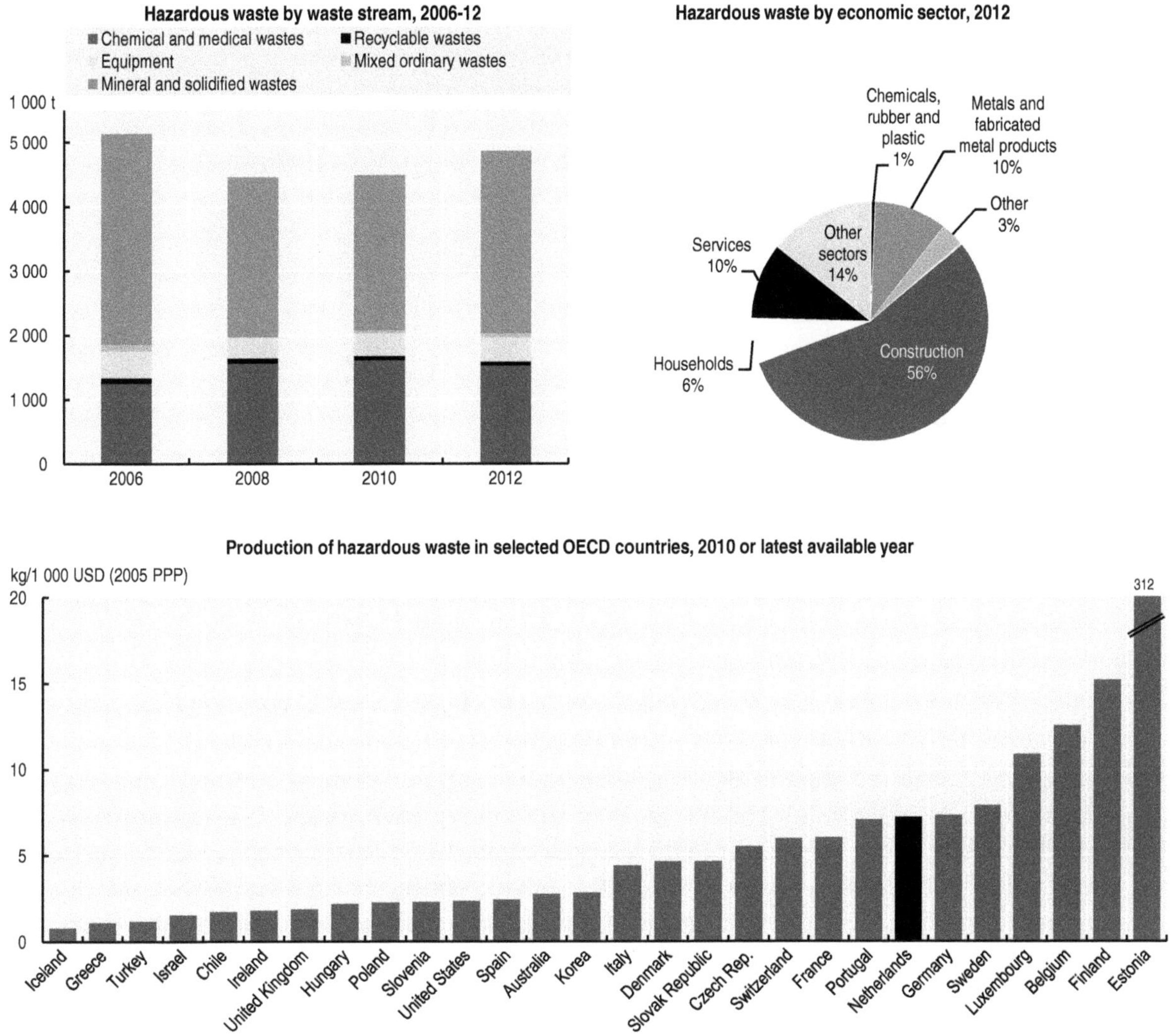

Note: Hazardous waste classified according to the Waste Framework Directive (Directive 2008/98/EC) which excludes radioactive waste.
Source: Eurostat (2015), *Eurostat Environmental Data Centre on Waste* (database); OECD (2015), *OECD Environment Statistics* (database); OECD (2013), *Environment at a Glance 2013: OECD Indicators.*

StatLink http://dx.doi.org/10.1787/888933280430

the energy rather than the waste sector (RIVM, 2013). GHG emissions from the waste sector have traditionally been a small contributor to overall emissions; in 2012, they accounted for only 2% of total GHGs (Chapter 1).

The composition of waste emissions has changed over time. In 1990, the bulk of emissions consisted mainly of methane (CH_4) from landfills, with a relatively low percentage of emissions from composting and incinerating. With the decline of landfilling after the ban in 1995, emissions from methane decreased steadily. From the early 2000s, emissions from landfills continued their downward trend, while stricter recycling measures reduced emissions further. Nevertheless, landfills continue to emit methane for decades after a site is closed. The Netherlands has therefore developed emission control systems that recover

Figure 5.4. **Marked shift towards incineration with energy recovery, 2000-13**

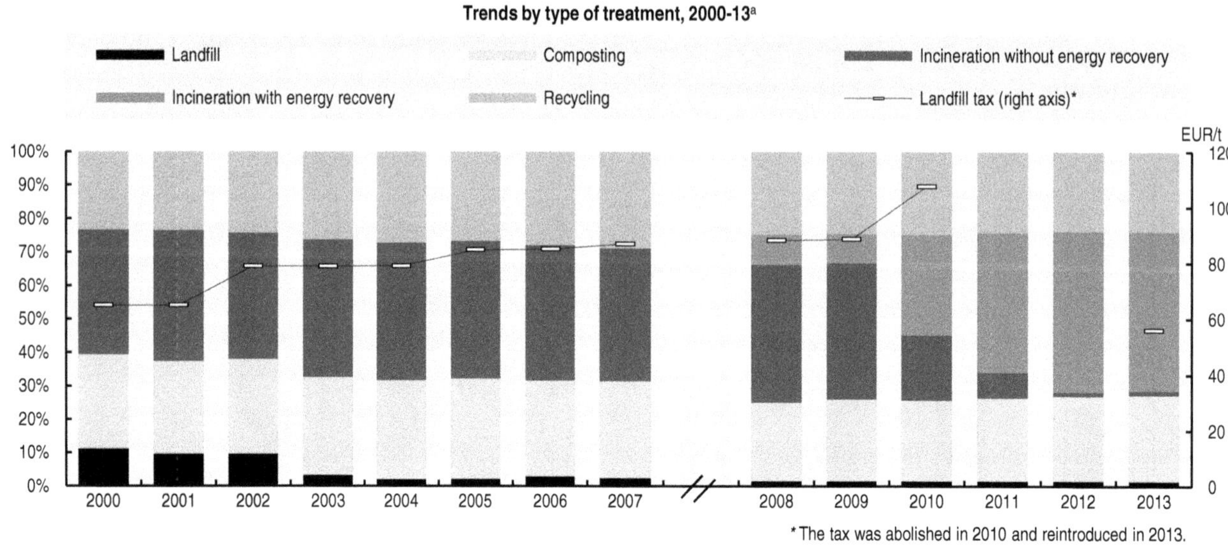

a) Waste collected by or for municipalities including household, bulky and commercial waste, and similar waste handled at the same facilities. Includes separate collection for recycling purposes. Up to 2008, data for total treatment exclude amounts undergoing mechanical sorting before further treatment/disposal.

Source: CBS (2015), *Statline* (database); OECD (2015), "Municipal waste", *OECD Environment Statistics* (database).

StatLink http://dx.doi.org/10.1787/888933280446

landfill methane before it is released into the atmosphere; it is used to generate electricity, which is an effective emissions reduction strategy (EEA, 2013; CE Delft, 2014a).

Since the second NMWP in 2009, the Netherlands has paid more attention to reducing emissions in product value chains. Most of the energy savings are due to improved recycling, while about one-third of emissions decreased as a result of the shift towards incineration with energy recovery. From 2010, methane emissions from landfills started to have less of an impact on the environment compared to emissions from incineration, which take the form of carbon dioxide (CO_2) and nitrous oxide (N_2O). These emissions were mainly caused by large volumes of plastics in the incinerated waste and the relatively low efficiency of incinerators. Studies have shown, however, that even highly efficient incinerators would only reduce emissions by about one-third compared to increased recycling. From this perspective, high-quality recycling or reuse of recovered materials should be preferred over incineration (Corstena et al., 2013). Although, emissions from incineration are balanced out by the avoided emissions associated with the recovery of energy (EEA, 2013).

3.3. *Materials consumption*

The Netherlands is one of the most resource-efficient countries in the OECD in terms of GDP per unit of domestic material consumption[4] (DMC) (Figure 5.5). It has a relatively low level of DMC per capita[5], compared to the EU average, which has declined over the review period. This is partly explained by the structure of the Dutch economy, which has a strong service sector and is less focused on manufacturing, which is relatively material-intensive. In addition, upstream raw materials, which are embodied in imports, are not reflected in DMC data. In a small, open economy such as the Netherlands, the impact of such factors on measures of resource efficiency could be considerable.[6] Figure 5.5 shows the breakdown of DMC across materials and the trends in DMC per capita for each category between 2000 and 2013.

Figure 5.5. **One of the most resource-efficient countries in the OECD**

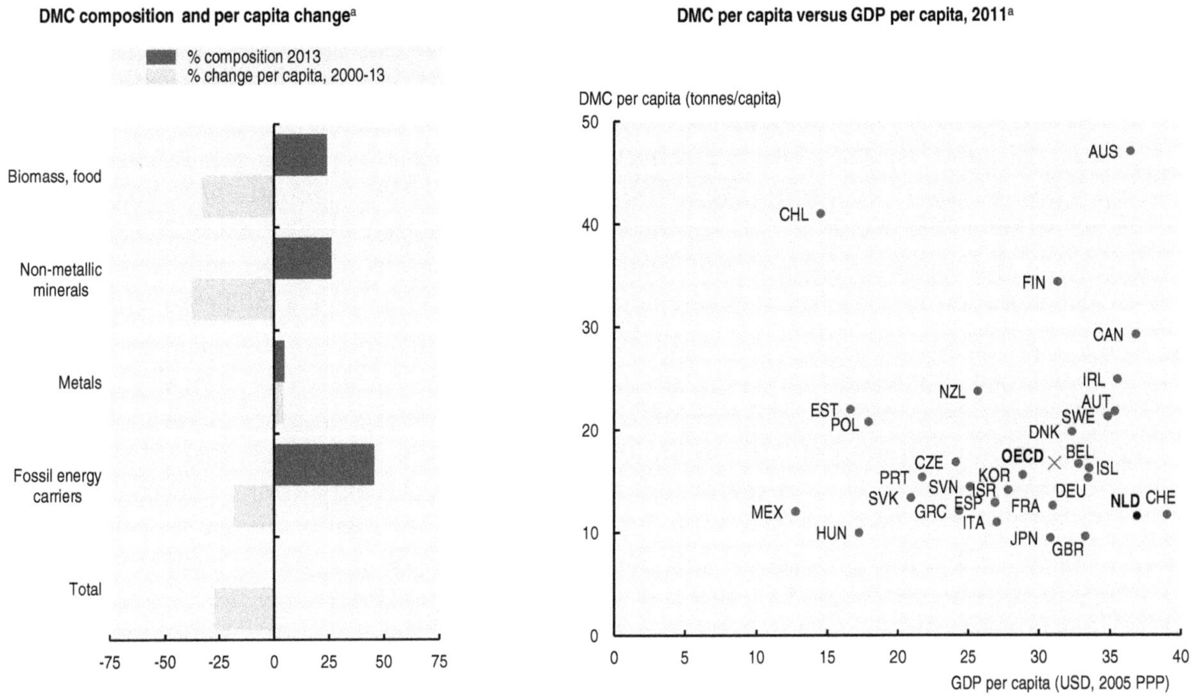

a) Domestic material consumption (DMC) designates the sum of domestic extraction of raw materials used by an economy and the physical trade balance (imports minus exports of raw materials and manufactured products).

Source: OECD (2015), "Material resources", *OECD Environment Statistics* (database); Eurostat (2014), "Material Flows and Resource Productivity", *Environment Statistics* (database).

StatLink http://dx.doi.org/10.1787/888933280453

4. Performance in managing waste

The Netherlands is one of the OECD's best performers in the area of waste prevention and management and has pioneered comprehensive planning and policy measures. It has set and achieved progressively ambitious targets to increase recycling and other useful forms of recovery (including incineration for energy recovery) across all major waste streams.

A recent evaluation of the NWMPs (CE Delft, 2014a) indicated that waste management costs have risen less than inflation over the period since the plans were in place. Costs have also risen less than in other countries with high-quality waste disposal, such as Germany, Austria and Belgium.

Several important measures put in place in the 1990s helped lay the groundwork for this strong performance. The Waste Decree of 1995 enacted a landfill ban on combustible or biologically decomposable waste if the waste might be reused, recycled or incinerated with energy recovery. The decree specified 35 categories of waste banned from landfilling (EEA, 2013), while a number of exemptions allowed for landfilling where alternative treatment capacity was lacking. To encourage expansion of alternative treatment, a landfill tax was introduced in 1995 (EUR 13 per tonne of waste[7]). In addition to the landfill ban and tax, the government introduced mandatory separate collection for household organic waste in 1994.

This section reviews the performance of various aspects of waste management, highlighting key issues over the review period.

4.1. *From landfilling to incineration for energy recovery*

The government took several steps to build on the progress made in the 1990s to shift waste treatment from landfilling towards recovery. The second NWMP set a quantitative target to eliminate landfilling of combustible waste. The landfill tax on combustible waste has been progressively increased over the 2000s, making it the most expensive method of waste disposal.[8] By 2010, the combination of the landfill tax and operator gate fees resulted in costs as high as approximately EUR 127/tonne compared with around EUR 90/tonne for incineration (ETC/SCP, 2012).[9] No equivalent tax for incineration was introduced during this time.[10] The number of categories of waste banned from landfill increased from 35 to 64. In 2000, the government introduced a moratorium on new landfills and landfill expansion.

The government also encouraged the expansion of incineration for energy recovery. The second NWMP set a target to increase the total waste recovery rate from 83% to 85% between 2006 and 2015. To that end, the government took a number of measures to promote investment in incineration for energy recovery and to liberalise the waste treatment market. First, it removed a moratorium on the expansion of incineration capacity in 2000 and eliminated the requirement for municipalities to use incineration capacity within their vicinity. Second, the government, waste incineration companies and other stakeholders signed a voluntary agreement to increase energy production from incineration plants by 23% between 1997 and 2004. Third, in 2007, the import of combustible waste for incineration (but not landfilling) was permitted. Finally, to reduce costs and share liabilities of investments in incineration for energy recovery, a number of municipalities signed long-term contracts with project developers for waste treatment.[11]

Three important external factors also aided the expansion of incineration for energy recovery within the Netherlands. First, Germany introduced its own landfill ban in 2005, eliminating the possibility for Dutch waste to be exported there and increasing waste available in the Netherlands for potential incineration. Second, the EU changed the rules in 2010 for classifying incineration for disposal and incineration for recovery. These changes allowed efficient incineration plants that produced heat and electricity to be classified as recovery installations, which affected all Dutch incinerators. Finally, with the introduction of renewable energy targets in the EU, the electricity and heat generated by the "biomass proportion" of waste incinerated could count towards national renewable energy targets.

Achieving targets for discouraging waste disposal and encouraging useful recovery have led to a number of side effects. Revenues from landfill taxes fell from nearly EUR 180 million in 2006 to just over EUR 40 million in 2010 (ETC/SCP, 2012). The tax was removed as of 1 January 2012 as a part of the Ministry of Finance's efforts to simplify the tax regime. The removal created a small "rebound effect", increasing landfilling slightly. The tax was re-introduced in 2014 to help defray landfill costs and extended to cover incineration.[12]

Another effect of the marked shift towards incineration for energy recovery has been overcapacity of waste incineration in 2005-10, which led to a significant increase in waste imported from other countries. Finally, measures to strongly encourage incineration for energy recovery may have thwarted progress towards higher rates of recycling (CE Delft, 2014a).

4.2. *Encouraging waste reduction, reuse and recycling*

Over the review period, the Netherlands has employed a range of policy instruments to encourage the reduction, reuse and recycling of waste. These include municipal charging schemes, separate collection requirements, voluntary agreements with industry, and extended producer responsibility schemes, among others. There have also been some efforts to promote the market for recyclables through compensation schemes and price supports for recycled materials.[13] This section reviews several of the key instruments.

Material recovery rates (including both recycling and composting) have not improved much over the review period. Composting makes up about half of material recovery rates of household waste, underlining the important role of mandatory separate collection of organic waste introduced in the 1990s.

One of the main policy goals of the Waste to Resource programme is to halve the volume of Dutch generated waste material that "leaves" the economy through waste incineration and landfilling (from 10 Mt to 5 Mt). This will require a significant increase in recycling rates of MSW and waste from business, government and services ("HDO"). To support this, the government has set targets for the separate collection of MSW and HDO waste aiming to reach 60-65% separately collected by 2015, 75% by 2020 and 100% in the longer term. Figure 5.6 presents the trends in separate collection of household waste in 2000-13. As the rate of separate collection of household waste was just slightly above 50% in 2013, the 2015 target appears out of reach. However, there have been some promising examples of municipalities that have made significant gains in separate collection rates.

Figure 5.6. **Rate of separate collection of household waste grew slowly, 2000-13**

Trends by waste stream, 2000-13[a]

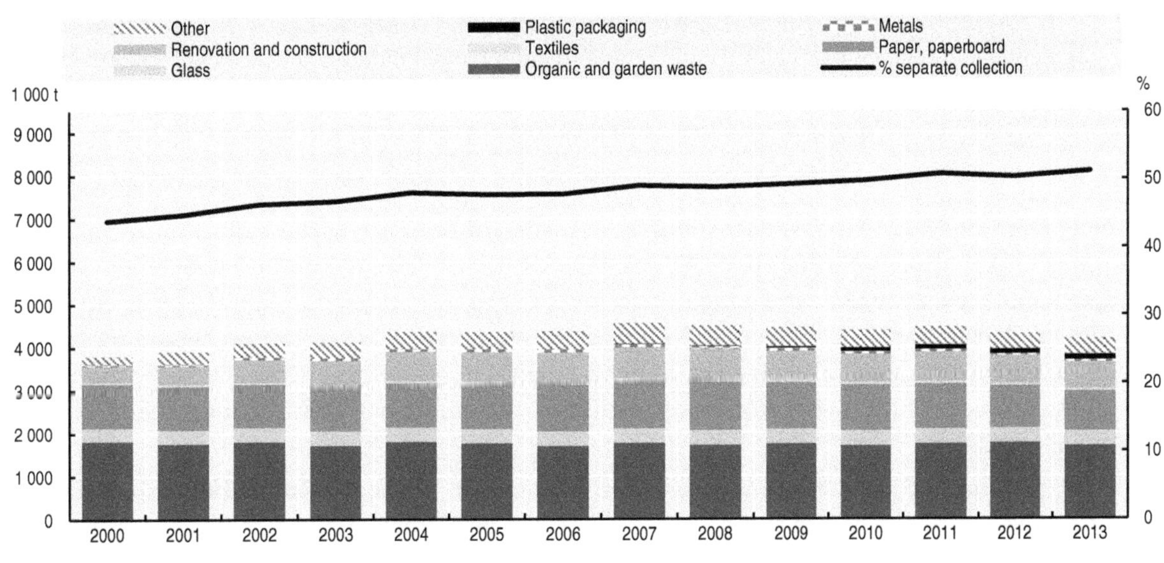

a) 20013: Preliminary data.
Source: CBS (2015), *Environmental Data Compendium* (website).

StatLink http://dx.doi.org/10.1787/888933280467

Municipal charging systems (along with extended producer responsibility schemes, discussed below) are a key instrument to encourage greater separation of household waste. There are several different types of municipal waste levies used in Dutch cities, described in Box 5.2.

In addition to differences in charging schemes, other factors contribute to differences in rates of separate collection between cities. High population density in large cities allows for "free-riding" in terms of waste separation. Lower-income levels in certain

Box 5.2. Municipal waste levies

Under Dutch waste law, municipalities operate and finance municipal waste management. While almost all municipalities impose a waste levy, charging systems and levies vary from town to town.

There are three main types of charging systems in Dutch cities:

- a fixed amount for each household
- a levy that depends on the size of the household
- a "pay-as-you-throw" levy that depends on the amount of residual and separated waste collected (called "Diftar", referring to "differentiated rate").

Overall, the evidence suggests the use of Diftar charging schemes is both more effective and more efficient than alternatives. The Diftar scheme encourages households to separate waste, reducing residual waste and generally leading to lower overall waste charges for households than non-differentiated rate systems. Costs are lowered because the consumer reduces the amount of post-collection separation involved for municipalities, and hence increases the value of the waste.

There are significant regional differences in rates of separate collection. In some areas, generally those using Diftar schemes, separately collected waste accounted for more than 60% of all household waste while it accounted for as little as 7% of household waste in others areas, generally those using fixed charges. This implies significant potential for the broader application of Diftar charging schemes to encourage higher rates of separate collection.

In 2013, 53% of municipalities used a levy based on the household size, 40% used Diftar systems and only 7% charged the same rates to each household. Use of the Diftar system has expanded steadily, up from only 13% of municipalities in 1998.

Source: Oosterhuis et al. (2009); Dijkgraff and Gradus (2014).

neighbourhoods can be associated with lower rates of separate waste collection. Finally, less available space for separate collection bins within the average urban households can also deter separation. Below-average performers in separate collection include large cities such as Amsterdam, The Hague and Rotterdam. Promoting post-collection separation of certain waste streams, like plastics, may be a suitable option to encourage recycling in large urban areas (CE Delft, 2011). Box 5.3 illustrates municipal waste management in a major Dutch city.

To promote the exchange of good practice between cities, a national benchmarking system is planned to assess and compare municipal performance in waste generation and separate collection. It is not, however, the intention to prescribe a particular system of charging.

Meeting the targets of the Waste to Resource programme will require increased recycling even in difficult categories such as plastics. Recycling plastics presents both economic and technical challenges. Plastic waste is bulky and low value, which increases costs for collectors. It is also difficult to process. Two recent studies covering deposit-refund systems for plastic bottles illustrate aspects of these challenges (Box 5.4). These challenges are common in other EU and OECD member countries where plastic recycling rates rarely exceed one-third of waste generated.

Despite these challenges, the amount of plastic waste separately collected in the Netherlands has increased significantly in recent years, particularly packaging waste. Extended producer responsibility schemes for packaging waste have contributed to this

Box 5.3. **Municipal waste management in a major Dutch city: The case of Rotterdam**

In Rotterdam, 610 000 people live in approximately 315 000 households. The city produces 290 kt of waste per year, or 475 kg per capita, just below the national average of 525 kg. Of this, 23% is recycled, 77% is incinerated and less than 1% is landfilled.

The main recipient of residual (non-recycled) waste is a recently privatised waste-to-energy plant within the city's boundaries (AVR). The energy generated from this plant produces electricity for the national grid, while a dedicated heat transportation network produces heat for the city. The city is a shareholder in the company that owns the heat transportation network.

Overall, annual costs of waste collection amount to EUR 100 million per year, towards which Rotterdam's households pay EUR 372.50.

Rotterdam has a generally low performance in separate collection. The main reasons are a lack of space in apartments, and the difficulty in monitoring and collecting separated waste from high-rise buildings. Social issues related to poverty also contribute (Rotterdam City Council, 2014).

The aim is to increase the recycling rate from 23% to 32% in 2012-18, while reducing waste management costs by 4%. One such option to achieve this is to provide a cash incentive to customers for separating waste (the "cash for trash" scheme). The city is also looking at options to improve post-collection separation, which may decrease costs, albeit at the risk of potentially lowering the overall quality of plastic recyclate (e.g. the output material from the recycling process) due to technical constraints.

Other cities, such as Arnhem, are promoting separate collection by making residual waste collection more difficult. The "reversed collection" scheme is aiming to do this by providing a higher service level for recyclables and a lower service level for residual waste.

Box 5.4. **Dutch deposit-refund systems for PET bottles**

Wageningen University (WUR, 2012) analysed Dutch deposit-refund systems for large (> 0.5 L) polyethylene terephthalate (PET) bottles in terms of costs, material and energy use. A life cycle analysis covering all processing steps revealed the Dutch system costs between EUR 25-45 million annually and yields approximately 21 kt of PET regranulate (rPET) flakes (or 19 k of regranulates). The analysis found that the economic efficiency of the deposit-refund system is limited, since the produced recycled PET regranulates costs roughly 1.2 to 1.8 times more than virgin PET granulate. Although the system helps reduce the environmental impact of beverage bottles in the Netherlands, its output (rPET) is more expensive than alternatives (virgin PET).

A more recent study on the same issue (CE Delft, 2014b), using a slightly different methodology, updated some of the costs. It suggested the costs of recycling large PET bottles are much lower than those estimated in the WUR study: 1.9 eurocents per bottle rather than 5.9 eurocents per bottle. This would mean that rPET is competitive with, or even cheaper than, virgin PET.

Source: WUR (2012); CE Delft (2014b).

positive trend. In addition, a packaging tax was in place from January 2009 until January 2013. Current plastic recycling rates still only represent around one-third of plastic waste produced (40% of plastic packaging) (CE Delft, 2011).

As discussed above, the rapid expansion of relatively inexpensive incineration for energy recovery may have stalled progress in increasing recycling rates (CE Delft, 2014a). The aim to promote higher recycling rates of Dutch waste is concurrent with the aim to avoid underusing the country's incineration capacity, which is currently too large for national waste treatment needs. Therefore, an increase in imports of residual waste is sought, thereby avoiding a conflict between the business interests of incineration facilities and government's goal of recycling more Dutch waste. The incineration tax, introduced in 2014, is charged on waste generated in the Netherlands, but not on imported residual waste (MRW, 2015).

Close co-operation between government and industry has also contributed to improving waste recovery rates, for example through a system of covenants and "Green Deals". The "Green Deals" programme launched in 2011 is an innovative way of working to remove obstacles to implementing environmental efforts by industry (Chapter 2). The deals consist of agreements between the government and various private parties that focus mainly on removing non-financial barriers related to regulations, legislation or licensing. Box 5.5 provides an illustration.

Box 5.5. **Green Deals to promote industrial recycling: The case of incineration ash**

Given the central role of incineration in waste treatment in the Netherlands, it is also a major producer of residual "bottom ash", which remains after the incineration process. This ash contains a range of materials, including metals and may only be reused under strict conditions.

To promote efficient and sustainable reuse of this ash, the Dutch government and waste incineration sector agreed on a Green Deal: in return for reprocessing (cleaning up) the bottom ash by 2020, the incinerators can market the (non-metallic) output as building material.

As a midpoint target, the deal aims to reprocess half of the ash by 2017. The agreement depends on the availability of necessary reprocessing technologies; the government and industry (operators of incineration and reprocessing plants) are working together on this issue.

Source: Dutch Waste Management Association (2014).

Given that recovery rates are already so high, the focus in recent years has been on increasing the quality (as opposed to the quantity) of recycled waste. One objective of the Waste to Resource programme is to help waste producers and traders better define when waste becomes product (e.g. "end-of-waste"). To support these efforts, the government has developed an e-tool for companies to make their own assessment of the quality and status of materials. The government also plans to develop further recycling standards for high and low quality waste. Such standards may be difficult to implement for waste that can be exported for treatment in other parts of the EU and beyond. The introduction of such standards in the Netherlands needs to consider the impact that overly stringent standards could have on waste exports.

Extended producer responsibility schemes

The Netherlands was one of the first OECD member countries to introduce extended producer responsibility (EPR) schemes in the 1990s and has benefited from experimentation with various approaches and extensive dialogue with stakeholders. Producers' responsibility was first referenced in a voluntary agreement on packaging waste in the 1990s (Box 5.6). Voluntary agreements for EPR were subsequently established for other waste streams, such as batteries, end-of-life vehicles (ELV) and waste electrical and electronic equipment (WEEE) (Box 5.7).

Box 5.6. **EPR scheme for packaging waste**

In the Netherlands, producers and importers of packaging are legally responsible for the prevention, collection and recycling of packaging and packaging waste. This producer responsibility is the implementation of the EU Directive on Packaging and Packaging Waste (Directive 94/62/EC); this directive has been implemented in Dutch national legislation by the Packaging Management Decree of 2014. To put the decree into effect, industry, municipalities and national government negotiated how responsibilities of producers and importers should be fulfilled, such as the recycling rates. This resulted in a private law arrangement, the "Packaging Agreement" in 2008-12 (Afvalfonds Verpakkingen, 2013). The agreement sets a number of recycling targets for packaging waste. Efforts to meet the targets are facilitated by a "Packaging Fund" organisation, which was a not-for-profit until 2012 and is now a private organisation.

The EPR scheme for packaging is one of the most important in the Netherlands in terms of tonnage and the impact on recycling, especially plastic. According to Eurostat, the volume of packaging waste generated in the Netherlands during 2003-12 has decreased by about 20% (from almost 3.5 Mt to less than 3 Mt). The targets of the EU's Packaging Directive (60% recovery and 55% recycling by 2014) have already been achieved in the Netherlands.

The most recent Packaging Agreement set ambitious national recycling targets for packaging materials in 2013: 43% of plastics, 90% of glass, 75% of paper, 85% of metal and 27% of wood. Each year, the targets for plastics and wood will be raised by 1% and 2% respectively until 2022, when the targets will be fixed at 52% for plastics and 45% for wood. The fulfillment of these plastic packaging collection targets would put the Netherlands among the world's best performers in terms of recycling rates. However, the cost of recycling plastics remains high. Therefore, the agreement contains incentives to reduce costs. The economic arguments in favour of higher recycling rates of plastics (see CE Delft, 2014b) are stronger if the full environmental costs of incinerating plastic waste instead of recycling it are considered. In purely financial terms, however, incineration is generally cheaper.

Source: CE Delft (2014b).

EPR schemes aim to increase collection and recycling rates of targeted waste and to shift financial responsibility of waste management from municipalities to producers.[14] In such schemes, producers manage waste generated by their products from production to disposal; this promotes the integration of environmental costs associated with goods' end-of-life costs into their market price. To meet the requirements of EPR schemes, producers organise and finance collective producer responsibility organisations (PROs) that collect or recycle end-of-life products on behalf of their members, or contract a third party to do so.

Several pieces of EU legislation refer to EPR as a recommended policy instrument, including the EU Waste Framework Directive and four other directives on collection and

Box 5.7. EPR scheme for waste electrical and electronic equipment (WEEE)

The Netherlands has an extensive network for the collection of WEEE and two PROs (Wecycle and WNL) work to collect and treat consumer WEEE. Other PROs are in charge of business WEEE. Under current EU rules (Directive 2002/96/EU), the Netherlands must collect 4 kg of WEEE per capita. This target was easily met and exceeded in the past decade, with the amount of WEEE collected in 2010 through official channels amounting to 7.5 kg per capita. Under the revised EU directive (Directive 2012/19/EU), the collection target will be a percentage of all WEEE produced in a country. By 2019, the Netherlands will be required to collect 65% of WEEE placed on the market or 85% of WEEE produced.

Lack of data on actual or estimated amounts of WEEE generated make it challenging to reach, and even measure progress towards, these targets. For example, WEEE can "leak" (be unaccounted for) if it is illegally shipped out of the Netherlands, hoarded in basements or left unrecorded as WEEE by recyclers. In 2012, Wecycle commissioned an extensive study to improve this information base (see Huisman et al., 2012).

Source: Huisman et al. (2012).

recycling targets in specific waste streams (packaging, batteries, ELVs and WEEE). Many of the Netherlands' EPR obligations derive from EU law, yet the national government has discretion as to how these obligations are implemented.

The systems in place for managing EPR schemes in the Netherlands have evolved considerably over recent years. Initially, for example, a number of schemes each covered a range of packaging materials. This led to problems with too many PROs covering too many separate waste streams. This approach, complex for both authorities and businesses, was replaced by a system of taxation that helped increase coverage of the waste streams, but also increased the regulatory burden. Finally, the system evolved to one based on PRO charging instead of taxation, with centralised control. Overall, this system enjoys both greater economies of scope (compared with having a large number of PROs) and reduced administrative costs (compared with a taxation-based system).

Over time, Dutch EPR schemes have been improved by broadening coverage (hence less "free-riding"), improving financial soundness (making charges broadly reflect costs), improving organisation and increasing transparency. The level of information available on certain waste streams has also improved through specific dedicated studies, in particular for WEEE.

Direct comparisons with EPR schemes in other countries are difficult (Bio, 2014), however, several general observations can be made. First, Dutch EPR schemes are, for the most part, based on the system of financial responsibility; producers pay for, but do not necessarily manage, them. Second, Dutch EPR schemes are relatively well-organised, with clear rules compared to other countries. Third, EPR schemes in the Netherlands are seen as highly effective, but may result in medium-to-high costs due in part to the aim for cost recovery through charges. In most cases, there is limited or no competition between PROs, which may, in theory, reduce incentives to reduce costs.[15] Finally, PROs will need to evolve in order to support the transition to the circular economy, which may require new activities.

4.3. *Managing waste trade flows*

The Netherlands' status as a major importer and exporter of waste expanded considerably during the review period. The main legislative instrument governing waste shipment is the European Waste Shipment Regulation (WSR). It regulates the shipment of waste within, to and from the EU with a view to protecting the environment both within the EU and internationally. The regulation applies directly to EU member states, but governments have some discretion in certain areas, such as how to supervise its enforcement. In the Netherlands, the WSR has been transposed mainly via the EMA and the Economic Offences Act. The Human Environment and Transport Inspectorate (ILT), Customs and the police service inspect several thousand waste shipments every year for compliance with legal requirements (Algemene Rekenkamer, 2012).

In 2012, the Netherlands Court of Audit released findings from an audit of the Dutch government's enforcement of the WSR. The report found the country complies with requirements to control waste shipments and imposes appropriate penalties. However, it also found the high percentage of decisions not to prosecute offenses was a matter of concern (Algemene Rekenkamer, 2012). Other areas for improvement highlighted by the findings include better information management to gain more insight into the impact and effectiveness of inspection and enforcement, as well as of the WSR system itself.

In line with the broader trend of increasing waste trade flows, trade volumes of hazardous waste increased substantially over the review period. By 2009, the Netherlands was the EU's largest exporter of hazardous waste and third-largest importer behind France and Germany (European Commission, 2012a). These trade flows reflect the level of specialisation of north-western European countries in different types of hazardous waste treatment. For example, the Netherlands is well-equipped to treat certain types of hazardous waste, like contaminated soil, while it lacks facilities to process other types, such as battery waste. Trade flows have also increased because hazardous waste previously landfilled is now increasingly destined for recovery. This facilitates trade, as EU rules for recovery are less stringent than those for disposal.

Under the WSR, trade in hazardous waste outside of the OECD is subject to significant restrictions, particularly with respect to disposal. Nevertheless, illegal trade does occur, and can have significant environmental and social consequences when exported to countries that lack environmentally-sound treatment facilities. In certain cases, lack of expertise of front-line customs and port staff, as well as unclear procedures for dealing with illegally shipped waste, can lead to errors. In the *Probo Koala* case of 2006, for example, Dutch port authorities turned away a shipment of hazardous waste, which was subsequently exported to the Ivory Coast (Box 5.8).

Another challenge in managing trade in waste for Dutch authorities relates to the broad definitions applied to waste by different countries, most notably to scrap metal, plastic and paper waste. Traders may wish to import and export this waste, but it may be categorised as hazardous in some cases. The EU's WSR does not always set quantitative limits on the level of contamination that classifies waste as "hazardous". This complicates the enforcement of waste shipment rules. The introduction of "end-of-waste" rules by the EU should help address these issues and simplify the legal trade of such materials within the EU and OECD.

In the future, a main challenge will be to ensure that similar types of waste are treated in an environmentally-sound manner in neighbouring countries. At the very least, countries that trade significant quantities of waste should use a common definition of recycling. There have been cases reported whereby waste exported for recovery is treated through certain waste treatment methods (e.g. backfilling[16]), which would not be permitted in the Netherlands (Zero Waste, 2014).

Box 5.8. **Waste shipment challenges: The *Probo Koala***

In July 2006, the *Probo Koala* tanker docked in the Port of Amsterdam to discharge sludge (washing water and oil residues released after cleaning with caustic soda) from its hold for processing. When the 550 cubic metre (m^3) hold was emptied, the sludge proved to be considerably more polluted than the ship's operating company, Trafigura, had stated. The recipient company was only prepared to accept and process the sludge at more than 10 times the cost originally quoted. The sludge (250 m^3) was pumped back into the tanker, and Trafigura reported to the Amsterdam Port Authorities that it would be managed safely elsewhere. Because the sludge had been pumped back onto the tanker, it became the *Probo Koala*'s cargo, and hence a waste shipment. The tanker sailed for Estonia, where the tanker took on a cargo for Nigeria. After delivering this cargo, the *Probo Koala* sailed to the Ivory Coast, where Trafigura found a local company willing to accept the sludge. The sludge was dumped at night in public sites in Abidjan, creating respiratory illnesses and reportedly several deaths (Eze, 2008; ECA, 2013).

The shipment of the sludge to the Ivory Coast violated the WSR. The Netherlands Court of Appeal found that Trafigura was aware of the chemical composition of the sludge and exported it illegally to the Ivory Coast. A fine of EUR 1 million was imposed on the company in 2011 (ECA, 2013).

The European Court of Auditors has cited this case to illustrate the importance of proper enforcement of the WSR. In short, the decision to pump the sludge back into the tanker should not have been permitted. A lack of clear communication between port workers and waste shipment experts contributed to this error. Therefore, the case highlights the importance of good communication between waste experts and customs officers, as well as the need to put in place comprehensive waste shipment training for front-line staff.

In light of this incident, front-line customs officers in the Netherlands were trained in the enforcement of the Waste Shipment Regulation and instructed on when to consult a specialist from the Environmental Inspectorate. Other front-line environmental or customs officers have been told to consult a colleague with special training in the enforcement of the WSR when dealing with actual or potential waste shipments.

Source: Eze (2008); ECA (2013).

Enforcement authorities also face the challenge of properly managing the risks related to trade in waste. To this end, Dutch authorities have introduced a risk-based enforcement and compliance system to assess the probability and potential impact of non-compliant waste shipments. Despite the relatively large number of inspections by customs, environmental enforcement authorities and police, illegal waste shipments still occur and cannot be eliminated completely. In 2010, for example, 20% of road haulage to Germany involved waste transport; an estimated 7% of the freights were illegal (Scharff, 2014), a figure in line with other EU countries (Joas and Gressmann, 2011).

The public prosecutor declines to prosecute about 30% of detected illegal waste shipments, well above the target of dropping 10% of cases involving environmental charges (ECA, 2013). As discussed above, this was noted as a cause for concern by the Netherlands Court of Audit (Algemene Rekenkamer, 2012). While these issues represent problems for all OECD member countries, they are particularly important for an open, trading economy with Europe's largest port, the Port of Rotterdam.

4.4. Strengthening waste management performance

The Netherlands has a long record of strong performance in waste management. The Netherlands Environmental Assessment Agency, PBL, considers waste management to be a well-established environmental issue, which it describes as being in "the monitoring and enforcement phase" (PBL, 2013a).

As a pioneer of sustainable waste management planning in the OECD, the Netherlands has generated a range of good practices for other countries to learn from. Furthermore, the Netherlands excels in a range of areas that have presented problems for other countries, including the provision of relatively high-quality waste data, monitoring and enforcement, and raising public awareness. The Netherlands has examined and applied a relatively large range of waste policy measures and instruments (economic, regulatory and information-based) since the 2000s, and has developed a good understanding of what works and what does not. Finally, the country is one of the best performers in the OECD in MSW management, while keeping household waste charges at some of the lowest levels in OECD Europe and achieving nearly full cost recovery (CE Delft, 2014a); this is a considerable achievement.

Co-operation between different levels of national, regional and municipal government, as well as stakeholders is impressive. The early and active involvement of stakeholders in decision-making processes is noteworthy. Waste management planning is comprehensive, in terms of broad coverage of the issues and the level of detail considered. Roles and responsibilities of the various actors are clear. The periodic revision of the NWMPs means that waste management planning is dynamic and flexible and can respond to emerging trends.

Some of the main challenges relate to setting future objectives, managing interactions among various policy instruments and trade-offs against other environmental and economic objectives, and accounting for regional dynamics. For example, progress in increasing material recovery (including both recycling and composting) during the 1990s stalled somewhat after 2000. At the same time, incineration for energy recovery has taken off, leading to overcapacity in the sector and likely thwarting efforts to increase recycling. The overcapacity in incineration has contributed to the significant increase in trade in residual and non-residual separated waste between the Netherlands and its neighbours. The import and export of residual waste for energy recovery is in line with the EU's proximity principle. But the growing level of imported residual waste, in particular from the United Kingdom, and indeed trade in hazardous waste between the Netherlands, Belgium and Germany, would suggest that regional waste markets are already a *de facto* reality. As such, these cross-border issues should be more fully considered in Dutch waste management planning.

As described in Chapter 3, the Netherlands could consider such an emission-based tax on incineration as an alternative to the input-based tax now in place. This would provide a much more direct incentive to operators of incinerators to limit as much as possible environmental damages related to the combustion process. The coverage could also be extended to include emissions from the combustion of imported waste, which cause the same environmental harm as those from domestic waste. The environmental damage caused by landfilling and incineration varies with the quality of the facilities. While it can be complicated to measure (some of the) actual emissions from a landfill, this is relatively simple to do (and is actually done) at an incinerator. More than ten years ago, for example, Norway introduced a tax on measured emissions of a number of pollutants from each incinerator.[17] Due to concerns about competition with Swedish incinerators, this tax has since been abolished.

Higher rates of separate waste collection and recycling could be encouraged by expanding Diftar charging schemes or other schemes, such as reversed collection. Large Dutch cities have some catching up to do in this area. The planned benchmarking of municipal performance can help identify and spread good practices. The implementation of the recycling targets could be assisted by a cost-benefit analysis that would support the economic case for ambitious targets.

In the area of EPR schemes, the country has benefited from a significant amount of experimentation and refinement over the years. Efforts to address information shortcomings about the flows of certain important waste streams, such as WEEE, are notable and an example for other countries facing similar problems. These efforts can also be expanded within the Netherlands to improve information on flows of other specific waste streams. In general, EPR schemes can be improved to make them easier to administer and to continue to reduce regulatory burden on firms.

Future challenges concern how EPR schemes can further encourage individual producer and or importer responsibility and promote the circular economy. To support the transition to the circular economy, it will be important to explore ways for EPR schemes to go beyond just waste management and promote systems that have an influence on sourcing, design and consumption phases, as well as improve the quality of recycling. Options to further promote the separation of plastic waste during collection without increasing costs of waste management should be explored. Greater competition between PROs could be considered once EPR schemes have matured.

In contrast with other waste streams, there are no specific targets for reducing hazardous waste in the NWMPs. An explicit objective for the reduction of hazardous waste in the next NWMP could encourage the exploration of cost-effective options to curb the growth on the generation of this waste.

Finally, the third NWMP expected in late 2016 will give greater attention to the quality of outputs from recycled waste. The Netherlands has some experience with encouraging markets for recyclates or recyclables. At the EU level, the development of such markets has been promoted by new rules on "end-of-waste". Promotion of recycling markets is in line with OECD guidance (OECD, 2007). It remains an open question, however, how recycling markets can be developed in the context of free trade in such materials within the EU and OECD. For example, it may be more effective to promote recycling standards at the EU level or within the OECD, rather than at the national level. Reaching common views on, for example, what is meant by recycling and landfilling and what standards should apply in a multilateral context may help the Netherlands meet its own targets.

5. Towards a circular economy

While the Netherlands has a long, strong record in waste management, policy efforts to move from "end-of-pipe" waste management issues to improving resource efficiency further up the material and product value chain are considerably less developed, as in other OECD member countries.

The concept of circular economy emerged to stimulate a departure from linear economic and industrial processes ("resources to waste") that deplete finite resources by making disposable products. The circular economy represents a life cycle approach to maximise value creation in each link of the system. The overarching goals are to enhance the restorative capacity of natural resources, improve the reuse and recycling of products and raw materials, phase out waste and hazardous substances, and transition towards renewable and sustainable energy supplies.

In recent years, the Netherlands has begun laying the groundwork towards a circular economy. It has formulated its own national policy, while actively contributing to international efforts to promote resource efficiency. This section reviews the main challenges in moving towards a circular economy, recent performance of the Netherlands and next steps that can encourage further progress.

5.1. *Main challenges in the move towards a circular economy*

The new focus on a circular economy has brought a number of policy design and implementation challenges compared to traditional waste management. First, in traditional waste management, the government has taken the lead in planning, target setting and implementation (at the appropriate level of government) of regulatory and economic policy instruments to meet objectives. While this approach has been very successful, a circular economy requires a different type of engagement with a broader range of actors influencing decisions about resource use. Specifically, it must engage a diverse set of companies, including those producing and selling products to end consumers; this is a much more diffuse group than those typically engaged in traditional waste management. Further, new business models may be required to put the circular economy into operation.

The role of government in a circular economy is also different than in traditional waste management. Since the early 2000s, the Netherlands has gradually shifted its approach to environmental policy formulation. Moving from "command-and-control" style planning, the government is now playing a more hands-off role using incentives and innovation to change business and consumer behaviour. Further, it recognises that the transition towards a circular economy is complicated and novel, requiring a certain amount of trial and error to reach a robust policy.

Moreover, the identification of realistic objectives, development of indicators and the measurement of progress for resource efficiency is complex. The choice of indicators to measure progress is still the subject of debate. In its 2011 Roadmap, the European Commission proposed a three-layered approach to setting performance indicators: one overarching or lead indicator based on resource productivity (DMC/GDP); a dashboard of macro-indicators focused on resource and environmental impacts and a third layer of thematic indicators (European Commission, 2011). However, PBL has criticised the use of the DMC/GDP indicator for a number of reasons[18] (PBL, 2013b). Given that in June 2014 the Commission put forward a proposed EU-wide target to reduce DMC by 30%, the outcome of this debate could have considerable consequences.

The discussion about appropriate targets raises a more fundamental question of what should be the ultimate aim of greater resource efficiency and the move towards a circular economy. While policy makers generally agree on the need to reuse resources and produce more with less, agreement on the extent of the desired change is more elusive. For example, PBL suggests that resource use in the Netherlands may need to drop substantially to reach sustainable levels (PBL, 2013b). Yet, it is difficult, if not impossible, to assess at what stage an economy has reached an "optimal" point in its transition towards a circular economy. With already relatively high rates of material recovery (recycling and composting), the Netherlands has made significant progress towards becoming a leader in improving efficiency in a linear economy; it still has much further to go in transition towards a circular economy. Potential gains in the transition to a more circular economy are still substantial for the Netherlands with important opportunities for improvement.

Further, existing legislation (in the areas of waste, chemicals) may create barriers in the move towards a circular economy. For example, strict rules exist on the definition of waste and when it can be considered a product. These rules serve to protect producers, consumers and the environment. However, they often cause secondary resources to be regarded as waste, which hampers the development of markets for these materials. The challenge is to facilitate these markets, while still meeting the objectives of the legislation.

Finally, there is also an important political economy dimension to this transition. The move towards a circular economy will result in winners (e.g. service companies and downstream product manufacturers), as well as potential losers (e.g. metal processing companies and primary extraction companies). The challenge for the Netherlands is how to navigate these political economy issues, including developing policies to minimise impacts on potential losers (PBL, 2013b).

5.2. *Accelerating the shift towards the circular economy*

Even without a formal, comprehensive resource efficiency policy, the Netherlands became more resource-efficient for most material groups over the review period. There was absolute decoupling for all categories except metal, which achieved relative decoupling (CBS, 2013).

Throughout the review period, the government set out a number of policy documents supporting the drive towards resource efficiency. Although the second NWMP continued to focus mainly on post-industrial and consumer waste, it signalled a shift from focusing on waste *per se* to focusing on resources more generally. The plan included a specific "chain-oriented" objective aimed at reducing the environmental impact of seven priority waste streams by 20% by 2015 (Box 5.9). A recent evaluation suggested it is doubtful this target would be met, or that it is even measurable.

Box 5.9. **"Chain-oriented" objectives and targets in the second NWMP**

One of the main objectives of the second NWMP was to reduce, by 20%, the environmental impact of seven priority waste streams in the Netherlands by 2015. These priority sectors included paper and cardboard, textiles, construction and demolition waste, organic/food waste, aluminium, PVC and bulky household waste. By applying the "cradle-to-cradle" (or full life cycle) concept to these waste streams, the policy aimed to achieve the environmental impact reduction target not only at the product's end of life, but also during its manufacture and use.

A recent analysis expressed doubt the 20% target would be met by 2015 and questioned the measurability of the target. It indicated the policy had had some positive environmental impact, even if difficult to measure and had promoted good co-operation among stakeholders. The study also noted that more progress was made in certain sectors (e.g. textiles) than in others (e.g. aluminium).

Source: CE Delft (2014a).

In addition to the "chain-oriented" objectives in the second NWMP, green public procurement has been used effectively to promote resource efficiency. In this area, the Netherlands is reputedly one of the best performers in Europe (CEPS, 2012).[19]

Several early voluntary initiatives and agreements have also been used to encourage resource efficiency and the sustainable use of resources. For example, the Sustainable Trade Initiative (IDH) is a private sector-led organisation, supported by the government, which aims to ensure raw material imports have been extracted or harvested sustainably. Another example is the Phosphate Value Chain Agreement (Bastein, 2013), a "Green Deal" concluded between the government and private companies in 2011 (Box 5.10). This agreement is unique in seeking to improve resource efficiency in a key economic sector while addressing the politically-induced security of supply issues, which continue to concern industrial users of raw materials.

Box 5.10. **Phosphate value chain agreement**

With its large agricultural sector, the Netherlands consumes substantial amounts of phosphates, a mineral used to manufacture phosphorus-based fertiliser. Phosphates are primarily mined in Morocco and China. Steep price increases in the late 2000s led to concerns over the potential impacts of a supply shortage on the food industry in the Netherlands and the EU in general, given their dependency on imported phosphates. Further, because phosphate mining is water-intensive, it was recognised that intensifying competition for water resources in a few water-scarce, phosphate-producing regions could disrupt phosphate supply chains.

At the same time, a number of Dutch stakeholders began to promote the possibility of "mining" secondary phosphate, for example from wastewater and manure. This could also help the Netherlands reduce excess phosphate in Dutch rivers and lakes, a source of water pollution.

In 2011, the government brought together 20 water, chemical, food industry and agricultural stakeholders through the "Nutrient Platform" to turn the Netherlands into a net exporter of secondary phosphate. The "Phosphate Value Chain Agreement", a "Green Deal" (see Chapter 2), was signed that same year.

There were a number of challenges to overcome. Success required bringing together stakeholders along the value chain that do not normally work together and promoting trust, even where certain parties might stand to benefit more than others and no government incentives (such as subsidies) were available. Legislation covering the use of recovered material (in particular if it contained heavy metals or other pollutants) also created a barrier. In response, the government set new rules for use of recovered phosphates as fertiliser in the Netherlands, which came into effect as of 1 January 2015.

Another challenge relates to promoting investment in a secondary phosphate market in the context of a highly volatile commodity market. For example, the price of phosphate rock rose from USD 50 to USD 450 in 2007-08 as a result of supply issues in China. The price then fell to USD 100 in late 2009. While price volatility can induce greater resource efficiency, it can also impede investments in alternatives. To this end, the Nutrient Platform aims to facilitate co-operation between innovative companies and financial institutions, with the objective of fostering innovation in the sector.

Finally, an additional factor affecting efforts was the significant drop in use of phosphorus per hectare (ha) in the Netherlands from almost 40 kg/ha in 1990-92 to just over 10 kg/ha on average between 2007-10 (OECD, 2014b). The impact of this decline on the development of the Phosphate Value Chain Agreement is unclear.

Box 5.10. **Phosphate value chain agreement** *(cont.)*

Overall, this agreement is an example of good practice in terms of how to promote resource efficiency through stakeholder co-operation without the promise of large state subsidies. It also illustrates the complexity of developing competitive secondary raw materials markets.

Source: Bastein (2013).

Recently, the government has taken further steps to support the move to a circular economy. It published the first Waste Prevention Plan in 2013 as required in the revised Waste Framework Directive (Directive 2008/98/EC). In the plan, the government outlines how it proposes to move beyond recycling and incineration measures to encourage better reuse of resources.

In January 2014, the State Secretary for Infrastructure and the Environment outlined the details of the Waste to Resource programme. The programme sets out eight high-level objectives and actions (summarised in Table 5.1). Sustainability at the front of the value chain is pursued through sustainable sourcing, ensuring the circular design of products, as well as closing local and global cycles. This consists of designing sustainable products that can be easily repaired and recycled. Closing cycles implies a more sustainable use of natural resources, such as land, water, ecosystems and raw materials.

Moving along the value chain, another key element of the programme is promoting more sustainable consumption patterns among consumers. This would be achieved through promotional campaigns and other methods, which need to be informed by a solid understanding of consumer behaviour. Another key element concerns more traditional waste management objectives. These include improving waste separation and collection by minimising the quantity of residual waste and simplifying laws related to reuse and recycling. Finally, the programme would be supported by financial and market initiatives (such as redesigning the landfill tax and other fiscal measures to promote circular economy objectives); by improving information about waste streams; and by developing indicators.

As the vast majority of actions are in progress or planned, it is too early to evaluate their impact. Nevertheless, some general observations can be made. Notably, the objectives and actions in the Waste to Resource programme directed at the early phases of the circular economy cycle are generally less detailed and concrete than those for waste management. For example, while there are time-bound targets for waste management, the proposed lines of action for the circular economy are generally less specific and lack time-bound targets. In certain cases, more analysis and exploration of options are proposed. In collaboration with stakeholders, the next steps will need to include developing more specific goals for each line of action.

While exploration makes sense in the early stages of development, the programme could elaborate more detailed measures for areas that are particularly important, such as promoting reuse and repair options. This area could bring a number of benefits in comparison with recycling. While the Waste to Resource programme encourages "reuse by strengthening the role of the retail sector, thrift stores and repair companies", it is not clear how this will work in practice and which actors will be needed to engage (e.g. electricians). This area is now part of an action programme (RACE), part of the Waste to Resource programme. As consumption patterns are often influenced by the relative difference between the cost of buying a new good and servicing an old one, the role of the services sector and the economic implications need to be further elaborated. Moreover, issues relating to product lifetimes, such as planned obsolescence and warranties, as well as the role of bring-back/product leasing schemes, are only mentioned for chemicals, but not other areas.

Aside from considering the design of the landfill tax, limited attention is paid to waste and resource taxation. Indeed, a resource tax could be unpopular and difficult to apply, even if its impact on heavy industry may not be as great as often claimed (PBL, 2014). Still, the Waste to Resource programme could elaborate more on how environmentally related taxes could support resource efficiency. The forthcoming progress report on the programme should shed further light on this.

Given the highly open nature of the Dutch economy, the programme could further incorporate trade considerations. For example, there is a specific reference to the "True Price Platform" in the programme. In this initiative, the environmental impact of Dutch consumption of imported cotton has been factored into actions to promote sustainable textiles. The general approach taken in such initiatives could be more broadly applied. Likewise, the influence that economic and security of supply issues can have on resource efficiency goals, such as those which came to light during the formulation of the Phosphate Value Chain Agreement, should also be considered.

In summary, putting the vision for the circular economy into action in a cost-effective way will require realistic targets informed by cost-benefit analysis. It will also require overcoming challenges presented in this new area, such as the need to develop new business models and approaches for working across whole product chains, dealing with commodity price volatility and defining a new role for the government. The development of a coherent roadmap for implementation, as well as indicators and monitoring, would be important next steps.

Recommendations on waste and materials management

- Maintain absolute decoupling of waste generation from GDP to avoid a potential rebound as the economy recovers by reinforcing efforts to reduce waste generation in the next iteration of the National Waste Management Plan. Consider an objective for the reduction of hazardous waste in the next iteration of the National Waste Management Plan, which was not done in previous plans.
- Consider the design of an emission-based tax as an alternative to the input-based tax now in place for the waste tax. This would provide a much more direct incentive to operators of incinerators to limit the environmental damages related to the combustion process as much as possible. Since environmental damages occur regardless of the origin of the waste treated, removing the exemption on imported waste could also be considered.
- Encourage broader uptake of schemes, such as "Diftar" charging schemes and reverse collection, which have been shown to promote greater separation of waste and lower the cost of treatment. There is significant scope for uptake in medium and large cities. Encourage measures to promote further separate collection of plastic waste, without increasing waste treatment costs.

Recommendations on waste and materials management *(cont.)*

- Explore ways for EPR schemes to support the circular economy by going beyond just waste management and promoting systems that have an influence on sourcing, design and consumption phases; improve the quality of recycling within EPR schemes.
- Continue to support and reinforce efforts to minimise illegal waste trade, such as through the use of the risk-based approach to identify possible waste shipments, as well as to ensure that such waste is properly handled once identified. This may call for further increased investment over the coming years to strengthen efforts to enforce EU and international laws on waste shipments.
- Develop a roadmap for specific actions to promote the circular economy and a timeline for implementation; strengthen product policies to deliver stronger incentives for designs that are conducive to the circular economy, such as through product labelling and information, as well as specific design criteria where appropriate; promote reuse and remanufacturing, including through fiscal incentives (such as lower VAT for repair services), minimum quality standards and warranties, legal requirements on the availability of information and spare parts for repair and facilitating (as appropriate) recycling, refurbishment, reuse and repair in the relevant legislation.
- Encourage innovation through the Green Deals approach; develop policies that can support the emergence of new business models conducive to the circular economy, such as those based on services rather than the sale of goods; explore dynamic standard setting that can spur innovation; use green public procurement to support the circular economy.
- Put in place policies and measures that help to overcome information barriers and issues with access to finance, in particular for SMEs where the capacity to identify and implement resource efficiency opportunities is more constrained.
- Prioritise the development of indicators to monitor resource productivity and progress towards a circular economy; consolidate and further develop material flow accounts by industry and improve the coherence between waste and material flow statistics (especially for secondary raw materials and recycling rates); encourage the inclusion of circular economy and resource productivity indicators (physical and financial data) in reporting by businesses and financial institutions.

Notes

1. The second National Waste Management Plan (2009-21) contains 84 sector plans.
2. In addition to the EMA, a number of other laws, decisions and regulations govern waste and materials management.
3. MSW is comprised of household and other municipal cleaning services/other waste. The vast majority of the latter comes from litter and similar organic waste.
4. DMC is the sum of domestic extraction of raw materials used by an economy and their physical trade balance (imports minus exports of raw materials and manufactured products).
5. DMC per capita declined from 12.6 to 9.2 kg per capita in 2000-13 (OECD Environmental Statistics).
6. For example, accounting for indirect use of raw materials (for instance in a "material footprint" indicator) could increase average materials consumption per capita significantly, as compared to the DMC measure. One recent study estimates the Netherlands' "material footprint" to be closer to 26 tonnes per capita or 427 Mt in total (Wiedmann, 2013), around two and a half times the DMC figure.
7. From 1998, the tax was linked to the landfill ban and differentiated according to whether the waste being landfilled was combustible or non-combustible. Combustible waste with a density under

1 100 kg/m^3 was charged at the high tax rate while non-combustible waste with a density over 1 100 kg/m^3 subject to the lower tax.

8. Initially, the landfill tax was set at just under EUR 30/tonne in 1996-98, but was more than doubled in 2002 to EUR 65/tonne. In 2005, it was raised further, to EUR 85/tonne (Oosterhuis, 2009).
9. Incineration gate fees subsequently fell as low as EUR 50/tonne in 2014.
10. The Netherlands did have an incinerator tax in place with the rate was set at EUR 0/tonne.
11. These projects were often established as not-for-profit organisations, whereby profits generated were redistributed back to municipalities. Public ownership of incineration by municipalities remained high until recent years.
12. The landfill tax rate was EUR 13/tonne in 2015. Landfill costs are estimated to be about EUR 18 million per year, including the maintenance costs of closed landfills. Together, the landfill and incineration taxes are expected to generate EUR 100 million per year.
13. For a description of the Norwegian tax on waste incineration, see OECD (2004).
14. For example, guaranteed prices were put in place for recycled paper, glass and other types of packaging.
15. A mix of policy instruments can be used, including product take-back requirements, economic and market-based instruments (e.g. deposit-refund schemes, material taxes, etc.), regulations and performance standards (e.g. minimum recycled content) and information-based instruments (e.g. product labelling requirements) (OECD, 2014a).
16. While competition in the area of EPR may have benefits from both an eco-design and cost perspective (OECD, 2014a), it is difficult to determine if competitive or centralised EPR schemes are more cost effective given the lack of comparable information on the performance of various EPR approaches (BIO, 2014).
17. According to the European Commission, "backfilling" means a recovery operation where suitable waste is used for reclamation purposes in excavated areas or for engineering purposes in landscaping and where the waste is a substitute for non-waste materials.
18. Among the criticisms of using a lead aggregate indicator is that it may have a cancelling out effect where a negative performance in one area is countered by a positive performance in another, even when the two variables are not strictly comparable. Second, since DMC is based on tonnes and not on the environmental impact of using the constituent materials, the indicator may discriminate against countries that use large amounts of certain material (e.g. gravel), which do not have a large environmental impact. Finally, DMC does not account for the materials and other resources used to make imported semi-processed and processed goods.
19. In 2009, the Netherlands, alongside Austria, Denmark, Finland, Germany, the Netherlands, Sweden, and the United Kingdom, were considered as the most advanced in the EU in terms of green public procurement.

References

Afvalfonds Verpakkingen (2013), Packaging Waste Fund website, *www.afvalfondsverpakkingen.nl/english/* (accessed 10 February 2015).

Algemene Rekenkamer (2012), "Handhaving Europese regels voor afvaltransport" [Enforcement of European Waste Shipment Regulation], Tweede Kamer, vergaderjaar 2012-2013, 33 418, No. 2. ISBN 978 90n 12 57593 5, The Hague.

Bastein, T. (2013), *Opportunities for the Circular Economy in the Netherlands*, TNO, Delft.

BIO (2014), *Development of Guidance on Extended Producer Responsibility (EPR), Final Report for the European Commission, DG Environment*, BIO by Deloitte, *http://ec.europa.eu/environment/waste/pdf/target_review/Guidance%20on%20EPR%20-%20Final%20Report.pdf* (accessed 31 March 2015).

CBS (2014), "Municipal waste; quantities", *StatLine* (database), *http://statline.cbs.nl/StatWeb/publication/?VW=T&DM=SLEN&PA=7467eng&D1=0-25,76-86&D2=0&D3=a&HD=100215-1537&LA=EN&HDR=G1,G2&STB=T* (accessed 30 March 2015).

CBS (2013), *Green Growth in the Netherlands 2012*, Statistics Netherlands, The Hague, www.cbs.nl/NR/rdonlyres/2C613080-F668-439C-B12C-98BF361B5ADF/0/2013p44pub.pdf (accessed 15 January 2015).

CBS (2012), *Renewable Energy in the Netherlands 2010*, Statistics Netherlands, The Hague, *www.cbs.nl/NR/rdonlyres/BED23760-23C0-47D0-8A2A-224402F055F3/0/2012c90pub.pdf* (accessed 30 March 2015).

CE Delft (2014a), "Evaluatie Landelijk Afvalbeheerplan LAP1 en 2", [Evaluation of Waste Management Plans LAP1 and LAP2], www.ce.nl/publicatie/evaluatie_landelijk_afvalbeheerplan_%28lap%29_1_en_2/1482 (accessed 30 March 2015).

CE Delft (2014b), "Kosten statiegeldsystemen voor grote PET-flessen" [Costs of Deposit-Refund Systems for Large PET Bottles], *www.ce.nl/publicatie/kosten_statiegeldsystemen_voor_grote_pet-flessen/1477)* (accessed 30 March 2015).

CE Delft (2011), "LCA: Recycling of plastic packaging waste from households", presentation at VDI Wissensforum, Amsterdam, 22 May 2014, *www.cedelft.eu/art/uploads/file/Persberichten/2014/Plastic%20recycling%20LCA%20CE%20Delft%20conference%20VDI%20may%20Amsterdam%2022-5.pdf* (accessed 31 March 2015).

CEPS (2012), *The Uptake of Green Public Procurement in the EU27, Report for the European Commission, DG Environment*, Centre for European Policy Studies in collaboration with College of Europe, *http://ec.europa.eu/environment/gpp/pdf/CEPS-CoE-GPP%20MAIN%20REPORT.pdf* (accessed 31 March 2015).

Corstena, M. et al. (2013), "The potential contribution of sustainable waste management to energy use and greenhouse gas emission reduction in the Netherlands", *Resources, Conservation and Recycling*, No. 77, August, Elsevier, Amsterdam, pp. 13-21, *www.sciencedirect.com/science/article/pii/S0921344913000888.*

Dijkgraff, E. and R. Gradus (2014), "The effectiveness of Dutch municipal recycling policies", *Discussion Paper* TI 2014-155/VI, Tinbergen Institute, Amsterdam/Rotterdam.

Dutch Waste Management Association (2014a), *Annual Review 2013*, *www.wastematters.eu/uploads/media/DWMA_Annual_Review_2013.pdf* (accessed 30 March 2015).

European Commission (2013), *Consultative Communication on the Sustainable Use of Phosphorus*, COM (2013) 517 final, European Commission, Brussels.

European Commission (2012a), *Report on the Implementation of the Waste Shipment Regulation*, SWD (2012) 244 final, European Commission, Brussels.

European Commission (2011), *Communication on a Roadmap for a Resource-efficient Europe*, COM (2011) 571 final, European Commission, Brussels.

ECA (2013), *Co-ordinated Audit on the Enforcement of the European Waste Shipment Regulation: Joint Report Based on Eight National Audits*, European Court of Auditors, Luxembourg, *www.eca.europa.eu/sites/cc/Lists/CCDocuments/other%20publications/Coordinated_audit_on_the_enforcement_of_ the_European_Waste_Shipment_Regulation.pdf.*

EEA (2013), *Municipal Waste Management in the Netherlands*, Publications Office of the European Union, European Environment Agency, Luxembourg.

ETC/SCP (2012), "Overview of the use of landfill taxes in Europe", *Working Paper*, No. 1/2012, European Topic Centre on Sustainable Consumption and Production, Copenhagen.

Eurostat (2015), *Treatment of Waste* (database) (accessed 20 March 2015).

Eurostat (2014a), *Material Flow Accounts* (database) (accessed 20 March 2015).

Eurostat (2014b), *Municipal Waste* (database) (accessed 20 March 2015).

Eurostat (2013), *Resource Productivity Statistics*, *http://ec.europa.eu/eurostat/statistics-explained/index.php/Resource_productivity_statistics, Eurostat, Luxembourg* (accessed 20 March 2015).

Eurostat (2012), *Waste Shipment Statistics*, *http://ec.europa.eu/eurostat/statistics-explained/index.php/Waste_shipment_statistics* (accessed 30 March 2015).

Eze, C.N. (2008), "The Probo Koala incident in Abidjan, Cote d'Ivoire: A critique of the Basel Convention compliance mechanism", in *Proceedings of the Eighth International Conference* (5-11 April 2008), International Network for Environmental Compliance and Enforcement, *www.inece.org/conference/8/proceedings/51_Eze.pdf.*

Huisman, J. et al. (2012), *The Dutch WEEE Flows*, United Nations University, ISP – SCYCLE, Bonn, 15 March 2012.

Joas, A. and A. Gressmann (2011), *IMPEL-TFS Enforcement Actions II, Final Project Report October 2008 – February 2011*, 2011/08, European Union Network for the Implementation and Enforcement of Environmental Law, Brussels.

Ministry of Infrastructure and Environment (2014a), "Implementation of the Waste to Resource programme", Letter to the House of Representatives, 28 January 2014, The Hague, *www.government.nl/documents-and-publications/parliamentary-documents/2014/01/28/implementation-of-the-waste-to-resource-programme.html* (accessed 30 March 2015).

Ministry of Infrastructure and Environment (2014b), "Implementation of the Waste to Resource programme", Letter to the House of Representatives, Annex I, 28 January 2014, The Hague, *www.government.nl/documents-and-publications/parliamentary-documents/2014/01/28/waste-to-resource-elaboration-of-eight-operational-objectives.html* (accessed 30 March 2015).

Ministry of Infrastructure and Environment (2013a), "Van afval naar Grondstof" [Waste to Resource], *www.rijksoverheid.nl/documenten-en-publicaties/kamerstukken/2013/06/20/van-afval-naar-grondstof.html* (accessed 30 March 2015).

Ministry of Infrastructure and Environment (2013b), "Afvalpreventieprogramma" [Waste Prevention Programme], *www.lap2.nl/sn_documents/downloads/07%20Afvalpreventieprogramma/Afvalpreventie programma%20NL%20final%202013.pdf* (accessed 30 March 2015).

Ministry of Infrastructure and Environment (2011a), "Landelijk Afvalbeheerplan" [National Waste Management Plan 2], *www.lap2.nl/downloads.asp* (accessed 30 March 2015).

Ministry of Infrastructure and Environment (2011b), "Meer Waarde uit Afval" [More Value from Waste], *www.rijksoverheid.nl/documenten-en-publicaties/kamerstukken/2011/08/25/betreft-meer-waarde-uit-afval.html* (accessed 30 March 2015).

Ministry of Infrastructure and Environment (2003), "Landelijk Afvalbeheerplan" [National Waste Management Plan 1], *www.lap2.nl/downloads.asp?c=./sn_documents/downloads/99%20LAP-archief/03%20LAP1_OrigineleVersie(2003)* (accessed 30 March 2015).

MRW (2015), "Dutch incineration tax expected to benefit RDF market", 2 February 2015, *www.mrw.co.uk/news/dutch-incineration-tax-expected-to-benefit-rdf-market/8677876.article#* (accessed 25 February 2015).

OECD (2015), "Municipal waste, generation and treatment", *OECD Stat Extracts* (database), *https://stats.oecd.org/Index.aspx?DataSetCode=MUNW* (accessed 30 March 2015).

OECD (2014a), The state of play on extended producer responsibility (EPR): Opportunities and challenges global forum on environment: Promoting sustainable materials management through extended producer responsibility (EPR), *Issues Paper*, 17-19 June 2014, Tokyo, Japan.

OECD (2014b), *Green Growth Indicators 2014*, OECD Green Growth Studies, OECD Publishing, Paris, *http://dx.doi.org/10.1787/9789264202030-en*.

OECD (2012), *Sustainable Materials Management: Making Better Use of Resources*, OECD Publishing, Paris, *http://dx.doi.org/10.1787/9789264174269-en*.

OECD (2007), "Improving Recycling Markets" (policy brief), OECD Publishing, Paris, *www.oecd.org/env/waste/38093900.pdf*.

OECD (2004), *Addressing the Economics of Waste*, OECD Publishing, Paris, *http://dx.doi.org/10.1787/9789264106192-en*.

Oosterhuis, F. et al. (2009), "Economic instruments and waste policies in the Netherlands. Inventory and options for extended use", *Report* R-09/01, Institute for Environmental Studies, Amsterdam.

PBL (2014), *Share of Raw Material Costs in Total Production Costs*, Netherlands Environmental Assessment Agency, The Hague.

PBL (2013a), *Changing Track, Changing Tack; Dutch Ideas for Robust Environmental Policy for the 21st Century*, Netherlands Environmental Assessment Agency, The Hague.

PBL (2013b), *Conditions for Greening the Dutch Economy*, Netherlands Environmental Assessment Agency, The Hague.

RIVM (2013), *National Inventory Report 2013 – Greenhouse Gas Emissions in the Netherlands 1990-2011*, National Institute for Public Health and the Environment, Bilthoven, the Netherlands.

Rotterdam City Council (2014), "(Household) waste management in the City of Rotterdam", presentation to the OECD, 17 October 2014.

Scharff, H. (2014), "Landfill reduction experience in The Netherlands", *Waste Management*, No. 34, Elsevier, Amsterdam, pp. 2218-2224.

Wiedmann, T. et al. (2013), "The material footprint of nations", *Proceedings of the National Academy of Sciences of the United States of America*, *www.pnas.org/cgi/doi/10.1073/pnas.1220362110*.

WUR (2012), "Analyse van het Nederlandse Statiegeldsysteem voor PET flessen" [Study on the Dutch Deposit-Return System for PET Bottles], Report 1316B, 10 April 2012, Wageningen University.

Zero Waste (2014), "And the best waste performing country in Europe is… Estonia!", *www.zerowasteeurope.eu/2014/04/and-the-best-waste-performing-country-in-europe-is-estonia/* (accessed 25 February 2015).

ORGANISATION FOR ECONOMIC CO-OPERATION AND DEVELOPMENT

The OECD is a unique forum where governments work together to address the economic, social and environmental challenges of globalisation. The OECD is also at the forefront of efforts to understand and to help governments respond to new developments and concerns, such as corporate governance, the information economy and the challenges of an ageing population. The Organisation provides a setting where governments can compare policy experiences, seek answers to common problems, identify good practice and work to co-ordinate domestic and international policies.

The OECD member countries are: Australia, Austria, Belgium, Canada, Chile, the Czech Republic, Denmark, Estonia, Finland, France, Germany, Greece, Hungary, Iceland, Ireland, Israel, Italy, Japan, Korea, Luxembourg, Mexico, the Netherlands, New Zealand, Norway, Poland, Portugal, the Slovak Republic, Slovenia, Spain, Sweden, Switzerland, Turkey, the United Kingdom and the United States. The European Union takes part in the work of the OECD.

OECD Publishing disseminates widely the results of the Organisation's statistics gathering and research on economic, social and environmental issues, as well as the conventions, guidelines and standards agreed by its members.

OECD PUBLISHING, 2, rue André-Pascal, 75775 PARIS CEDEX 16
(97 2015 14 1 P) ISBN 978-92-64-23999-9 – 2015-02

www.ingramcontent.com/pod-product-compliance
Ingram Content Group UK Ltd.
Pitfield, Milton Keynes, MK11 3LW, UK
UKHW051500290926
15471UKWH00008B/1322

9 789264 239999